STRATEGIC COUSINS

Strategic Cousins

Australian and Canadian Expeditionary Forces and the British and American Empires

JOHN C. BLAXLAND

McGill-Queen's University Press
Montreal & Kingston · London · Ithaca

ISBN 13: 978-0-7735-3035-5   ISBN 10: 0-7735-3035-5 (cloth)
ISBN 13: 978-0-7735-3064-5   ISBN 10: 0-7735-3064-9 (paper)

Legal deposit third quarter 2006
Bibliothèque nationale du Québec

Printed in Canada on acid-free paper that is 100% ancient forest free
(100% post-consumer recycled), processed chlorine free.

This book has been published with the help of grants from the
Centre of International Relations and the Defence Management Program
at Queen's University and from the Australian Army History Unit.

McGill-Queen's University Press acknowledges the support of the Canada
Council for the Arts for our publishing program. We also acknowledge
the financial support of the Government of Canada through the Book
Publishing Industry Development Program (BPIDP) for our publishing
activities.

Library and Archives Canada Cataloguing in Publication

Blaxland, J. C. (John Charles), 1963–
    Strategic cousins: Australian and Canadian expeditionary forces
and the British and American empires / John C. Blaxland.

Includes bibliographical references and index.
ISBN-13: 978-0-7735-3035-5   ISBN-10: 0-7735-3035-5 (bnd)
ISBN-13: 978-0-7735-3064-5   ISBN-10: 0-7735-3064-9 (pbk)

1. Canada – Armed Forces – Foreign countries – History. 2. Australia –
Armed Forces – Foreign countries – History. 3. Great Britain – Foreign
relations – 20th century. 4. Great Britain – Military policy – History –
20th century. 5. United States – Foreign relations – 20th century.
6. United States – Military policy – History – 20th century. I. Title.

UA10.B59 2006   355'.031   C2005-907509-0

This book was typeset by Interscript in 10/13 Sabon.

Contents

MAPS

CHARTS

Foreword

During most of the First World War, the French and the British armies fought together but separately. Not until late in 1917, as they faced defeat head-on, did the generals (under enormous political pressure) finally agree to create a unified Allied command. The Allied system in 1917 was imperfect but it provided a model of sorts for the unified command of Allied forces during the Second World War and, ultimately, for the North Atlantic Treaty Organization. Britain and the United States provided the leadership in this system of international command, efforts made possible because of their nearly identical political traditions, common language, and deeply shared values. "Like-mindedness," as it came to be called many years later, was and is the bedrock of this politico/military regime. It endures today in Iraq, Afghanistan, United Nations operations, and wherever the "anglosphere" of Australia, Britain, Canada, New Zealand, and the United States unite in pursuit of their common interests.

John Blaxland explores this broad and unique relationship – neither empire nor immutable alliance – in a study of the armies of "the strategic cousins," Australia and Canada. He examines the military histories of both nations, searching for the common threads that developed as the two nations matured from British colonies to, successively, independent "dominions" within the British Empire, sovereign states within the Commonwealth, and, today, members of an alliance of anglophone nations in consort with the United States.

The military links between the two armed forces are, from an operational point of view, tenuous. Though the armies fought near each other during the Boer War and in Korea, they stood on different ground during much of the First and Second World Wars and the Cold War. Indeed, from 1950 until 1989, the Canadian Forces had a closer association with British, American, and German soldiers than with any army south of the equator.

Yet the "Britishness" of the Canadian and Australian armies endures and provides a link that has persisted though all these years, exemplified by exchanges of officers for staff-college courses and collaboration in weapons development, military standardization planning, and senior military associations – a wide-range of military topics connected under the so-called ABCA arrangements.

Blaxland shows how these military facts are related to the strategic and political reality that, for much the same reasons, both Australia and Canada migrated from the British to the American sphere after the Second World War. He concludes that this aspect of national life has and will continue to shape their defence policies and armed forces. Australia moved first, immediately after the Japanese opened the war in the Pacific and the British (arguably) deserted the Australians, leaving them to find their own way. Circumstances thrust Australia into an American alliance then and maintaining that alliance – being noticed by being helpful – has endured as the keystone of Australian foreign and defence policy and military development ever since.

The Canadian Forces clung to British ways well into the 1970s: strongly in the navy, less so in the army, and hardly at all in the air force. This odd evolution reflected the separate nature of the services that had developed as a result of Second World War and Cold War missions. Slowly at first, but then rapidly after 1990, the Canadian Forces left the North Atlantic experience behind and turned its attention to Yugoslavia, Iraq, Africa, and Afghanistan and, in so doing, to American strategies and American-led operations.

Fate, it seems, has brought the sometimes estranged "strategic cousins" together in the home of their now newly favoured relative, Uncle Sam. This gathering of the military family brings with it advantages and obligations for Australia and Canada and, to a much lesser degree, the United States. Blaxland discusses this dynamic in detail, particularly the influence this uneven alliance has on the Australian and Canadian armies. Not only must they both adapt to the American way in warfare – the high command of the Canadian Forces deliberately made the transformation in just five years, beginning in 2001 – they must also adopt these mostly technical military consequences to the often ambiguous demands of national domestic attitudes towards the United States and its policies.

Yet there really is no other choice. NATO is increasingly quarrelsome, forcing Canadian politicians to choose between the country's North Atlantic traditions and its newly found western hemispheric destiny. The UN serves neither nation well, putting great demands on their limited armed forces with few returns for national interests. The United States, on the other hand, offers, at a price to be sure, leadership, technical military superiority, critical logistical and operational support, access to important policy forums in Washington, and, ultimately, national defence much like that the British Empire provided a century ago to both Australia and Canada.

These facts will inevitably draw the armed forces of all three nations closer together, mingling their blood and treasure in pursuit of common national interests. United Nations "alliances of the willing" may succeed in some circumstances, but alliances built on the same blood, on like-mindedness, and on family have always proved the stronger defence in a dangerous world. Leaders in the anglosphere should pay close attention to John Blaxland's work, not just as history but as an example of the shifts in ABCA strategies in the post-Cold War world. This study probably would not have been written in 1985 – the links were too faint – but in 2006 it is a work that could not and cannot be avoided.

Douglas Bland
Professor and chair of the Defence Management Studies Program
Queen's University, Kingston, Ontario

Preface

The idea for this book was planted in my mind in 1996 while I was attending the Royal Thai Army's Command and Staff College in Bangkok, Thailand. There I met my wife, Judith Steiner, a Canadian of anglophone and francophone background who was working in Bangkok for a Hong Kong-based international firm. One of the things that our relationship made me realize was how much Australians and Canadians have in common and just how little we both realize it. The Thais were very gracious and I made many enduring friendships during my time in their country. But it was towards those with whom I have more in common culturally that I was predisposed to gravitate in my spare time. This phenomenon, to me, was striking. While we were away from our own countries, what struck us most was our common ground, rather than the distinctive cultural and geographic nuances that are more apparent when one is at home.

Yet various social commentators have little use for a close focus on the ties that make such gatherings almost naturally occurring events. Instead, for instance, Australian academics, government policy writers, and social engineers spent much of the 1990s trying to convince themselves and the world that they were Asians. Clearly, Australia will always have a place in Asia, but that fact should not lead to a denial of cultural affinities and strategic predispositions that have for many years included alliance with the United States and close association with the world's English-speaking nations. In the meantime, Canadians, generally speaking, have experienced similar angst about their place in the world. Canadians appear to have spent many years trying to tell themselves that they are anything but Americans. Figuring out what is distinctive for Canadians or Australians has been a frequent topic of discussion for the members of these New World nations. Yet, apart from a select number of Canadian or Australian scholars, few have paid much attention to their commonalities.

Like Canadians, Australians tend to be preoccupied with the United States, thanks to the influence of U.S. popular culture and goods, let alone U.S. influence in foreign policy matters as well as in military affairs. Without doubt, the consciousness of Australians and Canadians has been strongly influenced by the United States. But, like a deer, or kangaroo, caught in a car's headlights at night, Canadians and Australians have tended to be fixated with the United States, seeing little else beyond the North American colossus to their respective south or northeast. What is more, when I told friends and colleagues that I was contemplating this project, many of the obvious differences between the two countries were quickly recited back to me, in an apparent attempt to discourage me from pursuing the comparison any further. The common view appeared to be that there was nothing worth exploring in the relationship between Australia and Canada that could be of any possible benefit for military affairs or foreign policy. Such ready dismissals only stirred my curiosity further.

Having worked in Washington, D.C., and having witnessed the attack on the Pentagon on 11 September 2001, I have developed a greater awareness of the sense of vulnerability as well as the span of responsibility, power, and ability of an aroused United States. In addition, I have come to appreciate how many things there are that Australians and Canadians share in common with Americans and what it is that sets Canadians and Australians apart from Americans. But I also have come to realize just how little Australia and Canada tend to feature in the public consciousness of the United States, particularly in terms of foreign and defence policy matters. (Australia arguably features more prominently in American public-policy consciousness in military terms and Canada in economic terms.) This limited consciousness of Canada and Australia in the United States is much like the limited awareness that Canada and Australia have of each other, since neither features prominently in the other's public consciousness either.

With this in mind, it occurred to me that there was scope for a considered examination of the parallel military histories of Canada and Australia. It occurred to me also that such a study could be relevant to military planners, strategists, and students of international relations interested in understanding the combined capabilities and limitations of the Australian and Canadian forces both in Ottawa and Canberra and beyond. It is this combination of circumstances that led me to want to write this book. But it was the foresight of the Australian Army that resulted in me being given the time to study in Canada and to see it through to fruition.

Acknowledgments

Although I alone am responsible for the arguments outlined in this book, I am indebted to many people who have inspired and challenged me along the way. First, I owe a debt of gratitude to Dr Ron Haycock, who was instrumental in challenging me to set my sights on such a broad canvas of shared heritage, and Dr Joel Sokolsky, with whom I had many stimulating discussions. I owe thanks as well to Dr Kim Nossal for providing me with useful advice, and Dr David Haglund for kindly reviewing a draft but chiefly for having encouraged me in my decision to write in Canada. I am indebted to several readers who have provided me with useful suggestions and guidance along the way, including Drs Jane Errington, Frank Milne, Alan Ryan, Walter Dorn, Albert Palazzo, Roy Rempel, Galen Perras, David Horner, (Lieutenant-Colonel) David Last, and (Lieutenant-Colonel) Doug Delaney; Mr Louis Delvoie; Reverend G.M.A. Blaxland (who also compiled the index); General Peter Cosgrove; Brigadiers William Mellor, Gary Bornholt (AS), and Don MacNamara (CF-ret); Lieutenant-Colonels (ret) Glen Steiner and John Marteinson (CF); and Lieutenant-Colonels Marcus Fielding (AS), Graeme Sligo (AS), Chris Field (AS), John Davidson (AS), Grant Iddon (AS), Warwick Austin (AS), Michael N. Smith (USA), Casey Haskins (USA), Randall Richert (USAF), Terry Loveridge (CF), and Don MacLean (AS).

Other colleagues have also provided me with helpful critiques on earlier drafts, including Commander Ian Moffat (CF); Majors Michael Boire (CF), Ian Rutherford (CF), Ray Stouffer (CF), Craig Braddon (CF), and Kenn Rodzyniak (CF); Lieutenants Steve St. Amant (CF) and Tonja Kerr (CF); and Emily Spencer, Robert Addinall, and Joshua Bennett. Brendan Sargeant of the Australian Department of Defence provided me with a useful perspective. Several people in Ottawa kindly assisted with useful feedback as well, including Mr David Elder of the Privy Council Office; Mr Daniel Bon,

Director General Policy Planning Group, Department of National Defence; Colonel Mike Cessford and Dr Brad Gladman of the Defence Directorate of Defence Analysis; Claude LeBlanc, Elizabeth Speed, and Hasit Thankey of the Defence Directorate of Strategic Analysis; and Jamieson Weetman of the Department of Foreign Affairs and International Trade, Defence and Security Relations Division. The staff at the Canadian Department of National Defence's Directorate of History and Heritage in Ottawa were helpful, as were the staff of the United States Army Centre for Military History in Washington D.C., as well as the staff at the Massey Library, Royal Military College, Kingston.

I am particularly grateful to the Australian Army for allowing me to conduct this study, and to those who hosted me during my stay in Canada, including Dr Charles Pentland and the Centre for International Relations at Queen's University, as well as my alma mater's sister college, the Royal Military College of Canada. I also wish to acknowledge assistance from the Australian Army History Research Grant Scheme in writing this book. Ms Louise M. Brooks also helped immensely with the mapwork.

The staff at McGill-Queen's University Press were gracious in assisting me convert a bulky manuscript into a more readable book. In particular, I would like to thank Dr Donald H. Akenson, Dr Roger Martin, and my editor, Dr Curtis Fahey. Getting it to publication could not have been possible, however, without the generous financial assistance arranged by Dr Doug Bland and Dr Charles Pentland of Queen's University (with financial support from the Security and Defence Forum of DND) and Roger Lee of the Australian Army History Unit.

The last debt I wish to mention is the one I owe to my incredibly selfless wife, Judith Steiner (COMHOMCOM!). She deserves my special thanks.

Finally, a disclaimer: this book is not an official account of the events described or of government policy. The views it expresses are my own and do not necessarily represent the views of the Australian Army or of the Australian Department of Defence.

Introduction

The community for which the United States speaks, includes at best, its
Anglo-Saxon cousins (Britain, Australia, Canada and New Zealand)
on most issues.

Samuel Huntington,
The Lonely Superpower

The refusal to address the question of force because we don't wish to use it merely
leaves us naked before those who may wish to use it against us.

John Ralston Saul,
Voltaire's Bastards

Australia and Canada are remarkably similar nations, many would say, and
this study examines a number of their broad similarities and notable differences. What follows is an explanation of how and why Canada and
Australia have employed expeditionary forces in support of their major security benefactors, Britain and the United States, from the Anglo-Boer War
to the modern-day "War on Terror." Examining old nationalistic myths
side by side may discomfort some readers. Yet such iconoclasm is often useful for re-evaluating preconceived ideas in an age when change is indeed
fast-paced. In explaining how and why Australia and Canada have used
their armed forces in the past, this work also sets out to show how their
forces may be able to collaborate more effectively with each other and their
major allies in future. I should point out in this context that, while my focus is on the armies of both countries, their air forces and navies are still
discussed. After all, a cross-examination of armies would not be complete
without at least passing reference to developments in the other services.

In a sense, this work revisits some of the issues of national identity,
policy, and strategic choices that first arose in the late nineteenth and early
twentieth centuries. In that earlier period, the focus for Australians and
Canadians was on Britain.[1] Indeed, several factors combined to indicate a

need for Canadians and Australians to seek haven in collective security within the British Empire. But even when calls for closer British imperial integration were strongest, considerable uncertainty prevailed about the ultimate nature of imperial relationships.[2] At the time, the two fledgling nations of Canada and Australia were not in a strong position to argue collectively against the political and diplomatic masters of the British Empire. More than a century later, though the focus of power has shifted from the British Empire to the United States, the issues of those times have a strangely familiar echo. Early in the twenty-first century, with mature instruments of state and the globalizing technology of the information era, Canadians and Australians are well placed to reconsider commonalities in the context of their relationship with the United States. This work sets out to conduct such a re-examination of the military affairs of these two remarkably similar countries of the West in an alliance framework.

In using the term "the West," I recognize what Canadian author John Ralston Saul describes as "the binding ties between Europe, North America and Australasia" which "can be seen in a series of fundamental shared experiences and convictions. From the Judaeo-Christian imprint through the Reformation, the Renaissance, the Industrial Revolution, the democratic and revolutionary crises, the West was formed."[3] Yet, in the aftermath of the u.s.-led war in Iraq, the West's binding ties have been strained. Many countries in the West have sought to reassess their relations with a "lone superpower" that appears ever wary of its potential "strategic competitors," and Canada and Australia have been in similar positions as they have done so. For Australia, however, the imperative to hold its course in maintaining good relations with the United States has been more enduring and strongly felt, although not completely constant, in order to buttress the security and stability of its region.

For Canada, the North Atlantic Treaty Organization (NATO) has for decades played the key counterweight role in relations with the United States. But the effectiveness of this counterweight has waned, in part because of Canadian neglect but also because of NATO's reduced military cohesiveness as the organization rapidly spread to include Eastern European nations.[4] The diminishing of NATO's prominence for Canadian foreign and defence policy was accentuated by NATO's exclusion from the running of the initial phases of the military campaign in Afghanistan in 2002 and from the war in Iraq in 2003. Such developments suggest that Canada and Australia may benefit from exploring closer relations with each other in order to promote common political objectives and to enhance their influence in the conduct of international affairs.

In addition, for both Australia and Canada, there have been numerous instances when their policies have not always followed in lock-step the American lead. For instance, Australia sided with Britain, not the United States, in the Suez Crisis in 1956 and opposed u.s. policy over independence for West New Guinea/Irian Jaya in the 1960s. The Canadian government initially balked at u.s. actions in the Cuban Missile Crisis and the Vietnam War. Yet, despite these sporadic strategic divergences between the United States and its two middle-power[5] strategic cousins, the diplomatic activity of Canada and Australia has almost invariably been premised on the need for responsible behaviour on the part of the United States in fostering international order. Thus, Canadians and Australians regularly seek to strengthen the international system.[6]

Since Canada and Australia are two geographically distant members of the international system with numerous historical and cultural ties, the nature of the relationship between them may be usefully analogized in terms of family ties. It would be going too far to describe the two countries as "siblings." Siblings tend to be very close to and highly conscious of one another, and this is not the case with Canada and Australia. The relationship might better be compared to that of cousins. Cousins usually attend family gatherings but are otherwise often indifferent to one another. Still, cousins can be friendly to one another without being close. The notion of "cousinhood," as it is being used here, was first enunciated as a grouping of people that share common beliefs but different approaches and centres on the Anglo-American alliance that emerged from the Second World War.[7] It serves as a useful way of considering Australia and Canada as part of the collective defensive grouping of the West. Although they may have diverged on some details, both usually showed up to defend their common global security interests, often far from their own shores. In terms of national strategy and the application of military force, therefore, the paradigm of "strategic cousins" is employed in this work to capture some of the broad filial ties between Australia and Canada. Such ties are most often spoken about by Australians and Canadians in terms of their relationships with either Britain or the United States, and not with each other. In that sense (and with the exceptions outlined in this work), this book covers largely unexplored territory.

Some have also argued that involving friends and allies in any major u.s. military effort contributes to and may even be a precondition for acquiring American domestic political support for such efforts.[8] With this in mind, and notwithstanding Canada's decision to refrain from supporting the u.s.-led campaign in Iraq in 2003, it could be argued that Canada may simply be too close to the United States to avoid having its security policy closely tied to it. Meanwhile, Australia may be too isolated to avoid relying on the United States as its security benefactor. In terms of security ties and alliance partnerships for these two so-similar New World countries, attractive alternative options are not easily found.

Alan Ryan has observed that "Australia's most important military relationship is with the armed forces of the United States of America. This relationship is not simply due to ties of culture, language and democratic ethos ... Australia's national security is inextricably linked with the fortunes of the United States and with other liberal-democratic countries around the world."[9] The same could be said of Canada. With these observations in mind, the argument presented here is, in part, premised on the understanding that Canada and Australia, by and large, have shared and continue to share an interest in maintaining close relations with their common security and defence benefactors, successively Britain and the United States. Support by Canada and Australia for Great Power benefactors comes despite their efforts to strengthen international institutions that hedge against indiscriminate use of power in international trade relations and other matters.

I take this relatively positive view of the significance and place of Canada/Australia relations with the United States despite deep-seated suspicion of Americans in some quarters of both countries, as articulated by certain leftist journalists and public figures.[10] The American scholar Andrew Bacevich has argued that the ultimate objective of the United States is the creation of an open and integrated international order based on the principles of democratic capitalism. His views resemble Michael Mandelbaum's three "ideas that conquered the world": peace, democracy, and free markets.[11] If Bacevich and Mandelbaum are largely correct, as this work contends, then Canada and Australia have a vested interest in remaining closely aligned with the United States. Canada and Australia also are in a similar predicament as they seek to find their own place in unequal relationships, and expeditionary forces often play an important part in establishing that balance.

Political scientists would look to hegemonic-stability theory to argue that post-war peace and prosperity can be, at least in part, attributed to the willingness of the United States to create and maintain an international economic order, a *Pax Americana*. It is to such an order, as Anne Capling has argued, that "Australians pay their dues" – often through the use of expeditionary forces.[12] While the merits of hegemonic-stability theory are debated, it is fair to say that Canada and Australia, in the main, are beneficiaries of American influence, and they share an interest in ensuring that the "American Empire" endures while at the same time protecting their own interests in unequal relationships.

From the American viewpoint, countries more closely aligned with the United States than these two "strategic cousins" would be hard to find. Canada and Australia have enduring shared strategic interests, to say nothing of shared cultures and values, with the United States. Britain's Lord Palmerston may have been correct in asserting that there are "no permanent allies, only permanent interests," but, for Canada and Australia, those security interests have been remarkably congruent for over a century, thus suggesting a close approximation to permanency alongside the world's major English-speaking powers, Britain and the United States.

While it is not that long ago that both Canadians and Australians were treated as though they were citizens of the United Kingdom, the British government now treats them substantially as aliens, and Australians and Canadians largely reciprocate.[13] In the early twenty-first century, Canada and Australia would probably balk at the idea of ever becoming part of a formalized "Anglosphere" group of nations, although informally such cultural-historic networks still exist, spanning many areas (including literary, economic, diplomatic, military, and intelligence matters) and stretching back to the ties originally formed during the heyday of the British Empire. Yet such objections do not rule out the merits of considering a closer bilateral relationship between Australia and Canada. After all, as the Australian scholar Owen Harries observes (and as Chart 4 appears to confirm), "despite the differences, no two other countries more closely resemble the United States in terms of language, culture and political values."[14]

EXPLORING THEIR MILITARY HISTORIES

This book sets out to conduct an examination of the military histories of Canada and Australia by using the research methodology of historians, but with an element of political science. In large part, it compares the literature on Canadian and Australian defence and foreign policy as it pertains to the use of armed forces. In doing so, it integrates the work covering both nations' histories, moving back and forth and striking comparisons along the way between the two.[15] The reader may benefit from examining Appendix 1 to help keep the two sides of the timeline in mind. In addition, given that secondary, or published, material is one of the major mechanisms for creating and nurturing beliefs in societies, this work gathers ideas concerning the use of armed force in the Australian and Canadian experience and tests them against each other.

By focusing attention primarily on secondary material, I also reconsider the way that such writers have interpreted history to date, challenging some of their introspective or single-nation-focused assumptions. Such a review requires extensive qualitative judgment of the literature in a field in which objectivity, some would say, is difficult to attain. For instance, post-modern[16] de-constructionist[17] critics may argue that such difficulties make an expansive book like this unworkable. On the basis of such views, however, readers would discount the works of ambitious yet sound and re-spected historians who dare to reach for a broad canvas of history.[18] In my own case, I have sought numerous reviews and critiques of my draft mate-rial in an effort to be as rigorous, cogent, and dispassionate as possible. Still, generalizations are inevitable for such a sweeping review of two nations' military histories over more than a hundred years. By the same token, one of this book's premises is that expansive works can and should be written if tired and unhelpful paradigms are ever to be reconsidered.

In conducting such historical analysis, the functional and dialectical planes are addressed.[19] With regard to the functional plane, the military staffs, unit organizations, and tactics are examined and compared at the tactical level, where appropriate, particularly on deployments abroad. On the dialectical plane, the political, social, cultural, and economic factors that helped form the two nations and their respective armed forces are also considered where applicable. After all, no army operates apart from these societal determinants. Reconciling the two planes on a national level and then comparing them with those of another nation is part of the analytical approach taken for this work.

With these dialectical and functional parameters in mind, the book's principal focus is on the expeditionary nature of the forces that Canada and Australia raised, trained, deployed, sustained, and modified on war-fighting and peacekeeping operations for over a century. In addition, while organizational structures are considered at certain junctures, I examine such matters only insofar as they pertain to the centrality and similarity of the expeditionary roles. Expeditionary operations involve the projection of military power over long distances to accomplish a specific objective. However, the term "expeditionary" is not frequently used by Australians or Canadians to describe their military formations deployed on opera-tions.[20] At times, owing to political sensitivities about the use of force be-yond their own borders, the governments of Canada and Australia have shied away from thinking about their armed forces in these terms. Never-theless, Australian and Canadian ground forces have been sent abroad – on expeditions – to fight their nations' wars and otherwise carry out their governments' policies. Certainly, troops have been raised, at times, for coastal defence and others have been used domestically for aid to the civil authorities. But such circumstances are only a fraction of the overall experience of the armies of Canada and Australia for more than a century.

Both Australia and Canada have numerous strategists and military historians who have written about their armed forces on such military operations abroad.[21] But a primary focus on understanding their own internal matters, in isolation from other's parallel developments, reveals a shortfall in the analysis thus far. Accounts tend to be lopsided, even jingoistic, at times, leaving little space for a broader appreciation of what the two countries have in common. For instance, the Australian First World War military historian C.E.W. Bean has been charged with having a partial perspective concerning the martial prowess of the Australian soldier.[22] Similarly, Canada's Sir Max Aitken has been accused of having "forged" a military reputation for Canada during the same period.[23] Their contributions helped foster what has been described as an "imagined community."[24] The wartime events described by Bean, Aitken, and others played a part in transforming Canadian and Australian notions of imagined community from being Empire-based to being locally based, centred thereafter on the federations of Canada and Australia respectively. Their work, however, while laudable, came at the expense of the greater imagined community (based on similarities in language, religion, customs, and traditions) that Canada and Australia have shared since their foundation as autonomous nations. No doubt, much can be learnt from a detailed consideration of one's own heritage, but there remains scope for further understanding by reflecting upon the similarities and differences between the two nations' forces (as well as the societies that nurture them). This work sets out, in part, to bridge that analytical gap primarily by comparing the experiences of the Australian and Canadian armies.

STRUCTURING THE ARGUMENT

As part of the parallel analysis, this work refers to a number of plausible alternative situations. Had circumstances been slightly different, such scenarios conceivably may have resulted in significantly different outcomes. The use of scenarios is important as an iconoclastic tool to help readjust the nationalistic paradigms[25] which have formed as a consequence of Canadian and Australian military historians focusing primarily on nationalistic historical interpretations of events as a means to establish their own national identity. Here, my goal in using alternative scenarios is not to construct alternative history per se but to prompt the reader to challenge present-day conceptions about the nature of Australia's and Canada's international relations. Like illuminating a dimly lit gallery with an extra lamp, this work sheds new light on the experiences of these two countries' forces with the intention of providing a fresh perspective on the experiences of both.

Against the background of this unorthodox methodology, the book is written chronologically. The first five chapters examine the historical experiences in parallel of the deployments alongside British forces from before the Anglo-Boer War to the Korean War. This historical review starts, in chapter 1, with an examination of events prior to the commencement of the First World War. Subsequent chapters cover the First World War itself, the inter-war period, the Second World War, and the commencement of the Cold War and the Korean War – the last war that Canadians and Australians fought together under a British commander and with British equipment, doctrine, and procedures.

The following chapters, 6 to 8, cover the period from the end of the Korean War to the War on Terror. Chapter 6 commences with a discussion of the divergence of force-development trajectories as Canada focused on NATO and peacekeeping and Australia focused on jungle warfare and Southeast Asia. Chapter 7 considers the post-Cold War era when there was a significant reconvergence in the force-development trajectories of Canada and Australia, with both becoming quite heavily involved in a remarkably similar series of military operations. Thereafter, in Chapter 8, the focus is on the period since the attacks of 11 September 2001, using the same comparative methodology as is in the preceding chapters.

The final part is a summary and overview, drawing out the broad conclusions and significant observations about the scope and limitations of closer collaboration between the forces of Canada and Australia. In addition, there are numerous appendices that support the main argument. Perhaps the most significant is appendix 8, which concerns the conceptual framework that is established by answering four questions: Why compare Australia and Canada? What do they have in common? What makes them different? And, particularly given the extensive similarities, why are the ties between them so limited? Appendix 8 also sets out to explain why these two countries, in contrast to any other likely candidates, are chosen for such detailed parallel consideration. Key to this is an assessment of the scope and limitations, in broad terms, of the similarities and differences between Canada and Australia that have affected the size, structuring, development, and use of their armed forces for what has turned out to be predominantly expeditionary operations. Appendix 8 establishes the value and legitimacy of the unorthodox comparative historical approach that is undertaken in this book.

Three observations emerge from my analysis. The first is that, in terms of historiography, the single-nation-focused accounts of warfare, peacekeeping, and defence and foreign policy written by Canadian and Australian historians tend to be unidimensional and could benefit by being put in a broader context. Secondly, despite the occasionally significant and widely recognized military contributions of Canadians and Australians, their actions, apart from when they have worked together, have barely featured in the "imperial" capitals of London and Washington. Finally, Canada and Australia are too distant to have been motivated to work with each other by cultural ties alone. Yet, as this book sets out to demonstrate, they can work more closely together if it can be shown that mutual cooperation will promote their own national interests.

Abbreviations

ABCA	America Britain Canada Australia
ABDA	American British Dutch Australian
ACT	Australian Capital Territory
ADF	Australian Defence Force
ADFA	Australian Defence Force Academy
ADHQ	Australian Defence Headquarters
AIF	Australian Imperial Force
ANZAC	Australia New Zealand Army Corps
ANZAM	Australia, New Zealand, Anglo-Malayan
ANZUS	Australia, New Zealand, United States
APEC	Asia Pacific Economic Cooperation
ARF	ASEAN Regional Forum
AS	Australia
ASD	Alternate Source Delivery
ASEAN	Association of South East Asian Nations
ASIO	Australian Security Intelligence Organization
ASP97	Australia's Strategic Policy, 1997
ASPI	Australian Strategic Policy Institute
AWM	Australian War Memorial
BAOR	British Army on the Rhine
BASB	Brigade Administrative Support Battalion
BCATP	British Commonwealth Air Training Program
BCC-K	British Commonwealth Contingent-Korea
BCFESR	British Commonwealth Far Eastern Strategic Reserve
BCOF	British Commonwealth Occupation Force
BCSS	Battlefield Command and Control System
CA	Canada

CANZ	Canada-Australia-New Zealand (ministerial trilateral meetings)
CAS	Chief of Air Staff
CBC	Canadian Broadcasting Corporation
CCEB	Combined Communications-Electronics Board
CDF	Chief of Defence Force
CDFS	Chief of Defence Force Staff
CDS	Chief of Defence Staff
CEF	Canadian Expeditionary Force
CER	Closer Economic Relations
CF	Canadian Forces
CF JOG	Canadian Forces Joint Operations Group
CGS	Chief of the General Staff
CJFA	Commander Joint Forces Australia
CMAC	Cambodian Mine Action Centre
CMBG	Canadian Mechanized Brigade Group
CMF	Citizen Military Forces
CMFZ	Commonwealth Monitoring Force-Zimbabwe
CMTTU	Commonwealth Military Training Team Uganda
CNS	Chief of Naval Staff
COMAST	Commander Australian Theatre
CSCAP	Council for Security Cooperation in the Asia Pacific
CSSB	Combat Service Support Battalion
DART	Disaster Assistance Response Team
DFAIT	Department of Foreign Affairs and International Trade (Canada)
DFAT	Department of Foreign Affairs and Trade (Australia)
DIO	Defence Intelligence Organization
DJFHQ	Deployable Joint Force Headquarters
DSD	Defence Signals Directorate
EATS	Empire Air Training Scheme
EU	European Union
FPDA	Five Power Defence Arrangement
FWMAO	Free World Military Assistance Organization
GATT	General Agreement on Tariffs and Trade
GOC	General Officer Commanding
HA	Humanitarian Aid/Assistance
HMAS	His/Her Majesty's Australian Ship
HMCS	His/Her Majesty's Canadian Ship
HQADF	Headquarters Australian Defence Force

HQAST	Headquarters Australian Theatre
ICCS	International Commission for Control and Supervision
ICSC	International Commission for Supervision and Control
IFOR	Implementation Force
INTERFET	International Force East Timor
IPMT	International Peace Monitoring Team-Solomon Islands
ISAF	International Security Assistance Force-Afghanistan
JIM	Joint, Inter-agency, and Multilateral
JTF2	Joint Task Force Two
LFC2	Land Forces Command and Control System
LWSC	Land Warfare Studies Centre
MAB	Munitions Assignment Board
MARCOT	Maritime Command Operational Training
MFO	Multinational Force and Observers
MINUGUA	United Nations Mission in Guatemala
MINURCA	United Nations Mission in Central African Republic
MINURSO	United Nations Mission for the Referendum in Western Sahara
MIP	Multilateral Interoperability Program
MNF	Multinational Force
MOLE	Military Operations in the Littoral Environment
MONUC	United Nations Observer Mission in the Democratic Republic of the Congo
MRG	Management Review Group
NAFTA	North American Free Trade Agreement
NATO	North Atlantic Treaty Organization
NBCW	Nuclear, Biological, Chemical Weapons
NDHQ	National Defence Headquarters
NORAD	North American Air/Aerospace Defence Command
NPCSD	North Pacific Cooperative Security Dialogue
NPAM	Non-Permanent Active Militia
NRMA	National Resources Mobilization Act
NZ	New Zealand
OECD	Organization for Economic Cooperation and Development
OEF	Operation Enduring Freedom
OIF	Operation Iraqi Freedom
ONUCA	United Nations Observer Group in Central America
ONUMOZ	United Nations Operation in Mozambique
ONUSAL	United Nations Observer Mission in El Salvador
ONUVEH	United Nations Election Verification Organization Haiti

OSGAP	Office of the Secretary-General in Afghanistan and Pakistan
OTN	Observer Team to Nigeria
PECC	Pacific Economic Cooperation Council
PJBD	Permanent Joint Board of Defence
PMG	Peace Monitoring Group-Bougainville
PPCLI	Princess Patricia's Canadian Light Infantry
R22èR	Royale Vingt-Deuxième Regiment
RAAF	Royal Australian Air Force
RAF	Royal Air Force (UK)
RAMSI	Regional Assistance Mission Solomon Islands
RAN	Royal Australian Navy
RAR	Royal Australian Regiment
RCAF	Royal Canadian Air Force
RCMP	Royal Canadian Mounted Police
RCN	Royal Canadian Navy
RCR	Royal Canadian Regiment
RFC	Royal Flying Corps
RIMPAC	Rim of the Pacific
RMA	Revolution in Military Affairs
RMC	Royal Military College (Kingston, Ontario/ Duntroon, Canberra)
RNZIR	Royal New Zealand Infantry Regiment
RTA	Restructuring the Army
SA	South Africa
SASR	Special Air Service Regiment
SEATO	South East Asia Treaty Organization
SERT	Special Emergency Response Team
SFOR	Stabilization Force
SHIRBRIG	Stand-By High Readiness Brigade
SOC	Senior Officials Consultations
SPADATS	Space Detection and Tracking System
SPPKF	South-Pacific Peacekeeping Force-Bougainville
SWPA	South West Pacific Area
TEAL	Trilateral Exchange and Liaison or Tactics, Equipment and Logistics (ABCA)
TMG	Truce Monitoring Group-Bougainville
TTCP	The Technical Cooperation Program
UK	United Kingdom
UN	United Nations

UNAMA	United Nations Assistance Mission in Afghanistan
UNAMIC	United Nations Advance Mission in Cambodia
UNAMIR	United Nations Assistance Mission in Rwanda
UNAVEM	United Nations Angola Verification Mission
UNBRO	United Nations Border Relief Operation-Cambodia
UNCI	United Nations Commission for Indonesia
UNC-K	United Nations Command-Korea
UNCMAC	United Nations Command Military Armistice Commission-Korea
UNCOK	United Nations Commission on Korea
UNDOF	United Nations Disengagement Observer Force-Syria
UNEF	United Nations Emergency Force in Egypt
UNEF II	Second United Nations Emergency Force in Egypt
UNFICYP	United Nations Force in Cyprus
UNGOC	United Nations Good Offices Commission in Indonesia
UNGOMAP	United Nations Good Offices Mission in Afghanistan and Pakistan
UNIFIL	United Nations Interim Force in Lebanon
UNIIMOG	United Nations Iran-Iraq Military Observer Group
UNIKOM	United Nations Iraq-Kuwait Observer Mission
UNITAF	Unified Task Force-Somalia
UNMCTT	United Nations Mine-Clearance Training Team Afghanistan/Pakistan
UNMEE	United Nations Mission to Ethiopia and Eritrea
UNMIH	United Nations Mission in Haiti
UNMIS	United Nations Mission in Sudan
UNMISET	United Nations Mission in Support of East Timor
UNMO	United Nations Military Observer
UNMOGIP	United Nations Military Observer Group in India and Pakistan
UNMOP	United Nations Mission of Observers Prevlaka
UNOC/ONUC	United Nations Observers Congo
UNOGIL	United Nations Observer Group in Lebanon
UNOMUR	United Nations Mission for Uganda-Rwanda
UNOSOM	United Nations Operation in Somalia
UNPREDEP	United Nations Preventive Deployment Force-Macedonia
UNPROFOR	United Nations Protection Force-Former Yugoslavia
UNSCOM	United Nations Special Commission
UNSMIH	United Nations Support Mission in Haiti
UNTAC	United Nations Transitional Authority in Cambodia

UNTAET	United Nations Transitional Authority East Timor
UNTAG	United Nations Transition Assistance Group-Namibia
UNTCOK	United Nations Temporary Commission on Korea
UNTEA	United Nations Temporary Authority in West Irian
UNTSO	United Nations Truce Supervision Organization
UNYOM	United Nations Yemen Observer Mission
U.S.	United States
USA	United States Army
USAF	United States Air Force
USMC	United States Marine Corps
USN	United States Navy
WTO	World Trade Organization

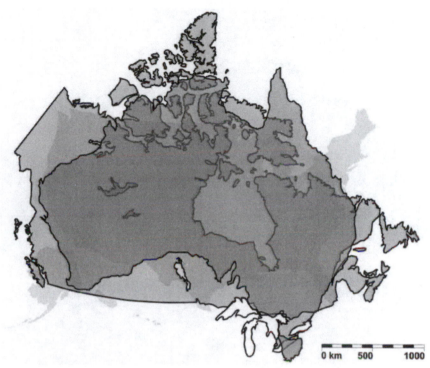

0 km   500   1000

Canada and Australia are remarkably similar in size, with similar geographic and demographic (and hence social and cultural) phenomena at work. In the map above, the outline of Australia is superimposed on the map of Canada, making it possible to recognize some of the more obvious geographic similarities between the two countries. A shaded outline of the United States has been added to the map, providing information not only on how similar the countries are in size but also suggesting the influence the US presence has had on both Australia and Canada.

Map 1
Australia and Canada in the Asia-Pacific region

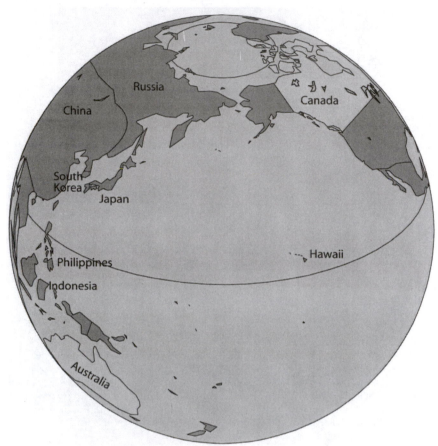

Canadian primarily looks to the United States and Europe, but, like Australia, it also has an interest in Asia-Pacific security issues – the two countries being virtually equidistant to potential flashpoints in northeast Asia. For instance, Canada deployed forces to Vladivostok (1919); Hong Kong, India, Burma, the Aleutians and Australia during World War II; South Korea (1950–1957); West Irian (1962–63); Cambodia (1993); and East Timor (1999–2000). Canada also sent ICSC monitors to Laos, Cambodia, and Vietnam (1954–1965 and 1973). If the twenty-first century is to be the "Asian Century," Australia and Canada may be drawn together even more so than during the last century.

Chart 1
Comparing Australia and Canada

Commonalities	Differences
BROAD SIMILARITIES	CANADA
– No revolutionary or civil war and no global *empire*	– Quebec culture and language main concern: internal unity
– Relatively small states (economy and demography) – AS: 1/15th and CA 1/9th size of U.S. population, but similar sizes geographically	– Membership of La Francophonie
– Membership in British Commonwealth	– Membership of G8, NATO, NORAD, and NAFTA
– Membership in ABCA armies and CANZ foreign affairs forums	– UN SHIRBRIG participant
– Membership in APEC, ARF, PECC, CSCAP, and OECD	– Next to US
– Membership in Western Europe and Others Group in UN	– Trade mostly land-borne with US
– Aligned with the United States and common UK/USA intelligence ties	– Lacks amphibious forces
– New World countries with Anglo-Celtic and European roots	– Smaller special and airborne forces
– Colonial experience and no hereditary titles	– No conventional military threat (arguably neither does Australia)
– Excluded from membership in other regional bodies – EU and ASEAN	– No strategic bombers
– Immigration and Multiculturalism	– No external secret intelligence service
– Widespread English usage	– Restrained "Mountie" stereotype
– Judaeo-Christian values with post-modern influences	– Founding Loyalist "myth"
– "Globalized" ideas, finance, capital, technology, and culture	
– Similar approaches to gun control, gender issues, and public health	AUSTRALIA
– Commonly recognized standards in education, law, medicine, etc.	– Remote from other "western" states
– Democratic practices	– Trade overwhelmingly seaborne
– Capitalist economic system	– Fought in Vietnam and Iraq
– Industrialised economies with comparable per-capita GDP	– Anzac Day
– Highly educated work forces	– Larrikin "digger" stereotype
– Federal bicameral (Westminster) parliamentary and legal systems	– Founding convict "myth"
– Heavily trade-reliant	
– Latent "anti-British-ness" in society	TOGETHER
– Idealpolitik and Realpolitik dynamics	– unilingual versus bilingual Canadians
– Large and often dry land masses (albeit with different geography)	– "general purpose" versus Canadian "multipurpose" capabilities
– Small populations on the rim with vast uninhabited hinterlands	– No formal military alliance with each other
– Middle power aims in foreign, trade, environment, and security issues	– Federal political orientations often at variance
– Priority on transport, industry, and social/health services	– Sporting preferences (ice hockey and baseball versus rugby, Aussie rules and cricket)
"MILITARY CULTURE" SIMILARITIES	
– Residual British influence on armed forces" ethos	
– Parallel shift in reliance from UK to US and stress on inter-operability	
– Security in collective defence	
– Similar defence budget and force sizes	
– Reliant on wide-area northern surveillance systems	
– Enlistment of aboriginals for regional surveillance	

Chart 1
Comparing Australia and Canada (*continued*)

Commonalities	Differences
BROAD SIMILARITIES – Priority challenge between defence at home or overseas – Lack of opportunity to excel militarily beyond the tactical level – Recently developed national-level military structures – Similar peace support operations experience – Small but skilled defence industries – ANZUS/Joint Facilities/AUSMIN versus NATO/NORAD/PJBD similarities – RMC Canada–RMC and ADF Academy similarities FORCES' SIMILARITIES – Similar land force structures (3 × regular brigades and reserve force) – Similar army equipment (Leopard tanks, LAVS, M113s) – Similar land-forces mix (special, light, and mechanized) – Similar air forces (F-18s, P3s, C130s) – Similar navies (frigates, submarines, inshore vessels) – Fought alongside in Boer War, World Wars, Korea, and Afghanistan – Contributed to many similar peacekeeping missions	TOGETHER – Opposite climates – Opposite hemispheres/ seasons

Chart 2
Cultural map of the world about 2000

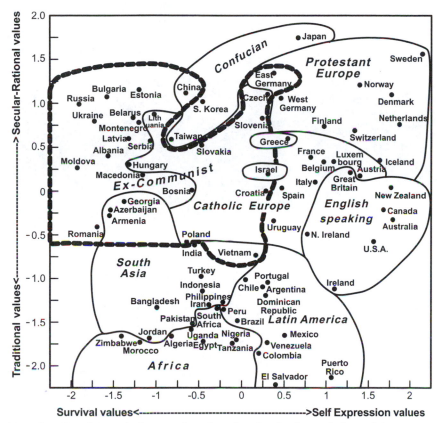

Note: Canada and Australia have similar values that also closely match those of the
United States.
Source: Prof. Ronald Inglehart, *World Values Survey*, University of Michigan, cited in
The Economist, 4 January 2003, 20. See also http://wvs.isr.umich.edu/, downloaded
26 May 2003.

South Africa, CA 1900. Eight men of the 2nd south Australian (mounted rifles) contingent, who fought in the Boer War. Left to right: Edward Richman, later lieutenant-adjutant of 5th contingent; trooper Frederick Solly-Flood, later no 19, corporal, 2nd contingent; trooper Harry Morant, no 37; trooper Hubert Fetch, no 51; trooper Harry Ogilvy, no 45; trooper Ramsay Nuttall, no 49; trooper Robert Bostock, no 75; trooper William Cuttle, no 2. Trooper Morant, later a lieutenant and known as "The Breaker" because of his experience in breaking horses, was court-martialled and executed in South Africa in 1902 for shooting Boer prisoners, some of whom were responsible for the murder of his friend and fellow officer, Captain Hunt.

HMCS *Magnificent* (seen here with fireflies on deck) was a British-built Majestic-class ship – like the Australian carriers HMAS *Sydney* and HMAS *Melbourne*. HMCS *Magnificent* arrived in Port Said in 1956 with aircraft, vehicles, stores, and personnel as part of Canada's contribution to the UN force in Egypt (UNEF). (USN photo – from http://www.hazegray.org/navhist/canada/postwar/magnific/)

Australian and Canadians on similar duties. Defence Public Affairs and Canadian Forces
Photo by MC Ken Allen

Australian Special Forces and Naval Forces. (Australian Defence Public Affairs)

STRATEGIC COUSINS

1

Prior to the First World War

At the dawn of the twentieth century, Britain stood as the pre-eminent global power. Then, however, following two debilitating world wars, it became a secondary power to the United States. This shift was matched by a concomitant increase of self-reliance, industrial maturity, and sense of independent identity in Canada and Australia (as well as elsewhere in the British Empire) that was fostered by wartime developments. Throughout this period, Canada and Australia continued to react to events, usually with little opportunity to influence strategy. Yet it was developments in the nineteenth century that set the tone for Australian and Canadian defence measures at the opening of the twentieth century.

NINETEENTH-CENTURY ANTECEDENTS

The military forces extant in 1901, when the Australian colonies formed a self-governing federation, are best understood in the context of events dating back to the formation of Canada's confederation in 1867, if not earlier. For both countries, the debates preceding union were often couched in terms of the mutual benefit that the colonies would gain through collective defence. In the last decades of the nineteenth century and the early years of the twentieth, it was Canada and not Australia that pressed most for changes in the imperial relationship, particularly in terms of constitutional issues. The same cannot be said of defence matters, where developments in Australia paralleled, and at times outpaced, those in Canada as both sought to respond to Britain's gradual withdrawal from its colonies.

Ever since the Crimean War in the mid-1850s and the turn to free trade, Britain had sought to reduce its commitments to imperial defence, particularly for those colonies with responsible self-government. In Canada, a

handful of volunteer companies were incorporated in the Militia Act of
1855, in part to offset the withdrawal of some British forces. Fear of attack
by Union forces during the American Civil War convinced the premier of
the colony of Canada, John A. Macdonald, that the Canadian military system was inadequate.[1] Consequently, by 1864, with the Civil War still rag-
ing to the south, military schools were established, employing local militia
staff as instructors to help improve military proficiency. These schools did
not long survive the conclusion of the war and the demobilization of u.s.
forces, however. Their closing, after a decade in operation, was largely due
to the enactment in London in 1867 of the British North America Act,
which signalled to the United States that Britain no longer was directly
interested in challenging u.s. interests in North America.[2] The United
States, under President Ulysses S. Grant, initially considered the creation of
Canada to be "an unfriendly act" that created a rival North-American federation based on monarchical principles. But such concerns would soon
abate. In the meantime, since the War of 1812, Canadians in Upper Canada
(now the province of Ontario) had fostered the myth that Canada could be
saved by the exertions of the local citizenry, and so little interest was shown
in raising permanent forces beyond a small cadre to train the part-time
militia. This approach, which had the great advantage of being cheaper
than the cost of maintaining a standing military, echoed views found in the
United States in the nineteenth century and during the earlier colonial
period – that a citizen military force of "unprofessional soldiers" would always be sufficient to defend the nation.[3] Besides, both countries distrusted
standing armies.

The Australian colonies did not face the challenge of a land border with
anyone except other British subjects like themselves, but "Loyal Associations" of free settlers were raised as early as 1800 to oppose riot and, in the
event the Irish convicts rebelled, revolution. Such troops helped suppress a
convict rebellion near Parramatta, a few miles west of Sydney, in March
1804. There also was a surge of martial enthusiasm with the outbreak of
the Maori Wars in New Zealand, particularly during the early-to-mid
1860s. For instance, the colony of Victoria dispatched the HMVS *Victoria*
to its sister colony. In addition, several thousand troops from the Australian
colonies volunteered to help out.[4]

In Canada, nearly four hundred men volunteered in French-speaking
Quebec to defend the Papal States in 1868 during the Italian civil war.
These "Pontifical Zouaves" returned in 1870 to an enthusiastic reception
from their French-speaking fellow citizens. That same year, which was also
the year in which British troops withdrew from the Australia colonies,

Canadian citizen forces were sent to the Red River settlement (now the site of the city of Winnipeg) in 1870 under the command of professional British military officers to preserve order and sovereignty in the face of a Metis[5] rebellion led by Louis Riel. Shortly thereafter, in 1871, Britain and the United States signed the Treaty of Washington, which resolved several outstanding boundary disputes. With the treaty signed, British Army regulars also withdrew from most of Canada in 1871.[6] Troops remained at the British naval base at Halifax on the Atlantic coast and returned to Esquimalt on the Pacific coast in the 1890s after having left in the early 1870s. This move reflected Britain's empire-wide efforts to economize with the use of its forces. Out of a similar desire for economy, as well as faith that Britain continued to be the ultimate security guarantor and a desire to encourage Britain not to "abandon" Canada militarily, the Canadian government declined Britain's offer of the regular-force Royal Canadian Rifles. It also assumed that the existing militia framework was sufficient to resist any American assault until reinforcements sailed from Britain. As one Canadian political observer noted, reflecting an enduring sentiment, "the best thing Canada can do is to keep quiet and to give no cause for war."[7]

In 1878 there was briefly a widespread fear of an impending war with Russia, with rumours of Russian warships off the coast of Canada and Australia. In Canada's case, an appeal for Royal Navy cruisers to defend the Gulf of St Lawrence on Canada's east coast was rejected in London. This apparent threat triggered some enthusiasm for warships and more substantial ground forces in both places. The Russian scare also prompted both Canada and Australia to create a series of coastal defences to guard ports.[8] On land, the first regular army troops were the garrison artillery units – "A" and "B" Batteries at Kingston and Quebec in Canada and "A" Battery in Sydney, New South Wales.[9]

Britain's Carnarvon Commission of July 1879 raised the question, for the first time, of the need for standardization of equipment, weapons, and ammunition throughout the British Empire. However, with the Russian threat ephemeral, the financial constraints were considered too great to maintain martial enthusiasm, particularly given the economic burden following the economic depression of the mid-1870s.[10] Neither Canadians nor Australians would remain focused on local defence.

When the Sudan crisis occurred in 1884 to 1885, 386 French-speaking and English-speaking Canadians, mostly civil boatmen (or *voyageurs*) from Canada's canals and waterways, were recruited. They went on the expedition sent up the Nile River to avenge the death of Britain's General Charles Gordon and to recapture Khartoum. Canadians won distinction in this distant imperial expedition, which paradoxically contributed to the impetus to full Canadian nationhood. The experience gave young Canadians a chance to judge themselves against men from other lands. Canada's government under Sir John A. Macdonald was hostile to the notion of directly supporting Britain's imperial policing tasks with Canadian soldiers, so the *voyageurs* were recruited and paid for by Britain. By contrast, several Australian colonies happily offered their own volunteer forces, although, ironically, the genesis of the New South Wales force, according to the Canadian historian Roy MacLaren, "was an indirect result of the recruitment of the *voyageurs*. An inaccurate report reached Sydney that six hundred Canadians would take over garrison duties in Britain to allow regular troops to help in the rescue of Gordon. The news of the decisions of the government of New South Wales to send to the Red Sea a contingent from its minute militia in turn encouraged Canadian militiamen to redouble their efforts to go to Egypt." The New South Wales offer of an artillery battery and five hundred infantrymen was accepted by London, but the expedition was short-lived and marked by boredom and death by disease rather than by any glory in battle. Nevertheless, its significance lay in the fact that colonial troops had been voluntarily raised and sent as distinct forces from Australia on an overseas military expedition. Australian enthusiasm for such expeditions reflected a stronger martial and imperial sentiment than existed in Canada. There would be many more such expeditions to follow for both nascent nations.[11]

Meanwhile, in Canada, the relatively quick and successful suppression of the Riel Rebellion of 1870 had served to satisfy most Canadians that little effort was required beyond the establishment of a paramilitary police force with a domestic mandate. Such a domestic mandate could be granted by the Canadian government without need for authorization from Britain, which retained authority over international and defence matters. Initially, this paramilitary organization was known as the North-West Mounted Police.[12] Another Metis rebellion occurred in 1885, this time on the western Plains, an event that revealed significant militia shortfalls in equipment and training but prompted only limited efforts at reform. Subsequently, the North-West Mounted Police became the Royal Canadian Mounted Police (RCMP), replete with military-style red tunics and paraphernalia. The militia, for its part, would remain largely unchanged, but it would serve as a handy patronage instrument, a means of social advancement, and a vehicle to facilitate the construction of public works rather than as an instrument of war.

Britain's Royal Navy stayed a while longer than most of the British Army units, operating out of Canada's Pacific ports until after the Anglo-Boer

War and the Atlantic ports until 1907, whereas the Australian naval station was independent, with its own squadron from 1884. On land, Canadian defence remained predicated on a defence against an invasion from the south. This task would be the responsibility of the militia from 1871, along with a small Canadian Permanent Force that would act largely as an instructional cadre from 1883 onwards. The final British Army-operated Atlantic and Pacific Ocean fortresses at Halifax and Esquimalt would be passed over to Canada in 1905 – one year after the inauguration of Britain's entente with France. War seemed a remote concern for Canadians. For them, European issues featured less than North American ones. Many considered that Canada's best interests would be served by avoiding a close identification with British policy while retaining the assurance of British military support in the event of crisis. Any imperative for Canada to build a strong army was further diminished by the growing Anglo-American entente that followed the peaceful resolution in 1894 of the so-called Venezuela Crisis (over demarcation of the Venezuelan border with British Guiana) between Britain and the United States.[13]

The net result of this reactive defensive approach was that the Canadian militia was a volunteer entity that was largely a police force of artillery, cavalry, and infantry with no service corps and haphazardly trained with obsolete and inadequate weapons. The militia would maintain this status until Sir Frederick William Borden was appointed Canada's minister of militia and defence in 1896 – a position he would retain until the fall of Sir Wilfrid Laurier's Liberal government in 1911. Borden set out to reform the military by applying the Swiss concept of a national army that involved, ideally, the total male population.[14] Borden's interest in Swiss practices matched that demonstrated by his successor, Sam Hughes, and by Canada's "cousins" in Australia. Australia's chief of intelligence, Colonel W.T. Bridges, had visited Switzerland in 1909 and reported back to Australia on the merits of applying a Swiss-styled military scheme.[15] The first steps in this direction were taken in Australia with the introduction of conscription in 1911, during the prime ministership of Alfred Deakin.

Awareness of Britain's continued eagerness to gain greater economy in its defence measures, as well as imperial support for similar economies, served to spur efforts to integrate Australia's separate colonial land forces. Efforts at military integration reflected the growing cohesion of the Australian colonies, cohesion that was fostered by the building of railways – a phenomenon also common to Canada and the United States. In addition, emphasis on defence of the Australian continent rather than the need for expeditionary forces made military integration acceptable to the colonial electorates.[16] Still, such sentiment did not prevent the Australian colonies from participating enthusiastically in one foreign adventure. In mid-1900 a multinational China Field Force was formed to suppress the Boxer uprising in China. This effort occurred at a time when American interest in Asian affairs was rising, with the annexation of the Philippines in 1899, and thus, not surprisingly, the United States was part of the multinational force. So were the Australian colonies. Victoria contributed its Auxiliary squadron of 200 men, New South Wales sent 260 men, and South Australia sent a ship, the *Protector,* with its 100-man crew. These expeditionary forces participated in some minor offensives but mostly carried out routine guard and police duties until recalled in March 1901.[17] Prior to their return, on 1 March 1901, Australia's colonial military forces, totalling just over 29,000 troops, were transferred to federal control and formed what would become known as the Australian Army.[18]

THE ANGLO-BOER WAR

Federation in Australia occurred in January 1901 while the Anglo-Boer War was under way in South Africa, having commenced in 1899. Initially, Britain was confident that, with its regular infantry troops, it could quickly defeat the apparently ill-disciplined Boers. But, after several significant setbacks in 1899, volunteers (particularly horsemen) were gladly welcomed from around the Empire, including Canada, Australia, and New Zealand. The Boers were eventually defeated in terms of conventional battles but at significant cost in casualties. Indeed, skirmishing and "guerrilla" type raids continued until British attrition tactics forced the Boers to surrender in 1902. By then, however, the skills acquired by Canadian and Australian volunteers in their relatively harsh and predominantly rural environments back home (particularly their ability to ride well, shoot straight, and live off the land) had made them ably suited to the kind of warfare embarked on in the latter stages of the war in South Africa.[19]

After federation in 1901, Australian colonial troops already in South Africa passed under federal control. Australia made a concerted effort to assert a measure of control over these troops, reflecting nascent nationalist urges that were particularly strong in the Australian Labor Party and the country's Irish community.[20] In Australia, the dispatch of forces to the Anglo-Boer War was widely supported, with several colonies sending troops who in 1899 and 1900 formed Australian units operating under British command. As in Canada, many of the troops were funded by wealthy benefactors,[21] but governments of the various Australian colonies were obliged to cover the costs in varying degrees. There was considerable opposition to the war from the Labor Party and the Catholic Church, whose largely Irish clergy tended to sympathize with fellow victims of British imperialism.

Similar antipathy was expressed in Canada, particularly by French Canadians. However, for Canadians, the debate over the war was more passionate and set a precedent for future tensions between the anglophone and francophone communities of Canada. The French Canadian prime minister, Sir Wilfrid Laurier, sympathized with the plight of the non-English-speaking Boers and, like Sir John A. Macdonald during the Sudan crisis, did not want to send a single soldier to aid Britain in its colonial war, particularly with French Canada pressing for Canada to avoid involvement. To Laurier, the battle with the Boers was nothing more than "a petty tribal conflict." But, since English-speaking Canada was predominantly enthusiastic about the conflict, the government settled on a compromise. In October 1899 it announced that it would allow unofficial contingents to go to South Africa, with British financial support on their arrival, and later it would support and fully fund official Canadian contingents. Perhaps most important, Canada insisted that Canadians be kept in their own units under their own officers and not dispersed among other British forces. This set a precedent that Australia also chose to follow following federation in January 1901.[22]

Henri Bourassa, French Canada's most articulate and influential war critic, played a leading role in denouncing the Canadian contribution to the war, arguing that a dangerous precedent had been set – a pattern for expeditionary warfare that Bourassa predicted would be repeated, as indeed it would be in 1914, 1939, and 1950. As Pierre Berton has observed, "the new war would force Laurier to indulge in the kind of tightrope act that every successful prime minister would have to master." In any event, the enthusiasm of English-Canadians for Canadian participation was supported by the British general officer commanding (GOC) the Canadian militia, Major-General E.T.H. Hutton, who had begun preparing a contingency plan for the dispatch of 1,200 Canadian men before Laurier had him replaced. Hutton, who had been commended for his appointment in Canada based on his success as the commandant of the military forces of New South Wales from 1893 to 1896, had hoped to lead the combined colonial forces of Australia and Canada. As it turned out, he would do exactly that, as Britain dispatched him from Canada to South Africa.[23]

During the Anglo-Boer War, Australian, Canadian, and New Zealand mounted infantry units were "brigaded" in a 6,000-strong force, the

1ˢᵗ Mounted Infantry Brigade. As a mark of distinction, the Canadians wore maple-leaf badges and the Australians a letter "A" badge on their slouch hats. Under Hutton's direction, Canadians and Australians gained their first experience of working together in battle, earning reputations as "a wild lot" who "love a fight at close quarters."[24] One Australian soldier wrote of the highly colourful and laudatory exploits of his Canadian colleagues in and out of battle.[25] Apart from a few such references, however, the readers of exclusively Australian or Canadian accounts of the war would find little evidence of these troops having fought alongside each other. To identify the common experiences, one would need to read the two countries' accounts in parallel (where an uncanny similarity between the forces contributed and the battles fought is evident) or refer to British accounts of the war. And British accounts tend to offer only passing reference to the "colonial" troops who fought in support of the British-led campaign.

The performance of colonial troops, while not always a series of triumphs, was remarkable. While most British troops were infantry, Australians as well as Canadians were predominantly horsemen, and the nature of the conflict demonstrated the merits of having good horse riders to fight against the mostly horse-riding Boers. At times, though, Canadians, with their wide-brimmed Stetson hats, mistook the slouch-hat wearing Australians for Boer horsemen. On one occasion, a Canadian inadvertently nearly shot Major Harry Chauvel, who would later become the first ever Dominion corps commander, leading the Desert Mounted Corps in Palestine in the First World War.[26]

As with the Australians, the relative success of Canadian arms, and the subsequent public criticism of the British Army, enhanced English Canadians' sense of distinctiveness and importance. However, the conflict exacerbated internal divisions in the country – between English, and predominantly Protestant, Canadians on the one hand and French and Irish Catholic ones on the other – to a more marked degree than was the case in Australia, probably because anti-imperial sentiment in that country was confined to a smaller and more dispersed proportion of the population. Canadian advocates of the war condemned anti-war French Canadians as "traitors and conspirators" who were impeding the Empire's mission. Such views were not representative of all English Canadians, since there were vigorous advocates of peace among Canada's Protestant community and among the Irish. But verbal violence (and, in one instance, during the three-day Montreal riot in March 1900, the violence turned physical) left a bitter legacy of misunderstanding and resentment. The conflict also helped launch the twentieth-century French Canadian nationalist movement that was already starting to react to rapid industrialization, urbanization, anglicization, and materialism. In addition, the war stimulated militia reform because the Boer system of defence appeared applicable to Canada. Imperial officers could lecture about the benefits of professional soldiery but the veterans who had witnessed the British Army's failures were not persuaded, seeing the loyal Canadian frontiersman and volunteer as second to none.[27]

Under the leadership of Prime Minister Laurier and Militia and Defence Minister Borden, Canada opposed imperial integration but supported imperial cooperation. Laurier, like most Canadian Liberal prime ministers, had little interest in military affairs, yet he and Borden were pragmatists, seeing imperialism and autonomy as complementary. They realized that Canada must pay its way but they remained eager to ensure that it did so without an unquestioning submission to imperial judgment. They also recognized an enduring feature of Australian and Canadian military entanglements: even when a dispute was not of immediate concern, the emotional involvement of some citizens could drag the country into it.[28] Thus, Borden had pressed for the first Canadian deployment to South Africa to be a full contingent, paid for, equipped, and transported by Canada. Yet Laurier was embarrassed at having to defend publicly, to sceptical French Canadians, the dispatch of troops for an imperial cause. Remarkably, given his concern over British actions, his government made no effort to influence the conduct or resolution of the war, despite poor British performance in the early stages. His hands-off approach would have echoes in the two world wars and beyond.[29]

POST-ANGLO-BOER WAR REFORMS

The Boer's concept of a nation in arms had exposed the weaknesses in British tactics, training, equipment, and leadership, and this bred a healthy scepticism of British military prowess in Canada, Australia, and elsewhere. The experience appeared to confirm the impression that war was a manly triumph over the obstacles of nature – not a matter of superior training or tactics – and, according to this view, courage, initiative, and intelligence were the hallmarks of a modern force. Such thinking fit well with the views of many Canadians and Australians, living as they did in what were still largely agrarian societies. For Canadians, there were also residual concerns over the prospect of American raids, last witnessed in the mid-nineteenth century; the Fenian raids of that time, according to Hereward Senior, "had aroused a martial spirit among Canadians that could be enjoyed without the cost of war."[30] In fact, many of the Canadian troops who departed for South Africa did so with the experience of the Fenian raids in mind. They embarked as "soldiers of the Queen," but their trying experiences in South Africa under poor British leadership led them to return as self-conscious Canadians.[31]

The parallel experiences of returning Australian troops resulted in a similar viewpoint about the role of the militia in Australia and the primacy of local tasks for the defence of the continent. For Australia, the war marked the birth of a military reputation noted for dash, courage, and the skills developed in the bush rather than on the parade ground, and the identity forged in South Africa would remain pervasive for a long time.[32] The execution of Peter Handcock and "Breaker" Morant, sentenced to death by a British court-martial for having killed detained Boers and a German missionary, also contributed to Australia's decision to adopt separate legal provisions for Australian troops. Those provisions were based on the British Army's legal code but they excluded the death penalty. Coincidentally, Handcock and Morant's defence counsel, the Australian Major James Thomas, had served with an irregular unit known as the Canadian Scouts. This unit had earned a reputation for savagery after having witnessed their commanding officer killed by Boers, and the incident left Thomas with a stark view of warfare. "War is war," he wrote, "and rough things have to be done." Major Thomas's experience with the Canadian Scouts suggests that a twist of fate could have made a Canadian the target of British military justice instead of Handcock and Morant.[33]

The dismissal of Canada's Colonel Sam Hughes from service in South Africa because of his strong public criticism of poor British military leadership produced bitterness in some quarters over British arrogance, a feeling similar to that felt in Australia over the Handcock and Morant incident. Certainly, it raised the issue of both government control and jurisdiction over their "nationals," although in Canada's case it did not lead to a change in the legal provisions concerning command authority.[34]

Following the war, the prime role of Canada's and Australia's part-time militias would be home defence and aid to the civil power – despite objections from the Australian Labor Party to the use of the militia in this capacity. But the expeditionary role would re-emerge whenever war approached to threaten national interests.[35] Despite the difficulties that British forces endured in the Anglo-Boer War, there was a sense in Australia and Canada, from this point on, that the colonials' contributions had been important in achieving eventual victory and that these contributions were recognized and valued by Britain. In peacetime, to be sure, neither country was eager to be at Britain's beck and call, but, as another war approached, both Australia and Canada – in response to pressure from their publics and also out of a sense that there was no other option – would resolve to come to Britain's aid should that be necessary. And they would do so, once more, as providers of expeditionary forces for overseas contingents.

For Laurier in Canada, the war in South Africa made him wary of attempts to fashion a centralized, imperial defence policy. He was concerned about the polarizing effect of such imperial commitments, which left him caught between French Canadian opposition to the war and the jingoism found in English Canada. Historian C.P. Stacey observed that "the rift between French and English Canada caused by the great external crises of 1914–18 and 1939–45 is painfully foreshadowed in the events of 1899."[36]

Reflecting a desire to avoid further rifts, Frederick Borden's plan was predicated on Canadian defence and not on an expeditionary force, but it was relatively inexpensive and it demonstrated that Canada was taking steps for its own defence. His plan required 100,000 sharpshooters, only one-third of whom would be uniformed troops required to attend annual camp for instruction. He set about creating other combat-support and service-support corps based on the British model and using British-pattern equipment, with some exceptions, including the Canadian-designed and manufactured Ross rifle.[37] British patterns provided the Canadian militia with the force structure necessary to maintain an army on deployment – capabilities that would prove invaluable in the years ahead.[38]

Meanwhile, similar post-Anglo-Boer War reorganizations were taking place in Australia. Lieutenant-General Hutton had returned to Australia as the nation's first GOC in January 1902, after serving previously in New South Wales, Canada, and South Africa. Hutton was charged with amalgamating, with as little expense as possible, the military forces of the six Australian colonies and to form the Australian Army as part of an imperial force for overseas service. He recommended the creation of a manufacturing department to produce its own small arms, guns, and ammunition. However, with financial cutbacks and martial enthusiasm waning after the end of the Anglo-Boer War, he faced a difficult challenge.[39] Still, Hutton was an assertive commander and he succeeded in laying the foundation of a modern military organization. But, as had happened in Canada, his eagerness to prepare imperial expeditionary forces and his reluctance to accept civilian political constraints on his influence led to his loss of favour.[40] Australia's first prime minister, Edmund Barton, had earlier made clear that "to establish a special force, set aside for absolute control of the Imperial government, was objectionable."[41] Nonetheless, the first Australian

Defence Act, of 1903, did allow for the formation of a special force to augment the government's regular forcers in time of war (s.118). Barton's position, like Laurier's in Canada, did not signify unwillingness to come to the
aid of Britain if the need arose.

When Hutton's appointment ended in December 1904, the Australian
government abolished his position and established the Military Board, consisting of the minister for defence, the chief finance officer in the Department of Defence, and the four senior army representatives. These moves
matched sweeping changes in the British Army's organization in the wake
of the Anglo-Boer War, changes that attempted to ensure civilian ministerial control over the forces while retaining professional military advice
through a chief of general staff (CGS). Despite Hutton's efforts to tie
Australian defence to imperial plans, the Defence Act that had come into
effect on 1 March 1904 restricted military service to Australian soil, mir-
roring the constraints imposed under the Canadian Militia Act. Australia's
Defence Act established the citizen-soldier as the basis of the Australian
Army and limited the role of permanent forces to administration, instruction, and garrison functions, once again matching developments in Canada.
This meant that any force contribution to an overseas commitment would
be made from volunteers, and an expeditionary force for overseas service
would have to await the outbreak of war to trigger its creation. In 1905 a
higher body, the Council of Defence, was created in Australia to advise
government on matters of policy. Hutton's organization of the field force
was scrapped in 1906, owing to weaknesses in the plan for mobilization. In
its place, units were grouped into five light horse brigades (two each in the
states of New South Wales and Victoria), two infantry brigades, and four
mixed brigades for the smaller states, with a view to facilitating regionally
based training exercises.[42]

In Canada, similarly, the Militia Act of 1904 gave the country its own
rudimentary General Staff, distinct from, but modelled on, the British
General Staff and responsible to the Canadian government as an advisory
body for the minister of defence.[43] Borden set about to reorganize Canada's existing twelve military districts into five larger regional commands,
not unlike those in Australia. One of Borden's last acts as minister was to
accept a plan for the dispatch of a Canadian contingent overseas. While
this plan deliberately avoided any politically unpalatable binding commitments that would have undermined the government's domestic standing, it
appeared to run contrary to Borden's efforts to assert Canadian sovereignty. Still, the plan reflected his growing awareness that a future war
would likely involve Canada. This reality led to military expenditure in

Canada rising dramatically from $1.6 million in 1898 to $7 million in 1911, with militia strength also increasing from 25,000 men in 1904 to over 57,000 by 1914.[44]

In Australia, an enduring debate had begun over how to reconcile demands for national self-defence, in a region with few natural allies and partners, and imperial commitments. Until 1905, fears of Russian and Japanese aggression were widespread, and the Russian naval defeat at the Battle of Tsushima left many uneasy about Japan's intentions. Although the Anglo-Japanese Treaty appeared to guard against immediate danger, many were concerned that it weakened Australia's security since it allowed Britain to reduce its naval presence in the Far East – Australia's "near north." Ironically, this eroding strategic situation made British naval strength the increasingly important condition of Australian security.[45]

Concerns over the prospects of war also helped spur military organizational reform. Thus, the British Army introduced a new General Staff system in 1906, with Canada following suit and Australia doing so as well three years later, in 1909. The staff model, which was a derivative of the Prussian-German system, provided commanders with the decision-making machinery for the increasingly complex art of war. In effect, it became a two-category structure – operations (G) and administration (AQ) – with the operations staff taking higher precedence.[46] This reform was a key development for future military interoperability in the Empire. In contrast, the United States followed the French numerical staff model, which numbered the staff branches 1 for personnel, 2 for intelligence, 3 for operations, and 4 for supply. The British-lettered system remained unchanged throughout the two world wars and beyond, providing for greater standardization and improved military efficiency – elements vital for the organization of vast armies in war. Canada's and Australia's staff model, based on the British one, endured for more than a half-century, until the numerical staff system became more widely accepted as the NATO standard. "Education in a common doctrine," Richard Preston argues, "was also a handy substitute for centralised command."[47]

CONSIDERING COMMON DEFENCE AS WAR LOOMS

The 1907 Colonial Conference laid the basis of future Commonwealth military structure and, recognizing the political limitations of the Empire, approved the principle of cooperation rather than direct commitment. At the conference, Australian Prime Minister Alfred Deakin agreed to standardize equipment and adopt the British force structure. This decision accomplished more to facilitate the integration of British imperial forces than any calls for imperial unity. For Deakin, Dominion equality with Britain was important in order to free Australia from the restraints of a single British department of state – the Colonial Office. His position contrasted with that of Laurier, who equated equality with unwanted responsibility for costly security and defence measures. While in London, Deakin stressed self-reliance as a way to limit the country's vulnerability. But, with a rising Japan, this approach was not enough to guarantee security, despite London's insistence that Japan was an ally. Australians were acutely aware of being in Asia but not of it. Like Canadians, but perhaps more so, they felt the conflicting pull of geography and history.[48] Altruism and nascent nationalism aside, economic dependency on Britain left both countries with little choice but to follow developments in British military doctrine and organization and to commit to fighting alongside British forces in the future.[49] By the same token, policy makers and elites were taken with the idea of *one* British Empire. However, the question that many in the dominions wanted to address was that of who would lead the Empire – Britain alone, or a consortium of states. This question, for the time being, was left unanswered. There would be little practical resistance to the notion of one Empire until the middle years of the forthcoming Great War when the question of responsibility and authority came to the fore.

In the meantime, following an invitation extended by Alfred Deakin to President Theodore Roosevelt, the Great White Fleet visited Australian ports in 1908, demonstrating the emergent power of the United States as well as the relative decline of British sea power in the Pacific.[50] Roosevelt, like his Australian counterparts, was concerned about growing Japanese power in the Pacific; the fleet's visit, which received an enthusiastic welcome, thus served mutual interests as a show of Anglo-Saxon solidarity in the Pacific. It stimulated interest in naval matters, and Deakin hoped that it would help persuade Britain to allow Australia to have its own fleet. As the largest display of naval power ever witnessed in the Pacific, it certainly raised Australian awareness of the significance of the United States as a Pacific power, even though few realized just how prominently the United States would feature for Australia in the years ahead, as it would for Canada also. By this time, too, Canadians were also becoming aware of growing American might. Canadian concerns over this development increased during the Alaska "Panhandle" dispute of 1902–05 – a dispute that illustrated Britain's willingness to sell out Canadian interests in order to curry favour with the United States.[51]

Also in 1908, marking a turning point in the path towards imperial integration, the Imperial Conference in London recognized the sole responsibility of the several parliaments of the British Empire to decide the nature and scope of their defence policy.[52] Answering to their own domestic constituencies, the federal governments of Canada and Australia would have to balance Britain's pressure for commitments with the domestic concerns of their local electorates. Shortly after the conference, in February 1909, the Australian government placed orders for its first warships. This development reflected revolutionary British concessions, which were driven by the need, in the face of a growing threat from Germany, to enlist support by whatever means possible while also recognizing Australia's lingering fears of Japan. Such fears among Australians had been exacerbated following Britain's fleet reorganization in 1904–05, which reduced the number, size, and quality of Royal Navy ships stationed in the Pacific and inauspiciously coincided with the Japanese annihilation of the Russian fleet at the Battle of Tsushima in May 1905, leaving the Japanese fleet dominant in the Western Pacific. After intense public lobbying in Australia, the Royal Australian Navy (RAN) was created in 1911 and its first, British-built ships arrived in Sydney Harbour in October 1913.[53] Australia was the first British Dominion to create an independent navy. The country's eagerness for its own fleet reflected geostrategic and domestic political concerns that were different from those of Canada.[54] It also reflected Australia's greater economic reliance on Britain for trade, industry, and finance and thus vulnerability to disrupted sea lanes. In the years leading up to 1914, both Canada and Australia were predominantly agricultural producers and exporters to the United Kingdom, from which they imported finished products, although Canada's trade with the United States was far greater. This economic relationship with Britain was to endure through the Second World War and served, for both countries, as a key realpolitik motivation for coming to Britain's aid in time of war.

As part of the deal with Britain, the ships acquired for the RAN were designed to fit seamlessly with the Royal Navy. When war came, Australia's flotilla was briefly engaged in attacking marauding German cruisers threatening seaborne trade in the Pacific and Indian Oceans. These encounters established the prestige of the fledgling navy, and thereafter Australian ships were faithfully sent in response to the Empire's call to duty far from the country's shores. In the end, Australian ships, controlled from London, played a marginal role alongside the British fleet, certainly when compared to the higher profile and more substantive role of Australian ground forces in Gallipoli, Flanders, and the Middle East.

In Canada, domestic pressure to establish an independent navy was less, because there were no immediate strategic imperatives to do so – despite the equidistance of Australia and Canada to Japan (see Map 1). By 1909, however, the Canadian government had adopted the premise of a navy controlled by Canada, in part as a concession to growing fears of German naval power – which appeared increasingly capable and prepared for conducting raids along the Canadian coast. In the end, the ships Canada managed to acquire were placed under arrangements similar to those governing the ships of the RAN – at the disposal of the Admiralty for general service with the Royal Navy.[55] What is more, the Australian precedent served as a model for the nascent Canadian fleet. Thereafter, the Canadian government would be encouraged to concentrate on providing assistance with ground troops, particularly given the long lead time for shipbuilding and fleet expansion.[56]

As war approached, the reality of the German threat spurred Australia and Canada into putting their military forces into better shape. In 1909 Australia set up a Commonwealth General Staff, but, unlike Canada's, it was styled not as a separate body but as a section of the British Imperial General Staff. Australia also started to introduce a system of universal service in 1909.[57] Lord Kitchener, considered the foremost soldier of the British Empire at the time, was invited to visit Australia, and in February 1910 he recommended an expansion of the national service system that was then being introduced.[58] Kitchener's scheme, which divided the country into ninety-two battalion areas, officially came into operation on 1 January 1911.[59] Critics observed, however, that Kitchener's plan, devised with a Anglo-Boer War-like scenario in mind, created an under-gunned force, with only 2.64 guns per thousand infantry as against 5.7 per thousand in the British Army. In addition, Kitchener placed little priority on staff training and development, since British professional officers were considered likely be able to be provided if needed. All this came to haunt soldiers and commanders in the early days of the forthcoming world war, when artillery shortfalls resulted in increased casualties and the lack of training opportunities left few openings for Australians in senior staff appointments.[60]

Kitchener also recommended the establishment of a Royal Military College, which opened at Duntroon, near the capital, Canberra, in 1911. The new college's founder, Major-General Sir William Throsby Bridges, was an Anglo-Boer War veteran who began his military career in Canada at the Royal Military College, Kingston, Ontario, prior to moving to Australia with his parents.[61] Bringing his memories with him, Bridges established a college that bore a striking resemblance to his alma mater. These two colleges were both modelled on the United States Military Academy at West Point, with its four-year curriculum, rather than Britain's one-year program at Sandhurst. While Bridges was building a military college, another Canadian, Brigadier-General G.M. Kirkpatrick, was tasked with supervising the development of the Australian compulsory training scheme.[62] In those days, the appointment in Australia of someone from Canada appeared not to be given a second thought. Shared standards and a sense of common identity were virtually taken for granted.

The issue of imperial centralization continued to be contentious, as did the issue of professionalization of the armed forces. The first Canadian to be appointed Canadian CGS was an Anglo-Boer War veteran, Major-General William Otter. Otter supported the reorganization of the Canadian militia into the six divisions that were considered necessary for Empire and home defence, recognizing, as Frederick Borden also did, that a Canadian infantry division and cavalry brigade might one day be required to fight alongside Britain in Europe. These measures reflected the changed strategic circumstances that added impetus to a fundamental shift in defence plans in Canada as war approached. In particular, the need became apparent for modernized, better-prepared, and better-equipped forces.[63]

The Conservative government of Prime Minister Robert Borden, elected in 1911 on a platform opposing free trade with the United States, was known to be more sympathetic to the idea of imperial cooperation. Thus, as tensions in Europe increased, military planners, such as British Colonel Willoughby Gwatkin, seconded to the Canadian General Staff, were encouraged to prepare a force for service abroad. Reflecting the need for preparation, in June 1911 representatives from Canada, Australia, New Zealand, and South Africa met with British staff at the War Office in London. There, they discussed exchanges, standardization of training and equipment, the operation of the imperial General Staff system, and the placement of Dominion officers at British staff colleges in Camberley and Quetta. Neither Canada nor Australia managed to establish regular-force command and staff colleges before the war. But, by the outbreak of war in 1914, Canada and Australia had twelve and four British staff college graduates respectively, with an additional two on loan to Australia from Britain.[64] On balance, the Canadians held an advantage, having commenced a rudimentary militia staff course in Canada in 1905. These exchanges set a precedent that was to become a feature of the British Commonwealth military system in the years that followed.[65] Indeed, British military practices were closely followed in Australia, Canada, and elsewhere in the Empire. Even in French Canada, militia regiments were fitted to be similar in appearance to British regiments. A modest exchange of officers was also established between Canada and Australia in the years prior to 1914.[66] These contacts provided some scope for cross-pollination of ideas and the emergence of a common school of military thought without challenging an individual government's right to control its own armed forces.

In Canada, despite these efforts at imperial coordination, Gwatkin's plans and those of Otter's successor as CGS, Major-General Colin Mackenzie, were largely thwarted following the appointment in late 1911 of the new Canadian minister for the militia, Sam Hughes – an industrious, leading Conservative Party figure, Orange Protestant, and Anglo-Boer War veteran. Hughes was a partisan proponent of amateurism, voluntarism, and the dispensation of favours to party cronies, and his vision did not include thorough planning along the lines proposed by Gwatkin. Hughes would preside as virtual commander-in-chief, having promoted himself to the militia rank of major-general. This state of affairs continued until he was removed from office in 1916, when his mismanagement of the forces in Europe, his disrespect for the principles of collective cabinet responsibility, and his continued confusion of civil-military roles turned him into a political liability. In the meantime, his heavy political clout, particularly in the province of Ontario, and wide support in the militia led Prime Minister Borden and others to give Hughes virtual carte blanche in the management of Canadian military affairs.[67]

CONCLUSION

The end result was that, prior to the outbreak of war in 1914, both the Canadian and Australian armies were remarkably similar in size, each with a small cadre of professional soldiers and a large group of militia: 2,906 Australians in the permanent force and 50,332 in the militia, compared with 3,038 Canadians in the permanent force and 57,338 in the militia – almost double the 36,000 members in 1904.[68] The professional soldiers in both armies had similar duties, forming headquarters staffs and providing instructors and administrators. They also worked closely with local militia groups, including the coastal forts. While Britannia still "ruled" the "waves," full independence was not yet tempting. To quote Margaret MacMillan: "As members of the British Empire, they were protected by the world's strongest navy and shared in the world's greatest power. Moreover, they had confidence in the ability of British statesmen to manage its affairs. That was about to change."[69]

2

The First World War

When war broke out in August 1914, the sentiment in Canada and Australia was remarkably similar. Canada's French Canadian opposition leader, Wilfrid Laurier, captured the mood of the time, declaring that Canada's answer to a call from Britain was "Ready, aye, ready." Even Henri Bourassa, who had opposed the Anglo-Boer War, favoured support for Britain in 1914. In Australia, Prime Minister Andrew Fisher announced that Australian resources were committed "to the last man and the last shilling."[1] Clearly, in 1914, Canadians and Australians viewed their place in the world quite differently from the way they would by war's end. Governments in both Canada and Australia understood that their forces would become part of the imperial army since British dominions were automatically committed once Britain declared war on Germany. Prime Minister Robert Borden of Canada proposed that his country would bear the full cost of its military contribution – a cost that added a billion dollars to the national debt by the end of the conflict. Borden, and most Canadians like him, still revered Britain and its institutions. The war was a test of loyalty they would proudly pass in 1914.[2] Australia likewise was to pay its own way, in part at least to advance Australian interests.[3]

EARLY CAMPAIGNS

Australia's early enthusiasm was reflected in the dispatch of the Australian Naval and Military Expeditionary Force, on 19 August 1914, to capture the German colonies of New Guinea and the Bismarck Archipelago north of Australia. This expedition would prove portentous, taking place in a part of Australia's neighbourhood that would be fought over much more intensively a generation later. In the meantime, the campaign ended with the surrender by the German governor on 13 September. However, British support for Japan's seizure of former German colonies north of the equator raised concerns that would remain for many years. Britain's interest and focus on European affairs led its foreign policy to be more conciliatory towards Japan than Australians considered appropriate – much as Britain's attitude over territorial disputes in North America had been conciliatory towards the United States at Canada's expense. This dichotomy of perspectives would haunt relations between Britain and Australia in the years ahead, particularly as Japan used these islands as bases for its southward assault in 1941 and 1942. Nevertheless, in 1914 Australians rallied in support of Britain, conscious that a triumphal Germany was not in their interests.[4]

The British War Office had initially asked Australia for four brigades to be sent for the war in Europe,[5] but the Australian government decided to send a division instead, so as to preserve the separate identity of its forces overseas. This move, paralleling steps taken in Canada, would prove important for Australia's role in the war and in the development of Australian nationalism.[6] When Australia announced on 3 August 1914 the raising of a volunteer expeditionary force of 20,000 men – a force that eventually would form one division of three infantry brigades plus a separate light horse brigade – the country had on hand over 87,000 rifles and plenty of basic gear with which to equip the force, thanks to the establishment of four government-owned factories in 1910 to manufacture small arms, cordite, leather goods, and distinctive clothing – items that the Australian troops insisted on wearing as a mark of identity, despite the availability of cheaper British-made uniforms. Nevertheless, the extent of manufacture in Australia was still not enough to equip a self-sufficient force. For instance, the 1st Australian Imperial Force (AIF) Division sailed with only thirty-six eighteen-pounder quick-firing artillery guns, and without the necessary support services and equipment such as medium and heavy howitzers.[7] Canadian forces experienced similar shortages in artillery in the early months of the war.

These shortcomings were sorely felt by the Australians at Gallipoli, from April to December 1915, where the "Anzac legend" was created – the legend of bravery, recklessness, and cynicism and disrespect towards authority outside battle but stern discipline under fire.[8] Still, only a minority of the Australian volunteers were from farming, mining, or frontier occupations, in this respect being much like the Canadians, as military historians Desmond Morton and J.L. Granatstein have observed. There were almost as many from clerical, sales, or professional backgrounds and a large portion were recruited from urban manufacturing, construction, and labour jobs.[9]

The incomplete divisional structure that Australia at first offered meant that the force could only be subsumed into the structure of the British Army. In addition, over-emphasis on providing combat forces without commensurate supporting elements resulted in a "teeth-to-tail" ratio weighed heavily towards front-line troops. This helps explain the disproportionate casualty rates that Australian, Canadian, and other British Empire troops suffered during the war – even when other troops were succumbing to periods of intense ill-discipline. Despite pre-war objections to an imperial commitment, the forces created by Canada and Australia were entirely dependent upon British support, and the force structures changed only incrementally over the course of the war, with Canadian and Australian military-organization modifications usually following British ones. All the while, the home armies in Australia and Canada withered, to the point of being considered virtually worthless. The citizen forces lost a steady stream of experienced men to the forces overseas.[10]

The initial force of Australians sailed on 1 November 1914, along with the first batch of New Zealanders. Although originally intended to sail to England, the force disembarked in Egypt on 3 December to train there instead. This arrangement became necessary because of the difficulties Canadians had experienced on the Salisbury Plain in England, with insufficient tents and supplies and days of torrential rain. The stop in Egypt occurred also because Britain had declared war on Turkey on 5 November, presenting a possible Turkish threat to the Suez Canal. Lieutenant-General William Birdwood, an Indian Army officer, joined the AIF in Egypt, along with a corps staff gathered from the Indian Army. This arrangement relieved Australia of the responsibility of providing for its own staff officers, something that, at this stage, was beyond the capacity of Australia and Canada alike. By January 1915, both the Canadian Expeditionary Force (CEF) and the AIF were undergoing extensive training while recruiting for additional forces continued at home.

The Australian 1st Division was commanded by Scottish-born and Canadian-educated Major-General Sir William Throsby Bridges. Its accompanying 1st Light Horse Brigade was commanded by Brigadier H.G. "Harry" Chauvel, the only Australian-born regular officer to receive a senior command in the original force. Soon, Bridges would become the first Dominion officer in the British Empire to command a division in battle, but early in the Gallipoli campaign of 1915 he was mortally wounded and he died at sea shortly afterwards.[11]

The campaign at Gallipoli was intended to be a strategic manoeuvre to overcome the stalemate of the Western Front in Europe, open a path through the Bosporus in order to support the Russian war effort against

Germany, and force Turkey out of the war. But, with preliminary naval bombardments removing the element of surprise, the Allied forces that landed on the beaches of Gallipoli faced substantial Turkish forces that were well led and equipped. Between 25 April, when the forces landed, and early December 1915, when the force withdrew, tens of thousands of Allied and Turkish lives were lost. Yet, for Australia and New Zealand at least, the "crucible" of fire helped forge a sense of national identity in battle that their peaceful path to self-government and independence had so far denied them.

The experience at Gallipoli was immortalized by the official historian of Australia's involvement in the Great War, C.E.W. Bean. His account portrayed Australian soldiers as typifying a rugged national character and reinforced a sense of the natural fighting qualities of such troops, despite the differing views of some British regular officers and historians.[12] This mythologizing of the Aussie "digger" lent added weight to the notion that militia-based citizen forces obviated the need to maintain professional standing armies in peacetime. Yet in Gallipoli it was not simply poor British generalship that cost the campaign. For instance, even John Monash, then an Australian brigade commander, suffered significant tactical setbacks along the way, learning hard and costly lessons in the process.[13] Canada's experience on the Western Front had a similar effect on the minds of Canadians. However, Canada was not represented at Gallipoli, except by Newfoundlanders, who would not be incorporated into Canada until 1949.[14]

In Palestine, the Anzac mounted troops formed the keystone of the defence in Egypt against German-led Turkish forces. At the battle of Romani, in early August 1916, the Anzac Mounted Division under Major-General Harry Chauvel achieved one of the earliest significant victories of British Empire land forces (the other being the campaigns in West Africa) and changed the face of the Middle East campaign. By April 1917, Chauvel had become the first Dominion corps commander, being appointed commander of the Desert Column. This was a mixed British Empire formation of three (sometimes four) divisions, including Australian and New Zealand troops, that was later renamed the Desert Mounted Corps. Chauvel's corps, as part of General Allenby's British Seventh Army, played a lead role in the advance through Palestine in pursuit of Turkish and German forces in 1917 and 1918.[15] The troops under Chauvel's command experienced a much more fluid form of warfare, where manoeuvre and combined arms tactics featured prominently. This had a lasting legacy on the Australian approach to war, and contrasted with the kind of attrition warfare pursued by the Canadians on the Western Front.[16] It was an experience, too, destined to be repeated in the next world war, when, unlike their Canadian counterparts, Australian troops fought in Egypt, Palestine, and the eastern Mediterranean (as discussed in chapter 4).

After Gallipoli, the rest of the Australian force expanded to five infantry divisions. General Birdwood, who commanded the Australian Corps at Gallipoli, was eager to appoint British officers as commanders of the new divisions, but Australia's defence minister, Sir George Foster Pearce, made sure that two of the three appointments went to Australians,[17] who also garnered the bulk of the brigade commands.[18] These adjustments led the rudimentary national-command and administrative arrangements to increase in size and complexity, which further reinforced Australian legal control of its forces.

Early in the war, while Australians were engaged in the Middle East and at Gallipoli, and while the first Australian troops were deploying to France, Canada's experience in the war prominently featured the controversial minister of militia, Major-General Sir Sam Hughes. Hughes was given broad authority to make the necessary arrangements for the CEF and he personally dominated its early administration. Hughes brushed aside most of the pre-war mobilization plans and exercised personal control over the raising of the expeditionary forces into region-based battalions (not unlike the approach adopted in Australia). Hughes also controlled the force's dispatch, commencing with a contingent of 33,000 men (nearly two-thirds of whom were British-born),[19] including the 1st Canadian Division, in October 1914. The contingent set sail one month before the Australian contingent departed.

Symptomatic of a gulf that would emerge between French- and English-speaking Canada, no French-speaking unit was formed until November 1914, when opposition leader Sir Wilfrid Laurier obtained Borden's consent to the raising of a single French Canadian infantry battalion, the 22nd. Meanwhile, under Sam Hughes's direction, those French-speaking recruits who were accepted at the Valcartier training ground were placed in English-speaking battalions. Hughes had a "singularly monolithic and English view of Canada," and his approach did more to divide the two cultures of Canada than to accommodate them. In particular, his approach to raising the CEF in 1914 undermined Quebec support for the war effort by refusing to make sufficient allowance for French-Canadian units.[20] Hughes's actions contributed to the subsequent divisive conscription debates after his dismissal from cabinet in late 1916. Anglo-French national unity had always been a source of *angst* for Canada, and it would continue to feature throughout the twentieth century both as a lasting source of concern and as an overriding determinant in foreign and defence policy.

Sam Hughes was still in charge when the 2nd Canadian Division joined the 1st Division in France in September 1915. The 3rd Division was in the line by March 1916. The 4th Division, raised from recruits training in Britain, deployed in August 1916. Throughout this period, Hughes controlled the force's actions in England and France, insisting that Canadian troops remain distinct as a "national army."[21] Moreover, he actively disliked professional soldiers, and his personal dominance undermined the principles of a professional merit-based force. His approach left little room for a logical restructuring of command-and-control arrangements until after he was dismissed in 1916.

When the Canadian Corps was raised in 1915 by the grouping together of the Canadian divisions, it followed the precedent set by the Australians and New Zealanders in the formation of the Anzac Corps. Sir Edwin Alderson, a British officer who had commanded Canadians in South Africa, was appointed to command the newest corps. Alderson's appointment made room for Arthur Currie, a Canadian from British Columbia, to take command of the 1st Canadian Division. Alderson was replaced by another British General, Sir Julian Byng, but full authority over Canadians in France was being reclaimed. An order-in-council in November 1916 created the Canadian Overseas Ministry along with a cabinet minister based in London. This arrangement helped ensure that the Canadian force was regarded and respected as a separate national entity, serving *with* the British Army rather than *in* it. While still reliant on British staff support and specialist units, Canada, like Australia, was paying, equipping, and maintaining its own troops, and so the Canadian and Australian governments felt justifiably responsible to their electors for their employment and their achievements. Such sentiment was reinforced following Prime Minister Borden's decision, in December 1915, to double Canada's contribution to the war effort, from 250,000 to 500,000 troops – a figure that eventually rose to 628,000. In reality, these figures would be difficult to achieve and to maintain, particularly given the high mortality rates and the waning enthusiasm for the war.[22]

THE MIDDLE YEARS OF WAR

With so many to train, Byng introduced a training regimen for non-commissioned personnel in the Canadian Corps that emphasized the need to be informed of battlefield objectives and the general flow of the battle. This would allow attacks to proceed despite heavy casualties and the loss of commanders, an approach encapsulated in the battle that took place northeast of

the town of Arras in northern France at a place called Vimy Ridge in April
1917. During the battle of Vimy Ridge, under Byng's command, four Canadian infantry divisions advanced in line, right behind an artillery barrage of
exploding shells, to capture, albeit with heavy losses, a brilliantly sited German defensive position that had evaded capture for years. In this battle,
tanks, guns, and airplanes helped, but not as much as flexible tactics and
leaders with initiative. The British military historian Paddy Griffith observes
that "here indeed was the happy consummation of all the tactical reforms
which had taken place during the winter." Similarly, the Australian military
commander Sir John Monash, speaking about the similarity of Australia's
and Canada's wartime experiences, remarked that it was impossible to over-
value the benefits from the close and constant association of all four divisions. "It was the prime factor in achieving the brilliant conquest of the Vimy
Ridge by that Corps."[23] Byng was promoted shortly after that success.

Yet the victory of Vimy Ridge in 1917 came after two years of warfare
during which the British effort was marked by what Griffith describes as
"the greatest amateurism, blundering and fumbling." It was the sacrificial
but ultimately vital French efforts in 1915 and 1916, when most of the
techniques of modern warfare were still in their infancy, that gave Britain
the opportunity to assemble its army and make tentative experiments in
how to use such a force. Australian and Canadian troops were equally beneficiaries of that "breathing space." Griffith also observes that by 1917 the
British were ahead of the Germans in practically every department, in quality as well as quantity. (No doubt, they were helped by the entry of the
United States into the war that same year.) Australians and Canadians,
once again, were beneficiaries of the technological and industrial advantages accrued by Britain and France.[24]

By this stage in 1917, it was clear that the Canadians wanted their own
corps commander, and the British commander, Sir Douglas Haig, without
consulting the Canadian government, appointed Lieutenant-General
Sir Arthur Currie to the post. Haig knew that, although Currie was not as
popular as Byng was after Vimy Ridge, Currie was the best Canadian
general in the war. Fearing political interference, Haig was reluctant to let
the Canadian government have any say over what he considered to be
operational matters.[25]

Currie's appointment to command the Canadian Corps reflected the
growing proportion of Canadian-born members of the CEF. Canadian-born
soldiers were supplanting the British-born immigrants to Canada who had
predominated in the first two contingents, a development that was paralleled in the changing composition of the AIF. In addition, the Canadian

Corps was coming to symbolize Canada's wartime identity. Greater resources combined with increased authority over command-and-control arrangements meant that, with his competent and experienced force, Currie
could exercise independent judgment in determining how best to accomplish his missions and serve Canadian national interests. In so doing, he
presided over a transformation of the CEF from an imperial to a national
Canadian force. Yet, while the British influence gradually diminished, it
was never eliminated entirely, for senior staff positions in the corps and
several staff positions in the four divisions were filled by British officers
until the end of the war. Moreover, as with the Australians, the Canadians
tolerated British illusions about imperial centralization because of the imperial sentiment aroused by the war, because the will to win made such
matters seem trivial,[26] and because of the Canadian Corps' heavy reliance
on British units.

Australia experienced an evolution of command relationships similar to
that of Canada, with Prime Minister William "Billy" Hughes, like Robert
Borden, strongly believing in the need to have an adequate voice in the making of the Empire's foreign policy. However, as with the Canadians, a succession of British generals remained in overall command of Australian forces. In
particular, the I Anzac Corps was commanded by Birdwood from the outset
and II Anzac Corps, raised in the first half of 1916, was commanded by Lieutenant-General Alexander J. Godley until 1917. This arrangement remained
until the Australian Corps was created in 1917 and Lieutenant-General Sir
John Monash was appointed its commander.[27] Meanwhile, technology and
tactics continued to evolve on the battlefield.

With the introduction of new equipment and the imperatives this generated, tactical innovation on the battlefield would prove to be a key force-
structure determinant in wartime. Adjustments had to be made once
troops deployed to the battlefields of France and Belgium. Steel helmets
were issued (unknown in Gallipoli), the Lewis machine-gun was introduced, and trench mortars, gas, tanks, "wireless" radios, and even three-
ton trucks acquired for movement of supplies created a demand for
instruction and innovation. To this list, in Canada's case, could be added
the motorized machine-gun brigade, with its machine-guns mounted
on truck chasses and commanded by Brigadier Raymond Brutinel. The
emergent professional self-awareness within the Canadian and Australian
formations (as well as in the one New Zealand division) was reflected
in tactical innovations that their troops put into practice.[28]

In the meantime, the war continued to grind on. In one instance, at the
Somme in July and August 1916, I Anzac Corps suffered terribly, with

23,000 casualties in gruelling infantry-artillery combat. Such experiences eventually would stand commanders like Monash and the Australian Corps in good stead, enabling the force to improvise, adapt, and overcome in battle. Similarly, for the Canadian Corps, the chances for tactical innovation were significantly greater in a relatively autonomous organization than in the British corps, for a number of reasons: first, because, the Canadians were unconstrained by the institutionalism evident among British cavalry and artillery; and secondly, because of the innovation that was engendered within a more cohesive body of troops led by a trusted corps commander who was promoted from among them and whose methods and abilities they knew and understood.[29] The same could be said for Monash and the Australian Corps.

Still, there were more devastating battles ahead, including the Third Battles of Ypres (otherwise known as Passchendaele) in 1917. As historians Robin Prior and Trevor Wilson note, the British political leadership was not interested in the lessons offered by the successes at Vimy and Messines – namely, that the key to victory was to use carefully planned artillery barrages to achieve limited objectives and to secure these before advancing farther, when troop exhaustion would set in and tenuous supply links were more likely to be affected by counterattacks. For British Prime Minister Lloyd George, these operations were of no account. He, too, wanted a sudden, smashing victory, preferably far afield – on the Russian front, in the Dardanelles, or at least on the French part of the Western Front – using non-British troops. But, until then, he would sanction the Passchendaele offensives in the autumn of 1917, involving the British, Australians, and Canadians – despite Currie's opposition to the campaign. The Canadians and Australians had last fought alongside each other when they had taken turns to capture the Pozières ridge in the Somme valley, to the south of Ypres, in 1916. At Passchendaele, all five Australians divisions would fight – although not yet as one corps – while the Canadians were initially held back while Australians, alongside British troops, pushed back the Germans. In the end, they took turns participating in eleven great attacks, the first five spearheaded by I and II Anzac Corps and the final four by the Canadians. The first Australian attack in Passchendaele was a great success, but it was not under overall Australian direction. On the whole, the battle cost over 200,000 British, Canadian, and Australian lives over a period of only four months. Over 55,000 of these were Australian casualties, while the Canadians, who eventually captured the heights of Passchendaele in November 1917 but were subsequently halted, had 16,000 casualties. Such figures indicate that, despite their skill and growing reputation, Australians and Canadians would continue to suffer severe losses to help break the deadlock of trench warfare. Ironically, what had taken four months to capture in late 1917 would be evacuated in three days in the face of the German spring offensive of March-May 1918. The ten Allied divisions consumed in the battle of Passchendaele would have been more than adequate to blunt such an offensive had they not been squandered in late 1917.[30]

Throughout these battles, artillery support usually took the form of short, sharp engagements to suppress or distract the enemy. Prior and Wilson contend that, "without wishing to detract from the bravery of the soldiers, it is our view that firepower was the great determinant of success and that the skill of the infantryman, their training, bravery and endeavour, was bound to count for little in an environment in which hostile machine guns and artillery shells were allowed to dominate the battlefield."[31] Indeed, for Canadians, perhaps more so than Australians (whose overall experience of the war was more varied than just the battles of the Western Front), one of the great tactical lessons of the war that was imprinted on the minds of the future commanders of the Second World War was the efficacy of relying on firepower to do most of the work in an offensive.

The Australians certainly also made their contribution, having escaped devastating defeat when the Germans initially struck in their final great offensive in March 1918, as did the Canadian Corps. The Australians had been less fixated with retaining the corps in one piece at the height of the crisis, and Monash was prepared to plug gaps in various British corps with his Australian troops, on a temporary basis at least – particularly during the trying days of March and April 1918. The deployment of Australian divisions to plug the broken British line in the face of the German offensive arguably "saved the channel ports." This act, some would claim, was Australia's greatest contribution in the war.[32] Currie's Canadian Corps was spared the March offensive, with the exception of Brigadier-General Brutinel's Canadian Machine Gun Brigade, which deployed that month.[33]

Australia had other successes as well that reflected developments parallel to those found in the Canadian Corps. Australians became renowned for their aggressive patrolling, euphemistically known as "peaceful penetration," whereby troops quietly reclaimed enemy ground with stealthy night-time raids and advances that required small-team tactical initiative and that came to occupy much of the soldiers' time between the major set-piece battles. They achieved such dominance in this kind of fighting that German commanders facing them worried about the moral ascendancy the Australians had gained over their trench divisions.[34] A British officer wrote in the Fourth Army's war diary that the Australian Corps had gained in the preceding months "a mastery over the enemy such as has probably not been gained by our troops in any previous period of the war."[35] According to historian Bill Rawling, Canadians were among the early practitioners of trench raids, conducting large and small raids that required individual initiative and resourcefulness, and predating the notoriety of the Australians and their "peaceful penetration."[36] Griffith argues that French Army Captain André Laffargue was "the father of infiltration tactics" and had realized its utility as early as 1915.[37] The Australians, it could be said, had simply taken it to a new level.

While these tactical innovations were developed between 1916 and 1918, Australian and Canadian troops fought alongside each other on the Western Front with a sense of being part of the Empire, even if rarely with a sense of close friendship. They rarely got along well with each other, perhaps because neither sensed the need to impress or to curry favour with the other. Australians were also perhaps too individualistic and rowdy for some of the more reserved Canadians.[38] Still, helped along by high-quality British staff officers assigned to their headquarters,[39] the Australians and Canadians had refined their fighting skills. Referring to the Canadian Corps (but the statement is equally apt for the Australians), historian C.P. Stacey stated that "the evidence is clear that the British staff officers made a great contribution to the Corps' efficiency, and Canadians who served with them remembered them afterwards with respect and gratitude."[40]

Rivalry appears also to have contributed to the lack of closeness between Australians and Canadians during the war. This is exemplified in the standard approaches to the question of who killed the German fighter ace, Baron Von Richtofen. The issue was long debated by Australians and Canadians, but Canadian Lieutenant-Colonel David Bashow argues that in fact it was the combined efforts of Canadians and Australians that led to Richtofen's demise in 1918. He contends that a Canadian pilot forced von Richtofen into the killing zone of the Australian ground gunners – located where Richtofen would otherwise never have considered flying because of the risks involved.[41] Clearly, teamwork pays off.

Britain had introduced conscription in early 1916. In Canada and Australia, the question was addressed in referenda, and the tense atmosphere surrounding these events was exacerbated by the Irish rebellion that began in 1916. In Canada, Borden sought to leverage Canada's war effort in the pursuit of its national interests and, arguably, to avoid being outdone by Australia, which fielded more divisions than Canada.[42] But then, as Borden knew, Australia was in certain ways more British than Canada.[43] Still, as Galen Perras maintains, "Borden also saw the war in increasingly apocalyptic terms as a true struggle to the death between good and Teutonic evil. To slacken the war effort meant breaking faith with the dead."[44] In this context, there could be no half-measures – and here is where Quebec presented a problem. French Canadian enlistment had always lagged behind that of English Canadians, which was hardly surprising given the attitude of anglophile pre-war militia commanders to say nothing of recruiting methods that stressed Canada's British ties. Eventually, after the referendum held in December 1917, in which conscription was overwhelmingly supported in every province but Quebec, Canada imposed compulsory military service, largely to increase the number of French Canadians serving in arms. But the scheme's late and poorly administered introduction resulted in conscription having virtually no effect on the outcome of the battles. Moreover, it appears that the manpower shortages would have avoidable with better resource management. Domestically, the introduction of conscription in this war – as in the next – was bitterly divisive, pitting English and French, patriots against "slackers," even though French Canadians saw themselves as the true patriots, seeing no reason to get killed in a war that appeared to them to have nothing to do with Canada. Many in Quebec felt that Canada was already doing too much, particularly given the country's internal divisions and competing demands for manpower. In the wake of conscription, Quebec abandoned the Conservatives cause and its hostility towards that party would endure for many years to come.[45] The Canadian liberal-nationalist and isolationist bureaucrat O.D. Skelton argued that the war commitments "proved too great a strain for the unfinished structure of Canadian unity."[46] In later years, those societal divisions would significantly constrain post-war Canadian commitment of resources for defence and especially for any prospective expeditionary force.

On a per capita basis, New Zealand had contributed the most of all the dominions, yet it introduced conscription out of a desire to overcome the relative injustice of, and uneven domestic responses to, the voluntary system. In contrast, Australia held two plebiscites over conscription in 1916 and 1917, both of which were defeated. In large part, the defeats were attributable to the efforts of the Catholic archbishop of Melbourne, Daniel Mannix, who tapped into the anti-war sentiment that was pervasive in the Irish population and among labour. (In Canada, Irish Catholics were not as much of a problem for the war effort, having been rallied to the flag by, in part, Bishop Michael Fallon of London, Ontario). But they also pointed to significant traditions of dissent in Australia, which would re-emerge on numerous occasions throughout the twentieth century and beyond when Australians again contemplated war. The unease was particularly felt by women, who, in Australia, had been enfranchised in 1902, in contrast to Canadian women, who were not entirely enfranchised outside Quebec until the early 1920s and inside Quebec until 1940 (although women in Canada associated with soldier's families were given the vote in 1917).[47] In any event, it is remarkable that, at a time when Britain and Canada were implementing conscription, the Australian forces, drawing on a significantly smaller population base than Canada, remained sufficiently well manned with volunteers to maintain their disproportionate presence in the fight against Germany. Conceivably, therefore, Borden would have been better served by following the Australian approach to conscription, and thus avoid the attendant social disruption, with its long-term and counter-productive ramifications for defence policy, that its introduction engendered.

Like conscription, the issue of discipline was of ongoing concern to commanders. The AIF did not fit the conventional British practices governing formal discipline and appearance. It proved to be a successful field army nonetheless, but its discipline was frequently questioned by those who did not understand the influence of egalitarianism and the volunteer ethos on the force. By and large, AIF commanders were not regular soldiers but men who, according to Australian historian Bill Gammage, "remained incorrigibly civilian" and so were disposed to accept the mores of the "civilians" they now commanded. For instance, the average number of convictions for desertion in the fifty-seven divisions of the British Expeditionary Force was 8.88 per division whereas for the AIF it was 34.2. One Canadian historian comments that "the leniency displayed by Australia had mixed results. While none of its soldiers suffered the death penalty, the Australian forces did have serious desertion problems, a hindrance to its otherwise exceptional performance during the war." In contrast, Canadians had a vastly superior disciplinary record, but, unlike the Australians, Canadian officials were prepared to see Canadian soldiers executed by British firing squads to achieve this. Twenty-five Canadians were executed during the war: twenty-two for desertion, two for murder, and one for cowardice.[48] Arguably, only the fear of execution could keep desertion rates low. But, for Canadians and Australians alike, the key to survival was not to let down one's mates – "that was the worst sin."[49]

With so much at stake, Canada and Australia maintained high-level representation in London to protect and further their national interests. Early in the war, Max Aitken was appointed as "eyewitness" for Canada in London.[50] Following events at Gallipoli in 1915, Australian Prime Minister Billy Hughes secured the admission of an Australian officer into the councils of the British War Office. For Hughes, the goal was to be able to stand up to the British and to ensure that Australia was consulted about military plans. In 1916 he also enlisted the support of Canada's Robert Borden to form a common Dominion position to press the British government to accede to Dominion requests for involvement in decision making. But it would be the feats of battle that added substance to their claims.

THE FINAL CAMPAIGNS

By 1918, both armies still served under British Field Marshal Sir Douglas Haig as commander-in-chief, but the Australians and Canadians now had their own commanders, their own organization, their own tactical "doctrine,"[51] and their own major ground formations in battle – the Australian Corps under Lieutenant-General Sir John Monash and the Canadian Corps under Lieutenant-General Sir Arthur Currie.[52] Each of these corps could have been organized into an army consisting of two smaller corps of two or three divisions. But, despite political pressure for such a restructuring that conceivably would have given their forces greater political profile, their commanders preferred to remain as united single-corps entities. Currie, for instance, strongly believed that a corps-level formation was better able to respond to the challenges of battle in its own sector and also avoided the duplicating of organizations at a time when fresh recruits were in short supply.

As the war progressed, technology and tactics evolved dramatically, making the organization of land forces a much more complex endeavour. The complexity was reflected in the growth experienced by the two dominions' corps. Units were added to the order of battle, including motor-transport companies, increased artillery and engineer battalions, reorganized and more sophisticated signals services, and – demonstrating the growing importance of aerial warfare – even anti-aircraft searchlight companies. To Monash, it was the formation of a national corps, complete with all accessory arms and services, that constituted the "paramount and precedent condition for the brilliant success achieved by these splendid troops during the summer and autumn of 1918." But it was by working together, as at the Battle of Amiens in August 1918, that the Canadians and Australians would play a pivotal role in the final stages of the war. They were able to do so not only because of their internal cohesion and their tactical and organizational innovations but also because the French and British forces were more thoroughly exhausted and the American forces were less battle-experienced.[53]

In 1918, when the British faced drastic manning shortages and were obliged to cut back their infantry divisions from twelve to nine battalions, the Canadians under Currie preferred to retain the corps structure but reduce the number of divisions from six to four, despite political pressure to retain the 5th Division still in Britain – Sir Sam Hughes's son, Garnet, was commander of the 5th Division. Australia faced similar pressures, but, with falling enlistments and without conscription, it followed the British lead on force reductions. The Australian 6th Division, raised in the United Kingdom in March 1917, was disbanded in September in an effort to minimize disruptions among the older battle-tested units and thus retain the older Australian divisional formations intact. Even with such measures, further cutbacks occurred. Similar manpower concerns led General Birdwood to decline Britain's offer to supply all the necessary equipment should the Australian forces be willing to supply the personnel for their own tank battalion.[54]

Unlike British units, where loyalty was to a regiment in addition to a battalion, Australian and Canadian troops appeared more strongly attached emotionally to the battalions they fought with. Their commanders had to take this into account. British commanders thought that Dominion forces should be used according to military convenience, but Dominion commanders realized that their national contingents were paid for separately and were increasingly an expression of their own nationhood – and so could not be dissipated piecemeal along with British units. Desmond Morton has argued that Currie made the Canadians into allies, not subordinates.[55] The same could be said for Monash concerning the Australians.

National sentiment was fostered by developments in the field, such as at the auspiciously timed Battle of Hamel, near the Somme River, on 4 July 1918. For this battle, the Australian Corps was commanded by Monash in his first big test as a corps commander. Monash initiated and meticulously planned the innovative battle, which Griffith describes as a larger manifestation of the "peaceful penetration" raids and indistinguishable from a formal all-arms assault complete with tanks, artillery, and machine-gun barrages. Monash did this with the blessing of his British commander, General Henry Rawlinson, and with the support of the British tank force commander, Brigadier-General A. Courage. The battle was the first Allied offensive of appreciable size in any of the theatres of war since the close of the Passchendaele fighting and the Battle of Cambrai in the autumn of 1917. At Hamel, the Australian Corps attack employed eight battalions, reinforced by four United States infantry companies in their first battle alongside British Empire troops since the pre-Revolutionary War period. The troops deployed on a frontage of almost 6,000 yards against three regiments ranged in separate tiers of defence, two of the regiments being from a German storm division. It was quite a feat.[56]

Chart 3
First World War, comparative enlistment figures

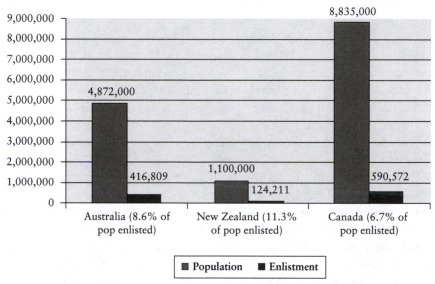

Source: General John de Chastelain, "The Canadian Contribution and the Conscription Crisis, 1914–1918," History honours thesis, RMC Kingston, 1960.

Chart 4
First World War troop contributions compared

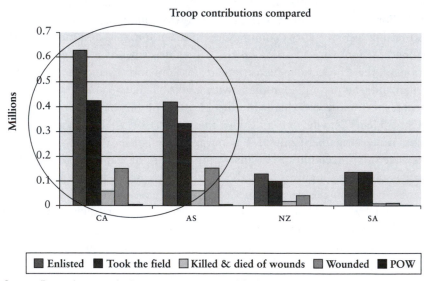

Source: Bean, *Anzac to Amiens*, 532.

The Battle of Hamel was like the Battle of Mount Sorrel for the Canadians – planned and executed by the corps, and its first real success of the war. The other, more famous Canadian battle, Vimy Ridge, arguably was more significant than Hamel to the overall outcome of the war, given Vimy Ridge's commanding view of the battlefield; but the wider tactical significance of Hamel would become evident in the forthcoming Battle of Amiens in August 1918. By the time of the Battle of Hamel, in contrast to the Canadian experience at Vimy, where the infantry were warned not to rely on the still unreliable tanks, improvements had finally made the tanks an important adjunct for the all-arms combat team. The successful outcome saw several tactical lessons learned and led to the publication of a widely promulgated British Army staff brochure – a well-established practice among the Allied forces on the Western Front to encourage the dissemination of new ideas. (Such reports often included details of German developments in weapons and tactics.) Yet, after Hamel, the Canadians continued to neglect the potential of tanks and preferred instead to concentrate on making their artillery more mobile, practising quick-movement drills.[57]

Hamel was followed soon after by a French counter-stroke at Soissons on 18 July that incorporated the use of Renault light tanks and that effectively recaptured all the ground lost to the Germans during their spring offensive in May.[58] One month later, it was the British Expeditionary Force's turn to attack, with the Australian and Canadian Corps as the vanguard. At Amiens, for the first time ever, a battle was fought jointly by Australians and Canadians as well as Britons, Americans, and Frenchmen.[59] However, as Morton and Granatstein observe, "Monash made a condition: his Australians deserved dependable troops on their flank. Canadians and Australians had not been friendly behind the lines but Monash respected Currie and the Canadian Corps was fresh, well trained, and backed by ten thousand reinforcements."[60] The two Dominion corps worked together, as part of the British Fourth Army, under the command of General Rawlinson – considered by some historians as the "star actor of the Amiens front."[61]

At Amiens, the two corps consisting of four Canadian and five Australian divisions worked superbly as a team to deliver, on 8 August, 1918, what the German chief of staff, General Erich Ludendorff, later described as "the black day of the German Army in the history of this war." As part of the Fourth Army, and using tactics that would portend the "combined arms" mechanized warfare of a later generation, the two corps launched a coordinated manoeuvre. They were equipped with new Mark III British wireless sets and supported by 2,000 guns, 470 tanks (allowing for a density of one tank for every forty-two yards), motor machine-guns, and aircraft – ninety-six of which were lost on 8 August. The Fourth Army also used dummy units to send false messages for deception, and the drone of aircraft noise was used to cover the pre-positioning of hundreds of tanks and to deliver a smoke screen for the advancing infantry. Platoons also had an unprecedented amount of their own firepower and were closely supported by artillery, trench mortars, and a plentiful supply of heavy machine-guns. In a single day the Canadians covered eight miles at a cost of 1,306 dead and 2,803 wounded, whereas the German frontline divisions virtually ceased to exist. In addition, the Australian Corps had captured 7,925 prisoners and 173 guns at a cost of 2,000 casualties over seven miles.[62] In total, over the period from 8 to 15 August, thirteen infantry and three cavalry divisions had destroyed or drawn into battle twenty-five German divisions. As one British historian notes, "it was the sort of scene of which generals had been dreaming ever since 1914." Contrasting the Canadians and Australians with the flanking British III Corps, the same historian states of the latter that "neither their recent experiences nor their innate characteristics kindled inside them the fire that made the 'Colonials' – the volunteer soldiers of the new-born nations of Canada and Australia – such irresistible attackers in this year of ebbing strength and spirit, 1918."[63] Desmond Morton, reflecting a national introspection as typical of Australian military historians as of Canadian ones, asserts that, for forty-seven days, the Canadians formed the spearhead of the British Army.[64] In fact, for the crucial Battle of Amiens, the spear had two sides – one Canadian and one Australian. The Canadian and Australian Corps together were ending the war by destroying the German Army.

The Canadian Corps relocated to the Arras sector after the initial battle ended on 15 August, but both corps continued in spearhead roles throughout the autumn of 1918. Further tactical innovations were applied, including the delegation of control over artillery sections to infantry commanders, the liberal use of smoke against machine-guns, and increasing the quantity of machine-guns for the pursuit of retreating German troops. The battles fought in these days included the Battle of Bellicourt and the breakthrough on the Hindenburg line, where infantry divisions from the II u.s. Corps were assigned to work alongside Australian troops, under Monash's direction. Monash observed that, despite their lack of experience, the American troops "showed a fine spirit, a keen desire to learn, magnificent individual bravery, and splendid comradeship."[65] Thereafter, Australian troops were pulled out of the line in October to recuperate in anticipation of the war continuing into 1919.[66]

Map 2
Western Front 1918

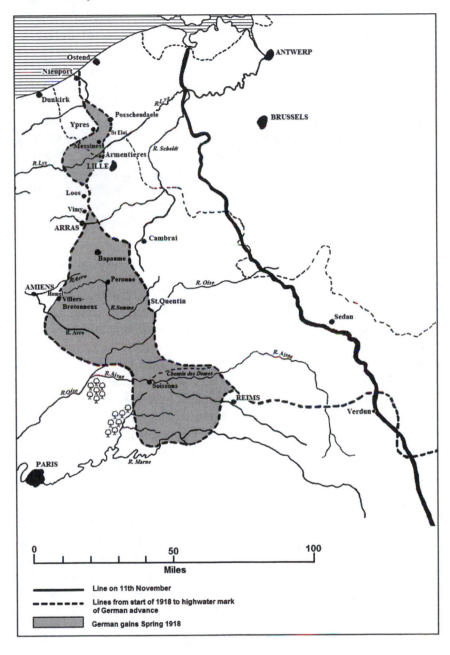

ANTWERP

Ostend
Nieuport

BRUSSELS

Dunkirk
Posschendaele
Ypres
St Eloi
Messines
Armentieres
R. Lys
R. Scheldt
LILLE
R. Lys

Loos

Vimy
ARRAS
Cambrai

Bapaume
AMIENS
R. Ancre
Peronne
R. Oise
Hamel
Villers-
Bretonneux
R. Somme
St.Quentin

R. Avre
Sedan

R. Aisne

R. Aisne
Chemin des Dames
R. Oise
Soissons
REIMS
Verdun

PARIS
R. Marne

| 0 | | | 50 | | 100 |
Miles

————— Line on 11th November

- - - - - Lines from start of 1918 to highwater mark
of German advance

▨ German gains Spring 1918

The remarkable performance by the Dominion forces is due, at least in part, to the stability of the Australian and Canadian Corps. The permanence and size of the Canadian and Australian forces, combined with their *esprit de corps* and emergent national consciousness, gave them opportunities to learn and innovate together. In essence, the dominions' hard-won military prestige in 1917 and 1918 was "a very real thing."[67]

In his *War Memoirs*, British Prime Minister Lloyd George (who intensely disliked Field Marshal Haig, who, in turn, had no deep affection for obstreperous colonials) suggested that Monash would have been a potential commander-in-chief, with Currie as his chief of the general staff, if Haig, with his substantial support in British political circles, could have been dismissed. Such remarks are easily made in hindsight and do not necessarily reflect what would have happened if Lloyd George had had his way at the time. Still, J.L. Granatstein contends that, while Currie "was no Napoleon," he was "the best soldier Canada ever produced."[68] The same can be said, in Australia's case, of Monash.

As the war neared its end, both Canada and Australia, among other nations, contributed to the Russian expeditions. Australia contributed nine soldiers to the 560-strong "British" (but largely Canadian) military mission to the north Russian port of Murmansk and Archangel in 1917 following the communist revolution. The mission faced insurmountable local challenges by March 1919 and was to be withdrawn, but, with the situation deteriorating, a relief force was recruited which included 100–200 Australians. By late September, the force had evacuated the military mission and the Australians had won two Victoria Cross awards for gallantry. By then, Canada had decided to send a contingent of about 5,000 troops, also taking two British infantry battalions under command, to form the British contingent of a Japanese-led multinational expeditionary force that deployed via Vladivostok. As well, the United States moved 10,000 troops into eastern Russia to watch the Japanese, with the expectation that they would moderate British and French plans to become more deeply involved in the Russian Civil War. Short on successes and with failing public support, the force was withdrawn in 1919.[69] Overall, however, these events had little impact other than to indicate that there were cracks in the façade of Empire unity, particularly in Canada, that would be further exposed in the inter-war years. Nonetheless, they demonstrated how Canadian and Australian troops would again, virtually by accident, end up working alongside one another.

Meanwhile, repatriation of hundreds of thousands of troops took many months to organize, based on the shortage of shipping. Two Canadian divisions would form part of the Army of Occupation in Germany, and Australia also offered two divisions for the task.[70] The Australian offer was withdrawn, however, once Prime Minister Hughes began to realize that the soldiers, who wanted to return to Australia quickly, would be in Germany for some time if they participated in the post-war occupation.

WAR'S END

Throughout the war, Australian and Canadian troops had fought alongside each other with a sense of being part of the Empire but also with a growing sense of distinctive national identities that was reinforced by British insensitivity to the dominions' desire for recognition and respect. By war's end, both Canada and Australia had suffered approximately 60,000 soldiers killed – a total proportional to the 600,000 soldiers of both sides who perished during the American Civil War. By contrast, the United States suffered 53,000 soldiers killed in the First World War. These figures, of course, pale in comparison with the 1,397,000 French combat deaths during the war.[71] Still, almost one in one hundred Canadians was killed by enemy action, while Australian and New Zealand losses were proportionately higher. As Desmond Morton argues, "although imperial solidarity survived the war, it would be among the conflict's casualties."[72]

A heightened sense of national identity was emerging in both Canada and Australia – born of a greater maturity, self-awareness, and reluctance ever again to let a great power dictate policies and strategies on their behalf. Many still liked to think that they were British as well, but most men in the Dominion forces had outgrown the anonymity of imperial deference to Britain. At the Imperial War Cabinet in July 1918 (which the Canadian and Australian governments had called for), prime ministers Billy Hughes and Robert Borden resisted pressure to remain subservient to Britain, claiming that the dominions were nations of equal status with Britain and that this relationship must be recognized, both in Britain and on the world stage. With Canada's significant contribution to the final battles of 1918 in mind, Borden pressed Britain to allow for representation at the post-war negotiations, arguing that Canadians "feel that new conditions must be met by new precedents." Similarly, when the Australian prime minister, Billy Hughes, went to Versailles in 1919 to represent Australia, he did so as "the little digger" who could, like his Canadian counterpart, declare his right of place with the claim: "I represent 60,000 dead." Dominion performance in battle had fostered military competence as well as military autonomy, which in turn was matched by more self-assured national identities and the birth of aspirations for independence status within the British Empire.[73] By their actions, Canada and Australia had gained equal and unprecedented leverage at an important juncture in world affairs. But, at the same time, "the British were the necessary intermediaries through whom Dominion aspirations achieved recognition at the Paris Conference." What is more, the hard-nosed but tactless realism of Australia's Billy Hughes butted up against Woodrow Wilson's American exceptionalism. Hughes (whom Margaret MacMillan describes as a "scrawny dyspeptic") certainly failed to ingratiate himself with Wilson. In contrast, Canada's Borden was more circumspect in his dealing with the American president, being acutely aware of the merits of a partnership between the British Empire and the United States and of the proximity of the latter to Canada.[74]

The First World War also had engendered a professional military approach within the Canadian Corps that was marked by detailed planning, thorough preparation, exhaustive training, pronounced reliance on intense artillery preparatory fire, and a lesser emphasis on manoeuvre and the use of armour. For Australia, a similar nascent professionalism emerged but with less emphasis on discipline and more on initiative, as reflected in the popular tactics of peaceful penetration. In addition, as we have seen, the experience of the Desert Mounted Corps troops under command of General Chauvel in the Middle East would leave a legacy of a more fluid form of warfare than that experienced for most of the time on the Western Front.

Having examined some of the many historical parallels between the Canadian and Australian forces during the First World War, I wish now to consider a plausible alternative situation that might have arisen. Imagine, for instance, if Major-General Bridges had not died from wounds received at Gallipoli in 1915 and had lived on to command forces in battle on the Western Front in Flanders and France. C.E.W. Bean claims that, had Bridges lived, "it is probable that he would have emerged the greatest of Australia's soldiers, as he was certainly the most profound of her military students."[75] He would have been the senior general in the Canadian and Australian forces, and so, conceivably, a Canadian-Australian Army Group could have been formed in 1917 with a Scottish-born officer, and a former Royal Military College (Kingston, Ontario) cadet, in the Australian forces at its head. Arguably, neither Currie nor Monash could be appointed to such a position because they were peers. One could not be expected to be subservient to the other, given the nascent nationalism at work in Canada and Australia. But perhaps this would not have been the case with Bridges, had he lived. The point of such a hypothetical scenario is to illustrate that the differences between the Canadians and Australians may be less significant than most historians have acknowledged to date.

Yet, in fact, Canadian and Australian leaders during the First World War were not sufficiently broad-minded to realize that, as I will argue in subsequent chapters, a pooling of their combined efforts would have made good use of their scarce diplomatic and military resources to further their own national interests. It was a great opportunity missed.

3

The Inter-War Years

By 1918, a heightened sense of identity had emerged in Canada and Australia. For both countries, the end of the war marked their coming of age as they asserted their national identity and exercised more prominent roles on the world stage. This was illustrated by their signing their first international treaty – the 1919 Treaty of Versailles – as distinct nations, albeit as part of the British Empire delegation. As Australian Prime Minister Billy Hughes asserted, the event signalled Australia's entrance into the family of nations on an equal footing. "We had earned that, or rather, our soldiers had earned it for us." Canada's prime minister, Sir Robert Borden, had worked with Australia's Billy Hughes to insist on separate Dominion representation at the Versailles Conference, but Borden, like others, found Hughes abrasive and bombastic. President Woodrow Wilson of the United States viewed Hughes as "a pestiferous varmint" who too strongly supported French calls for crippling war reparations and pressed for the annexation of German New Guinea, as the spoils of war and also to shield Australia from any possible future Japanese aggression in the Pacific.[1] To Hughes, however, this was little compensation for the Australian lives lost in the war.

POST-WAR FALLOUT

The sacrifices made on the fields of battle left indelible scars on Australia and Canada, and nowhere were the scars worse than among the returned veterans. Soldier-settler schemes were introduced in both countries, but most measures were inadequate to meet the veterans' needs. For Canada, a mythology of the Great War developed in the 1920s that highlighted the merits of avoiding mass casualties by keeping a distance from European affairs and seeking the protection of the United States. The general sense of security was captured in Canadian Senator Raoul Dandurand's remark to the League of Nations that "we live in a fire proof house far from inflammable materials." The refusal of the United States to join the League of Nations also seemed to justify Canada's reluctance to make firm military commitments. With Germany defeated and the United States no longer perceived as a military threat, the Canadian forces found it hard to argue against rapid moves to disarm and reversion to pre-war habits. Canadians felt secure in North America, and to many it appeared that the lessons of the Great War could be forgotten at little risk.[2] Canada-Australia relations were often competitive, as between rivals rather than strategic partners. With Canada better positioned by geography to enjoy influence with Britain and the United States, Canadians tended to be disinclined to support isolated Australia's diplomatic positions.

The different perspectives towards defence were reflected in their opposing stances towards the renewal of the Anglo-Japanese Naval Treaty in 1921. By now, Australia's earlier criticism of Britain's conciliatory approach to Japan had, essentially, been overtaken by events. After all, in the First World War, Japan had provided naval escorts to Australian troop ships crossing the Indian Ocean. What is more, Britain's relative weakness after that war made it clear to many Australians that considerable effort needed to be made to stay on-side with Japan if at all possible. For these reasons, Australia pressed for the treaty's renewal – a position that placed it at odds with Canada. Prime Minister Arthur Meighen of Canada sensed American unease at the prospect of the British Empire continuing to align itself with Japan, and he feared the prospect of being caught in the middle should the treaty be invoked in a Japanese war against the United States. Many Australians subsequently blamed Meighen and Canada for the demise of the Anglo-Japanese alliance. Moreover, in 1921 Britain signed the Washington Agreement, which replaced the Anglo-Japanese alliance and defined the "One-Power Standard" of naval strength. Following the agreement, the cruiser and destroyer that Britain had given Canada for its postwar navy were scrapped, with two small but new destroyers taking their place. From the perspective of Australia (which lost its flagship HMAS *Australia* as a result of the treaty's provisions), the Washington Agreement effectively hobbled Britain's ability to defend its oceanic Empire and awarded the Japanese naval supremacy in the Pacific. Yet, ironically, the agreement also angered Japanese imperialists – since it did not grant Japan equal status with Britain and the United States – and fed their ambitions.[3]

Galen Perras aptly describes Australian-Canadian diplomatic relations during this period as being of "parties long estranged."[4] Such a relationship helped constrain these imperial "cousins" from developing closer ties. Essentially, the estrangement resulted from divergent interests being narrowly defined in terms of immediate concerns. In terms of longer-term interests, this estrangement could have been avoided. But to have done so would have required Australian and Canadian national leaders to maintain a broader appreciation of the common strategic concerns of these two so-similar emergent Anglo-European middle powers.

While political differences endured, both Canada and Australia continued to experience similar phenomena in their military organizations. For instance, they both continued to rely on predominantly militia-based citizen forces as the mainstay of their armies. Early successes in the Anglo-Boer War and the First World War led to the myth that their citizen-soldiers were born fighters. But beyond the myth, as D.S. McCarthy points out, "Australia's historical reliance on citizen soldiers resulted from cultural (the English tradition of distrust of standing armies), financial (citizen soldiers were cheap) and particularly strategic circumstances."[5] He could equally be writing about Canada.

After the war, Australia decided to maintain only a small permanent-force training cadre for the citizen force and no regular-force combat units.[6] In Canada, the best prospects for a reorganization of the militia in the post-war period lay in the hands of General Sir Arthur Currie, appointed to head the militia in November 1919. Canadian military planners were eager to capitalize on the hard-earned prowess and capability of the CEF. However, given the pervasive sense of confidence over Canada's security prospects, their views were soon marginalized and only three permanent-force infantry battalions – the Royal Canadian Regiment; the 22nd Battalion, renamed the Royal 22nd Regiment (soon afterwards renamed in the French language); and the Princess Patricia's Canadian Light Infantry – as well as two cavalry regiments would remain in being. As a consequence, debates over military affairs in Canada tended to be more about internal Defence Department politics than any form of grand strategy.

As details of the origins of the war were released after the war, public perceptions became increasingly anti-militarist, leaving little popular support for the senior military commanders' post-war plans. The Canadian government, much like its Australian counterpart, also found itself preoccupied with post-war reconstruction. Canada's and Australia's largely nominal land-force establishments for most of the inter-war period were similar to the pre-war part-time militia establishments. In Canada, the government decided that it was better to re-emphasize the earlier peacetime precedent of ministerial control and a collegial general staff system, despite the experience with the fiery Sir Sam Hughes in the first years of the Great War and the diluting effect of these arrangements on the definite lines of authority found in traditional military chains of command.[7]

With funds scarce, both Australia and Canada faced significant squabbles between their naval and army chiefs as well as between senior officers and their respective governments. For instance, the CGS in both Canada and Australia unsuccessfully called for the disbandment of their respective navies.[8] For Australia, this clash revolved around the country's decision to rely on Britain's Royal Navy for protection, encapsulated in the Singapore Strategy (discussed below), instead of building up its own land and air forces against the prospect of a Japanese invasion.[9]

Facing so many constraints, military professionalism in Canada declined throughout the 1920s and staff training and field-training exercises were minimized. By the mid-1920s, a malaise had set in that resulted in most units and officers being unable to employ effectively even the most basic platoon- and company-level tactics. The onset of the Depression in 1929 made matters worse as permanent-force regimental and combined-arms training was halted, not to be revived until 1938. Australia experienced similar challenges, although such pressures were tempered fractionally by an enduring concern over Japan's longer-term intentions.[10] Still, there seemed to be a sublime faith in the powers of Britain's navy and an enduring misconception that the 300,000 men who had comprised the AIF in the First World War would somehow still be available for years afterwards. But, even within a short time after the war, this notion had become unrealistic, there being no legal or practical means to recall such troops in event of a crisis.

In the minds of some, a military contribution from the Dominions appeared to be required in the Chanak Crisis of 1922, which was triggered when Turkish troops threatened a beleaguered British occupying garrison on the Dardanelles. Britain, with no prior warning, sought to rally Dominion support in handling the crisis by calling for expeditionary forces from Australia and New Zealand and, inadvertently, Canada as well.[11] Canada's opposition leader, Arthur Meighen, initially responded with Laurier's ringing pre-war phrase "Ready, aye, ready!" but he was widely criticized for it. In the end, the group-unit concept of Empire "bobbed like flotsam in its wake."[12] As British historian Nicholas Mansergh says, Chanak "was a warning against thinking of joint responsibilities without ensuring full, prior joint consultation."[13] The mishandling of the Chanak Crisis by Britain was symptomatic of the growing administrative neglect of overseas governments and brought discredit both upon the Empire's consultative machinery and upon the British government charged with its oversight. In Australia, however, Prime Minister Hughes had commissioned the army to draw up plans for the dispatch of a one-division expeditionary force – Plan 401 – before the incident was resolved diplomatically. Hughes's position reflected Australian concern to continue to pay its dues to Empire security and to protect the chain of communications through the Middle East on which the bulk of its trade was dependent. (Incidentally, Plan 401 would form the basis for raising the 2nd AIF in 1939.) In 1927 Canada's Defence Minister, Colonel J.L. Ralston, would approve "in principle" the completion of a similar administrative outline for the mobilization of a large expeditionary force that required discreet coordination with the British Army. Yet little would be done about developing such plans into more definitive capabilities, particularly since they were opposed by the External Affairs mandarin and anti-militarist Irish anglophobe O.D. Skelton – Prime Minister Mackenzie King's most important adviser.[14]

This arms-length approach to contingency planning went hand in hand with an ongoing, dramatic reduction in personnel and a reluctance to spend on military matters that endured for two decades. For instance, the Canadian government only grudgingly accepted Britain's offer to return the equipment (apart from mechanical transport) of the four Canadian divisions and the cavalry brigade of the First World War. By 1922, the Canadian permanent force, authorized to number 10,000 troops, could muster less than 4,000. The non-permanent militia fared just as poorly. Even by 1939, only about 47,000 would attend the annual training camps – significantly less than the 58,000 who did so in 1914.[15]

Similar declining troop number trends were evident in Australia. Once the AIF was demobilized, the force ceased to exist, in effect leaving Australia without an army.[16] This was due to the legal paradox of the Defence Act, which prohibited the dispatch of citizen forces abroad despite the enduring formal links with the British Empire. By 1919, there were 45,000 enrolled in Australia's part-time forces. In 1920 the Australian Staff Corps was established – a step not followed by Canada, which retained formed units in the permanent forces instead. The creation of the Australian Instructional Corps followed the next year. These bodies provided the nucleus of the permanent-force cadre to oversee military training and plans for the remainder of the inter-war period.[17]

Paradoxically, it was also in these years that the place of the army – the dominant service in terms of troops involved – was imprinted on the national psyche of both nations. In Australia, the "digger" myth emerged, consolidating a sense of nationhood while helping to rationalize the incredible waste of war. For Australians, the key event was Gallipoli, which the popular Australian historian Patsy Adam-Smith effusively compared to Thermopylae, where three hundred Spartans tried to repulse thousands of invading Persians. While such portrayals are overwrought, the Gallipoli experience did indeed help to bind together the new Australian nation, creating a strong sense of national identity in place of the colonial heritage. Meanwhile, for Canadians, the comparable event was the Battle of Vimy Ridge in April 1917. However, in Canada's case the event was not celebrated in anything like the sense of "Anzac Day" in Australia. Probably because of the country's earlier martial history – particularly the French/British and Indian wars of the seventeenth and eighteenth centuries – Vimy Ridge did not hold such a prominent place in the Canadian consciousness.[18] Indeed, the bitter domestic political fallout of wartime conscription also contributed to limit Vimy Ridge's appeal as a national symbol – it being associated, for some, as much with the unmaking of Canada as with the making.[19] This mixed legacy in Canada would be reflected in the political party system – which was ever mindful of the divisive effects of costly imperial commitments on electoral prospects, particularly in the province of Quebec.[20]

DEBATES OVER STRATEGY

Ironically, as Britain's naval power was diminishing, the Australian government reverted to a predominantly naval strategy in 1923. This "Blue Water" strategy relied on the protection of the Royal Navy and the naval base at Singapore and was used to excuse Australian thrift. Successive governments recognized the strategy's flaws, and staff exercises clearly demonstrated them.[21] By agreeing to this policy, the Australian government had implicitly acknowledged its need to support Britain, with at least a garrison in Singapore, but the Defence Act continued the prohibition against sending soldiers to serve overseas, except as volunteers. In the meantime, the Australian government remained eager to export raw materials rather than to antagonize such an important, albeit secondary, trading partner as Japan.[22] Arguably, Australia had no option but to follow this naval strategy owing to the continued dominance of trade with Britain, which obligated its government to support British plans. Moreover, successive Australian governments appreciated that defence efforts in peacetime were easier to support if money spent on material was spent at home instead of abroad. The government's reaction was to encourage investment in technology. Nevertheless, Australia's inter-war defence strategy featured an enduring concern over Japan's intentions which resulted in slightly higher per-capita defence expenditure than in Canada. In the 1923–24 financial year, for instance, Canada's military expenditures were $1.46 (Cdn.) per capita, Australia spent the equivalent of $3.30, and the United States and Britain spent $6.51 and $23.04 respectively.[23]

While the defence-strategy debate raged in Australia, military matters rarely became the primary focus of attention in government. For the Liberal politician W. L. Mackenzie King, for instance, his concern throughout the inter-war period would remain protecting his Quebec political power base and ensuring his re-election, which meant downplaying defence issues whenever possible. Thus, in 1921, while opposition leader, King acidly scolded government efforts to return to pre-war defence spending levels, declaring that "there is no menace ... The minister says that expenditure is needed for the defence of Canada – defence against whom?" Australian politicians had earlier shared similar sentiments about their own place in the world. In 1852, for instance, the Scottish-born republican John Dunmore Lang responded to his own query whether an Australia independent of Britain could protect itself against foreign aggressors. "For who, I ask, are the enemies with whom the Australian colonies, if free and independent, would have to contend? Is it the Aborigines of their own territory? ... Is it the New Zealanders [Maoris] or the South Sea Islanders? Is it the Malayans of the Indian Archipelago or the adventurous subjects of the Emperors of China or Japan? These inoffensive and unwarlike people could never find their way to the Australian colonies." Lang's view would eventually lose favour in Australia, and Mackenzie King's, in turn, would, in a few short years, also be exposed as unduly optimistic. But King's question would have an enduring echo in Canadian defence- and strategic-policy formulation. As James Eayrs notes, "the Great War brought Canadians to Europe, but left Europe remote to Canadians ... To the protection of the oceans – Admirals Atlantic and Pacific – might be added that of the Monroe Doctrine ... Isolationism in Canada was the product of geography." In addition, from 1921 onwards, Canada's new Mackenzie King government (see appendix 1) was far less sympathetic towards the military than the previous administration.[24]

Despite the parallels, differing geo-strategic imperatives led Canada and Australia to come up with different priorities for their naval forces: the former, seeing little obvious threat, was content to contribute a few ships to the Royal Navy, while Australia, in a more vulnerable position, was eager to establish a fleet of its own. The contrasting postures reflected the lack of consensus within the British Empire about its nature as well as about the extent of mutual-security obligations. The strategy of imperial defence that was, broadly speaking, orthodoxy in Australia and New Zealand was considered by the government in Canada to verge on heresy. This reluctance on Canada's part to join any "orthodoxy" was seen by Britons, Australians, and New Zealanders as "calculating aloofness." Yet, when the British government, without consultation with the Dominions, signed the European Treaty of Mutual Guarantee, known as the Locarno Treaty in 1926, it effectively declared itself against imperial unity. This marked another step in the inter-war process of unravelling the Empire.[25]

Canada, in a manner similar to that of the United States, expressed no interest in any League of Nations collective-security measures and vociferously opposed the League Charter's collective-security article. As far as Mackenzie King was concerned, the Australians and New Zealanders were "imperialist propagandists" and could not be trusted – reflecting a coolness towards Canada's fellow Dominions that endured throughout his terms in office. Dominion enthusiasm for defence expenditure was further dampened by Britain's rolling "no war for ten years" policy, practised throughout the 1920s, formalized in 1928, and not abandoned until the mid-1930s. The Great Depression in 1929 sealed the fate of plans to invigorate peacetime forces in Canada and Australia, let alone Britain, with its expensive-to-maintain 200,000 constabulary troops spread throughout the Empire. Canada's other services fared even worse. A little navy of only three former Royal Navy warships survived. The two submarines were decommissioned and sold off in 1922.[26]

Although a Canadian air force was approved in 1920, it was not established on a regular basis until April 1923, despite many thousands of Canadians having enlisted in Britain's Royal Flying Corps and Royal Naval Air Service during the First World War. (Tellingly, although the Australians did establish their own flying corps during the war, the Canadian government had rejected the idea.). Australia's air force was formed in 1921 as the successor to the Australian Flying Corps. The new Royal Australian Air Force (RAAF) followed the training and procedures adopted by the Royal Air Force in Britain, as would the Canadians once they formed their own. The eventual creation of the Royal Canadian Air Force (RCAF) would be facilitated in large part by a British gift of war surplus and an American gift of flying boats left in Halifax after the war. The RCAF was organized by the mid-1920s with eight stations, but Canada placed more emphasis on support to civil aviation than on military aviation. The RAAF faced similar constraints.[27]

STATUS WITHIN EMPIRE

During the inter-war period, the status of Britain's self-governing Dominions, including Canada, Australia, New Zealand, South Africa, and the Irish Free State, changed significantly as the notion of empire lost favour in the face of the Dominions' growing dynamism and self-confidence. Britain's own attitude towards the Dominions was ambivalent, with the Colonial Office and Foreign Office disagreeing on the merits of pursuing a "centralist" policy line. The decentralizing dynamics, particularly resulting from demands for more control from South Africa and the Irish Free State, as well as Canada to a lesser extent, led to the Balfour Declaration at the Imperial Conference of 1926, proclaiming separate responsibility in foreign policy and leading to the use of the term "Commonwealth" instead of "Empire." With its wide-reaching trade ties and heavy burden of war debt, Britain was eager to advocate global free trade and unwilling to champion free trade solely within the Empire at the expense of outsiders. Thereafter, the Statute of Westminster was signed by King George V on 11 December 1931, redefining Commonwealth relations and legally granting the self-governing Dominions virtual autonomy from Britain. The statute, in effect, conferred the status of minor but not yet "middle" or world powers. As Canadian historian C.P. Stacey states, "the whole achievement had its origins on the battlefields of France and Flanders ... And if one seeks a date on which Canada became independent, there is no other to be had than December 11, 1931." Nonetheless, as Francine McKenzie indicates, "constitutional confusion was compounded by ambiguities about the national identity of each of the Dominions." Indeed, the Dominions still "lacked the symbols of nationhood, such as flags, currency, anthems and parliamentary traditions, and a unique head of state." And besides, "in the eyes of the rest of the world, Britain still dominated the association ... Continued association in international affairs with the mother country perpetuated the belief that the dominions belonged to the category of advanced colony."[28]

Australia would wait until 1942 to appropriate the Statute's provisions, remaining eager to ingratiate itself with Britain – its major trading partner and security guarantor. Furthermore, as McKenzie points out, Australians still did not see themselves as sovereign or separate because they thought of themselves as British. In contrast, although Canada had established preferential tariffs on British exports as early as 1897 (Australia followed suit in 1908), from 1922 onwards it became more reliant on investment from the United States. Nevertheless, given an enduring American tariff wall, this shift in the balance of trade did not stop Canada from signing trade agreements with Australia and other Commonwealth countries in the 1920s and 1930s. For instance, the 1932 Ottawa agreement for imperial trade preference marked the high point of interdependence, entrenching the imperial preferential system at the expense of other foreign markets. Even with preferences, there was little interest in promoting inter-Dominion trade because Australian, New Zealand, and Canadian exports largely were competitive, not complementary. Still, in the face of savage American tariff increases under the Smoot-Hawley Act of 1930, the Commonwealth's member states grasped at imperial trade preference in order to foster trade.[29] This infuriated American officials because it discriminated against u.s. goods. For the next fifteen years, American officials worked hard to destroy such economic blocs, despite their own counter-productive tariff policies. Generally, however, Australian diplomatic efforts to rally Canadian support for Commonwealth-wide measures were not welcomed by their Canadian counterparts. Stacey argues that the general agreement between the United States and Canada in 1935 was the trade agreement of greatest significance for Canada in the inter-war years. It marked the beginning of a rapprochement which was to go on for many years and also led to a fundamental alteration in Canada's traditional international position. However, that alteration would take several more years and another world war to take full effect.[30]

WORSENING SECURITY PROSPECTS

While trade agreements were being made, international security affairs worsened, particularly following Japan's seizure of Manchuria in 1931. The British chiefs of staff, in their annual review of 1932, saw that the naval facilities at Singapore and Hong Kong were incomplete and indefensible. Britain, however, was facing tight financial constraints, a still war-weary electorate, and the hope that further disarmament efforts would alleviate international tensions. Attempts at rapprochement, particularly with Japan, appeared the only viable approach that Britain could afford in order to engage Germany and Japan while simultaneously seeking to maintain a balance of power. Yet, following the Japanese abrogation of the Washington Naval Treaty in 1934, even these efforts to engage Japan were largely abandoned.[31]

The Australian government recognized the deteriorating security situation and announced a rearmament program in September 1933 that succeeded in restoring the defence-budget allocation in 1934–35 to its 1920s levels. This program allowed for Australian land forces to plan for a division-sized expeditionary force for overseas service within three months in addition to a nucleus of three lightly armed divisions for a "Defence Against [Light] Raids Contingency." This "raids contingency" was predicated on British naval protection and envisaged only up to two hundred lightly armed troops on Japanese cruisers getting through the Royal Navy's cordon to land in Australia.[32] Admittedly, plans were also in place to send one division to fight alongside British forces overseas, but the army was not allowed to spend funds on acquiring the necessary heavy equipment for this purpose. Moreover, the Treasury worried about the extravagance of the armed services. Its concern grew as expenditure increased, consuming about 9 per cent of federal revenue by 1936–37.[33]

The Australian CGS throughout the 1920s – the former commander of the Desert Mounted Corps, Lieutenant-General Sir Harry Chauvel – insisted on planning for contingencies against a more robust adversary.[34] His successors, Julius Bruche and John Lavarack, clashed with the chief of the naval staff, Admiral Sir George Hyde, and with his supporter, the secretary of the Australian Department of Defence from 1937 to 1956, Sir Frederick Shedden – an ardent imperialist whose friendship with and admiration of the British secretary of the Committee of Imperial Defence, Sir Maurice Hankey, earned him the nickname "pocket hanky." Shedden was convinced that Australia had to rely on British sea power as its first line of defence, and possibly the United States if it were faced with multiple enemies.[35]

Lavarack wrote a highly critical rebuttal to Shedden's ideas. Yet, despite Lavarack's piercing analysis, his acerbic nature left him without the necessary political support. Lavarack sought to make mobile forces the first priority by unsuccessfully disguising the true purpose of expenditures under his control. Tensions were apparent, and mistrust bred a degree of dysfunction between military staffs and civilian Defence Department officials.[36] This pattern of behaviour obstructed efficiency and effectiveness and endured beyond the beginning of the Second World War, once again paralleling the problems faced in Canada.

In Canada, A.G.L. McNaughton, experiencing similar challenges, also faced off against the navy in a bitter interservice dispute. Lavarack's views were like those expressed by Canada's Colonel H.D.G. (Harry) Crerar, who recognized that, if Japan used Canadian territory to attack the United States, American public opinion would "demand what would amount to a military occupation of British Columbia by U.S. forces." Eventually, Lavarack's views emphasizing a military capable of fighting at home and overseas, like McNaughton's and Crerar's in Canada, would prevail, but the delays would be costly in lives and resources in the coming war.[37]

In the meantime, until Australia's industrial capacity gathered pace as war loomed, the Australian army remained a hollow, part-time militia-based force. Like its Canadian equivalent, it retained the equipment and force structures of the First World War while keeping abreast of British doctrinal developments. Such measures were obviously cheap, convenient, and politically acceptable. However, when rearmament gained momentum on the eve of war, the Uniformity of Armaments Agreement with Britain meant that overseas orders almost invariably had to be filled by British firms. This arrangement was complicated by British companies' inability to meet Dominions' orders because of the surge in domestic demand. When British companies could not deliver, there remained pressure to produce locally, using British equipment patterns.[38]

There were feelings of imperial kinship throughout the armed services, but these were strained at times by patronizing British officers. As Eayrs states, such attitudes were found at the highest levels of government in London. "Colonial peoples were like children and were to be treated with 'all the kindness and severity of the Victorian parent.' This was hard to take. Canadians exposed to the Englishman's sense of effortless superiority, his condescension, his ignorance of other peoples ways ... these were hard to overcome." The high commissioner for Canada in the United Kingdom from 1922 to 1929, P.C. Larkin, observed that "it accords better with their dignity that we should continue in the eyes of the world as dependents."[39]

Despite these tensions, in the military at least, regular exchanges of individuals helped maintain bonds that would ease later cooperation through friendships and common values. Both Canada and Australia lacked their own higher command and staff training for their small regular cadre, so training continued to be carried out at British staff colleges at Camberley and Quetta. This training provided opportunities for a select few to see large formations on exercise – something that could not be experienced in Australia or Canada. The net effect of this policy in both Canada and Australia was to ensure that force structures, doctrine, and equipment remained "British through and through," with only minor differences imposed by purely local conditions. Quarterly liaison letters were also passed between the general staffs of Britain and the chiefs of general staff of Australia, New Zealand, South Africa, and Canada, and the same sort of relationship prevailed between Britain's naval and air forces and Australia's and Canada's sister services. Consequently, while the "alliance" was not based on specific commitments, it had a certain vitality generated through shared allegiances, customs, institutions, and ideals that reflected the political facts of life of the time.[40]

Such helpful connections notwithstanding, reports in 1935 indicated the perilous state of defence in Canada, with its limited stock of equipment, the obsolescent and defective quality of the equipment it did have, and the lack of practice in their use. Consequently, Canada was unable to make a significant contribution to the Allied military effort for years after the Second World War was to commence. In an effort in part designed to stave off further cuts, the army set up defence-related public work camps for the unemployed – a scheme that closely resembled the u.s. Army-administered Civil Conservation Corps.[41] Eventually, administration of the scheme was transferred to the Department of Labour.[42] Although as cash-strapped as the Canadians, the Australians avoided such a scheme, remaining more focused on the development and maintenance of war-fighting skills – skills that would prove their worth in the years ahead.

When Mackenzie King's Liberal Party won office in Canada in 1935, the newly appointed CGS, Major-General E.C. Ashton, warned the government that Canada was essentially powerless to defend itself. King recognized the domestic political priority of avoiding all international commitments in advance, while preparing for home defence and rearmament, but, as Stacey states, "he had never had any connection with the armed forces. He was un-military and anti-military."[43] Defence contingency plans drafted in the early 1920s were updated. By now, "Defence Scheme Number 1" – a fanciful plan based on non-existent forces for war against the United States, premised on a repeat of the War of 1812 – had been destroyed (as of 1933), but the u.s. equivalent, "Plan Red," which was equally divorced from American national policy, was not declared obsolete and burned until 1937. The most enduring and realistic plan was Canada's "Defence Scheme Number 3," which covered a seven-division expeditionary force and home defence in a major war.[44] This scheme, which had some of the hallmarks of similar Australian plans, was given limited sanction, but without public acknowledgment. The secrecy was due to the government's preoccupation with national unity.[45]

Apart from focusing on local defence through most of the 1930s, Canada, along with Ireland and South Africa, expressed only nominal interest in common imperial security measures. Given domestic political concerns, Canadian political leaders were not in a position to offer material support or definite commitments. Further, although insisting on separate defence policies, they were prepared to spend little themselves on defence. In Canada and, to a lesser extent, Australia, it was possible to entertain the idea that isolation presented an alternative to collective defence. In Australia, however, remoteness from Britain always meant that promises of protection by the Royal Navy could only be tenuous and conditional.[46]

As in Canada, the Australian electorate had reacted against their "Depression governments" by voting them out of office, but in Australia's case the move was from left to right (to the conservatives under Prime Minister Joseph Lyons in 1932),[47] as opposed to Canada's shift from right to left (under liberal nationalist Mackenzie King in 1935 – as illustrated in appendix 1). Thus, in Canada the party most sympathetic to "Empire" was in opposition before the war while in Australia it was in power. Yet even the nationalist Australian "left" under Labor Party leader and First World War anti-war campaigner John Curtin was prepared to contemplate a degree of imperial solidarity that was unacceptable in peacetime Canada. This concession was, in part, because Australian nationalism was more practical and socio-economic than cultural and emotional. The Australian left was socialist in orientation – a product of geographical conditions and the needs of an industrial-age, landless, and immigrant population. Kinship was the unifying bond that held together people of disparate views and socio-economic status. This was in contrast to the more parochial nationalism characteristic of the Quebec *habitant*.[48]

Ongoing Japanese expansionism in China and the Pacific, combined with Britain's relative military decline in the Pacific, resulted in a divergence of interest from Britain that eventually forced Australia to explore political and military ties with the other major power in the Pacific, the United States. In 1935 Australian Prime Minister Joseph Lyons attempted to involve the United States in a broad security pact embracing "all the nations bordering on the Pacific Ocean." Lyons's overtures paralleled Canada's and Britain's trade rapprochement with the United States following President Franklin D. Roosevelt's Reciprocal Trade Agreements Act of 1934, which set out to reduce tariffs in bilateral trade. Lyons also discussed Pacific defence problems with Roosevelt in Washington in 1937. But, without an independent diplomatic service, and with competing agricultural produce as well as British opposition to such moves, the Australian government could not effectively promote such extra-imperial initiatives.

In Australia, despite the growing evidence to the contrary, there remained an overriding belief in the supremacy of naval power and the Singapore Strategy as the basis for Australian defence. This view was encouraged by a government eager to contain defence expenditure.[49] For Canada, the emergence of the Japanese threat was of more peripheral concern, although of sufficient gravity to warrant Mackenzie King's support for rearmament for

home-defence purposes.[50] Despite its Pacific seaboard, and despite the fact
that the distance between Canada and Japan was the same as that between
Australia and Japan, Canada (with the exception of British Columbia)
looked at world affairs with the Atlantic in mind, conscious that any Japanese threat would invariably trigger an American response. In contrast,
Australia judged events in their Pacific context, with no clear indication
that American support would be forthcoming.

Canada's isolationist imperatives, which marked one of the strongest distinctions between Canadian and Australian policies in peacetime, were reduced by 1937 in the face of German, Italian, and Japanese aggression.
However, they would continue until after April 1939 when Germany over-
ran the remainder of Czechoslovakia. Mackenzie King's appeals to substitute reason for force would continue through August. Until that point, the
Canadian government, fearful of a fragile national unity, sought to ensure
that a large dissenting minority, particularly in Quebec, did not feel that
they had been rushed into a war that was not, in their view, in Canada's interests. The royal visit to Canada in May and June 1939 helped consolidate
public opinion in support of Britain and France if there was another German act of aggression. The Canadian position was, in part, constrained by
British contracts for the use of docks for the Royal Navy on the Atlantic
and Pacific coasts at Halifax and Esquimalt respectively. This constituted a
practical obstacle to populist calls for neutrality, as did the British Commonwealth Air Training Program (BCATP), based in Canada, which itself
indicated a growing awareness on the part of the King government that
neutrality was likely not a viable option. The prospect of munitions and
foodstuffs contracts also helped encourage Canadian industry and government to think of the desirability of participation alongside Britain in any future war with Germany.[51]

AS WAR LOOMS

The chief Canadian foreign-policy mandarins, O.D. Skelton and Loring
Christie, were eager to minimize association with British military plans and
to assert instead an essentially neutralist foreign policy, arguing that Canada
had no defence problem. In 1937 Christie maintained that "Canada does not
go in for defence alliances. Such a policy is not feasible or necessary in her
circumstances." Skelton and Christie also objected to participation in much
of the crucial interdepartmental planning in the years leading up to 1939.

In contrast, by 1939, the Canadian service chiefs were displaying a level
of unity of purpose unmatched since 1918. Their belief in cooperation

demonstrated an enlightened self-interest, since they had gained greater efficiencies by working together than they had ever experienced when working apart. While air force planners prepared for what would eventually be an Empire-wide aircrew-training scheme, Canada's army chiefs drew up plans for expeditionary forces that included a maximum deployed effort of six divisions – one more than would actually be sent overseas by 1945. As CGS, Major-General Ashton enjoyed high-level access to cabinet, much to the chagrin of Skelton and Christie. To them, confrontation in international politics was an evil; collective security, an anathema.[52]

The attitudes of Skelton and Christie stand in contrast with the views of the man most comparable in the Australian bureaucracy in the late interwar and wartime years – the secretary of the Department of Defence, Sir Frederick Shedden. In Australia, Shedden's role went far beyond that of the traditional public servant. He would be the key confidant of two successive Second War War prime ministers, Robert Menzies and John Curtin, and would become, by 1942, the trusted link between Curtin and General Douglas MacArthur of the United States. Particularly during the 1930s, his views were more pro-British than those displayed by his Canadian counterparts.[53] Yet Shedden, like his Canadian counterparts, evinced little concern about leveraging Australia's relationship with Britain for a better "seat at the table" on the world stage.

The conflicting departmental views of two Canadian government departments, Defence and External Affairs, reflected enduring mutual distrust and interdepartmental cultural differences that also had parallels in Australia. But in Australia's case the differences came without the heartfelt anti-imperialist impulse evident in Canada. Still, the differing interdepartmental perspectives had similar consequences in both places – pulling foreign and defence policies in opposite directions, particularly in peacetime when security imperatives were not prominent. Public perceptions of safety through the 1920s and early 1930s contributed to the atrophy of military capabilities, but changes in these perceptions eventually made rearmament and support for Britain an unavoidable imperative for Canada as much as for Australia.[54]

The imperial connection was essential to the economic well-being of Australia, but it was less so for Canada because ties with the United States had grown stronger since the turn of the century. As trade between the two countries grew, the United States, under President Franklin Roosevelt, implemented a "Good Neighbor" policy with Canada on civil and commercial matters in 1935, thus providing Canadians with an even greater sense of comfort. This was followed in August 1936 by Roosevelt's first public pledge, at Chautauqua, New York, of defence assistance to Canada, a pledge accompanied by his declaration that "our closest neighbours are good neighbors ... they know that we can and will defend ourselves and defend our neighborhood." Appearing to regard Canada as a natural part of an American-led regional hemispheric system, Roosevelt may have been motivated by a concern that Canada's weakness could potentially hurt U.S. interests as well. He realized that the United States could not afford Canada to become a strategic liability, and Mackenzie King, for his part, could see that Canada could not afford to have the United States think that way either. Consequently, King quietly supported a modest rearmament program in February 1937. The following year, at a speech delivered in Kingston, Ontario, in August 1938, when the Czech crisis was in the headlines, Roosevelt offered the assurance that "the United States will not stand idly by if domination of Canadian soil is threatened." King was worried over the consequences of "letting" the United States defend Canada, and so, a few days after Roosevelt's Kingston address, King replied by saying that Canada, too, had its obligations to ensure that "enemy forces should not be able to pursue their way ... to the United States across Canada."[55] Like Borden before him, King also was eager to bring the United States and Britain into closer accord, and he saw his remarks as a first step in that direction. Canada was being drawn into a permanent American embrace, while Australia still looked almost exclusively to Britain for its military and economic security, albeit with increasing apprehension. Canada's steps also would have parallels with Australia's shift towards the United States, a shift that began in the mid-1930s and accelerated once Britain's weaknesses in the Far East were fully exposed with the fall of Singapore to Japanese forces in February 1942.[56]

For Australia, Britain remained the greatest market for primary produce throughout the 1920s and 1930s. Australia was also one of the largest customers for British goods and had the largest amount of British capital invested of any single overseas country. As a consequence, Australia had to ensure that trade and trade routes remained undisturbed. In peacetime this was taken for granted. But, as war approached, government and military planners prepared forces to protect vital trade links, particularly through the Mediterranean and across the Indian Ocean. At the same time, Australia was determined to prevent an armed clash between Britain and Italy that would potentially threaten the Suez lifeline. Australia's overriding economic needs, then, gave coherence and direction to its foreign and military policy. Its priorities were essentially unencumbered by a need to conciliate substantial cultural minorities – unlike in Canada. Even the strongest nationalist recognized Australia's need for imperial solidarity. In addition, Australia supported the policy of appeasement with Germany for clear national interests. After all, as long as appeasement worked, the British fleet remained free to sail to the Far East, and, if it did not work, nothing had been lost because of the efforts made to ensure Australian industrial self-sufficiency. The contrasting Canadian position left Australian politicians baffled. For instance, the conservative Australian politician and diplomat R.G. Casey declared that "no one man can claim credit for having done as much as Mackenzie King to damage what remains of the fabric of the British Empire. His efforts to make political capital out of his domestic nationalism are analogous to a vandal who pulls down a castle in order to build a cottage." As Perras observes, the u.s.-educated Mackenzie King "preferred 'the American road' rather than a British one." Yet, as Eayrs points out, "in defence affairs, what was needed was co-operation, not non-co-operation; compliance in a common cause, not a stubborn assertion of autonomist rights. Canada's response to the menace of the Axis was to voice with unaccustomed fervour her approval of appeasement, while resisting improvements in imperial defence. It brought the worst of both worlds." On the other hand, the Canadian diplomat John Holmes commends Mackenzie King, contending that "once the war started, King's policy on commitments was widely reviled as 'pussyfooting,' but it has been justified – and denounced – as a calculated strategy for bringing Canada as united as possible into a war that seemed inevitable ... Christie could speak sarcastically of 'an English-Speaking Mission to oversee the universe.' King believed in that mission even though he was reluctant to see it established by force."[57]

As war loomed, the economic consequences of preparing for high levels of threat daunted the Australian government. The Australian military chiefs outlined the additional requirements for the "Defence Against Light Raids" contingency, and also what was needed for defence against heavy raids, to a Council of Defence meeting on 5 July 1939. But the government was unwilling to adopt such costly measures in peacetime. Not-yet-fashionable Keynesian economic policies would have been required to fund such measures, and, in any case, the Australian government was unwilling and effectively unable to take this route because of tight constraints imposed by powerful British financial institutions. After all, Australia's currency was tied to Britain's. Calls were made for a two-brigade permanent force of 10,000 troops that could expand at the outbreak of war. Instead, the government authorized the expansion of the part-time militia from 35,000 to 70,000, the intensification of training for part of the militia, and the creation of a permanent-force Darwin Mobile Force to protect its otherwise defenceless yet vital northern port city.[58]

Canada and Australia both claimed that they provided for their own defence in the event of direct aggression against them, but it was expeditionary forces that were required as war broke out in Europe in 1939. Plans for expeditionary forces were quickly dusted off and prepared by army staffs in both countries. Thereafter, a volunteer expeditionary infantry force came to represent the main focus of the Australian and Canadian ground-war efforts, particularly in the first years of the war. The system of defence cooperation based on standardized organization, equipment, and training came to the fore once again because there was broad agreement on the nature of the common danger.[59] However, since both countries had spent most of the inter-war years preoccupied with the politics of mere survival, they faced a formidable task in preparing for war, one that would take months if not years and would tax their abilities to the utmost. It would also dramatically affect their relationships with Britain as its power declined, eclipsed by an emergent United States.

CONCLUSION

The similarities between the inter-war experiences of the armies of Canada and Australia are sometimes obscured by the fact that, in terms of foreign-policy objectives, the two nations had been at loggerheads for most of the inter-war years. Canadian officials were never convinced of the Australians' arguments about Empire solidarity and mutual defence, and usually considered Australians themselves brash, unsophisticated, and, because of their remoteness, unimportant to Canada's national interests. While Canadian military officers understood the need for teamwork and interoperability, as far as the Canadian External Affairs officials were concerned, certain words had always created difficulties at imperial conferences, including "Empire" and "Defence Committee." For Mackenzie King, it was better not to mention them at all, yet, for Australia and New Zealand, they appeared the most significant issues on the agenda.

The years that followed would demonstrate that the armed forces of Canada and Australia continued to share more in common than either side fully realized. But, even so, the political leadership of both countries could not see beyond their own domestic views and concerns, unaware that it was in their shared self-interest to help keep the world safe for their enduring security benefactors, Britain and the United States. Indeed, beyond keeping the Germans and the Japanese down, Canadians and Australians could not agree on much.[60]

Still, as war approached, the long-held ties with Britain gained renewed prominence for both Canada and Australia, as epitomized in the remarks of the conservative Canadian economist and humorist, Stephen Leacock: "If you were to ask any Canadian, he said, 'Do you have to go to war if England does?' he'd answer at once, 'Oh, no.' If you then said, 'Would you go to war if England does?' he'd answer, 'Oh, yes.' And if you asked, 'Why?' he would say, reflectively, 'Well, you see, we'd have to.'" Such sentiments reflected a continuing Canadian imperative for expeditionary forces that would continue to be matched in Australia. For Australia, more so than Canada, the Second World War would be the catalyst and crucible for the creation of a genuinely national foreign policy.[61]

4

The Second World War

The Second World War of 1939–45 presented the Australian and Canadian forces with challenges that were on a greater scale than those they had faced in the Great War of 1914–18. Both countries were unprepared for hostilities, partly because their inter-war defence policies were based not on the likelihood of war but on the people's wish for peace. Both struggled with their response to this challenge, establishing separate departments for air, navy, munitions and supply, and national war-support services. Over the course of the war, four in five Australian men of military age would be in uniform, and the Australian Army, like Canada's, would grow to more than half a million troops. In each country, over a million citizens would serve full time in the three armed services – assigned to remote locations around the world – while Britain would have nearly five million men in arms by 1944.[1]

For Canada, the foreign postings included Burma, Hong Kong, the West Indies, the Aleutian Islands (in the northern Pacific), Britain, northwest Europe, Italy, and even Australia, and, for Australia, they included Britain, North Africa, Palestine and Syria, Greece, Crete, Malaya, Singapore, the Dutch East Indies, East Timor, Burma, Papua and New Guinea, and even Canada. Yet, in the case of both countries, the people who made decisions about the use of their troops in battle usually were Britons or Americans, not Australians or Canadians.[2] Owing in part to the "tyranny of distance,"[3] neither Canadian nor Australian leaders had seriously considered pooling their diplomatic or military resources in order to have a greater combined say in determining their own destinies. There would be several opportunities to do so during the war, but not many would be taken up, leaving Canada and Australia with relatively fewer gains in terms of diplomatic clout in 1945 than they had gained by 1919, following their significant military contributions in the closing days of the First World War.

ORGANIZING THE FORCES

Australia's and New Zealand's declaration of war was immediate upon Britain's declaration on 3 September 1939, a demonstration that, in Australia's case at least, Prime Minister Menzies supported the notion of the "indivisibility of the crown" and that an overwhelming majority of Australians and New Zealanders wished their declarations to be prompt and unequivocal. Australians were not yet prepared to exercise the constitutional prerogative that allowed them to choose for themselves if and when to follow Britain's lead. Yet Menzies's support was more equivocal – more "business as usual" – than Andrew Fisher's had been in 1914 when he proclaimed that Australians would stand beside Britain "to our last man and our last shilling." Menzies's approach reflected the fact that he had been strongly pro-appeasement. It also reflected what Menzies described as Australia's view that its "primary responsibilities and primary risks" were in the Pacific, where Britain's forces were dispersed and relatively weak. And yet the Australian government believed that the defeat of Britain would eventually threaten the overthrow of Australia, either by Germany or by Japan. Hence, Australians felt a sense of obligation to contribute to the war effort.[4]

In contrast to Australia's immediate declaration of war, Canada chose to wait until 10 September. Its stance reflected the value it placed on the autonomy accorded the Dominions under the Statute of Westminster, as well as more finely balanced political dynamics and a desire to receive military-equipment orders from neutral u.s. suppliers before an American neutrality embargo came into effect.[5] The delay confused American officials, who believed that Canada had to be at war as soon as Britain declared war. Still, while the legal obligation was gone, for the majority of Canadians, the moral obligation and the wish to help Britain in any major war were still so great that many considered that "Canada *had* to fight." By and large, French Canadians did not see it that way, believing instead that their country was Canada and that it owed nothing to Britain or, for that matter, France. On the other hand, by 30 March 1939, even Mackenzie King's most prominent French Canadian minister, Ernest Lapointe, had publicly acknowledged the need to support Britain. In addition, despite the growing economic ties with the United States, the prosperity and security of Canada were still closely linked with the prosperity and security of Britain.[6]

Once war was declared, the Australian military forces found themselves with two armies, much like the situation in 1914, since the Defence Act still allowed conscription for domestic service only. The Australian government mobilized just a portion of the militia, and mobilization plans were described as being in a condition of considerable confusion.[7] The fleet of the Royal Australian Navy (RAN), consisting of only slightly more ships than it had in 1914, once again was placed at the disposal of the British Admiralty.[8] By contrast, the four available destroyers of the Royal Canadian Navy (RCN) would not be put at Britain's disposal until after the fall of France was imminent in May 1940. Canada's arrangements for its ships allowed for cooperation with the British "to the fullest extent" but avoided Australia's more subservient position. The RCN would be retained largely for tasks directly affecting the security of Canada, particularly in the north Atlantic, and would be based in Canadian ports; however, a lack of experience, obsolescent equipment, and sometimes weak leadership would make for significant difficulties in the years ahead. As for air power, the RAAF consisted of 14 squadrons with 280 pilots flying obsolescent Hanson and Wirraway single-engine aircraft and Anson bombers. An additional 450 Australians, predominantly pilots, were already serving in Britain in 1939.[9] More would soon be in training in Canada.

At the same time, the Australian government did move quickly to create a standing force of 20,000 volunteers that would become the 2nd AIF. The decision to dispatch the force, however, would not receive cabinet approval until 28 November 1939 – following the government's discovery that New Zealand had already secretly offered an expeditionary force. The first formation raised was the 6th AIF Division (there being four divisions and the components of a fifth in the militia). This formation, like its equivalent, the 1st Canadian Division being raised at the same time, included many "breadliners," since the war offered unemployed men the chance to join the army.[10] Command of the 6th AIF Division went to Major-General Thomas Blamey, who, like Canada's McNaughton, had served in relatively senior appointments on the Western Front in the First World War. Blamey had been Monash's chief of staff in 1918 and "second" (or deputy) CGS in 1925 before leaving the army.[11] His appointment was a reasonable one, for, although he was a militia officer, he was an experienced former regular officer and, also like McNaughton, considered by temperament to be well equipped for handling politico-military problems.[12]

An almost inevitable consequence of the British connection for Australia and Canada was that no tri-service (later termed "joint") force was created in either country. This lack of interservice cooperation would have significant ramifications for later deployments and force-structure decisions. Until the American military forces became a significant factor, planning by Canadian and Australian military chiefs was carried out at the single-service level with collaboration on a service-to-service basis with their British equivalents. Australia's navy, for instance, never fought as a separate entity, but it did fight with distinction alongside the British in the Mediterranean and alongside the U.S. Navy in the Pacific. The RAN was used primarily as a pool of vessels that British and American war leaders could draw on in support of missions which they had decided on and to which their own countries made by far the greatest contribution. The same could be said for the RCN. On the other hand, while the RAAF had a forty-fold increase during the war, and suffered a distressingly high level of killed, wounded, and taken prisoner, the service did little to show that Australia could rely on it for its defence, as a result of its often obsolescent equipment and its being "penny-packeted" out under Allied-control arrangements.

The armies of Canada and Australia fared better than their air force or navy equivalents.[13] In Canada and Australia, the higher command elements were eager to retain a degree of control over the operational role of their land forces.[14] The contrast between the armies and the other services is telling, but the lack of interservice coordination of efforts was perhaps of greater consequence in the long run, particularly in terms of limiting the political and strategic leverage gained from single-service contributions to Allied objectives. In fact, the consequences of such limited interservice cooperation would linger long after the war ended, since both Canada and Australia emerged from the war with disunited command-and-control arrangements that provided for little coordination between their navy, army, and air forces. These disjointed arrangements and the legacy of disparate wartime experiences would hinder subsequent attempts at enhancing interservice cooperation and integration. Without such internal cohesion between the three armed services of each nation, the individual services would perpetuate a subordinate mindset in international military relations. In the meantime, national commanders would face many challenges in the intervening years at war as competing pressures were placed on them by British and American commanders.

General Blamey would be Australia's best practitioner at this difficult task when he deployed to the Middle East in 1940 armed with a "charter" that reflected a de facto recognition of the Statute of Westminster and the concomitant national responsibilities that flowed from it. The militia would remain a part-time citizen army until the Pacific war began in December 1941. However, partial conscription was reintroduced in late 1939 and many who went to camp with the militia in 1939 would remain in the military for the remainder of the war. Yet the Australian Labor Party (in office from 1941 to 1949) would refuse to permit the use of conscripted

Australian troops outside Australia or its territories until January 1943, and then only in a legally prescribed "South-West Pacific Zone."[15]

Most of the officers appointed to Canada's and Australia's expeditionary forces were formerly militia officers, but they included the fresh graduating classes from the military colleges of Kingston and Duntroon. In Canada's case, RMC graduates had come to dominate military appointments by the early inter-war years, whereas graduates from Australia's younger RMC, at Duntroon, did not reach senior levels until later.[16] After the initial surge, however, most officer appointments for the expeditionary armies of both countries would be by promotion from the ranks. In addition, training centres for the various army specialties and for officer training sprouted in support of the expeditionary forces overseas as well as in the homelands. Military planners recognized that individual and unit training for modern warfare required higher standards than had been acceptable in 1914. The soldier in 1939–45 needed to have a working knowledge of a wider range of complicated weapons and equipment, and these skills could be mastered only with long and careful instruction. If there was doubt that such efforts were necessary, the German blitzkriegs in 1939 and 1940 and the Japanese advances in 1941–42 laid it to rest.

The Australian decision to commit forces abroad was not made until Britain promised to secure further trade concessions for Australia's primary industries.[17] Once a trade agreement was secured, Australia deployed the first contingent but insisted on sending them to the Middle East, where the 2nd AIF would gain experience in modern warfare. Britain had wanted the force deployed to Singapore, but, unlike Canada, the Australian government saw more national and military value in fighting Germans and Italians than in sitting in a remote British colony. Experience in battle would, it was thought, be invaluable in the likely event that Japan entered the fray – a concern of less apparent consequence to Atlantic-focused Canadian planners.[18]

The Menzies government was concerned that an over-commitment to the 2nd AIF would have a detrimental effect on the stay-behind militia.[19] Consequently, universal service, abandoned in 1929, was reintroduced for militia homeland-defence tasks. In total, about 100,000 men had volunteered for the three Australian services by March 1940, out of an eligible male population of 600,000 men aged between twenty and twenty-nine.[20] Two AIF brigades were in Britain by the time of the fall of France and would remain there for several months, forming the nucleus of the 9th Division under Major-General H.D. Wynter. This Australian force would prove a useful reinforcement to the army defending England, which, immediately after Dunkirk, contained only one fully armed and trained force – the

1st Canadian Division.[21] A twist of fate had once again conspired to place Australian and Canadian troops alongside each other in the defence of Britain.

Meanwhile, in Australia, the Australian Volunteer Defence Corps was created in July 1940. The corps would include men too old for service overseas, many with experience in the First World War. They would perform roles similar to those of the Veterans Guard of Canada, which was created in May 1940 to protect defence installations but which also provided guards for prisoner-of-war camps.[22]

In seeking to raise substantial forces for another major war, Canada faced problems similar to those of Australia. About 10,000 men in the Mobile Force of two militia divisions from the Non-Permanent Active Militia (NPAM) were placed on active service on 30 August 1939, to operate the coastal defences and protect vulnerable points. However, since section 68 of the Militia Act stipulated that no man could be required to serve in the field continuously for more than a year unless he had volunteered, a legally distinct Canadian Active Service Force (CASF) also was raised. The distinction between the NPAM and CASF units was made by parading NPAM units and calling for volunteers for the new force. Most volunteered, re-enlisting "for overseas service." Thereafter, the remaining NPAM men would be re-designated as the Reserve Army, consisting of eight brigades.[23]

Six days after declaring war, the Canadian government decided that one division would proceed to England. The creation of an even larger Canadian Army would be approved after the fall of France. Thereafter, integration of British and Canadian formations proved relatively easy because of common organization and procedures. To oversee this process, the Canadian government recalled Lieutenant-General McNaughton to active duty, much as the Australian government did with Blamey. Like Blamey with the 2nd AIF, McNaughton never forgot that he was more than a military commander – he was the de facto representative of the home government for the deployed forces. British commanders observed that McNaughton, strangely enough, had an "ultra political outlook" but was "devoid of any form of strategic outlook."[24] Still, McNaughton observed in 1940 that "our relations with the British Expeditionary Force [are] in marked and pleasant contrast to 1914 when we came over practically as strangers." Despite good relations, however, J.L. Granatstein observes that "it was the Canadians' good fortune that they were not yet part of the British Expeditionary Force [in early 1940] because, as ill-trained as the division was, as ill-led by men who still thought in terms of the Great War, it could not have done well in action, if indeed it could have survived." In addition, they were legally distinct forces, unlike their counterparts of 1914. A Visiting

Forces (British Commonwealth) Act recognizing the issues that arose in the First World War had been passed reciprocally for Britain and Canada in 1933. This act enabled their troops to serve together "in combination" and under the operational command of a British general. Australia and the other Dominions would enact similar legislation in 1939.[25]

Canada also faced challenges with those of its troops conscripted for service under the National Resources Mobilization Act (NRMA) that was passed in June 1940. Like Australia, the Canadian government had sought to handle the issue of conscription delicately while facing increased military manpower requirements. By 1942, the NRMA forces included 34,000 troops who stood guard against the possibility of a Japanese invasion of Canada's west coast. Like their militia equivalents in Australia, the NRMA conscripts could be used for home defence only, leaving the Canadian Army with two classes of soldiers. In a plebiscite held in April 1942, about 64 per cent of Canadian voters agreed to allow the government to conscript for overseas service, a power it would hold in reserve until November 1944; however, only about one-quarter of Quebec voters were supportive. Some favoured Irish-style neutrality or a clerical-fascism of a Spanish or Italian type. Quebec separatists would cite the 1942 plebiscite as an example of the dangers of remaining a minority in a predominantly "Anglo" country. Ironically, as in 1917, internal readjustments probably would have been sufficient to obviate the need for conscription.[26]

LOOKING TO AMERICA

While these events transpired, Canada was being drawn increasingly into the U.S. orbit, as it had been for much of the inter-war period. As early as 1923, the Halibut Treaty between Canada and the United States had been signed in Washington by a Canadian government minister – the first time a Canadian had done so alone on behalf of his country – and this event opened the way to separate Dominion control over foreign relations. At the same time, by 1939, American capital accounted for 60 per cent of foreign investment in Canada, whereas in 1914 it had accounted for only 23 per cent – far behind that of Britain, which then furnished 73 per cent of the country's foreign investment.[27] The growth of American influence in Canada resulted not just from trade and business ties but from heightened U.S. defence interest in the Pacific coast and in Alaska as bulwarks against a growing Japanese threat.

After the fall of France, Canada had an added incentive to align itself with the United States given the precarious position of Britain. In effect,

Britain's military weakness forced Canada to look to the United States for its security. The end result was the 1940 Ogdensburg Agreement, signed by President Roosevelt and Prime Minister Mackenzie King, which led to the creation of the Permanent Joint Board on Defence (PJBD), through which Canada and the United States vowed to consider, in the broad sense, the common defence of the northern half of the western hemisphere.[28] King's aide, Leonard Brockington, thought that adding Britain, Australia, and New Zealand to the PJBD would prove beneficial – a view like that expressed by Australian Prime Minister Joseph Lyons in 1935. But, once again, the United States objected. The secretary of state at the time, Cordell Hull, declared his country was not ready for a military alliance in the Pacific.[29] In addition, the United States evidently believed then (as it still does) that Canadian weakness could potentially endanger American security. In any case, Canadian prominence from the Washington perspective was short-lived. Britain, once again, soon came to dominate the transatlantic relationship as the United States prepared to enter the war.

Despite such sentiments, and the fact that the United States remained sympathetic but formally neutral until December 1941, the continuing expansion of North American trade led to an agreement that Mackenzie King and O.D. Skelton had strived for since 1935 – the Hyde Park Declaration of April 1941 – which integrated Canada into the United States orbit of industry and defence production. Furthermore, unlike Australia, which in 1939 already had a negative trade balance with Canada and the United States, Canada was not subjected to the Lend-Lease Agreement and the Hyde Park Declaration helped consolidate the country's favourable trade position. The Lend-Lease scheme would also undermine the imperial trade-preference arrangements, thus helping to ensure the eventual dismantling of the British Empire.[30] That dismantling, in turn, would drive Australia and Canada towards a closer security relationship with the United States.

Despite the progress achieved on economic matters, Canada would struggle to convey – for the remainder of the war – the message of its changed diplomatic status to the United States. Unable to get Roosevelt's attention, the Canadian government was increasingly suspicious of American intentions. Indeed, it was in Britain's interest that this ambivalent arrangement should continue, because, by standing on the shoulders of the Commonwealth, Britain could remain at eye level with Russia and the United States. Without a like-minded strategic partner (such as Australia) with which to collaborate, Canada's efforts to gain influence in Washington would be limited. In addition, for Canadians, the United States was both the "fabled city on a hill" and a feared rival.[31] Australians felt the same way but to a lesser degree, because of geography. The Americans, for their part, would feel no compulsion to formalize bilateral military arrangements with Australia until the Philippines fell to the Japanese in 1942.

Australia took a little longer than Canada to acknowledge the implications of shifts in strategic-alliance dynamics. It did not establish its first diplomatic mission to a foreign country (that is, outside the British Empire) until 1940. The Japanese advance towards Britain's Singapore base offered an effective inducement to further Australian rapprochement with the United States, though, as was also the case with Canada, American deference to Britain inhibited moves towards greater independence.[32]

Australia had a similar if not stronger need than Canada to realign itself with the United States, given Britain's weaknesses and Australia's vulnerabilities in the Pacific. In addition, the United States had a clear interest in using Australia as a springboard for its counter-offensive against the Japanese. With these concerns in mind and while the debacle in Singapore was occurring, Australian Prime Minister John Curtin declared that "Australia looks to America, free of any pangs as to our traditional links or kinship with the United Kingdom ... we shall exert all our energies toward shaping of a plan, with the United States as its keystone ... until the tide of battle swings against the enemy."[33] Curtin's speech was strongly criticized by Churchill and the leading figure in Australia's Opposition, Robert Menzies, much as Churchill and Arthur Meighen, Canada's Opposition leader at the time, had condemned the Ogdensburg Agreement. Indeed, Curtin's speech has been seen by many as a turning point in Australia's foreign relations, just as the Ogdensburg Declaration was in the case of Canada's. But the speech did not translate into a breach with Britain or the Commonwealth. Essentially, Curtin was looking to the United States to supply aid that Britain could not possibly supply. Australian diplomatic historian Alan Watt observes that "it is open to argument that the scars left by these disputes never healed completely, that from this period onwards ... British-Australian relations never recovered fully their degree of intimacy." Yet Australian politicians, like their Canadian counterparts, were not being disloyal by looking after their domestic interests. National interests were understandably being placed highest in the scale of priorities of Australian and Canadian governments. Conversely, Canadian and Australian interests were, quite reasonably, secondary to Churchill. He admitted as much afterwards when he stated that "the Australian government could feel very little confidence in the British conduct of the war or in our judgement at home."[34] Not surprisingly, therefore, the traditional ties with Britain gradually would become less important for Australia (as they would also for Canada), although Australia would seek to involve Britain in the planned offensives in the Pacific late in the war as well as in post-war policy formulation for the area.

Before Pearl Harbor, Australia's diplomatic objective had been to avoid finding itself at war with Japan without the United States at its side, so R.G. Casey's diplomatic role in Washington as head of the Australian mission had been crucial to the country. But, as Alan Watt observes, the Japanese decision "to bomb American territory solved this problem." Shortly after the attack on Pearl Harbor, Brigadier-General Dwight D. Eisenhower, one of General George Marshall's principal staff officers at the time, placed Australia sixth on a list of eight "things that are highly desirable," as opposed to necessary, for the ultimate defeat of the Axis Powers.[35] Still, Eisenhower did indicate that Australia was the nearest base to the Philippines that the United States could hope to maintain. And maintaining Australia as a base meant protecting Hawaii, Fiji, New Caledonia, and New Zealand as an essential line of communications. Marshall replied to Eisenhower: "I agree with you ... Do your best to save them." Reflecting on this calculus, Australia's T.B. Millar writes: "Had Japan conquered Australia and New Zealand, the Allies would have had an immensely more difficult task, even though the final outcome would undoubtedly have been the same. The United States thus did not really come to the *aid* of Australia; it came to *use* Australia, and in using her, keep her safe."[36] In essence, therefore, even when facing its most dire predicament, American support appeared to have been equivocal. The realization that Australian had but a tenuous hold on the list of American security priorities would significantly affect the country's defence- and foreign-policy priorities for the remainder of the twentieth century and beyond in a more strongly felt way than that experienced by more comfortable and secure Canadians.

The Australian most directly charged with this responsibility during the war was Prime Minister John Curtin. Curtin was the first representative of the Irish Catholic minority to come to power in Australia. Arguably, Curtin's anglophile predecessor, Menzies, would have found it more difficult to make such a leap into the "arms" of the United States. Regardless, Curtin's appeal for an Australia-United States partnership was initially not welcomed by Roosevelt any more than it was by Churchill.[37] A few months later, in March 1942, the United States Army commander from the Philippines, General Douglas MacArthur, arrived in Australia, taking command of the Allied forces in the South West Pacific Area (SWPA). The SWPA included Australia and the islands stretching north to the Philippines but excluded New Zealand, the Solomon Islands, New Caledonia, and Fiji, which were assigned to the U.S. Navy's Hawaii-based Pacific Command under Mac-Arthur's rival, Admiral Chester Nimitz. Their rivalry would come at some strategic cost to all concerned, including Australia and New Zealand.[38]

MacArthur's headquarters were established initially in Melbourne, with Australia's General Blamey as his Land Forces Commander SWPA – since, at that stage, Australia provided the overwhelming majority of the land forces at MacArthur's disposal.[39] Yet, despite Blamey's apparently powerful position, the position of principal Australian adviser to the prime minister was reserved for the secretary of the Department of Defence, Frederick Shedden – an arrangement that Blamey found extremely frustrating.[40] Thus, while Australia's defence shifted from being an imperial responsibility to being an American duty, Blamey's authority was diminished.[41] Curtin had eagerly accepted Roosevelt's decision to make Australia a major base against Japan. This followed Roosevelt's and Churchill's decision, without prior consultation with Australia, to carve up global responsibilities, leaving the United States with jurisdiction over the Pacific area. The Churchill-Roosevelt diarchy meant that Australia, like Canada, had virtually no say in the Allies' higher direction of the war from 1942 to 1945, although, in Canada's case, Mackenzie King also sometimes did not want to know. Stacey notes that "in the strategic discussions during the war Churchill assumed that he was entitled to represent the Dominions and to give them as much or as little information about events as he chose."[42]

The short-lived unified command arrangement for the American-British Dutch-Australian (ABDA) Command was one such issue that, in Churchill's mind, required little Australian input. In 1941 ABDA Command was based in Java, but it collapsed early in 1942 under the weight of Japan's assault. MacArthur then was given broader powers, including exclusive strategic and operational responsibility in the SWPA. He made no provision for a balanced, combined staff at his headquarters, or for much of a voice for Australia in the higher direction of the war in the Pacific theatre – despite the wealth of experience of Australian commanders and staff returning from the Mediterranean. MacArthur's SWPA headquarters functioned as an American, not an Allied, body. His approach made the earlier arrogance and aloofness of senior British military officers appear tame by comparison – and his manner irked Blamey. At the same time, MacArthur's generalship had one great merit: it never put Australian troops in such a hopeless position as the British had done in the Greece, Crete, and Singapore disasters.[43]

MacArthur shared the traditional American distrust of British aims and policy, which appeared to extend to Australians as well. Yet, by accepting MacArthur's appointment, the Australian government had made a notable surrender of sovereignty, and Curtin accurately remarked that "it does not appear that the [Australian] Government has any place in the set up as laid down." In effect, the Australian government's reliance upon MacArthur "had a stultifying effect on its ability to develop its own strategic view." By 1943, Curtin would come to hope that a British force would re-enter the Pacific theatre to help reduce Australia's dependence on the United States. This view reflected similar balance-of-power concerns as those felt by Canada's leaders – concerns that conceivably could have been alleviated by closer inter-Dominion collaboration.[44] The presence of a Canadian force of division size or larger (discussed later in this chapter) may have altered the dynamics of command away from its lopsided acceptance of MacArthur's control. Had Canada established more of a presence in the Pacific, it is possible that MacArthur would have been forced to concede more to his Allied partners and to be less overbearing.

But this, of course, did not happen. Instead, as with Australia, Canada's pattern of leaving direction to the Great Powers was repeated when the United States entered the war. For instance, when Churchill and Roosevelt met off Argentia, Newfoundland (then still British territory), to issue their Atlantic Charter in 1941, Canada was not invited to participate and, like Australia, resented being excluded from grand strategy and the higher-level decision-making process. Yet Canada's slowness to organize forces and to equip them to act as an extension of its foreign policy rendered it largely incapable of exerting significant influence on the direction of the war. This was despite Mackenzie King's late conversion to the merits of Allied cooperation and his determined, albeit belated, efforts to increase Canada's access to the seats of Allied power. Even in 1944 Canada was excluded from the Allied integrated military staff in Europe, especially from Eisenhower's headquarters.[45]

Canada had not developed a mature and independent foreign or strategic policy before 1939 and found it virtually impossible to assert one during the war. Mackenzie King's position was not enhanced by his character, described by Canadian historian R.A. Preston as "lacking the grand manner and speech of a public hero." Nor was his position enhanced by the small size of the military force Canada initially had at its disposal. Still, the creation of the Permanent Joint Board of Defence was the first step in Canada's slow but significant reorientation from the United Kingdom to the United States – with dramatic ramifications for the structure of its military.[46]

In contrast, the wartime Australian-United States alliance was born of immediate military necessity but not at the permanent expense of continuing ties with Britain. Despite the theoretical equality between two sovereign countries, relations with the United States would be strained by difficulties that arose out of unequal international status and national power. This strain was at least in part due to Australia's desire to maintain preferential trading arrangements with Britain and the Commonwealth. After all, throughout the 1930s, over two-thirds of Australia's exports were to other Commonwealth countries – predominantly Britain. With u.s. dollar reserves in limited supply in Australia, government officials were eager to minimize reliance on costly American imports. Still, although not as substantial as Canada's, Australian reciprocal aid, arranged under the u.s.-initiated bilateral Mutual Aid Agreement that Australia signed in September 1942, approximated one-quarter of Australia's war expenditure in the last two years of the war. This arrangement offset most of the costs of Australia's military effort, amounting to a "reverse Lend-Lease."[47]

During the remaining years of the war, Australia, too, would increasingly become part of the u.s. economic and security orbit. However, in contrast to Canada, whose formal military and economic ties with the United States were secured in 1940 and 1941, the United States would not see the need formally to integrate Australia and New Zealand into its alliance system until after the onset of the Cold War.[48] Moreover, trade and security ties with Britain would still feature prominently for Australia and New Zealand following the end of the Second World War. After all, as economic historians John Singleton and Paul Robertson argue, "Australia and New Zealand were core members of the global web of financial, economic, political and military ties characterised by us officials as the 'British complex.'" These ties with Britain would endure while Australia remained in the British sterling financial bloc and until Britain joined the European Common Market in the early 1970s. Financially, Australia's position was unlike that of Canada, where American manufacturers (particularly the auto industry) could take advantage of preferential duties with the Empire-Commonwealth to export to Australia, Britain, and elsewhere in the sterling bloc. In 1948, for instance, President Harry Truman would permit recipients of Marshall Plan aid to make purchases in Canada as well as the United States.[49]

Australia, like Canada, was operating under apprehensions about its place both as a part of the Empire and as a separate national state, and, indeed, its apprehensions on this score may have been more acute than Canada's. The Australian government contributed with air and sea power to help fight for Britain's cause, but its more noteworthy and publicly identifiable contribution was with ground forces.[50]

Chart 5
Commonwealth casualties in Second World War

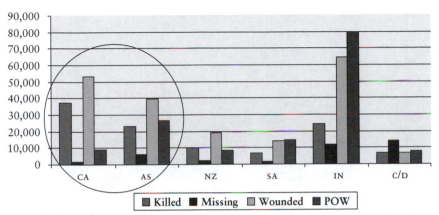

Source: Nicholas Mansergh, *The Commonwealth Experience, Volume Two: From British Commonwealth to Multi-Racial State* (London: Macmillan 1982), 94.

(SA = South Africa, IN = India, C/D = Colonies and Dependencies)

FORCES DEPLOY

Canadian ground forces briefly deployed to France in 1940, and in fact Defence Minister Norman Rogers had meetings in France in April 1940 concerning a possible Canadian base there. But the Canadian forces were withdrawn when France sought an armistice with Germany in June. Canadian troops also were sent to garrison Bermuda and Jamaica and would later contribute to the recovery of the Aleutian Islands, southwest of Alaska, from the Japanese. Still, the vast majority of Canadian troops would end up concentrating in Britain during the following years. These would include five divisions and ancillary units, which were structured along British organizational lines. The militia – renamed the Canadian Army in 1940 – sent the 1st Canadian Division to England in December 1939, with a shortfall in equipment that was surprisingly similar to the shortfall of the Australian's 6th AIF Division.[51] Like the Australian force, it would include brigades representing the national regions, but, unlike the Australian force, it would also include regular-force artillery brigades.[52]

While Canada's forces were concentrating in Britain, Australian forces in the Mediterranean expanded to three divisions – the 6th, 7th, and 9th AIF divisions. The 8th deployed primarily to Malaya and Singapore, and the

Map 3
Mediterranean

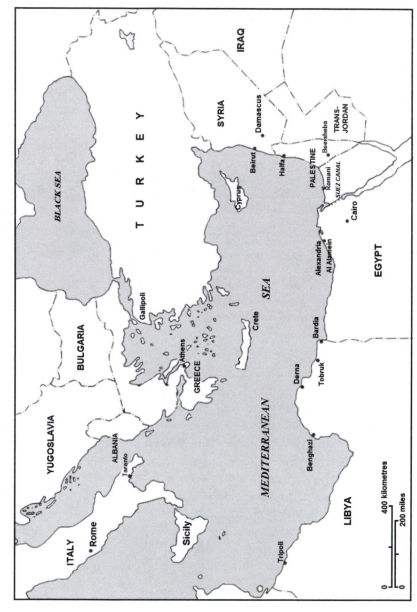

Map 4
Asia-Pacific

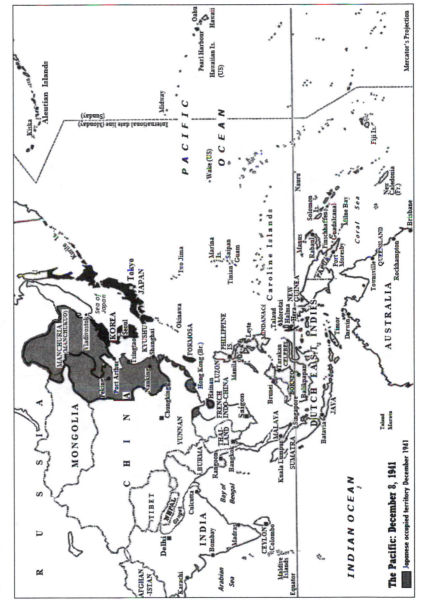

The Pacific: December 8, 1941

▓ Japanese occupied territory December 1941

1st to 5th divisions, being militia formations, were retained in Australia.[53] With the increases in span of command, a corps headquarters and corps troops were raised to support the 2nd AIF in the Middle East.[54] This force saw extensive service under the command of Lieutenant-General Blamey. The Australians fought successfully against the Italians, then with less success once the Germans entered North Africa, Greece, and Crete, although the first defeat of the Germans in the war arguably occurred when they failed to seize Tobruk in the face of predominantly Australian defences from April to December 1941. In addition, the Australian 9th Division played a crucial role at the battle of El Alamein in 1942. Australians also fought successfully, albeit after a surprisingly difficult struggle, against the Vichy French in Syria.[55]

In general, the Canadian government was not prepared to get "into the fight" early in the ground war, being unwilling to commit troops to the North African campaign. General McNaughton, with Mackenzie King's backing, refused to divide his corps in Britain.[56] Thus, Canada missed fighting in North Africa and trained in England, watching as the armies of Britain, Australia, New Zealand, South Africa, and India (as well as the United States, from 1942 onwards), refined fighting skills and, more important, replaced inadequate commanders while fighting the Italians and before facing the better-equipped and organized, and more challenging, Germans. That said, though Canada ended up suffering higher casualties during the war than Australia (see Chart 9), the benefits of having integral armoured forces would be amply demonstrated in the campaigns in Italy and northwest Europe from 1943 to 1945. Without them, Canadian casualties likely would have been significantly higher.

Like Canada, Australia also raised armoured and motor formations. These were more complex organizations than infantry divisions and required a significant input from local industry. After Japan's intervention, and with Australia fearing an invasion, the newly created armoured formations were retained at home. Thereafter, the merits of armoured forces for Australia would be again demonstrated in the battles against well-dug-in Japanese troops in the jungles of the Pacific. But such successes would occur only after unprecedented setbacks against the Japanese in 1942.[57]

Both Canada and Australia deployed small numbers of soldiers in isolated locations in Asia, seeking in vain to hold back the Japanese surge while their main force contributions were otherwise occupied in Britain or the Middle East.[58] The majority of Australia's 8th AIF Division (19,000 troops) deployed to Singapore – where they joined 120,000 other British,

Indian, and local forces. The remainder of the 8th Division was dispatched to the Dutch East Indies islands of Ambon and Timor, with a battalion also sent to the island of Rabaul, northeast of New Guinea. These dispersed forces were captured by the Japanese in February 1942, with none of the smaller garrisons causing Japan so much as a day's delay.

This defeat occurred only a few weeks after two raw and ill-equipped Canadian garrison battalions were sent to Hong Kong. Mackenzie King had opposed sending troops to the South Pacific and North Africa but, apparently lacking a grand vision of how to use Canadian forces, ended up committing troops in a piecemeal manner. Canada's contribution in Hong Kong, for instance, was in response to a British appeal in 1941 to reinforce the one British and two Indian battalions. This combined force was overwhelmed and captured by the Japanese in early 1942. Stacey suggests that "a more active policy might have achieved more respect for the forms, rather than the substance, of Canadian sovereignty."[59]

Arguably, had Australia and Canada considered pooling their scattered resources prior to the events of December 1941 and January 1942, these Asian debacles might have been replaced by a more stout defence of, say, Singapore. Such a plausible alternative situation serves to illustrate the limited vision of both Australian and Canadian leaders, who failed to grasp fully the strategic consequences of dispersing their forces. Menzies, in some ways, was like Mackenzie King – both were criticized for having had no combat experience and little direct acquaintance with the armed forces. But King's desire to distance himself from notions of Empire would happen even at the expense of his fellow travellers, the Australians. Caution, not heroism, was a Mackenzie King hallmark – to the irritation and disappointment of his Australian contemporaries. For instance, while Menzies was still the Australian prime minister, he saw Mackenzie King as a key ally and had visited Ottawa in May 1941 calling for an imperial war cabinet that Australians, Canadians, and others could participate in. But, as Stacey states, "Mackenzie King was not Borden, and when Menzies called in at Ottawa on his way home he wholly failed to sell King on this device, which the Canadian told him would bring the Dominions merely 'responsibility without power.'" Menzies expressed frustration at the two countries' inability to work together in a common cause, describing King as "no war leader." But, unlike Menzies, King had to contend with an unenthusiastic Quebec, the base of his Liberal Party's support, which wanted to weaken, not strengthen, political links with Britain. Mackenzie King observed that Menzies "would rather be on the War Cabinet in London than Prime Minister of Australia." He went on to predict ominously, and accurately, that Menzies's affection for "the environments of high society places, etc ... will cost him, perhaps, dearly in the end."[60] Menzies lost office soon afterwards.

By early 1942, with Menzies's successor prime minister, Curtin, in power since October 1941, Allied forces had been defeated throughout most of east and southeast Asia and Australia's circumstances had drastically altered – invasion of Australia seemed possible. Some Australian territory in New Guinea had been captured in the first few months of 1942 (Rabaul and New Ireland in January, Lae and Salamaua by March, and the Buna-Gona area by June), Japanese submarines were reaching Australian shores, penetrating Sydney's harbour defences in May 1942, and Japanese bombers were repeatedly bombing Darwin and other northern Australian coastal cities. Canada's experience with such relatively harmless challenges as balloon bombs on the west coast led to an exaggerated precaution of deploying three home defence divisions there – a far greater force than Australia could spare for the defence of places like Darwin.[61]

As these events were unfolding, Canadian Major-General V.W. Odlum arrived in Australia on 8 January 1942 as Canada's new high commissioner to Canberra.[62] Odlum had a strong sense that Canada and Australia faced the same threat in the Pacific. Responding to an appeal from Prime Minister Curtin, Odlum suggested – without consulting Ottawa – that Canada might be able to provide practical help to Australia, including the dispatch of a brigade group or a division to operate as a mobile reserve to supplement the five remaining Australian militia divisions still in Australia and so "enable Australia to adopt a bolder policy than it otherwise could."[63] In the meantime, the first batch of 4,200 U.S. troops, having been diverted from the Philippines, had already arrived in Australia, receiving a rapturous welcome in Brisbane on 22 December 1941. By June 1942, there would be about 60,000 American and 410,000 Australian ground troops in Australia. Over the course of the war, about half a million American servicemen would spend some time in Australia.[64]

Senior Australian government officials and military officers were eager to receive such support as Odlum appeared to offer. To support Odlum's case, the Australian chiefs of staff sent an assessment of the defence needs of Australia and the adjacent areas to help persuade Canada of the merits of cooperation.[65] But it was for naught. New at the game of diplomacy, Odlum was forcefully instructed to refrain from making such offers and told instead to draw Australia's views on this matter to the Combined British-American Chiefs of Staff Committee and the Munitions Assignment Board

(MAB). Canada's increased industrial capacity, it was argued, was already committed to the support of Britain and the United States, and their agreement would be required if resources were to be diverted to Australia.[66] Little thought appeared to have been made to Canada making an independent decision on this matter.[67] Meanwhile, Australia's high commissioner to Canada, Sir William Glasgow, appealed to the Canadian government for the shipment of Canadian-produced equipment to Australia. Initially, Canada would agree to supply only Catalina flying boats. Clearly, Odlum had overstepped the limits of his authority, and scholars have long derided him for his missteps. But several officials in Canada could see the mutual benefit of two small powers like Australia and Canada pooling resources. Canada's defence minister, Colonel J.L. Ralston, for instance, suggested sending a brigade to Australia, although the chiefs of staff in Ottawa argued against such a move. In addition, Canada's Opposition leader, R.B. Hanson, demanded that the Canadian government commit a division for Australia in late January 1942. Clearly, therefore, Odlum's ideas were not that far-fetched. If they had been acted upon, they might well have helped both countries to gain greater strategic leverage at their respective "seats at the table" in Washington or London. In any event, matters were not helped by Mackenzie King's prevarication: first, he indicated to Glasgow that he was "favourably disposed toward rendering assistance wherever possible in the Pacific area";[68] then he delayed repudiating Odlum's offer until Australia's brilliant but fiery external affairs minister, Herbert "Doc" Evatt, could be told the news in person when he visited Ottawa in April 1942.

The fact that both Australia and Canada faced the same reorientation away from Britain and towards the United States during this period was not lost on officials in the two countries. In addition, they both disliked the Washington-London partnership that left them with little voice in the direction of grand strategy. Australia, as much as Canada, it seemed, was now an American strategic responsibility, but there was a feeling of resentment in Australia that, having had its hopes raised, Canada did not respond with commitments of support in 1942. Odlum's successor as Canadian high commissioner to Australia, T.C. Davis, would observe in mid-1945 that "many Australians to this day feel badly that the British Commonwealth as a whole was not able to send assistance [in 1942] and the main burden of support fell on a non-British Commonwealth country [the United States] ... The feeling grew that Canada, a sister Dominion, should have done exactly the same thing." Canada's Department of External Affairs dismissed this idea, revealing an ignorance of the classic Clausewitzian dictum that "war is an extension of politics by other means," declaring that such "token forces are of political rather than military value." It appears that the governments of Canada and Australia could not overcome their predisposition for working directly with Britain or the United States rather than pursuing their own national interests in a mutually supportive manner. By the same token, Australia's diplomatic inexperience contributed to the troubles between Australia and Canada. Australia's political culture valued an adversarial plain-speaking style that contrasted with and failed to appreciate the nuances of the Canadian approach under Mackenzie King.[69]

At this juncture, one might object that Canada could not have afforded to split its forces to support Australia in the Pacific, particularly given the well-established "beat Hitler first" policy. But that policy did not stop the United States or Britain (let alone Australia or New Zealand) from engaging in major military operations in the Pacific and southeast Asia. Moreover, Canada did indeed split its forces anyway, between northwest Europe and Italy. It also deployed, as recounted above, two infantry battalions to Hong Kong and contributed to the expulsion of the Japanese from the Aleutian Islands in the north Pacific. Even with multiple Canadian divisions committed in Italy, at the time of D-Day, three more Canadian divisions were assigned Juno Beach and these forces captured the bridgehead essentially on their own. Such forces also were sufficient for Canada to be given command of an army-sized formation in northwest Europe in 1944 and 1945.

Conceivably, if Odlum's vision of Canada's obligations to its other ocean, the Pacific, had been given greater weight in Ottawa's deliberations, the two divisions in Italy could have deployed to the Pacific, where division-sized battles in the Pacific islands had greater prominence and, arguably, greater strategic consequence than their equivalents among significantly larger ground formations in Europe. As it was, Odlum's views were rejected and Odlum himself was replaced, providing a classic example of why better Canadian and Australian cooperation did not and perhaps could not take place.[70] Given the conventional view of Canada having little interest in Pacific affairs at the time, such a view may seem reasonable. But, like Australia, being a "two-plus-oceans" nation, Canada always has had an interest in security affairs in the Pacific region and would demonstrate those interests repeatedly with the deployment of Canadian forces in the post-war years.

While dramatic events unfolded in the Pacific war against Japan, President Roosevelt, under strong pressure from the Australians, proposed the creation of an international advisory council on Pacific matters, known as the Pacific War Council. This council would provide a forum where political representatives could at least seem to be having a say in Allied decision making. Its first meeting was in Washington in April 1942, with representatives from the United States, the United Kingdom, Australia, New Zealand, Canada, China, and the Netherlands in attendance. John Robertson argues that Roosevelt probably saw the body as a means of appeasing his minor Pacific allies.[71] There, Australia's Evatt, inspired by Odlum's offer, advocated Canadian participation in the Munitions Assignment Board as a reciprocal gesture for Canada's support of Australian participation on the same board. Mackenzie King, having already snubbed Evatt by repudiating Odlum's offer of troops in support of Australia, further missed the chance to placate the Australians by refusing to cooperate on MAB membership. King instead declared that Canada "would not wish this representation on the score of being there to protect the interests of any particular part of the Empire." Australians had earlier experienced the consequences of Mackenzie King's lack of solidarity with Australia during the imperial conferences of the 1930s, when it became evident to them that Canada would not support efforts at collective defence. In September 1939 this point had again been reinforced when the Australian government sought to have Canada take delivery of aircraft, which it had on order from the United States, until the Canadian state of belligerency came into effect a few days later. The Canadian government refused, claiming that such action might have undesirable consequences for its relationship with the United States.[72] Now, with King's 1942 decision regarding the MAB, yet another opportunity for mutually beneficial cooperation appears to have been missed, arguably because the decision makers in Canada did not appreciate the advantages of working with the Australians in a way that was consistent with their own national interests – interests that included having a greater say in the deliberations in Washington and in the establishment of the post-war international order.

Australia's overtures for Canadian help in 1942 reflected its sense of shock and helplessness as Japan advanced southwards, but Australia first had to reflect on its own convoluted defence arrangements. The Australian militia divisions, including volunteers and an increasing number of conscripts, had been legally barred from service outside Australian territory and maintained a separate chain of command, reporting to the Military Board and the minister. These divisions were initially mobilized for a rotation of three-month training camps until Japanese advances forced the government to increase the tempo in December 1941 and bring the five infantry and two motorized cavalry divisions to full strength – 246,000 troops.[73] Eventually, however, several of these formations would end up fighting the Japanese beyond Australia's shores in the southwest Pacific.

Meanwhile, the prospects of a Japanese onslaught had prompted the Australian government to return its forces from the Middle East to the Pacific, but by December 1941 over 100,000 Australian troops remained in the Middle East, much to the chagrin of Prime Minister Curtin, who was eager for their prompt return. Blamey returned to Australia in early 1942, after having vigorously defended Australian interests in the face of conflicting British demands. His experience with the higher-level political aspects of command prepared him for his new position of commander-in-chief of Australian Military Forces.[74] This position was created to provide command for both the AIF and the militia (renamed the Citizen Military Forces, or CMF).[75] By April 1942, a series of new commands were raised to control the growing number of military forces spread around the country.[76]

As the armed forces grew, one area where Australia set out to make a significant and unique contribution was intelligence. The Australian government had been concerned about being poorly informed about Japanese intentions, dispositions, and capabilities. As a result, a wartime intelligence apparatus was developed in Australia that would play a significant role in shaping Allied strategy in the Pacific. As David Horner points out, (reflecting Australian parallels with the Canadian notion of functionalism, whereby Canada has sought to be granted a status in accordance with its expertise and capabilities – including its military contributions), "for a relatively small expenditure on manpower and equipment, Australia was able to contribute to the allied war effort in the Pacific to a degree out of proportion both to her military strength and to the role allowed to her military forces. Mutual confidence was developed and the basis for future intelligence co-operation was established." By war's end, Australia had made an important contribution in the field of special intelligence, establishing, with MacArthur's forces, an Allied Intelligence Bureau that included a wide array of capabilities.[77] The bureau would operate in many parts of the archipelago to the north of Australia. Moreover, most of these capabilities were built upon Australian Army foundations, with the Australians providing the majority of personnel. Horner concludes that "it may well be that present day intelligence co-operation has proved to be the most lasting and important legacy of Australia's experience of coalition warfare in the Second World War."[78]

No such comparable national-level and multifaceted intelligence apparatus was developed in Canada. However, Canada did contribute to Allied intelligence capabilities during the war, for example, through the deployment in March 1945 of the Canadian Army No. 1 Special Wireless Group to Darwin as well as a select number of volunteers to other operations, including the

Allied Intelligence Bureau. But Canada's geography and sense of relative security did not dictate the same degree of urgency to the development of intelligence-related capabilities.[79] Instead, Canada's forté was in the air.

During the war, Canada contributed massively to the Allied air effort through the Empire Air Training Scheme, known in Canada as the British Commonwealth Air Training Program. This scheme, conceived by the Australian and Canadian high commissioners to Britain – Australia's Stanley Bruce and Canada's Vincent Massey – would see tens of thousands of British Commonwealth airmen trained and sent on to fight the air war over Britain and Europe and, to a lesser extent, against Japan. However, at first, its designers appear not to have realized that what they had created was essentially a recruiting scheme for the RAF.[80] Canada placed more emphasis on the BCATP than the other countries did, providing 51 per cent of its graduates. It also agreed to create twenty-five squadrons within the RAF, while Australia undertook to create eighteen squadrons under similar arrangements that did not include ground crew or full payment of all expenses. In the end, the scheme left Canada and Australia with little opportunity to gain political leverage from such significant national contributions – although Canada was not as subsumed by the RAF as the Australians were because of the formation of the relatively cohesive No. 6 (RCAF) Group in Britain's Bomber Command. From the standpoint of Australia's national-defence policy, the scheme was a disaster. Australia lost control of its airmen and its experienced squadrons, leaving the nation largely unprotected except for limited United States air support in the critical days of 1942. The same was not the case for Canada, which entered the war with less enthusiasm for imperial matters but emerged from it with a significant air force and air industry.[81]

Air power also played an important role at sea, particularly with the naval battles of the Coral Sea in May 1942 and Midway in June 1942. But after these battles, the threat of a Japanese invasion of Australia receded and the country's army began making preparations for taking the offensive. Before the war, the army's chiefs had contended that Australia could not support more than seven or eight divisions at full strength in active operations, and events were to prove them right. Although Australia raised fourteen divisions, only seven of them would be maintained for war-fighting abroad in New Guinea and the Pacific from the end of 1943 onwards, as compared to the twenty-four divisions of the U.S. Army and Marine Corps in the Pacific theatre. The army's unsustainably large force of fourteen divisions had to be scaled back to allow over 100,000 workers to return to civil industry. Canada faced similar challenges during the summer of 1943, and two divisions were disbanded as Canadian industry reached its greatest expansion. By the end of 1943, Australia's prime minister, Curtin, had determined that further cuts were required. Thereafter, Australia's war effort would consist of two armoured brigades and six infantry divisions – three AIF and three CMF – for active operations in the southwest Pacific. In addition, the RAN would be maintained at its extant capacity, and the RAAF with fifty-three squadrons.[82] At that time, Canada (with a population of eleven million) had two divisions in Britain and two on the way.[83] In the meantime, the process of force expansion and contraction would be significantly affected by developments in tactics and equipment.

TACTICS AND EQUIPMENT

The tactics and equipment necessary to fight the lightly armed but determined Japanese in Pacific island jungles differed from those required for fighting more heavily armed and armoured German forces. Australians considered fighting on the plains of Europe to be more "conventional." Not surprisingly, therefore, jungle fighting against Japanese troops had an effect on the tactics and organization of the Australian forces unlike anything experienced by Canadians and others fighting in Europe. Australian divisions that had been equipped and organized as British formations for desert warfare were rearranged – for the first time – using Australian-designed models tailored for jungle operations.

Unlike their Canadian equivalents preparing to face German forces in the Mediterranean and in Europe, Australian force structures and tactics moved away from heavy reliance on armour and mechanized forces. Adjustments in force structure and tactics made in response to specific Japanese actions were complemented by improved equipment for the Australian troops. In addition, logistic capabilities, long considered secondary because of reliance on access to British supply and support, became of primary importance to sustain troops in the battlefields of New Guinea. In the meantime, exchange officers kept each other's armies abreast of developments in jungle- and armoured-warfare techniques.[84]

Jungle operations meant less reliance on motorized vehicles and anti-aircraft weapons (particularly once the Japanese air threat had been largely eliminated) but a greater reliance on machine-guns, native porters, easily carried (and Australian-designed and produced) twenty-five-pounder-pack howitzers, and close air support. Still, vehicles with off-road capacity, such as tanks and Canadian-built scout cars, did have an important – if limited – role to play. Australians found that tanks dispersed in support of infantry provided a decisive advantage in jungle attacks against emplacements where Japanese soldiers would fight to the death. Indeed, in the Pacific theatre of operations, even the light tanks built in Australia in 1939, with their obsolescent two-pounder main guns, were capable of defeating Japanese tanks. As Major-General Hopkins observed, "it had been amply demonstrated that armour was not only a feasible proposition for jungle fighting; it was as essential to success in the New Guinea jungles in 1942 as it had been in the highly developed machine-gun defences in France and Flanders in 1917. In contrast, the European (and hence Canadian) experience during World War II emphasised mass effects of tanks, heavier calibre armaments, and avoidance of dispersal of armoured assets (at least until effective anti-tank weapons became prevalent) to fight infantry battles."[85]

These different experiences would influence the post-war organizational developments in both Canada and Australia. Canada would structure forces with a European continental conflict in mind, and, for more than a decade after the war, Australian forces would similarly revert to British organizational structures. Yet the latter's experience in the Pacific would lead them to re-emphasize jungle-warfare skills that relied on dispersed small-unit actions and some amphibious capability.[86] For Canadians, by late 1944, personnel-carrier-borne troops and tanks worked together regularly, foretelling what would become a standard Canadian mechanized approach during the post-war years when troops would be stationed in Germany.

Notwithstanding that the Australian forces were well placed to fight the Japanese, Australia's war efforts in the Pacific from 1943 onwards were marginalized and dwarfed by U.S. Navy and Army operations, and the Australian Army was frozen out of the campaign to recapture the Philippines – although the RAN was included. Under General MacArthur's direction, there was little room for Australia's ground forces other than to play a supportive role on the edge of the theatre, mopping up Japanese resistance with a series of anti-climactic amphibious operations.[87] This marginalization occurred despite the valiant and laudatory performance of the Australian troops who had borne the brunt of the hard fighting against the Japanese in 1942 and 1943 in Papua and New Guinea.

MacArthur also consistently sought to claim Australian successes for his own advancement by invariably describing specifically them as more generic "Allied" successes. His approach reflected a mindset similar to that of General Eisenhower in the European theatre, who claimed that "security requirements" made it inadvisable to mention the Canadians by name in a broadcast announcing the Allied invasion of Sicily in 1943. However, unlike MacArthur, Eisenhower had the grace to allow the announcement to be corrected. What these instances show is that, on their own, Canada and Australia simply carried little diplomatic muscle and their wishes could often be overlooked by their more powerful partners. To be sure, their military and political leaders were not as "pushy" as the equally diplomatically and militarily marginal French leader, General Charles de Gaulle.[88] With their forces dispersed in different theatres, the Australians and Canadians were not in a position to reinforce each other's positions, even if they had recognized the value in doing so.

Following the fall of France, Canada's reluctance to join the fray in the Mediterranean by 1942 left the Canadian ground forces to wait in vain for an increasingly unlikely invasion of Britain. With the exception of the 1st Brigade, which was briefly deployed to Brest on the French Atlantic coast in June 1940, Canadian forces had been left out of battle since the war's commencement in 1939.[89] Concerns about troop boredom, as well as the belief that Canadians should be seen to be making a contribution, soon led to disaster: Canadian forces were chosen to launch a raid on the coast of France at Dieppe in August 1942 – where thousands of soldiers of the 2nd Canadian Division were killed or captured. Lieutenant-General Harry Crerar appreciated that there were imperial and political reasons for getting Canadians into the fight, and he not only demanded that Canadians be picked for the raid but also participated in the decision to attack on 19 August. Afterwards, Crerar defended his decision, arguing that the Dieppe operation had a "sobering influence" and taught many important lessons for the eventual assault at Normandy. However, this was a costly way for Canadians to fight, for so little gain.[90]

Against the background of such traumatic events, Canadian forces continued to train in England, numbering almost a half-million by war's end.[91] Many of these were part of the First Canadian Army.[92] Their prolonged exposure to life in England arguably left Canadians predisposed towards a European focus in the post-war years. European military operations had featured armoured forces in 1940, and this experience drove the Allies to develop sufficient armoured counter-weights to the German military machine. Like their Australian counterparts, who contributed about one-third of the Allied infantry divisions in the Mediterranean and North African campaigns in 1941 and 1942, the Canadian Army faced pressures to disperse its forces on a variety of fronts.[93] By 1943, despite the debacle at Dieppe, Canadian officials felt concern that post-war influence would be undermined unless Canadian troops were committed to action. Canadian troops had played a useful role in immobilizing German forces along the coast of France from 1940, but comparisons with Australia and others were creating a stigma. Indeed, there were complaints from Australia about Canadian inactivity. Also, officers were being promoted, becoming brigade, division, and even corps commanders, "without having smelled powder" since 1918.[94]

With growing Canadian domestic disenchantment at being left out of the action, Canadian troops of the 1st Canadian Infantry Division and the 5th Canadian Armoured Division eventually were deployed to Sicily and Italy in 1943 and 1944 as part of the 1st Canadian Corps. But they arrived when Allied interest in Mediterranean operations was already waning. Having missed the moments of "glory" in North Africa, Canadian forces played what was an extremely hard-fought but arguably minor role in Allied grand strategy. Yet the Canadian Army suffered heavy casualties and was pressed to find sufficient reinforcements. Some described the battles at Ortona, in Italy, for instance, as reminiscent of the morass of Passchendaele in 1917. Thereafter, in the race to Rome, Canadians "demonstrated their lack of experience in fluid battle conditions." Of the nearly 93,000 Canadian soldiers who served there, nearly 5,500 were killed and 20,000 wounded. Such heavy casualties were worse than the Australians experienced fighting against the Japanese during this period and led the Canadian government to introduce conscription – a move that severely strained the Canadian body politic.[95]

As a consequence of Canada's earlier ambivalence, by the time of the Normandy invasion in June 1944, few of the Canadian officers who would fight in Normandy had gained sufficient operational experience for the tasks ahead. The root problem appears to have stemmed at least in part from a number of regimental officers whose attitude was casual and haphazard rather than urgent and scientific. Others say that blame is better assigned to the high command, with its paucity of talent. Still others maintain that, in terms of defects in weapons, training, doctrine, and commanders, the First Canadian Army was no worse than its American and British counterparts, both of whom experienced similar problems.[96]

For the Australians, in contrast, many battalion and brigade commanders had been given plentiful opportunities to gain experience early in the war. By the time they faced the Japanese in New Guinea, the Australians also were gaining experience at independent command at higher levels, albeit with errors made along the way. Indeed, most of the ground fighting in the southwest Pacific was conducted by Australian soldiers in the first two years. Much of this was at platoon and company level with limited artillery and logistic backup and only a handful of tanks (for bunker busting), simply because of the difficulty of the terrain. Their efforts gave the u.s. Sixth Army the time it needed to orient and prepare itself for jungle war and seaborne envelopments after much of the hard fighting had been completed.[97]

In contrast, Canadian assaults were dependent on aerial bombardment on narrow frontages and barrages with fixed timing. Here Canada was following British trends then still popular and considered important in order to achieve the breakthrough battle. But, for the Canadians at least, these factors combined to stifle flexibility and reduce options for infiltration and battlefield manoeuvre. In addition, tensions between senior officers exacerbated institutional problems.[98] Canada's lack of experience with more fluid forms of warfare left them with a mindset still dominated by the experience of 1914–18. Its key commanders, McNaughton, Crerar, and Guy Simonds, were gunners whose artillery-dominated plans encouraged caution and discouraged initiative in battle.[99]

McNaughton, who commanded the Canadian Army until he was relieved in 1943,[100] assumed that military knowledge was less a result of a tactical and operational-level military education than a matter of technical efficiency. Consequently, non-technically minded infantry and cavalry officers were unappreciated by McNaughton and faced poor prospects, in part because they had been bypassed in selection for Staff College in the interwar years and thus made ineligible for higher command.[101] (The contrast with Australian commanders points to some interesting conclusions. By and large, Australian divisional and corps commanders had more varied backgrounds, and their track records were generally good.) Moreover, the dominance of gunners and engineers in the Canadian high command appears to reflect the legacy of the stronger preference for heavy artillery support evident in the Canadian Corps in 1917–18, as compared with the more prominent use of "peaceful penetration" and patrolling by the Australian corps during the same period. In the end, the Canadian ground contribution boiled down to a force that represented five of the ninety Allied divisions fighting across Western Europe, playing a difficult but relatively minor role on the edge of the drive through France to Berlin.[102]

Apart from conventional ground forces, Canada and Australia, like their British and American partners, created special forces to meet the unusual demands of world warfare. Australian independent companies began training at Wilson's Promontory on the south coast of the state of Victoria in March 1941. Eleven such units, renamed as commando units, were formed, as well as Services Reconnaissance Department units (or "Z Special Units"). Such units operated as stay-behind forces in the islands north and east of New Guinea and in Portuguese Timor, provided support to Australian and

American conventional forces, and conducted daring raids on Japanese shipping. Canada's special forces during the Second World War were more closely aligned with U.S. forces. Following the creation of the 1st Canadian Special Service Battalion in June 1942, the unit was dispatched to train with American troops in the United States. The unit became part of the combined First Special Service Force created in 1943 – a combined force that was important for political as well as military reasons.[103] Both Canadian and Australian special forces would be disbanded by war's end, but Australia would look to re-establish such capabilities by the mid-1950s.[104]

Throughout the war, doctrine and organization remained British-dominated, but both countries' force structures came under stronger U.S. influence as British military and economic power waned. For instance, in August 1943, Canadian forces conducted their first land campaign in the Asia-Pacific region since committing troops to the futile defence of Hong Kong in 1941. The Canadian 13th Infantry Brigade stormed ashore on the Aleutian island of Kiska only to find that the Japanese already had decamped. This northern Pacific operation was launched in part to defuse criticism (including from Australia) of Canadian inaction in the European theatre of operations. But, unlike their counterparts in Europe, the troops had trained with U.S. weapons and equipment, setting a precedent for later coordination with American forces.[105]

Also in 1943, the Australian war cabinet made renewed overtures for Canadian recognition of the importance of the military effort in the Pacific, arguing that "it is imperative that this view be accepted by the United Kingdom and the other Dominions, especially New Zealand and Canada." Jungle Warfare Liaison letters were dispatched from Australia to keep Allied forces informed of developments in tactics, organization, and equipment. Also as part of the effort to improve collaboration and share experiences, Canadian officers were attached to U.S., Australian, and New Zealand forces in the Pacific from February 1944, as well as to the British-led South East Asia Command fighting in Burma.[106]

When it came to the counter-strokes in the Pacific from 1943 onwards, C.P. Stacey observes that the decision as to whether or not Canada should participate was political and moral rather than strategic. Another scholar, John Holmes, argues that "splitting the Canadian forces in two at that critical point [in 1942] merely to make a token demonstration would have been bad strategy ... Unlike the Australians, who felt a need to protect their homeland, Canadians, in spite of some panic on the west coast after Pearl Harbor, continued to see Europe as the major threat." But Holmes's assessment misses the point. Canada did split its forces, albeit within the broader

European theatre, committing two and at times more divisions and sustaining heavy casualties in the Italian "sideshow" while maintaining several divisions on Canada's west coast. The issue should rather be viewed in terms of Canadian national interest. In this sense, Canada had good reason to pursue a greater role in the fight against Japan. In fact, Holmes later virtually concedes this point, arguing that "non-involvement in the Pacific war encouraged a Canadian disposition to leave the Pacific and Far East to the Americans, a situation which for some time after the war notably differentiated Canadian attitudes towards Asia [and the opportunities it presented] from Canadian attitudes towards Europe."[107] After all, a greater participation by Canada in the Pacific war would arguably have been as strategic as any of its other commitments of troops in Asia in the twentieth century, ranging from Hong Kong, Australia, and Kiska in the Second World War to Vietnam in the 1950s, West New Guinea in the early 1960s, Cambodia in 1993, East Timor in 1999, and Sri Lanka in 2005. Even with these post-Second World War military commitments in the Asia-Pacific, many observers could ask: "What was the Canadian interest at stake in such deployments?"[108] The point worth noting here is that, as much as Canadians may protest about Canada's lack of sufficient interests in the Asia-Pacific region to warrant greater military efforts there, Canadians still show up in the area, repeatedly, and often in the same manner as the Australians – and with similar objectives. Consequently, the question becomes a matter of considering the common outlooks and interests of Canadians and Australians which repeatedly draw them into making military commitments in the Asia-Pacific region and elsewhere.

By June 1945, ninety-five Canadian Army officers had experience in the various Pacific theatres and over four hundred had spent time on attachments with the Australian forces. These included radar technicians servicing Canadian-built equipment and signals and intelligence personnel working with the No. 1 Special Wireless Group based near Darwin.[109] One Canadian report highlighted how much the armies still had in common. "Training, Staff Duties, organization and administration is in nearly every instance identical with our training," this report stated. "Officers could be rapidly interchanged and be able to carry on whatever appointment they held." The judgment was that "there are naturally many 'tricks to the trade' learnt in fighting the Jap [sic] that we can profit by, but it is certain that our 6 Canadian Div [re-raised on American organizational lines with over 24,000 troops] could do well in this type of warfare against the Jap." In fact, there were Australian exchange officers in Canada as well. For instance, one Australian Intelligence Corps officer, Major R.W.T Cowan, was even attached as an instructor to the Royal Military College, where efforts were made to retain him at the end of his posting.[110]

Like Australia, Canada offered forces (a division and ancillary troops compared to Australia's three divisions) as well as naval and air elements to participate in the invasion of Japan. In contemplating this action, the Canadian prime minister noted that "we may be sure we will get little credit for anything we do, either on the part of the u.s. or Great Britain."[111] The same applied for Australia. Yet, had the two countries' leaders understood each other's predicament better, appreciated the merits of working together, and pooled their resources, they may have gained greater operational flexibility and strategic prominence – much as they had done virtually by accident at Amiens in 1918. Clearly, such broad-mindedness was missing on this occasion.

In the meantime, MacArthur blocked British requests for Australian divisions to assist in the British-led fight on the southeast Asian mainland. Instead, he favoured the idea of a British Commonwealth force of three to five divisions from Canada, Australia, and Great Britain.[112] Yet he would accept such a force only if it was organized and equipped according to u.s. standards, arguing that the logistic burden of maintaining separate force types was untenable.[113] The surrender of Japan obviated the need for such forces, but the developments reflected the early stages of a reorientation to American equipment and standards and growing American influence. That reorientation would later be confirmed in Recommendation 35 of the Permanent Joint Board of Defence, which switched the military model for Canada from Britain to the United States.[114] But, because of financial constraints, it would not be until the later stages of the Korean War that this policy could be implemented.

Australia and Canada clearly were pursuing similar courses of action, although largely independent of one another. In the end, Australia would contribute forces to the occupation of Japan and Canada would decline, having already undertaken a commitment for the first stage of the occupation of Germany. Still, Canada would be represented on the Far Eastern Advisory Commission (later the Far Eastern Commission) on Japan – a body the United States wanted to use to forestall Soviet pressure for a four-power governing council in Japan. As Holmes notes, "that was an American wish Ottawa had no interest in frustrating." But the Canadians in Europe would find that the Great Powers were not interested in sharing control of the occupied territory.[115] Similarly, the Australians stationed on occupation duties in Japan would face little scope for influence beyond the prefectures assigned. This would lead to common frustrations for both

Chart 6
Commonwealth military strengths, Second World War

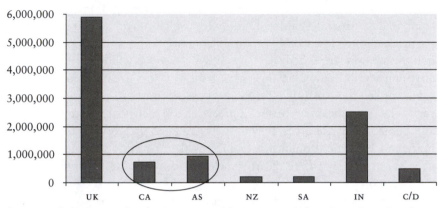

Source: Nicholas Mansergh, *The Commonwealth Experience, Volume Two: From British Commonwealth to Multi-Racial State* (London: Macmillan 1982), 94.

(SA = South Africa, IN = India, C/D = Colonies and Dependencies)

Canadians and Australians – frustrations that, once again, could have been ameliorated if they had collaborated in seeking to leverage their influence within the Grand Alliance.

Canada's reluctance to get "into the fight" early on in the war illustrates the effect of one of the key differences between the two countries. Australian voters were eager supporters of the war (and especially the war in the Pacific), while Canadians – particularly French Canadians and Liberal nationalists – were less enthusiastic. Canada was obsessed with the idea of status and with the fear of the national split between English and French Canada that would follow the introduction of conscription – which was, in fact, implemented, in November 1944, without triggering – though it was a close-run thing – a national crisis. Yet Canada also was increasingly frustrated, as the war progressed, over its being denied any real say in how the war was conducted.[116]

Given the massive military contributions of the major Allied powers, the Australian and Canadian forces played a proportionately decreasing role in the war effort. For Australians, service in Papua, New Guinea, and the islands of the Dutch East Indies remained arduous and resulted in significant casualties, while Canadians experienced even heavier casualties against bitter German resistance in Italy and in the Dutch homeland territories along the northern flank of the Allied advance in Europe. At the same time, the contrasting experiences of Australia and Canada in the Pacific and Europe pointed to divergent trends in force structure that would continue into the post-war period. Even though Australia had raised an armoured corps during the war, no armoured formation above brigade size was deployed on operations; instead, the Australian experience was predominantly with lightly equipped dismounted troops, initially in desert and Mediterranean climes and later in the jungles of the Pacific. In contrast, Canada's experience in Europe saw great concentrations of artillery and far more armoured resources, including armoured troop carriers that would presage the prominence of armour in Canada's post-war involvement in NATO.

Wartime pressure to employ women in the services and in industry triggered a social transformation that would have significant social effects after the war. For instance, women in the Australian Army Nursing Service served in all the major theatres during the Second World War. In addition, women served in the Australian Army Women's Medical Service, which developed out of the need to place the maximum number of men in fighting units, and the Australian Women's Army Service, where they provided critical support in specialist fields such as searchlight and radar operation and cryptography. In Canada, the only women who served in army uniform in 1914–18 were the nurses of the Army Medical Corps. But by 1945, 47,000 women had joined the Canadian Armed Forces. For both countries, the transformative social effects of these developments are well known, but their effect on military organization was also significant. Although women were quickly demobilized after the war, they were soon reintroduced into the services, having made their mark during wartime, and slowly would become integrated into almost every facet of the armed forces.[117]

SEEKING A POST-WAR "SEAT AT THE TABLE"

By 1945, as by 1918, Australian and Canadian ground forces had played a key role in their nations' wartime strategies. But, while their military contributions were even greater than those made in the First World War, their impact was less than it could have been when it came to major international policy decisions. From the American viewpoint, the most important among the wartime allies on the periphery of the British-American coalition, in political if not military terms, were not Canada and Australia but two militarily less significant contributors to the war's outcome: China and France. Further, the intimate and friendly relations between the United States and Canada, on the one hand, and Australia and New Zealand, on the other, served to counterbalance British influence among the three and tended to establish an atmosphere of reliance and good faith.[118] While this arrangement was favourable to the United States, it came without benefits significant enough to compensate Canada, Australia, and New Zealand for the loss of British influence. Canada and Australia failed to demonstrate solidarity with each other as a manifestation of mutual, enlightened self-interest. Not surprisingly therefore, both were effectively shut out of higher-level decisions concerning the post-war international political order. From then on, Canada and Australia would have to learn the realities of power politics in the absence of Britain's diplomatic cover. Their marginal influence at the conclusion of the war would be reflected in the discussions at the United Nation's founding conference at San Francisco in 1945.

Australia's Evatt worked vigorously to put Australia on the international map, particularly at San Francisco. But his flamboyant manner was the antithesis of that of his Canadian equivalents, who envied Evatt for saying what Canadians thought and consequently getting all the credit for it. To quote John Holmes, after the San Francisco conference and the acceptance of France as a great power (despite its marginal role in the war's outcome), "it was agreed that France would have to be on the Central Committee. It was tactfully decided to use the occasion to admit Canada as well – in August 1946. The Russians had seconded the United States resolution to admit France and Canada, but they opposed an Australian resolution that would have admitted three further countries, Australia, Brazil and Yugoslavia." Evatt's single-minded approach undermined Canada's place as the apparent leader of the small powers and seemed to have deprived it of a seat on the Security Council. Moreover, Canada's refusal to support Evatt's attempt to block a Great Power veto on the new Security Council, despite several Canadian delegates agreeing with the notion, led an angry Evatt to label Canada's representative an "American pawn in the move to defeat the Australian case." One Canadian diplomat, Charles Ritchie, said of Evatt that, "like many Australians, he seems to regard Canadians as mealy-mouthed fence-sitters. He is also very jealous of any Canadian initiative or achievement. Despite all this I much relish my contacts with the Australians. They are such pungently lively company and don't give a damn for the proprieties. The New Zealanders may be nicer but they are tamer." Clearly, incompatible diplomatic styles, mixed with mutual envy, limited the scope for cooperation between Canada and Australia on the world stage at this critical juncture, and both countries were the losers for it. Their ability to achieve their diplomatic objectives was limited in part because they viewed one another as rivals instead of partners. Neither saw sufficiently past their minor differences to exploit the potential benefits of working together.[119]

Despite the difficulties in working together, the experience of two world wars had finally demonstrated to both Canada and Australia the merits of maintaining regular ground forces in peacetime for contingencies that might arise. Both before and after 1918, budgetary and political concerns along with flawed strategic thinking had led governments to neglect their armed forces' capabilities. The experience of the Second World War, however, demonstrated the nexus between foreign policy, military capacity, and international leverage, with the result that full-time combat-capable forces would be maintained thereafter as an instrument of government policy – essential for a state claiming the status of a "middle power."

The fact that neither Canada nor Australia raised forces to fight as an integrated national team of army, navy, and air force elements certainly contributed to a shared malaise in the mastery of the higher art of war. Douglas Bland, commenting on Canada, makes an observation that largely applies to Australia as well: "Canada may have joined the war by an independent act, but she willingly pursued the war as a dependant because the country lacked a strategy and defence structure that would have allowed it to do otherwise." In a similar vein, David Horner concludes that "the lack of balance in the Australian forces stemmed not merely from an inability to concentrate elements, but also from inadequate preparation before the war ... Military credibility is also determined by performance on the battlefield. There is a need for a high level of expertise both in battle and in staff work ... During the Second World War Australia failed to obtain full political value from the use of its armed forces. Not only did they lack balance and, in the case of the RAAF, an adequate command structure, but also the army was afflicted by the division between the AIF and the militia."[120] He could just as easily be referring to the Canadian forces. The full political value of armed forces appeared not to be fully appreciated by Canadian or Australian senior political leaders, who, without detailed deliberation over the effect on their national interests, left the strategic direction for the war in the hands of Britain and the United States. But Horner's observations can be taken one step further. Canada and Australia remained virtual accidental allies throughout the Second World War. On their own, they were regularly sidelined or marginalized, including at Singapore and Hong Kong in the early days of the Japanese offensives. Together, if they could have agreed to cooperate in the use of their forces, be it in Singapore, New Guinea, or elsewhere, they would have been of "European great power proportions" – as their combined feat of arms in August 1918 had once demonstrated.[121]

Horner also observes that, during the Second World War, Australia's strategic decision making made two important steps forward: demanding some influence over the strategic use of its forces, and contending with the leaders of the Grand Alliance in a global context.[122] Although Mackenzie King made little effort to influence Allied strategy – seeing Canada as not directly threatened in the same way that Australia was – Canada essentially took the same steps as did Australia. Both countries recognized the necessity of surrendering some individual choice for the accomplishment of Allied grand strategies.

At the 1944 Prime Ministers Conference, while their troops were still fighting, Australia's prime minister, John Curtin, proposed an extensive Commonwealth-wide defence cooperation arrangement. Canada's Mackenzie King scotched the idea, since the proposal called for more cooperation than he was comfortable with. King's approach was reminiscent of his stand on Commonwealth-wide schemes in the 1930s.[123] Yet, after the war, Canada would seek the safety in numbers that Australia had earlier sought, as a kind of trans-Pacific "New World" or Commonwealth entente. However, Canada found this safety (until the end of the Cold War, at least) in the opposite direction – eastwards, rather than westwards, with the United States and the countries of the "Old World," through NATO. Further defence cooperation between Canada and Australia would have to await post-war British or U.S.-led initiatives. Nonetheless, as John Holmes observes, "the [world] wars left Canada an industrial power of consequence, but as ever dependent on world trade and increasingly aware of international order as the national interest of a great trading nation. One of the new features ... was a frank recognition that practically everything in international politics was of interest to Canada."[124] Virtually the same could be said for Australia. In the post-war years, this broad interest in international affairs would drive Canada and Australia to establish regular forces readily capable of conducting expeditionary operations in support of national objectives.

5

Cold War Onset

As the armies of Canada and Australia demobilized after the Second World War, their two nations separately sought to establish affordable post-war defence plans. In Canada, under Defence Minister Brooke Claxton, a policy paper entitled *Canada's Defence 1947* outlined the enduring roles of the armed forces. These roles, which remained largely unchanged in the post-war era, were to defend Canada against aggression, to assist the civil power in maintaining law and order within the country, and to carry out any undertakings that Canada voluntarily chose to assume in cooperation with friendly nations or under any effective plan of collective action under the United Nations (UN).[1] The roles assigned to the Australian Army were similar: UN missions, including regional commitments; British Commonwealth defence; the maintenance of a pool of skilled personnel capable of training a larger force, should the need arise; and the local defence of mainland Australia. As in Australia, Claxton's third role presaged a series of post-Second World War expeditionary-force operations that Canada would contribute towards (as listed in appendix 4). But in Canada's case, the issue of civil law and order featured more prominently, affecting priorities in equipment acquisition and assignments. Indeed, there also was little interest in Commonwealth defence, in contrast to the situation in Australia and New Zealand.[2]

For the "cousins down under," the British connection would remain important as a consequence of powerful social, cultural, and trade links, and, for Britain, imperial ties remained critical to bolster its claims to be a leading power. In addition, the sterling bloc countries like Australia helped Britain pay its bills, providing resources through trade and thereby avoiding further indebtedness to the United States. For Australia, the security dimension of its relationship with Britain also regained significance after the war. Australia was eager to strengthen its security by joining the nuclear "club," following the lead of Canada, which had nuclear facilities at Chalk River, Ontario. But, with American unwillingness to include Australia in the "club," and no security guarantees from the United States, there was a view in Australia that, in the atomic age, the Commonwealth should act as a unit. Consequently, prime ministers from Curtin to Menzies would work to forge strong ties with Britain, which, in the military area, meant pressing for standardization of organization, equipment, and training of the armed forces. The incentive to work closely with Britain would continue until after the Suez Crisis in 1956 and the eventual withdrawal of British forces from "East of Suez" in the late 1960s. Only then, with Britain's power fading and the United States seeking closer defence ties and "more flags" in Vietnam, would Australia turn to the United States to a similar extent as Canada did at Ogdensburg in 1940. In the meantime, Canada's cooperation with the Commonwealth, when it was interested in cooperating at all, was restrained by its formal security ties with the United States.[3]

DEMOBILIZATION AND REORGANIZATION
FOR PEACETIME

As the ramifications of these strategic realities were becoming clear, post-war demobilization took some time to put into effect. Canada avoided most of the post-war occupation responsibilities, preferring to expedite the return of its service personnel. The resulting inability of Canada to acquire a meaningful say in Allied policy concerning Germany left Canadian planners bitter. In contrast, Australia chose to contribute the 34th Infantry Brigade, consisting of between 10,000 and 12,000 troops, to the 37,000-strong British Commonwealth Occupation Force (BCOF) in Japan. The BCOF also consisted of British, Indian, and New Zealand personnel, but no Canadians. In addition, Australia contributed to the forces required to supervise, repatriate, and/or prosecute for war crimes surrendered Japanese troops in Borneo and the Dutch East Indies, and Australians garrisoned Dutch and British territory until early 1946 when Dutch and British troops could relieve them. This task occupied four Australian brigades in 1945–46 in the Dutch East Indies alone.[4]

The new United Nations, meanwhile, soon commenced asserting itself in international-security affairs. From the outset, Australia and Canada were enthusiastic supporters of the UN. Canadian policy, for instance, stressed that "in the United Nations there is the beginning of an organisation which may be developed progressively into a great instrument for peaceful co-operation." But the abrasiveness of Australia's minister of external affairs, "Doc" Evatt (whom Lester B. Pearson of Canada described as "an extraordinarily rude fellow"), left little room for close cooperation with his Canadian counterparts, even though their policies were similar. Evatt and Curtin, as well as Curtin's successor (after Curtin's sudden death in 1945), Ben Chifley, were eager to reshape the Commonwealth, whereas Mackenzie King preferred to keep it at arm's length. Moreover, to a certain extent, the countries were rivals, for, as Andrew Cooper points out, each was attempting to become the leader of an emerging constellation of middle powers after the Second World War. Such sentiments not only made for tensions between Australia and Canada; they even made for difficult interdepartmental relations within each country. As Desmond Ball and David Horner have observed, some people in Evatt's External Affairs Department regarded those in Defence to be uncritically pro-British and pro-American and incapable of distinguishing Australia's interests from those of Britain or the United States. Defence, for its part, concerned about increased Soviet espionage, was equally aghast at some senior External Affairs officials' tolerant views about communism in Asia, the importance (or otherwise) of Australia's traditional allies, and the significance of intelligence and security matters.[5]

Similarly, Alan Watt argues that Evatt miscalculated the Great Power dynamics at work during the onset of the Cold War. For example, Manus Island was part of the Australian-mandated territory north of New Guinea that had been used by the United States Navy during the Second World War. Its abandonment by the United States, according to Glen St J. Barclay, "represented a disaster for Australian security, as well as the total collapse of Evatt's hopes for tripartite defence arrangements in the South Pacific." (The fulfilment of this dream of tripartite arrangements among Australia, Britain, and the United States would take place under Evatt's more mild-mannered conservative successors.) Evatt had pushed too far, demanding reciprocal access rights to other American naval bases when Manus was of only peripheral importance to the United States. Watt concludes that "the balance of available evidence suggests that Australia lost ground between 1945 and 1949 in her relationships with the United States ..." Richard Casey, who would become minister for external affairs during the early 1950s, later reflected on the events of 1945, saying with regard to Manus that "Australia lost what I think was a tremendous opportunity to retain the military interest of the world's greatest power in a position of immense value to us ..." But, as T.B. Millar maintains, American links with the South Pacific lacked the historical foundation of the u.s. sphere of influence in the Americas. The point really was that, however much Australia and New Zealand might see NATO as a precedent, the United States just did not want to take on such an obligation in the Pacific, and saw no reason why it should. According to Millar, for the Americans, at least prior to the Korean War, the "perimeter" excluded Australia and New Zealand just as much as Korea. Thereafter, Australian diplomatic efforts would focus on tying Australia's defence to that of Britain while also seeking to redress the initial post-war downturn in relations with the United States.[6] The maintenance of expeditionary forces would be a key instrument used in pursuit of this policy.

Reflecting this focus in Australia, for instance, in early 1946 the vice-chief of the General Staff, Lieutenant-General S.F. Rowell, presented the first post-war policy, which stressed that the army would have to be organized on the basis of overseas service. Efforts such as his helped ensure that the interim army arrangements that immediately followed the cessation of hostilities in 1945 would be replaced by standing combat formations by 1947 and establishments with higher percentages of regular soldiers than in the past. In Australia's case, this would come to include a permanent field force of one independent brigade group (based on the forces in Japan), a citizen field force of two infantry divisions, and an infantry and an armoured brigade group and selected corps units as well as the necessary supporting establishments. This type of structure would be better placed to respond to regional security concerns that might arise at short notice than had its predecessors prior to 1939 (though its effectiveness was hampered by the fact that recruiting fell short of the targets set). But, as in the United States Army, where the introduction of atomic weapons seemed to forecast the demise of ground combat, the Australian and Canadian governments were reluctant to invest heavily in their armies for difficult-to-envisage post-war conflicts.[7]

With concerns about security in the Asia-Pacific region in mind, Australia's secretary of defence, Sir Frederick Shedden, tried to raise Canadian interest in a Pacific Defence Pact in 1947, notwithstanding that Chifley had already discounted Canada as a defence partner. Brooke Claxton and the secretary of state for external affairs, Louis St Laurent, responded coolly to the idea. Claxton argued that it was up to the United States to initiate a Pacific regional-security system, while St Laurent's successor, Lester B. Pearson, stressed that the greater threat in the Atlantic precluded substantial commitments in the Pacific.[8] Australia still placed emphasis on British Commonwealth defence measures, but Mackenzie King, Canada's prime minister until 1948, was eager to remain at arm's length from the British

Empire and even from the United Nations. Unlike his British and Australian counterparts, he did not perceive a common threat that made cooperation essential. What is more, the absence of any formally established mechanisms for cooperation and combined planning or policy left Canadian and Australian policy makers excessively at the mercy of strong personalities. Preoccupied with their immediate self-interests, they were unable to see the longer-term benefits of working more closely with each other out of mutual or "enlightened" self-interest.

Such military cooperation in the Pacific theatre and diplomatic cooperation at the conferences called to establish the post-war economic and strategic world order conceivably would have given both countries greater diplomatic leverage to further their own national interests. Yet the time for closer Canadian teamwork with Australia had not yet arrived; fence mending between the two countries would have to wait until the departure of both Mackenzie King in 1948 and Evatt in 1949. Shortly afterwards, the outbreak of the Korean War led Canada to recognize once again the existence of a a common threat. At that point, both Canada and Australia would affirm the principle that the defence of their nations was best achieved as far away from their own shores as possible.

Exacerbating the difficulties in the immediate post-war years were challenges of international trade. Eager to pursue greater multilateralism to resolve its chronic trade imbalances and to offset overwhelming American power, Canada was prepared to negotiate away its imperial trade preferences. But Australia's new Labor Party prime minister, Ben Chifley, seriously doubted the u.s. government's ability or willingness to make sufficient trade concessions to warrant a reduction of Australia's restrictive preferential access to Commonwealth markets. Such concessions appeared to threaten Australia's policy of industrial diversification and development and would quickly lead, it was thought, to American economic hegemony in Australia and, at worst, subject the country to the consequences of another world-wide depression.[9] And so, here too, Canada and Australia found themselves occupying starkly different positions in the early post-war years as they sought to establish their place on the international stage. In military terms, this meant that Australia remained more disposed than Canada to prefer British equipment over American.

Notwithstanding these differences, Canadian and Australian foreign and defence policy in the immediate post-war period was similar in two important ways – and these similarities endured for the latter half of the twentieth century and beyond. First, foreign policy in both countries has tended to stress distinctiveness within an alliance context while supporting multilateral agreements and bodies such as the United Nations. In contrast, defence policy, for sound military reasons, has emphasized the merits of enhanced interoperability of Australian and Canadian armed forces with their main alliance partners, initially Britain and then the United States. For both Canada and Australia, this dichotomy has resulted in varying degrees of foreign- and defence-policy dysfunction, as foreign-policy officials stress distinctiveness while their military equivalents inadvertently work to diminish that distinctiveness by focusing on enhanced interoperability with their major alliance partner. The result has been frequent changes in the direction of national-security policy, which in turn has helped shape the armies of Canada and Australia in a frequently disjointed manner.[10]

But, to return to the post-war period, the exposure of Soviet spy rings immediately after the war demonstrated the aggressiveness of Soviet intelligence and the need for vigorous counter-measures. In Ottawa, Soviet agent Igor Gouzenko defected in September 1945,[11] and in Canberra, code breakers, using decrypted Soviet intelligence reports, uncovered a Soviet spy ring that operated from the late war years through to the late 1940s. Australia's left-leaning Labor Government, under Prime Minister Chifley and External Affairs Minister Evatt, initially discounted fears of espionage until the evidence mounted and British and American political pressure for action increased.[12] Later, in April 1954, the Soviet embassy's Canberra-based cipher clerk, Vladimir Petrov, defected, and he helped corroborate the extent of Soviet espionage in Australia.[13]

These developments awakened the governments of both Canada and Australia to the post-war realities and spurred the creation of several intelligence and security organizations. In Australia's case, the Australian Security Intelligence Organisation (known as ASIO), the Defence Signals Branch (for signals intelligence, or eavesdropping), and the Joint Intelligence Bureau (for military intelligence analysis) were created on the foundations of their predecessor wartime organizations.[14] Canada would create comparable organizations for eavesdropping and analysis that would focus primarily on the Soviet Union and Warsaw Pact countries. However, unlike Australia, Canada did not create a Secret Intelligence Service, choosing instead to focus on counter-espionage, which, by definition, is passive not aggressive. Despite the differences, both Canada's and Australia's intelligence organizations collaborated with Britain and the United States as well as New Zealand as part of the UKUSA agreement.[15] Such organizations would also play important supportive roles for subsequent expeditionary forces, as their predecessor organizations had done during the Second World War.

On 5 March 1946 Winston Churchill, in his famous "Iron Curtain" speech, argued that "the only hope of stemming this [communist] tide is a fraternal association of the English-speaking peoples. This means a special relationship between the British Commonwealth and the United States." Churchill went on to state that Anglo-American unity was probably the only means by which the United Nations would achieve its full stature and strength. His focus, as usual, was on Britain and the United States, but Australia and Canada would come to play a significant contributing role in support of such aspirations in the years that followed. For Australia, events were brewing relatively close to home as well, when communist insurrections broke out in Malaya and Indonesia in 1948.[16]

With the commencement of the Malayan "Emergency" in 1948, and following a request from Britain, the Australian government decided to base RAAF bombers in Malaya from 1950 onwards. From the viewpoint of the Australian Defence Committee, a body including the minister of defence and the chiefs of staff of the three services, this forward defence posture was adopted in order to prevent Soviet bombers from being able to penetrate south of Malaya. The decision to base bombers rather than ground troops reflected an emphasis on air power as the means of choice for the atomic era, as well as a reluctance to spend scarce resources on maintaining large standing armies. Indeed, Australian historian Wayne Reynolds notes that "Australian defence planners, generally, saw forward defence not in terms of soldiers fighting conventional or counter-insurgency wars, but as involving the despatch of bombers, equipped with atom bombs, to wage global war as part of the defence of the empire."[17] Of course, Australia never acquired atomic weapons. Consequently, given that the capabilities of these aircraft were limited to conventional weapons, the forward defence strategy could be applied most effectively largely through the dispatch of expeditionary ground forces instead, as events in Korea would demonstrate.

Before the decision to deploy RAAF bombers to Malaya, the emerging Cold War most prominently manifested itself in Berlin, where, in June 1948, Soviet troops blockaded the city, leaving air transport as the only means to resupply the city from the west. Australia offered ten Dakota air-transport planes with RAAF crews to participate in the Berlin airlift. In the end, Britain accepted the offer of forty-one airmen – who flew from September 1948 to August 1949 – but declined the offer of aircraft as impractical. Australia's action provoked controversy in Canada, where the government had declined the British request for assistance. A senior Canadian External Affairs official, Escott Reid, reported to Lester Pearson that a contribution "could be interpreted in certain quarters in Canada to mean that Canada is behaving very much as a colony ..." Both Mackenzie King and his successor as prime minister, Louis St Laurent, balked, according to Eayrs, "not for reasons of state but for reasons of status." Perras contends that Mackenzie King also was terrified that, if Canada participated in the airlift, it might be helping to bring on a third world war.[18]

Despite Canada's unwillingness to support the Berlin airlift, the Canadian government under St Laurent played an important role, alongside Britain, in the initial discussions about the formation of NATO. Canada's Escott Reid advocated the inclusion of Australia, New Zealand, and South Africa in the alliance "to preserve the unity of the Commonwealth" and to "remove the possibility of criticism of the pact by Commonwealth minded people in Canada." However, Canada's ambassador to Washington, Hume Wrong, considered Reid's proposal to be impractical. For Wrong, the focus on domestic security was of greater importance; he argued that, "if the North Atlantic is bridged by a new defensive alliance, the problems of North American defence would become a small part of a larger plan." Indeed, the term "NATO" was chosen, at least in part, "to prevent efforts of Latin Americans, Australians and others to adhere to the treaty" since "this would make the arrangement unwieldy, especially as none of those are now directly threatened by Soviet communism." In accepting the rationale for establishing NATO, St Laurent observed that foreign policy "must be based on recognition of the fact that totalitarian communist aggression endangers the freedom and peace of every democratic country, including Canada. On this basis ... we should be willing to associate ourselves with other free states in any appropriate collective security arrangements."[19] Such a commitment appeared politically sensible and, at first, economical, since the basing of forces in Europe would be unnecessary as long as the United States perceived that it had a huge nuclear superiority. In the meantime, another trend was becoming apparent.

In 1949 the United Nations Military Observer Group in India and Pakistan (UNMOGIP) was established in Kashmir, and Canada and Australia contributed military personnel.[20] This undertaking was one of the earliest post-war peacekeeping missions, and many more would follow in the years to come. Indeed, even by 1949, the precedent had been set with UN-sponsored monitors in Indonesia and Korea (see appendix 4).

The increasing requirements for such military contributions, combined with the escalating Cold War confrontation, made apparent the necessity for more personnel, equipment, and money to maintain a permanent and more substantial force in peacetime than had been maintained following the end of the First World War. With the experiences of two world wars in mind, and conscious of the limited place given to them by the Great Powers in the post-war international order, Canada and Australia decided that ready combat forces would be required. Such forces would, at least partly, enable foreign policy to be matched with extant military capabilities and thereby advance national interests and enhance the two countries' middle-power status. They would also help prevent a repetition of the experiences of the two world wars – with the inordinate number of casualties arising from the sending of half-trained and ill-equipped forces against determined and professional enemies. Indeed, events would soon put these ideas to the test.

THE KOREAN WAR

The Korean War commenced on 25 June 1950 when North Korean troops crossed the 38th parallel and invaded South Korea,[21] and it ended more than three years later with an armistice that came into effect on 27 July 1953. In between, the war see-sawed. The North Koreans initially pushed the South Korean and American forces to a perimeter around the southeastern city of Pusan. By launching a surprise amphibious assault at Inchon, near Seoul on Korea's west coast, MacArthur's forces outflanked and surprised an overstretched North Korean force, driving them back north well past the 38th parallel, to the point that the war virtually seemed over. But MacArthur's pursuit invited a Chinese reaction as the UN-mandated forces approached the Chinese border at the Yalu River. Thereafter, a massive Chinese invasion caught the stretched UN forces under MacArthur by surprise, pushing them once again south of the 38th parallel. The front line would continue to change back and forth until mid-1951, when it stabilized near the present demilitarized zone. From then on, for the next two years, there was a battle of wills reminiscent of the trench warfare of the First World War. In this war, Australian and Canadian forces played small but significant roles in support of their key security benefactors and the United Nations.

At the outset of the Korean War, the Australian government committed itself to an emergency Three Year Defence Plan and the expansion of the army, including the introduction of national service for home defence only.[22] Canada similarly raised defence expenditure and set out to expand the force by 12 per cent, to 47,185 troops. In contrast, the Australian Army had an authorized permanent-force strength of 19,000, but by June 1950 the number of soldiers on full-time duty was only 14,651. This number would grow to 29,104 during the Korean War, supplemented by 29,250 national servicemen per year trained for homeland defence and the Citizen

Military Force (CMF). Canada's new (since Mackenzie King's retirement in 1948) and more internationalist and anti-communist Prime Minister, St Laurent, argued in support of the war from a realist perspective, saying, "I am simply asking you to pay an insurance premium that will be far less costly than the losses we would face if a new conflagration devastated the world." By the same token, Canada was eager for the endorsement of the United Nations Security Council. Canadian historian Denis Stairs argues that "without this formal involvement of the United Nations the government in Ottawa would no more have embroiled itself in the conflict in Korea than it did later in the war in Vietnam" (his assessment would prove accurate for the war in Iraq in 2003 as well). According to Stairs, "Canadian officials felt it was essential to moderate and constrain the course of American decisions. In attempting to do so, they acted in concert with other powers of like purpose, and their instrument was the United Nations itself. They met with only marginal success ..." The official remarks from 1951 and Stairs's observations appear to be timeless, reflecting Canada's cautious foreign-policy approach. They also reflect a continuing contrast with the willingness of Australia to gain political mileage from its relatively small contributions of expeditionary forces. As a classified official Canadian report contended in 1951, "we prefer not to make commitments we are not reasonably certain we can carry out. For this reason we frequently have no definite policy on a question until almost the last minute. This makes it difficult for our representatives to engage in discussion with the Americans before American policy has become too firm to be altered ... Despite what we have done and are planning to do ... many Canadians have a somewhat unconscious feeling that we may not be doing our full share. This puts us on the defensive in our dealings with Washington and leads us to adopt what may be an unduly sensitive attitude."[23] Such last-minute thinking also tends to preclude much attention being given to cooperation with Australia.

Australia had held federal elections in December 1949 and Chifley's government had been replaced by a Liberal (conservative) one led, again, by Robert Menzies. Like the St Laurent government in Canada, Australia's Menzies was initially reluctant to send Australian troops to Korea. His concern was to keep troops available for the Middle East, consistent with the strategic contingency plans that envisaged Korea as a possible precursor to the outbreak of a wider war. But, while Menzies was travelling outside the country, his external affairs minister, Percy Spender, quickly responded to the news that Britain was preparing to commit forces; in the belief that a commitment of forces to the conflict would have a positive diplomatic effect on relations with the United States, Spender announced that Australia, too, would make a contribution. Under Menzies, Australia committed a squadron of aircraft and several ships to the conflict. The Mustang fighter aircraft of 77 Squadron RAAF was the first British Commonwealth force to see action – on 2 July 1950 – and one of its pilots was the first British Commonwealth serviceman killed in the war. Australia was relatively well placed to contribute air, sea, and ground elements to the conflict, having stationed forces in Japan since 1946 as the lead participant in the BCOF. The force had been scaled back in 1948, however, and what remained had been about to withdraw completely when the war broke out. Australian and Canadian naval ships also joined the fight early on and comfortably integrated under the operational control of the Royal Navy in the Yellow Sea on Korea's west coast or in Task Force 77, under the United States Navy in the Sea of Japan, to the east of Korea. The two countries also contributed ships to the Inchon landings near the South Korean capital of Seoul in September 1950. Though Australia sent a smaller number of ground-combat troops than Canada, there was greater awareness in the United States of the Australian contribution, the Australians having arrived in Korea five weeks before the Canadians landed.[24]

That greater awareness also sprang from the fact that Australia, along with Britain and New Zealand, announced its commitment before Canada did. In fact, the announcements from these three countries prompted the Canadian cabinet to review the Canadian position. Then, on 7 August 1950, the Canadian government announced its decision to recruit the brigade-sized Canadian Army Special Force, including three infantry battalions, each designated the second battalion of Canada's three active force infantry regiments: the Royal Canadian Regiment (RCR); the French-speaking Royal 22nd Regiment, or Royale Vingt-Deuxième Régiment (R22ÉR), commonly known as the "Van Doos"; and the Princess Patricia's Canadian Light Infantry (PPCLI). In addition, the force included one regiment of artillery, a field ambulance, an infantry (repair) workshop, a transport company, and two light detachments carrying supplies and provisions. The first element to deploy would be the 2nd Battalion Princess Patricia's Canadian Light Infantry (2PPCLI).[25]

On 18 February 1951 the 2PPCLI joined the 27th Commonwealth Brigade under a British commander. This formation predominantly used common British-pattern equipment and organizational models and included infantry battalions from Australia, Canada, England, and Scotland, as well as a New Zealand field-artillery regiment and an Indian ambulance unit. The Canadians had contemplated re-equipping with items of U.S. origin, but, with most of the force consisting of Second World War veterans, much of their expertise would be nullified by having to retrain on unfamiliar equipment.[26] Denis Stairs observes that, until that time, there had been no record of any other brigade – or force of similar size – composed of so many contingents from different Commonwealth countries. In fact, such an arrangement would not be repeated until the International Force in East Timor (INTERFET) in 1999 constituted its "Westforce," based on the Australian 3rd Brigade.[27]

From February 1951 on in Korea, the Australian and Canadian land forces fought alongside each other, for the first time since 1918. That April, near a place called Kapyong, a significant battle took place on a cleft between two promontories that marked one of the invasion routes into South Korea. Fighting as part of the 27th Commonwealth Brigade, the 2PPCLI and the 3rd Battalion, Royal Australian Regiment (3RAR), earned United States Presidential Unit Citations for their combined role in blunting a Chinese offensive. They did so alongside the New Zealand gunners and troops from the 72nd U.S. Heavy Tank Battalion. Intelligence reports indicated that the attack had been launched by an estimated 6,000 troops from two Chinese regiments.[28] Once again, Canadian and Australian accounts provide little coverage of, or comparison with, each other's forces, despite their similar experiences and the fact that the outcome would not have been successful without their combined efforts.[29] While Australian troops bore the brunt of the Chinese attack for the first part of the battle, they would have been easily outflanked and cut off had they not been effectively supported by the Canadian battalion on their left flank. When compared with the fate of the British Gloucestershire Regiment nearby on the Imjin River, the combined feat of arms at Kapyong is put in stark relief. At the same time as the battle of Kapyong was unfolding, the Gloucesters, essentially alone and surrounded by Chinese forces, were eventually overwhelmed.[30] A similar fate likely would have befallen the Australians and Canadians had they not been defending in mutual support of each other.[31]

As the Korean War reached stalemate, Canadian and Australian air and naval elements continued contributing to the U.S.-led campaign. The RCAF's 426 Squadron joined the American airlift to Tokyo – the main supply base and launching point for operations – in late July 1950 (they stayed until 1954), but Canada's air contribution was primarily through some twenty pilots and several technical officers seconded to the U.S. Air Force. These men were credited with a total of more than twenty Russian-made jet fighters destroyed or damaged. In contrast, the RAAF's 77 Squadron was committed to the conflict directly from its base in Japan. In addition, both

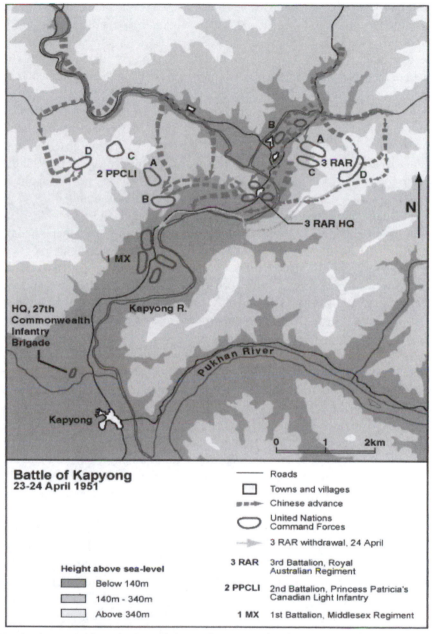

Battle of Kapyong
23-24 April 1951

———	Roads
☐	Towns and villages
▰▰▰➤	Chinese advance
⬭	United Nations Command Forces
➤	3 RAR withdrawal, 24 April
3 RAR	3rd Battalion, Royal Australian Regiment
2 PPCLI	2nd Battalion, Princess Patricia's Canadian Light Infantry
1 MX	1st Battalion, Middlesex Regiment

Height above sea-level

	Below 140m
	140m - 340m
	Above 340m

Battle of Kapyong: by Lieutenant Slade Crooks (CF). Used with permission. The Battle of Kapyong was not just a Canadian or Australian feat of arms. It was the second "ABCA Battle" involving a US tank battalion, and a New Zealand artillery battery, as well as a British infantry battalion in depth and a British brigade commander.

countries contributed forces to the only integrated ground formation of Commonwealth countries, the 1st Commonwealth Division, consisting of three brigades (the 25th Canadian, the 27th and later the 28th Commonwealth, and the 29th British), in mid-1951. This occurred despite the St Laurent government's initial reluctance to have Canadians grouped with the other Commonwealth forces, preferring instead to stress Canada's United Nations affiliation. The division included an integrated British, Canadian, Australia, and New Zealand headquarters as well as divisional and line-of-communications signals units. Its official historian observes that "the division achieved a remarkable degree of homogeneity. A formidable fighting force of over 20,000 all ranks, it remained to the end of hostilities a key formation along the line of hills defending the 38th parallel."[32]

Canada's main contribution as part of the division, the 25th Canadian Infantry Brigade, was commanded by an Australian-born veteran commander of Canadian troops in the northwest Europe campaign of the Second World War, Brigadier John M. ("Rocky") Rockingham. Thereafter, the division's three brigades included one British and one Canadian (the 25th Canadian Brigade), along with the 28th Commonwealth Brigade (including two British and two Australian infantry battalions and New Zealanders gunners). The 28th Commonwealth Brigade was commanded successively by British Army brigadier J.F.M. Macdonald and Australian brigadiers T.J. Daly and J.G. Wilton. These brigades took turns in defensive positions along the Imjin and Sami-ch'on rivers near the 38th parallel – including the well-fought-over "Hook" area. In addition, the predominantly British divisional-support units incorporated Canadian, Australian, New Zealand, and Indian members in their organizations.[33]

Occasionally, Australian infantry units complained when taking over from the Canadians that Canadians had not dominated "no man's land" by patrolling. In fact, according to the Canadian historian David Bercuson, "Canadian commanders were guilty of using inappropriate patrol tactics, of generally allowing patrols to become routine and meaningless, and primarily, of inadequate reconnaissance. All these failings can be linked to the absence of an effective patrol doctrine." One Canadian officer reflecting on the fighting in March 1953 declared: "Our tactics have a stereotyped quality that deprives us of initiative and forewarns the enemy. We rarely trick the Chinaman. We do not use deception and have lost our aggressive spirit. Commanders and men are dug-out minded. The fear of receiving casualties deadens our reactions and lessens our effort. We are thoroughly defensive minded but not thorough in our defence."[34] On occasion, this mindset allowed the Chinese to prepare detailed assaults from no man's land. For instance, on 23 October 1952, B Company 1 RCR's position at Hill 355 (known as "Little Gibraltar") was overrun; it was soon retaken, but with significant casualties.[35]

In contrast, the Australians had developed a tradition of patrolling and dominating no man's land as a form of aggressive defence. This approach had been illustrated in the successful defence of the North African city of Tobruk in 1941 – where a German armoured-infantry thrust was effectively stopped for the first time in that war by Australian infantry and British artillery. At Tobruk, dominance of no man's land and the fearless and meticulous investigation of the terrain had become an Australian forté.[36] In contrast to the Canadians, according to Jeffrey Grey, the Australians in Korea "erred in the other direction, patrolling too aggressively" and exposing themselves to greater casualties by straying into places from which it was difficult to extricate. Other complaints by Australians were that Canadians left their positions in unsanitary conditions and with the camouflage and concealment weakened by the disposal of rubbish on the forward slopes of defensive positions, including reflective tins that helped make their positions attractive targets. The Canadian response was that "they saw little point in trying to conceal their positions from the enemy, who certainly knew where every rifle pit and crawl trench was – as the Canadians in fact knew of the Chinese positions." Bercuson believes that "the magnificent effort of the [Canadian] troops was undermined by an improperly prepared divisional front and poor defence doctrine." The latter stemmed in part from the Canadians' experience in fighting the Germans in Italy in 1943 and 1944, where the actions were more fluid and the requirement had not been for defence in depth. As for the division level, says Bercuson, "Commonwealth Division HQ never imposed a uniform defensive doctrine along its front." Brigadier Jean V. Allard was the Canadian brigade commander for the last three months of the war (and was later, in 1966, Chief of Defence Staff [CDS] at the same time as his fellow brigade commander, John Wilton, was in the equivalent Australian post). Allard vigorously rectified many of the faults he observed in the third rotation of battalions on assuming command. He also was scathing about the preparedness of his soldiers and critical of his company commanders, who were "brave and loyal" but rapidly rotated and lacking in knowledge of defensive battle, particularly patrolling skills.[37]

Despite these differences, the Commonwealth forces still supported each other's efforts as a matter of course, whenever possible. In October 1951, for instance, when the Australians in 28th Commonwealth Brigade attacked Hill 317 (Maryang Sang), north of the Imjin River, the 25th Canadian Brigade swept forward on the Australians' left, seizing their designated objectives.[38] Also, during this period, Australia and Canada started shifting to equipment, if not doctrine, of U.S. origin. However, for both countries, the purchase of U.S. equipment was kept minimal on account of political and economic constraints arising from a national balance of payments that favoured the United States. In terms of doctrine, the American approach to defensive positions called for establishing a "Main Line of Resistance," built largely as a line along the lower or forward slopes of the hills being defended. These lines were complemented by strongly held outposts that invited attack and resulted in heavy American casualties. In contrast, the Commonwealth troops shared the view that the best place to defend from was on the hilltops – or "Forward Defended Localities" – with all-round defence, interlocking fire plans, plunging fire for the lower slopes (instead of forward-placed "main lines"), and small standing patrols that could be withdrawn at short notice. When Commonwealth and American units replaced each other on the front, the result was a great deal of alteration of positions, with much unnecessary digging and filling. On the Hook, for instance, such alterations resulted in a compromise in the defensive positions that would be exposed by Chinese attacks. For the Commonwealth troops, the view was that any battle that caused equal casualties on both sides left the Chinese with the advantage.[39]

Indeed, U.S. Army doctrine was often considered inappropriate for the smaller Commonwealth forces, including the Canadians and Australians. Like the U.S. Marines, who drew on a smaller recruiting pool than their army equivalents, the Commonwealth Division troops, for both manpower and political reasons, could not afford to sustain the continuous heavy casualties likely to arise from occasional "fool-hardy stunts which had no military purpose." Such "stunts," which occurred on U.S.-sectors of the front, included defending outpost positions at any cost. According to the British commander of the 1st Commonwealth Division, Major-General Sir Archibald Cassells, this was what the U.S. Army Corps commander had requested – unsuccessfully – from the Commonwealth Division.

By the same token, as the war reached stalemate, the United States Army also became more casualty-averse and was forced to modify tactics accordingly. Moreover, according to Grey, it manifested "the penchant for senior commanders to play squad leader." Such inclinations reflected a seeming reluctance to trust non-commissioned officers and a predisposition to micro-manage minor tactical incidents. This predilection was complemented by attrition or "meat grinder" tactics aimed at negating the Chinese numerical superiority by taking advantage of overwhelming American airpower and artillery dominance. Even the employment of Commonwealth (that is,

Canadian, Australian, British, and New Zealand) artillery and u.s. field artillery contrasted sharply. Commonwealth artillery relied on decentralized command and control of the guns through more senior-ranking forward observers (artillery captains), assigned to rifle companies and with direct communications to their assigned artillery assets, and battery commanders (majors) assigned to work with infantry battalion commanders (lieutenant-colonels). In contrast, the u.s. approach was to concentrate command and control at the artillery battalion headquarters, allocating only junior officers and enlisted men as forward observers, with little delegated authority.[40] Indeed, with artillery and other aspects of combined-arms warfare, the American tactics of mass-effects required little finesse from troops on the ground. Exposure to this kind of warfare discouraged Canadians and Australians from abandoning their British-derived tactics in favour of the more expensive and resource-consuming American ones. The American resource-intensive approach would have a similar effect on the frugal-minded Australians in Vietnam, over a decade later.

By late 1951, the entire 25th Canadian Infantry Brigade had deployed to Korea. Australia's ground contribution peaked in 1952 with two infantry battalions in the 28th Commonwealth Brigade, a major contribution to the British Commonwealth Forces Korea logistical-support base, and small groups assigned to divisional units. In August 1950 Brigadier F.J. Fleury was appointed the senior Canadian officer in the Korean theatre, thus becoming the founding head of the Canadian Military Mission, Far East.[41] Fleury's position involved considerable liaison with the Australians, who were providing much of the administrative support for the deployed forces. This support came largely from Japan through the Australian-led BCOF, the residual elements of which later formed its successor organization, the British Commonwealth Forces-Korea (BCF-K). Fleury had been invited to be the BCF-K chief of staff, and he was eager to accept the appointment. But Canadian authorities preferred to limit his responsibilities, fearing that his role as chief of staff would undermine his independence in safeguarding Canadian interests. Grey points out that "it was an unfortunate decision" that led to occasional misunderstandings. Moreover, Grey argues, had Fleury been appointed, the "train of events surrounding the Koje-do incident [when Canadians were called in, without consulting Ottawa, to help subdue prisoners-of-war who had seized a u.s.-administered detention camp] might never have happened, and certainly would not have caught the Canadian government unprepared." The official historian of the Canadian Army in the Korean War, Lieutenant-Colonel Herbert Fairlie, admitted later that, although "Canada made too much fuss over the affair," the real lesson was "the vital necessity for prior consultation between allies when unusual activity of any sort is being contemplated." Grey further observes that "personalities were as important as policies, with differences in the former often being used to justify disagreements in the latter." Unfortunately, such short-sightedness prevented key figures from seeing the merits in closer collaboration. For instance, the Canadians "were so concerned to preserve a distinctly Canadian position that they did not coordinate their actions with the Australians, to their mutual cost on occasions."[42]

This situation was exacerbated by differing financial arrangements. Canada was not a member of the sterling bloc and thus felt financially unconstrained by the arrangements made under the BCOF and was certainly not attracted to the diet of mutton, bully beef, and biscuits to which the Australians, New Zealanders, and Britons were subjected. Not surprisingly, therefore, the Canadians were alone among the Commonwealth units in making regular use of American food rations. In contrast, financial constraints predisposed the British and New Zealanders to work through the administrative arrangements in place from the war's outset through their sterling bloc partners, the Australians. But rations aside, the Canadians, like the British and New Zealanders, found that the ease of Commonwealth logistic arrangements, based on Australian support elements originally located in Japan, meant that the establishment of a Commonwealth formation made eminent sense. This was particularly the case given the plethora of other national contingents, each with unique requirements that had to be imposed on the American supply system.[43]

After the armistice, Canadian and Australian troops would remain alongside each other as part of the composite Commonwealth force until the major combat units returned home in 1955 and the final elements were withdrawn in 1957. In the end, 26,791 Canadians served in Korea and took 1,588 casualties, including 516 dead and 32 captured. Australia suffered 339 killed and 29 taken prisoner. Chinese and North Korean casualties were likely more than a million, while United Nations casualties numbered some 490,000, including 33,000 American fatalities. South Korea suffered 66,000 soldiers killed.[44]

On the diplomatic front, Canada and Australia were included in the United Nations Committee of Sixteen, which started meeting in Washington in January 1951. Denis Stairs states that "there was considerable esprit de corps among the non-American participants, but there was never advance collusion against the American officials. The Canadians, British, and Australians were especially close and often lunched together beforehand for general discussion, but the views even of these three were seldom unanimous." He also notes that "Canadian diplomacy during the Korean War can be interpreted very largely as a manifestation of the attempt to support the core, while simultaneously containing the extremities of American policy, and to ensure that military forces operating under UN auspices but delegated to U.S. command, were prevented from being drawn into a larger Asian war ... The central preoccupation of senior Canadian policy makers was ... they wanted the Americans to stop acting – or at least to stop *appearing* to act – unilaterally ... [But] the Americans were paying most of the piper's bill. It followed that they were calling most of the piper's tunes."[45]

Complementing the diplomatic manoeuvring were the tactical actions of troops such as the Canadians and Australians that proved so costly in lives but that also had some significant strategic effects. For instance, it was during the Korean War that Australia and New Zealand negotiated a military alliance with the United States. The ANZUS Pact between the United States, Australia, and New Zealand had become negotiable owing both to the reassessment of American strategic security interests following the outbreak of the Korean War and to the military cooperation offered to the United States in conducting it. The treaty was signed during the month that Australia decided to commit an additional infantry battalion to Korea and shortly after the combined Canadian and Australian successes at Kapyong in 1951. It was ratified in 1952, although it did not include complementary military planning staffs or dedicated troops, as the NATO agreement did, or an automatic commitment of support in time of crisis. In addition, as Barclay observes, "probably nobody in Canberra had ever conceived an alliance with the United States as a partnership between equals." Still, it had the effect of reassuring Australians, who were anxious about the non-punitive terms of the peace with Japan. The treaty also justified the limiting of Australian defence expenditure, much as the American presence assured Canadians that they could afford to restrict defence spending. As Australia's official Korean War historian Robert O'Neill indicates, "the major dividend of participation was diplomatic rather than military or strategic." The ANZUS Pact also pointed to the growing focus of the Australian forces on increased interoperability with their U.S. counterparts, much as their Canadian counterparts were also doing. Interestingly, Canada's Progressive Conservative Party in the House of Commons also had considered an anti-communist Pacific treaty to complement Canada's membership in NATO. The British did propose a joint Commonwealth military presence in Malaya or Hong Kong, and Australia and New Zealand supported the idea, but, despite its Pacific coastline and enduring interests in Asia-Pacific security, Canada still considered itself primarily a North Atlantic nation. Consequently, NATO would remain Ottawa's priority for the remainder of the Cold War and beyond.[46]

Nonetheless, for the Australian and Canadian militaries, the Korean War had led to the emergence – for the first time in their histories – of professional expeditionary forces, the leaders of whom at all levels returned to barracks in 1953 as experienced combat-tested veterans.[47] The Korean War had once again demonstrated that, despite the predilection for looking to the United States for equipment and procedures, the Canadians and Australians would continue to find ways of conducting military operations that were more suitable and more like each other than their bigger cousin's. The subsequent fifty years would see the concept of maintaining professional expeditionary forces undergo significant challenge and reorganization, but it would remain a proven and enduring instrument of state – for peacekeeping, war-fighting, and the plethora of "grey area" missions in between that Canadians and Australians would be repeatedly called upon to perform. The Korean War also demonstrated that, notwithstanding official statements to the contrary, Canada's real national interests would at times compel it to consider the situation of, and deploy forces to, the Pacific region. Conceivably, if the Canadian and Australian governments had recognized this, greater cooperation could have been sustained between their respective military forces.

REFLECTIONS ON CANADIAN AND AUSTRALIAN "WAYS OF WAR"

Many writers have noted that, in the first half of the twentieth century, Canada vacillated in its approach to national strategy and security issues during peacetime and wartime. The shift was from support for British imperialism before the First World War to isolationism and only local defence measures in the inter-war period and then to internationalism as the Cold War set in.[48] The broad parallel with Australia is striking. In peacetime, Canadian and Australian governments have favoured local defence measures and small military establishments to save resources for public needs, while also showing reluctance to accept international responsibilities. This conduct was particularly evident prior to 1950. Yet, during wartime in the same period, huge contributions were made to collective or "forward defence" by both countries. Throughout, these efforts resulted in the raising and deploying of surprisingly similar expeditionary forces.

The overall trajectory of the two countries' armies reflects a parallel attempt to grapple with the issue of professionalism and the military. Both countries produced outstanding commanders in the First World War who emerged from the pre-war militia forces. In the inter-war years, their success led to an excess of confidence in the "natural" fighting qualities of men bred in the outback or the woods and prairies, an outlook that reinforced the myth that wars could be won by militiamen.[49] In the Second World War, such confidence proved misplaced in several instances, as both armies suffered setbacks arising from their lack of preparedness for modern warfare against determined, well- equipped, and professional enemy forces from Germany and Japan.

The dual-track approach – military retrenchment in peacetime and rapid militarization in wartime – left both countries ill-prepared for the military crises in 1914, 1939, and 1950. Yet, at the same time, both countries gradually began to discover their own self-interest and learned how to "serve" two "masters" – Britain and the United States. Not surprisingly, similar circumstances produced similar force structures, of relatively small size and with limited funding. These similarities were evident despite at times contrasting Canadian and Australian foreign policies.

While similarities were numerous, differences were equally apparent. For instance, both Canada and Australia developed its own "way of war" that was strongly influenced by British models, but their experiences and their outlooks left different legacies. The Canadian way, as Granatstein points out, reflected a disposition that was "uptight and lacking confidence" and characterized by staff-driven and top-down control, concerned with preventing a repetition of the horrific casualties of the First World War and invariably featuring heavy artillery preparation and small-scale objectives.[50] This style of warfare remained focused on combat requirements in Western Europe. In contrast, during both world wars, the Australian way was influenced more by experiences with desert warfare, where battlefield manoeuvre was both feasible and common. The Australian way also featured fighting in the jungles to the north of Australia, where light forces, limited availability of artillery (and a concomitant increased reliance on close air support instead), and small-team actions, including assertive patrolling, featured prominently. For much of the time, such tactics were driven by resource constraints – shortages of suitable equipment and adequately trained personnel – as much as by the inaccessibility of the inhospitable terrain where the fighting took place. The combination of these factors led to a greater emphasis by Australians on battle cunning and local initiative – an approach that would come to be considered "manoeuvrist."[51] Australia's experience, while it contrasted with that of Canada in the Second World War, was similar to Canada's nineteenth-century romantic idea of the *petit guerre*, with its stealthy hit-and-run raids, that had its roots in the wars of conquest in North America of the seventeenth and eighteenth centuries.

After two world wars, and despite a common commitment to support the United Nations and other emerging alliance commitments, the forces of Canada and Australia would take somewhat divergent paths in terms of operational orientation and force development "trajectories." While both countries remained committed to maintaining expeditionary forces that in many ways still looked like each other's, Canada would focus on predominantly mechanized forces in Europe, as well as on peacekeeping, while Australia's main focus would be on dismounted light infantry and special forces in southeast Asia. In addition, for Canada, the attitude towards Britain would be much different from what it had been during the two world wars. The shift would be from not wanting to participate actively in the Empire (although arguably needing to do so) to no longer even needing the Empire. For Australia, such a transition would take a little more time, as the following chapter explains.

6

Cold War Divergence

While divergence became more apparent after the Korean War, particularly where Canada's and Australia's forces focused their efforts, similarities between the two nations' armies did indeed continue. For instance, Canada and Australia adhered to a short-war, forces-in-being military doctrine that placed priority on ready regular forces instead of militia-based reserves. For Canada, the focus was NATO and Europe, while, for Australia, it was southeast Asia and the Middle East (where in fact, as discussed below, Canadians rather than Australians would deploy in 1956). Neither Canada nor Australia felt that they could disengage militarily from the outside world as they had done in the inter-war years and both saw themselves as participants, together with other countries, in international-security affairs rather than as independent military actors on the world stage. After the advent of intercontinental bombers and missiles, Canada was no longer a "fire-proof house" and Australia felt similarly about the prospect of possibly becoming the last "domino" to fall following any communist Russian or Chinese thrust southwards. With these security concerns in mind, Canada signed the North Atlantic Treaty in 1949 and the Canadian Defence White Paper of November 1949 stressed that "the best place to defeat the enemy is as far away from Canada as possible."[1] This view echoed sentiments in Australia and would permeate Australian and Canadian defence- and foreign-policy thinking for decades to come. The "forward defence" approach to national security would also reinforce the need for expeditionary forces.

ESTABLISHING A PLACE IN THE WESTERN ALLIANCE

In the Cold War years of the 1950s, it was evident that Australia and Canada were firmly entrenched in the Western bloc. Australia's prime minister (from 1949 to 1966), Robert Menzies, and external affairs minister (from 1951 to 1960), Richard Casey, enjoyed the company of Canada's Louis St Laurent (prime minister from 1948 to 1957) and Lester Pearson (minister of external affairs from 1948 to 1957, and prime minister from 1963 to 1968). Indeed, Casey was far less abrasive than his predecessor, Evatt, had been. All these men were "eager to compare notes ... without fear of stepping on great and powerful toes." They even initiated an exchange of officers between their departments of external affairs. Both countries were grappling with the question of how to maintain good relations and develop appropriate policies with Britain and the United States, despite being pulled in different directions. Moreover, both supported collective-defence arrangements and recognized communism as a major threat to non-communist Asia and thus supported major American policies in Asia. By and large, they had similar world-views and subscribed to similar analyses of the great events affecting Asia. There was a broad consensus between them on what the threat was, even though they may have disagreed on some details.[2]

Similar strategic outlooks, however, did not outweigh other factors that would produce significant divergences between the armies of Canada and Australia. Such divergences, indeed, would become more prominent as the Cold War progressed, reflecting certain foreign-policy distinctions and resulting in different force-development "trajectories." For Australia, the paramount concern was the increase in post-colonial revolutionary movements to its north, which led the Australian Army to maintain and refine its expertise in jungle warfare. By contrast, Canada's commitments in Europe led to greater reliance on mechanized forces which emphasized group skills over individual and small-unit initiative – a reflection of increasing u.s. influence on doctrine, equipment, and force structures.

The key to Canada's Cold War security was NATO, with its ties to Europe and the United States. In Europe, Canadian troops were placed with the British Army on the Rhine (BAOR) as a counter-balance to the integration and absorption of Canada's forces by the United States in North America – the RCN was becoming increasingly oriented to the u.s. Navy and the RCAF was operating with the u.s. Air Force. The chief of the general staff, the United Kingdom-born Lieutenant-General Guy Simonds, argued that the Canadian Army preferred to work with the British than with the Americans, continuing an association that had existed in two world wars and that had been profitable and deeply satisfying to both parties. In addition, placing Canadian troops with British ones allowed for more interaction with the smaller NATO armies, thereby counteracting the preponderance of American power in the NATO decision-making apparatus. The Canadian

Brigade eventually followed a predominantly British organizational model with a mixture of u.s. equipment, including 105-mm. howitzers, 81-mm. mortars, M113 armoured personnel carriers, Belgian-designed self-loading rifles, and British Centurion tanks as well as Ferret and Saracen scout cars – much like their Australian "cousins" would do. Both Canada and Australia also later acquired the Bell Kiowa (OH58) light-observation helicopters and the "Carl Gustav" 84 mm.-anti-armoured recoilless weapon. The similar procurement patterns helped perpetuate their forces' uncanny resemblance. As for the Canadians, it appeared to one American that they "speak British, organize British, and think British, but with an American accent."[3]

The ground contribution alongside British troops was balanced by grouping Canada's air division in France (a force of twelve squadrons of aircraft by 1952) under American command. Thus, according to Canada's Chief of Air Staff Air Marshall Wilfrid Curtis, "it would be clear that Canadian forces were not aligned with any particular power." All this led to Canada spending more on defence than Australia. But, as Roy Rempel contends, "most Canadian leaders ... never understood the full political worth of the country's military presence in Germany. In consequence, the value of that presence to Canada, both politically and economically, was never fully appreciated and therefore never fully exploited. Indeed, in many instances, the lack of understanding of the political importance of the Canadian military commitment in Europe ensured that Canada's diplomatic and military policy actually worked at cross-purposes." The contrast with Australia points to one of the significant differences, in terms of defence policy, between Canada and Australia. Australia's military commitments abroad were frequently weighed in terms of their political and economic consequences for the welfare of the country – as insurance policies for those living in a more "remote" and apparently less benign corner of the globe than Canadians. Reflecting on this contrast, one American military officer argues that "Canadians find fighting distasteful and their leaders consequently look down upon their military. Australia prides itself on not picking fights, but it has no intention of ever losing or being thought a pushover. Aussies thus respect their military, and their leaders consider it a proper tool."[4] Nonetheless, Canadians still weighed its commitments in terms of broader trade policies, and such considerations underscored the need for defence and security policies to complement governments efforts to foster economic ties in North America.

As benign as Canada's part of the world was, there developed an increased awareness of its proximity to the Soviet threat. By the end of 1953, the Mid-Canada Line of radar systems was under construction across the

55th parallel to support the combined American and Canadian air-defence capabilities. Canada's ties with the United States also led to the construction of the Distant Early Warning (DEW) Line, completed in 1957 along the 70th parallel in Canada's far north. The DEW Line was constructed to give U.S. Strategic Command sufficient warning time to mount retaliatory strikes against potential transpolar Soviet bombing raids. Such efforts led eventually to the North American Air Defence Command (NORAD) agreement, formalized in 1958.[5] NORAD was created separate from NATO because the United States preferred bilateral dealings to prevent interference with its own ability to exercise control. Joel Sokolsky argues that Canada also had to be concerned, in the early days of the Cold War, with its new position as part of the immediate strategic defensive foreground of the United States. By participating in NORAD (and, to a lesser extent, in North American naval operations), Ottawa believed that it was contributing to overall Western collective defence. Such contributions were costly and, in a sceptical democracy, some convincing was required, particularly for French Canadians. Prime Minister St Laurent, who was considered a very good communicator, argued that significant defence expenditure in peacetime was the only way to avoid war. After all, hanging back (the lack of preparedness) had not stopped the previous two wars. Rather, it helped precipitate them.[6]

In addition to outlays on defence, both Canada and Australia again accepted some loss of foreign-policy independence in return for alliance security led by "powerful friends." This made the transfer from Anglo-centric defence to the American alliance relatively easy. More so than the land forces, at least, Canada's and Australia's navies were reared in the tradition of British and American seapower. Consequently, according to Canadian Rear-Admiral Fred Crickard, they found it easier than the other services to adjust to the Cold War balance of power in alliance with the United States. However, a further consequence of such alliance commitments was that the respective forces' capabilities narrowed to the point where they became able to act only as a contribution to a larger enterprise. This approach left the force structure not necessarily suited to national needs. Canada's navy, for instance, focused almost exclusively on its anti-submarine warfare capabilities, leaving no room for the development of balanced naval forces for self-reliant Canadian operations (like the Suez operation, discussed below, which Canada was still able to manage in 1956).[7] Both Canada and Australia would allow their naval force structures to be driven in large part by such alliance requirements, although Australia would maintain a more diversified fleet.[8] In Australia's case, such requirements were informed by the Radford-Collins Agreement of March 1951, which preceded the ratification of the ANZUS Alliance (on 29 April 1952). This agreement placed priority on trade protection and the defence of shipping,[9] establishing peacetime surveillance operations and wartime contingency plans for the escort of shipping in the western Pacific and east Indian oceans. The ANZUS Pact signalled that the Americans had replaced the British as the protectors of Australia and New Zealand, although, for more than a decade after its enactment, the United States was unwilling to allow ANZUS to become the means for formulating military plans in the Pacific.[10]

In addition to the role of Canadian naval power in the alliance context, Canada was considered "a very important piece of real estate"[11] and, accordingly, it prepared to contribute modest forces to assist in monitoring the air and maritime approaches to North America. However, like Australia, Canada would not place a high priority on homeland-defence issues during the Cold War, largely relegating such tasks to the part-time militia forces. Technically, Canada also raised full-time ground units as the "Mobile Ground Forces," structured, notionally at least, to support defence of the homeland, but these were considered more likely to be assigned the task of supporting NATO should the Cold War turn hot in Western Europe. The perceived need for such domestic-security efforts in both Canada and Australia would wane even further in the initial post-Cold War years and would not regain prominence until after 11 September 2001.[12] Until then, both Canada and Australia would see homeland defence as a strategic backwater. Yet, while Canada appeared to be nonchalant about the United States not focusing its military forces on the direct defence of North America, Australia sought to coax the United States to value its security concerns more highly.

By 1954, the strategic divergence between Australia and Canada was becoming increasingly apparent with Canada's acceptance of the NATO Military Committee's strategic-concept document known as MC48. Canada's three ground-force components – the Mobile Strike Force, the 25th Brigade (which had served in Korea), and the 27th Brigade – were converted into four interchangeable brigade groups for operations in conventional and nuclear environments in the defence of Europe.[13] This focus on Europe would remain in place for Canada's forces for nearly four decades, until after the end of the Cold War.

While Canada was becoming involved in NORAD because of its geographic position between the Soviet Union and the United States, it was also seeking to create a triangular relationship in which it would be regarded as an equal by its atomic partners, Britain and the United States. But in 1946, with the United States objecting to Britain developing its own atomic bomb, the latter concluded that a British-led nuclear project in Canada – where the Canadians were pursuing an independent policy at odds with British interests – should be closed down. A nuclear plant in Australia, however, offered mutual benefits to Britain and Australia, and Canada provided Australia with a model for its own atomic development. Australia made arrangements to work with the British on its own atomic-weapons testing program, known as the "Joint Project," using facilities in the remote South Australian outback at Woomera and Maralinga as well as off the west Australian coast, at Monte Bello Island.[14] Canada did not participate in the Joint Project, being more closely tied to the U.S. nuclear-weapons program. But ties with Britain and Australia remained in other fora.

The Commonwealth was one such body in which both Canada and Australia maintained an interest. Attention to Commonwealth affairs complemented, in part, their concerns about Cold War communist expansion. This interest was manifested, for instance, in their contributions to the Colombo Plan – the world's first aid program for the developing world. The plan was put together in Ceylon (now Sri Lanka) by the leading Commonwealth nations of the time, Britain, Canada, Australia, India, Pakistan, New Zealand, Ceylon, and South Africa. It aimed at countering the influence of communism in poorer countries in Africa and Asia in the 1950s and 1960s through economic development and education assistance. To make it work, Britain pledged to contribute U.S.$300 million annually, and Australia and, eventually, Canada agreed each to contribute $U.S.25 million annually as well. While small compared to the $12-billion Marshall Plan in Europe, the scheme made a modest contribution. It was Australia's main instrument of aid, next to aid to Papua New Guinea.[15]

Australia was also responsible for the mandated territories of Papua and New Guinea. This brought with it a unique set of challenges, including fostering an indigenous defence force in anticipation of Papua New Guinea independence, which was granted in 1975. This set of circumstances was more akin to the British colonial experience than the experience of their Canadian "cousins."

For Canada, distance from Asia facilitated a more sympathetic position in relation to non-aligned nations such as India as they sought to find a place in bodies such as the British Commonwealth of Nations. While Menzies appeared to mourn the decline of the old British Empire, Canada, under St Laurent, embraced the new Commonwealth. Canada's approach also made it easier to play a role as the West's proxy in the International Commission for Supervision and Control (ICSC) in Indochina. Admittedly under U.S. pressure, Canada contributed military and civilian monitors in Vietnam and the rest of Indochina from 1954 until 1973 and to the ICSC's successor, the International Commission for Control and Supervision (ICCS), in early 1973. This commitment was in recognition of the need for a supportive but acceptable nation to represent the West in a triumvirate arrangement that also included representatives from a non-aligned nation, India, and a communist state, Poland. Canada's participation reflected a willingness to contribute to communist containment in a low-key manner. But the ICSC's mandate was crammed with ambiguities and its commitment to impartiality would create diplomatic difficulties for Canada. As Eayrs points out, "of all its expectations, none was to prove more ill-founded than the belief that Canada could serve in the spirit bidden by its mandate without in the course of that service complicating, eventually fraying, Canada's relations with the United States." Early on, Canadian officials recognized their difficult predicament, as Canadian delegates regularly passed information to Washington. At times, the Canadians acted as messengers for the United States to the North Vietnamese leadership. Given the difficulties this commitment was generating, in 1955 Canada approached Australia and New Zealand with a request that they replace Canada on the ICSC. Its overture was greeted, according to Eayrs, by "somewhat hysterical laughter by the Australians and New Zealanders." The antipodeans could see Canada's difficult predicament and had no interest in placing themselves in an equally awkward position. After 1956, Canada would retain a token presence in the ICSC to keep an eye on what the communists were doing. But, by 1972, there would be only nineteen Canadians left on the body. This was one-tenth the number involved in 1955, although the number would temporarily increase in early 1973 to facilitate the Paris accords between the United States and North Vietnam.[16]

THE SUEZ INTERVENTION

The Suez Crisis occurred in 1956 when Britain's prime minister, Anthony Eden, together with the leaders of France and Israel, conspired to bring down the Egyptian government of Gamal Abdel Nasser and to reverse the abrupt nationalization of the Suez Canal. But, before the scheme was hatched, Australia's prime minister, Menzies, led a delegation to Egypt, representing eighteen nations, which was initially endorsed by Canada. Menzies hoped to reason with Nasser, but his position was compromised by secretly coordinated military actions by Britain, France, and Israel which he was not briefed about. The situation was further complicated by President Eisenhower, who was determined to avoid resuming the wartime closeness with Britain which gave that country added prestige. Thus, once the invasion of Egypt commenced, he responded swiftly, threatening the British and French with financial ruin. In effect, Eisenhower, with Anthony Eden's blundering help, badly split the alliance. As Robert Kagan observes, "when President Dwight Eisenhower undermined and humiliated Britain and France in Suez in 1956, it was only the most blatant of American efforts to cut Europe down to size and reduce its already weakened global influence." Similarly, Canadian diplomat John Holmes notes that the British, who had "doggedly stood by the Americans out of loyalty as well as dependence, were told to abandon their Commonwealth obligations – mocked as nostalgia for imperial glory – and set themselves up in Europe." As Nicholas Mansergh comments, "there was a link in psychological terms between the traumatic experiences of 1956 and the manner of the British application for membership of the Common Market six years later, even if the latter was dictated chiefly by economic considerations."[17] These events had a sobering effect on Canadian and Australian views of their future relations with their two security benefactors. In effect, the Suez Crisis "marked the de facto end of the British Empire in Canada" as Canadian actions set it in support of U.S. objectives but against the policies of its two former colonial "masters" – Britain and France.[18] The crisis also, according to Canadian historian B.J.C. McKercher, "redefined the North Atlantic triangle [of Britain, Canada and the United States]." It is even credited with having destroyed French chances to put down the rebellion in Algeria and led to the rise to power of the "recalcitrant" – on the Algerian issue – General de Gaulle. Through it all, Canada was the willing surrogate of the United States, eager to play a constructive role. But Canadian and Australian positions were at odds. For instance, unlike Menzies, St Laurent had an instinctive dislike of colonialism that was separate from his concerns to keep in step with the United States. Yet, even in the midst of their differences, when Egypt broke off diplomatic relations with Australia, Australia's External Affairs Minister Richard Casey approached his Canadian counterpart, Lester Pearson, asking for Canada to act as "protecting power" so far as Australian interests in Egypt were concerned – a request to which Canada agreed.[19]

Canada played a distinctive role under the guidance of Lester Pearson. Pearson recognized the need for a trusted go-between to defuse the crisis in relations between the United States and its key European allies, Britain and France. Accordingly, the Canadians provided the lead elements for the

United Nations Emergency Force (UNEF) in Egypt in 1956 – a force that, with contributions from seven nations, would reach 6,615 personnel of all ranks. While the United States provided a large portion of the funding for UNEF, it was Canada that led the way on the ground. Troops were drawn from a number of countries not strongly aligned with either superpower, and the forces were under instructions to use their weapons only in self-defence. The mission clearly established the concept of large-scale interpositional peacekeeping operations in buffer zones between contenders, and Canada contributed with gusto. At the same time, the mission demonstrated the weakness and limitations of such neutral peacekeeping missions, since Egypt's Nasser reasserted control over the Gaza Strip within two days of it being transferred to the United Nations. Nonetheless, the Canadian Armed Forces' lead role in UNEF denoted a high-water mark in terms of their utility as distinctive national instruments of power. Canada contributed the force commander, Major-General E.L.M. Burns, who had been in command of the United Nations observers in Palestine (his initial reconnaissance to Egypt also included an Australian Army officer). In addition, Canada contributed a significant proportion (one-sixth) of the force that deployed, including armoured reconnaissance, signals (for command and control), transport squadrons, an infantry (maintenance) workshop, and an air-transport unit (including cargo and short-take-off-and-landing aircraft).[20]

Pearson won the Nobel Peace Prize for his efforts, and his approach to peacekeeping and the use of expeditionary Canadian armed forces in UNEF set a precedent for liberal internationalism. This precedent would be a distinguishing feature of the Canadian experience for the remainder of the Cold War era. Canada's actions brought prestige internationally and economic rewards from the United States. Yet, as Roy Rempel maintains, "it was Canada's military capabilities in the mid-1950s that made the entire operation, and hence Pearson's diplomacy, possible." Similarly, Andrew Cohen notes that Pearson "saw the need for power – a real army – in uncertain times, especially in support of the United Nations." He further observes that "much as Pearson was a Nobel laureate, however, he was no pacifist. He knew the uses of power, the necessity of force, and the rule of international law. He embraced the idea of collective security …"[21]

The crisis marked perhaps the starkest contrast ever in Canadian and Australian foreign policy. Both Canadian and Australian external affairs ministers opposed the Anglo-French invasion of Egypt in 1956. However, Australia, at the time, happened to be on the United Nations Security Council and Australia's anglophile prime minister, Menzies (a personal friend of Eden), strongly supported Britain's position in the Suez Crisis.

Menzies has been harshly criticized for his support of Britain over Suez. But, according to polls, a 61 per cent majority of public opinion was on his side. In the estimation of Australian diplomatic historian W.J. Hudson, Menzies's filial loyalty to Britain "to a significant degree was blind," involving "hazard to other loyalties and interests." Hudson's contrast with the Canadian position is worth noting as well: "In 1956 Ottawa ministers, for example, saw Canada as a British state in terms of origins, values, institutions and Commonwealth membership but did not feel constrained on that account to rally to a United Kingdom which, in their view, was pursuing foolish policies. Australian ministers, on the other hand ... accepted that they were not just a British state in the Canadian sense but a British state junior to the United Kingdom." Yet Menzies also saw Egyptian nationalization of the Suez Canal, which led to the crisis, as a threat to Australian national interests, particularly because a major portion of Australia's trade passed through the canal. In a sense, the Suez Canal had a significance for Australia not unlike that of the St Lawrence Seaway for Canada. It was the route through which most of Australia's international seaborne trade passed. In addition, as Wayne Reynolds contends, "the Suez crisis occurred when Maralinga and the Joint Project was about to enter the place in which nuclear deterrent weapons would be deployed. It was, moreover, a great test for empire defence, at least that was the view in Canberra."[22] Menzies also could see that failure to support Britain at this juncture would only further undermine Britain's ability and willingness to contribute thereafter to stability and security in southeast Asia. This was a matter of concern because the Malayan "Emergency" was ongoing and defence and security ties with Britain remained important for Australia, covering parts of the country's near north which United States security commitments explicitly did not cover. These long-term ramifications of wounding Britain over the Suez Crisis were not fully appreciated even by the sharply anti-colonial Eisenhower administration, particularly in terms of the Cold War balance of power and the future stability of the Middle East, let alone southeast Asia – where a few years later the United States would be looking for assistance (particularly from the British and French whom it had earlier spurned) to support its actions in Indochina.

In essence, then, Canada differentiated itself from Australia during the Suez Crisis because it believed that it could afford to do so. Despite the views expressed by Hudson, Australia, under Menzies, was not blindly following Britain's lead. Indeed, in the Suez Crisis, Australia had real interests at stake, whereas Canada did not. Canada was therefore free to take the moral high ground with no sacrifice involved.

There is considerable irony in the fact that Canada acted as the surrogate for the United States in Suez while it received the kudos for its distinctive and innovative approach to problem-solving through peacekeeping. Arguably, also, the Suez Crisis provides an instance when the "cousins" failed to appreciate fully each other's national interests and the enlightened self-interest that they all shared in a stable and peaceful order in the Middle East that was pro-West or at least not anti-West.[23] Thereafter, Australia was considered unable to contribute to UNEF because it was not seen as an "honest broker." But Canada found itself having to spend additional money to retain forces stationed in Suez for more than a decade as a consequence of having contributed to the undermining of Britain's position. And so, in the end, Canada contributed to a peacekeeping venture without comprehending its full ramifications for the broader shared interests of "the cousinhood" and the West in general. It could even be said that Pearson's Nobel Peace Prize was a pyrrhic victory since Canada's broader self-interest was not served by having Britain and France humiliated and weakened at the height of the Cold War and the Middle East radicalized.

The Suez Crisis had presented the Western alliance with a significant challenge to its *raison d'être*, as key allies were pitted against one another, leaving scope for the Soviets to suppress the 1956 uprising in Hungary uninterrupted by united opposition from the West. Clearly, the United States had an interest in quickly resolving its differences with its key NATO allies. The ending of the British-Australian Joint Project at Maralinga would be one of the consequences of the British-American rapprochement following the summit held at Bermuda in March 1957. Afterwards, the United States resurrected the wartime atomic relationship, agreeing to share nuclear technology with Britain, but to the exclusion of Australia. As compensation, British Defence Minister Duncan Sandys promised essentially what had been promised before the war, except, instead of a fleet of battleships being sent in an emergency, V bombers carrying atomic bombs would be dispatched to Singapore if the need arose. But even this promise had to be jettisoned after Britain's military withdrawal from "East of Suez" a decade later.[24]

Following the Bermuda summit, Australia, like Canada, was prepared to rely on the U.S. nuclear deterrent and decided not to pursue the development of an independent nuclear-weapons program. It took this decision even though, again like Canada, it had substantial natural deposits of uranium and a sufficiently sophisticated industry to develop nuclear-weapons capabilities on its own, a route taken by, for instance, France.[25] The United States would later engage Australia with a series of other intelligence and military-support arrangements that paralleled those made with Canada.

These included agreements on the North West Cape communications station in 1963, the National Aeronautics and Space Administration (NASA)
tracking station at Tidbinbilla, near Canberra, in 1965, and the satellite- intelligence facilities at Pine Gap in 1966 and Nurrungar in 1969. Australian
defence-policy academic Desmond Ball argues that these arrangements
became the "strategic essence" of the ties between the United States and
Australia. As with Canada, such arrangements helped ensure that Australia
also was valued for its real estate and remained within the U.S. security orbit.[26] But at times Canada and Australia were uncomfortable with where
this led. For instance, in a speech in 1954, the U.S. secretary of state, John
Foster Dulles, had responded to the apparent Soviet efforts at encirclement
and strangulation with a strategy of "massive retaliation." This strategy
depended primarily upon a great capacity "to retaliate, instantly, by means
and at places of our own choosing." Allies like the Canadians had no
forewarning of or prior consultation concerning the new policy, leaving senior officials shocked.[27] Such developments pointed to the benefits of
fostering other international fora to protect and further Canadian and
Australian interests.

PEACEKEEPING, SECURITY OBLIGATIONS, AND REORGANIZATION

Several years later, in May 1967, the mission in Egypt would be abruptly
cut short when Egyptian President Nasser ordered the withdrawal of the
United Nations force from the Suez. Nasser's actions demonstrated that
prolonged deployments are no guarantee of conflict resolution. Nonetheless, from 1956 on, involvement in UN peacekeeping missions became a
major part of the Canadian identity, while also helping to "fight" the Cold
War by "other means." Canadian deployments were usually to strategically
significant places and continued to complement the efforts of others to
contain Soviet expansion.[28] In addition, unlike their unilingual English-
speaking Australian equivalents, French-speaking Canadian troops were
well suited to peacekeeping missions in francophone countries like the
Congo, one of the world's few sources of nuclear-grade uranium – and
hence of strategic significance in terms of the Cold War balance of power.
Ironically, though, in the Congo "peacekeeping" would come to look remarkably similar to counter-insurgency operations, which were more familiar to Australians. For instance, in the Congo, the United Nations
"observers" (UNOC) resorted to offensive ground operations supported by
bombers and fighter aircraft. Yet, at the same time, such missions (listed in

appendix 4) were portrayed as a form of *idealpolitik* that distinguished Canada from its neighbour to the south without undermining the European and North American defence roles. After four years, the UN forces in Congo withdrew, having restored a semblance of law and order and at least temporarily forestalling the country's disintegration. By 1965, the United States had replaced Belgium as the dominant foreign power in the Congo. Reflecting the difficulty of the mission in the Congo, the ONUC has been described as the United Nations' Vietnam. Still, from the Canadian perspective, the involvement of the UN in the Congo "was unquestionably right and perhaps inevitable" because, it was thought, the crisis had the potential to boil over into a major conflict.[29]

In contrast to the complex and bloody troubles in the Congo, UN peacekeeping missions usually involved modest-sized contingents that faced little risk of significant numbers of casualties and often were deployed for relatively short periods (frequently only a few months). Canada's deployment of interpositional peacekeeping troops to Cyprus (alongside Australian police contingents) for over thirty years of generally predictable deployments is the most noticeable exception, although other missions also involved long-term commitments, frequently alongside Australians as well.[30] In Cyprus, Canada's contribution in support of the West was notable and Canada's actions were appreciated by the administration of United States President Lyndon Johnson.[31] (Cyprus was a strategically important Cold War nuclear-bomber base in the 1950s and 1960s.) Louis Delvoie contends that Canada's peacekeeping commitments had policy rationales "firmly grounded in Canada's national security and policy interests" – particularly until the end of the Cold War. Peacekeeping, he says, provided Canada with the means to practise leadership at the international level while gaining world-wide esteem. In addition, Delvoie argues, peacekeeping helped preserve Canada from the effects of a global thermonuclear war that might have arisen from the escalation of regional conflicts. It also helped maintain the integrity of NATO.[32] In Cyprus, for example, Canada's contribution forestalled Soviet efforts to build closer Turkish links and helped contain tensions between two NATO partners, Greece and Turkey. Similarly, Denis Stairs believes that Canada's contribution helped "NATO and the Americans out of a jam in Cyprus." In several instances, such deployments were made largely using Canadian sealift, including the aircraft carrier HMCS *Bonaventure* – at least until it was decommissioned in 1970.[33]

Peacekeeping missions also served as a handy justification for budget cutbacks and reductions in force size and capabilities. Furthermore, they were a convenient way to ensure that – while containing military expenditure –

Canada's forces operated as an extension of policy by other means in order to help retain "a seat at the table." The dictum appears to have been: "maximum political return for minimal military investment."[34] As Sokolsky maintains, "while Canadians often viewed peacekeeping as a neutral activity in the context of the dominant East-West struggle, Washington welcomed and appreciated Canada's participation precisely because Ottawa was a loyal Western ally." Clearly then, Canada was not neutral.[35]

Granatstein observes that peacekeeping became the sine qua non of Canadian nationalism. "Peacekeeping was so popular," he argues, "because it was useful, to be sure, but primarily because it was something we could do and the Americans could not."[36] Meanwhile, Canada appeared to have a greater freedom to choose how it structured its forces since planners did not have to face the heavy consequence of error that their American equivalents faced. This liberal and apparently "altruist" approach helped to perpetuate the myth of Canada as the honest broker, yet it was something that its more remote and less self-confident and vulnerable "cousins" "down under" could not readily afford.

Despite this prominence of peacekeeping in the Canadian experience, the common view among members of the Canadian military was encapsulated by a former CDS, who said in 1967: "I do not believe we should ever design our forces for peacekeeping only. We should design forces for war as we know it and then adapt them to the peacekeeping role or any other role that happens to fall to them in line with Canada's National Defence Policy."[37] Such views echoed Australian sentiment, but Canada would find them increasingly difficult to live up to as the Canadian Armed Forces downsized, particularly in the 1970s and 1980s, from an army of 52,000 troops in 1962 to 29,300 by 1978 and only 19,300 by 2002 (see appendix 6) and as peacekeeping operations continued to be one of Canada's major instruments of foreign policy. Compounding Canada's problem was the increased tendency to cannibalize units, that is, making specialist contributions to dispersed peacekeeping operations while leaving units back in Canada without the key capabilities that they needed to function effectively.[38]

Australia refrained from Canada's enthusiastic embrace of peacekeeping missions largely because of its security preoccupations in southeast Asia, but pressures for change were as strongly felt there as in Canada. Particularly after the Bermuda summit in 1957, it became increasingly apparent to Australian defence planners that Australian weapons, equipment, and procedures would have to be standardized with those of the United States. As Australia adjusted to its changed strategic and economic circumstances, its army went through a series of reorganizations from 1957 to 1965. The

1957 reorganization resulted in a regular force of one brigade group that
was immediately available, one battalion group as part of the Far Eastern
Strategic Reserve, and supporting units. In addition, the part-time Citizen
Military Force would consist of three divisions. But the CMF would undergo significant change, with the abolition of the ten-year-old National
Service Training Scheme in 1960 (the same year that Britain abandoned its
National Service scheme). Experimentation began in the same year with the
"Pentropic" organization – which revolved around a pentagonal battalion
and divisional structure ostensibly designed to be air-portable and floatable
for operations in the tropics. The new organization eliminated brigades in
favour of expanded all-arms "task forces" based on five rifle-company infantry battalions. Restructuring both the regular and part-time forces in
this manner served to transform the Australian Army further, from an essentially part-time force or CMF into a regular and more readily employable
force.[39] The model for the Pentropic experiment was the radical U.S. "Pentomic" model – a pentagonal division structure designed for dispersed
"atomic" warfare that was briefly adopted by the U.S. Army.[40] However,
the model did not work, for it pushed military doctrine and organization
beyond what was technically feasible on the battlefield and placed too
much emphasis on increasingly unlikely nuclear tactical scenarios. Developed as a U.S. hybrid force structure, and introduced shortly before the
U.S. Army abandoned its "Pentomic" organization, the Pentropic model
was jettisoned just in time to commit regular ground forces to Vietnam in
1965. The change to smaller battalions would provide a windfall, allowing
the army to raise twice the number of regular infantry battalions.

The period of these reorganizations in Australia marked a strategic re-
alignment with the United States that was reflected in changes to military
structure and equipment (although only to a limited extent with tactics
and doctrine), with occasional forays into the adoption of European ideas
and technology. It also coincided with the decline of the Commonwealth
sterling bloc economic community as Australia's trade diversified and as
Britain sought to adjust to a shift in its trade relations from the Commonwealth to the European Common Market. This alternative had been made
stark by French President de Gaulle, who was adamant that Britain must
abandon the Commonwealth in order to enter the European Economic
Community. By 1966, Commonwealth economic ties were effectively cut as
Australia entered the dollar bloc.[41]

During these years, Canadian defence expenditure was declining but
Australia's increased, particularly as a result of concerns over a volatile
Indonesia and the Vietnam War. The rise in Australian defence expenditure,

however, was from a base much lower than that of Canada in the early 1960s. Even at the height of the Vietnam War, Australia would spend only u.s.$1,294 million on defence compared to Canada's u.s.$1,763 million.[42]

With financial constraints and competing pressures, cuts had to be made somewhere. One area where the Australian Army felt that it could make savings was with its part-time force, the CMF. Through the Pentropic reorganization, a major cutback of CMF strength was put into effect. This had a debilitating effect on the CMF, with only seventeen infantry battalions out of thirty-one left unscathed by the reorganization in 1960.[43] As mentioned earlier, the crippling effect of this change was not unlike the effect experienced in Canada when the militia forces were allocated to unpopular national-survival (civil-defence) tasks in 1960. These tasks stripped combat units of war-fighting roles and equipment and, as in Australia, left militia commanders despairing for the future of their forces.[44]

In the meantime, Australia's security relationships, particularly after the political and military eclipse of Britain's Empire at Suez in 1956, left it with little counterweight to its "great and powerful friends." As with Canada's contribution to NATO, which helped to give Canada a European diplomatic balance to the United States in its "North Atlantic Triangle," Australia contributed forces to the British Commonwealth Far Eastern Strategic Reserve (BCFESR) based in Malaya. This contribution was under the auspices of ANZAM – the Australia, New Zealand, and Anglo-Malayan defence agreement of 1948. Through ANZAM, Australia assumed responsibilities on behalf of the Commonwealth that went beyond comparable arrangements in the inter-war years. But this time, Australia assumed its responsibilities as a full strategic partner of Britain.[45]

Its contribution alongside British forces also served to bolster Australia's support for another military organization that was intended to echo the capabilities of NATO but that never lived up to such expectations – the South East Asia Treaty Organization (SEATO), which Australia joined in 1954. Canada sent observers to the preliminary discussions in Washington but opted out of joining the organization, preferring to remain focused on its NATO commitments. However, in reality, most SEATO members contributed little to the alliance, and SEATO quickly became militarily irrelevant, although for a dozen years u.s. officials (as well as Australian and other "Free-World" ones) used this supposed collective-security pact to justify military commitments to Vietnam.[46] Still, Australia saw a benefit in continuing to appear to contribute to SEATO. After all, as Prime Minister Menzies stated, for Australians, if the battle against communism was to be effective, "it must be won as far north of Australia as possible."[47]

Reflecting this disposition, and in addition to the RAAF elements deployed to Butterworth on the Malayan peninsula from 1950, an infantry battalion group and support elements were stationed in Malaya, following the withdrawal of troops from Korea, from 1955 onwards. The RAN also conducted annual visits with frigates and an aircraft carrier. These force elements deployed as part of the BCFESR but there was a deliberate degree of official ambiguity over Australia's intended purpose in stationing such forces in southeast Asia. After Malayan independence in 1957, Australia "associated" itself with the Anglo-Malayan Defence Agreement (AMDA) in 1959.[48] However, even with this different range of commitments, requiring different forces, Australia's military engagement remained significantly smaller than Canada's commitment of forces to NATO and the defence of Western Europe and the Atlantic.

While Australia was preoccupied with its Pentropic experiment and developments in southeast Asia, Canadian ground forces worked together with the BAOR – an organization with a striking resemblance to the BCFESR in Malaysia and Singapore. Yet, with the BAOR in Europe, Canadians, like their British counterparts alongside, saw little immediate imperative to follow the U.S. Pentomic model. Canada's forces had developed specialized roles within the NATO and NORAD contexts, with the navy focusing primarily on anti-submarine warfare, the army on its mechanized battle group in Germany, and the air force on its nuclear-strike, reconnaissance, and air-defence roles. These specialized commitments alongside allies paralleled the arrangements made between the Australian armed services and their British and American counterparts in Asia. In both cases, such arrangements left little scope for either increased flexibility or operational integration of a tri-service interoperable national force focused on the exclusive needs of either Canada or Australia.

Canada's "relatively great influence" with the United States and NATO during the 1950s, according to Jon McLin, was due at least in part to the relatively large size of its military contribution. But this was a temporary factor owing to Europe's war-induced weakness.[49] As Europe revived, and Canada's contributions waned in relative importance, its influence decreased as well, although aspirations remained high. In addition, Canada's territory was of declining importance to the United States following the introduction of intercontinental ballistic missiles in 1957.

The problems caused by waning influence were worsened under the government of Conservative Prime Minister John Diefenbaker. Diefenbaker's poor personal relationship with President John F. Kennedy seems to have reinforced both his suspicion of American intent to "push the Canadians around" and his determination to resist. Diefenbaker's situation was worsened by what Peter Haydon describes as his "singularly insular leadership style," which arose from his distrust of senior civil servants and senior military officers. The Diefenbaker period saw the integration of Canada into NORAD. But it also was marked by a series of defence calamities, including the demise of the indigenously designed and built Avro Arrow jet aircraft,[50] the fiasco over acquisition of Bomarc missiles (designed exclusively for use with nuclear warheads that were not initially acquired with the missiles),[51] and the dysfunctional control of the armed forces during the Cuban Missile Crisis,[52] all of which heightened awareness of the new realities faced by Canada.[53]

On one extreme, the disparity in size and power between Canada and the United States led some to react by calling for Canada to be a "peacemaker" rather than a "powder-monkey" – that is, for Canada to leave NATO and NORAD, reduce military expenditures, and adopt a neutral posture.[54] Such views also reflected one extreme of the internal policy debate between the more hawkish Canadian Defence officials and their External Affairs counterparts – who argued that Canadian acquisition of nuclear weapons would be strategically destabilizing and would damage the nation's international reputation. Despite the expression of these pacifist views, both sides of mainstream Canadian politics saw the inherent dangers of the "peacemaker" approach and rejected it, as evidenced by Canada's enduring commitment to NATO and NORAD beyond the end of the Cold War. Indeed, following the demise of Diefenbaker's Conservative government and the election of Lester B. Pearson as Liberal prime minister in 1963, Pearson quickly ended the controversy over Diefenbaker's incoherent nuclear-weapons policy by reaching an agreement with the United States to acquire the Bomarc nuclear warheads.[55] While these deliberations were under way, the acquisition of nuclear weapons was also considered in Australia. Indeed, Wayne Reynolds argues that the Canberra bomber was purchased with a view to being able to carry atomic bombs and "by 1963 the Menzies government had enough information to allow the purchase of the F-111 on the understanding that it could carry nuclear weapons."[56] The purchase of U.S.-built F-111 aircraft reflected the increased Australian orientation towards American procurement, much like that experienced in Canada, which continued to drive reorganizations in the Australian Armed Forces in the early 1960s.

With Pearson's election, the Canadian Armed Forces also faced reorganization. The new defence minister, Paul Hellyer, saw the need to adjust to the new geo-strategic circumstances, particularly since the Cuban Missile Crisis had shown that a gulf had apparently emerged between the military and their civilian masters. In addition, he was eager to eliminate waste and duplication in the armed forces and improve their ability to operate autonomously, but as a team. With this in mind, he drafted a new White Paper in December 1963 which outlined his philosophy and rationale for the forthcoming unification of the armed forces. Having absorbed a casual remark by General Simonds that Canada needed a kind of "Marine Corps" to meet its needs, Hellyer saw unification as a way to build a Marine Corps-like armed-forces team. Hellyer also wanted to assert civil authority over the squabbling military hierarchy and unification seemed a good vehicle to achieve such a goal. Beyond such rational reasons for reform lay the dynamism and personal ambition of the new minister, who appeared determined to impose his will on the department and to use it as a stepping-stone to higher office.[57]

Still, Hellyer's actions were not *ab initio*. For instance, his predecessor from 1946 to 1954, Brooke Claxton, had introduced a tri-service system of military law and pushed the Department of National Defence towards a unified rank and pay scale.[58] Indeed, during Claxton's tenure, the Royal Commission on Government Organization (or the Glassco commission) had outlined areas for improved administrative efficiency in government, particularly the management of defence matters. Hellyer relied on the Glassco commission's report to strengthen his proposals for unifying the forces.[59] But he wanted greater and faster change too. His dogged determination to force through coldly rational reforms that dismissed concerns about military traditions met with less than complete success and caused significant internal trauma within the Canadian forces. This was in part because of his unwillingness to deviate from his rigid, albeit largely practical and utilitarian, vision of how to unify the forces.

Unification and integration were unique features of the Canadian military experience from the mid-1960s onwards. Bill C-90, passed in 1964, went further than the 1922 and 1946 consolidations of Defence into one department and beyond the creation in 1953 of the position of chairman of the chiefs of staff (a step taken belatedly in Australia in 1958 with the appointment of Lieutenant-General Sir Henry Wells as chairman of the Chiefs of Staff Committee). The new Canadian bill involved integration of the various single-service functions and appointment of a CDS to replace the chairman of the chiefs of staff (a step Australia did not take until 1976 with the appointment of General Sir Francis Hassett as chief of defence force staff – CDFS).[60] Bill C-43, which came into effect in February 1968, unified the Canadian services, replacing the army, the RCAF, and the RCN with land, air, and maritime components of the unified Canadian Armed Forces (now formally renamed the

Canadian Forces [CF]). The terms "army," "navy," and "air force" were not officially sanctioned again in Canada until 1980.[61] But, with financial constraints, widespread opposition, and a single-service focus more on interoperability with the United States than with the other Canadian services, the plan for unification never quite reached Hellyer's grand goals of a fully integrated and effective tri-service team. Indeed, part of the problem was that there was no unified mission for the three services. The closest thing to a unified mission was the responsibility to reinforce Norway in the event of the outbreak of war in Europe, but this plan was untenable since the capabilities required to deploy the force across the Atlantic did not exist in the Canadian forces' inventory. Indeed, Canadian air, sea, and ground forces would continue to operate as discrete force contributions to other allied forces and not as a single Marine Corps-like team.[62]

Still, significant measures were taken, including the merging of the single-service staff colleges into the Canadian Forces Staff Course at Armour Heights, Toronto.[63] But as far as the Canadian Army was concerned, Hellyer's reforms, as Granatstein notes, may have speeded up the Americanization process "by dealing a killing blow to the Army's system of corps and its distinctive and much-loved uniforms buttons and badges. The Army had been the least Americanized of the forces by the mid 1960s, proud of its regiments and traditions. The dark green uniform that came with unification homogenized the Canadian military and weakened the land forces' psychological defences against Americanization." According to the New York *Times*, "nearly all experts agree that the changes reflect Canada's continuing search for a national identity and her attempt to adjust old loyalties and traditions to a modern frame."[64]

There appeared little enthusiasm for other countries to follow suit, although at least nine countries set up military study groups to observe the Canadian experiment and receive briefings on the workings of unification. Britain and New Zealand specifically rejected it. Australia reviewed it, including in the *Australian Army Journal*, but was similarly critical – although recognizing the merits of closely watching the Canadian experience. As one Australian bureaucrat commissioned to study the Canadian experiment observed, "unification is not an optimal solution for a number of reasons. The solution to a proper grasp of combined operations lies not in unification but in strengthening the concept of a joint staff; derived from the service experts, but owing some higher allegiance to a common cause."[65] Indeed, this Australian position is one that Canada has come to embrace after nearly forty years of unification.[66]

Conscious of the trauma generated by the Canadian approach, Australia followed a much slower route towards unification, or "jointery," of the services.[67] Australian efforts at more closely integrating the armed services also were held back early on after the Second World War by Sir Frederick Shedden, who objected to a dilution of his power at the hands of a prospective commander-in-chief of the three services. Horner notes that "Shedden wanted to preserve the authority of his position," but, by focusing on maintaining centralized control, "he overlooked the need for someone to command joint operations." Despite the experience of the Second World War, Horner comments, "for the next 30 years the Services gave little attention to joint operations." In the Korean War, the Malayan "Emergency," the confrontation with Indonesia, and the Vietnam War, Australian army, navy, and air force units tended to serve alongside those of allied services rather than as part of a joint Australian force.[68]

In 1964, for instance, Australian troops in Malaysia were used against Indonesian paratroop and seaborne raiders. Then, in 1965, Australia committed forces to support British and Malaysian efforts aimed at preventing cross-border raids from Indonesian Borneo. Australians easily integrated with British and other Commonwealth forces (Malaysians and New Zealanders), although in other respects the Commonwealth was becoming more unwieldy as former colonies gained independence and swelled the ranks of member nations. In the meantime, Canadians, according to John Holmes, were "immaculate and fastidious about our peacekeeping. We could not consider helping our Malaysian brethren resist aggression from Sukarno because it was not a UN operation. The blunt fact, of course, was that anything that could, however distortedly, be called a defence of empire would raise all kinds of local hornets."[69] Australian infantry, artillery, engineers, and communications teams contributed to the combined efforts aimed at containing Indonesian incursions. In addition, Australia's special forces unit, the Special Air Service Regiment (SASR), gained a reputation for stealth and skill on a par with that of the best special-forces soldiers in the world.[70] In contrast, Canada's armed forces were not designed for limited war, the focus being instead on nuclear war, which, arguably, nobody really expected to fight. For Canada, this less likely but potentially more dangerous nuclear-warfare contingency was preferable to preparing for the more likely and therefore more dangerous contingency, in practice, of limited war as experienced by Canada's partners in southeast Asia.

THE VIETNAM WAR

Australia's military commitment to Vietnam had commenced in 1962 with the dispatch of thirty (later up to 100) military advisers with the Australian Army Training Team Vietnam.[71] The United States had eagerly courted

Australian support in Vietnam, particularly because, after the Korean War, the United Nations had become increasingly unresponsive to its overtures. The 51 original UN member states had grown to 114 by 1965, and the United States thus could no longer assume support from a majority of the UN General Assembly. Consequently, the support of close allies like Australia, outside the United Nations, was of increased significance.[72]

Underlying Australia's commitment to Vietnam was an ongoing concern over its apparent strategic vulnerability, particularly as Britain's regional influence was waning and the United States seemed prepared to ignore Australia's perceived security needs. The sense of Australian isolation that these developments generated was made acute by the United States decision to bow to Indonesian pressure for territorial expansion in West New Guinea (later renamed Irian-Jaya) in 1963, after Australian diplomatic action to the contrary through the 1950s.[73] Australian concerns, from the Washington perspective, were trivial; the Indonesian nationalist movement appeared non-communist in character and the United States remained eager to avoid politically destabilizing the regime in a way that would give the powerful Indonesian communist forces the upper hand. In addition, Indonesians produced commodities necessary to American industry. The sum of these factors made Australian officials realize that Australia had little leverage in Washington on matters it considered to be strategically important, notwithstanding the closer relations with the United States evinced by the non-nuclear Mutual Weapons Development Agreement signed in 1960.[74]

This concern over the region to Australia's immediate north was made all the more acute because it was apparent that Australian diplomatic weakness had been the consequence of military weakness – a state of affairs that Menzies had helped create. But Menzies at least recognized this and saw the need to align Australia more closely with the United States to circumvent the kinds of problems that had emerged.[75] Reflecting the high priority that foreign and defence policy now attached to securing a U.S. commitment to local defence, Australia, in addition to contributing troops to fight alongside British forces in Borneo and Malaya, purchased frigates from the United States and committed an RAAF fighter squadron (with F-86 Sabres – common to the RAAF and RCAF aircraft inventories at the time) to serve alongside U.S. forces in the defence of Thailand, which it did from 1962 to 1968. Menzies also agreed to commit combat troops to fight with the United States, for the first time without Britain alongside, in Vietnam, a commitment that endured from 1965 until 1972.[76] The reasoning, according to Barclay, "was that it might not be true that Australia was at all times and under all circumstances more important to the

United States than Indonesia. But it was undoubtedly more important so long as Vietnam was a matter of concern for Washington."[77]

This move in support of U.S. forces in Vietnam, followed by the ending of the period of confrontation with Indonesia after the fall of President Achmad Sukarno in 1966, allayed Australia's sense of insecurity. Yet, despite this ease in security concerns, for the first time the government implemented conscription for overseas service – and for the benefit of the regular forces instead of the CMF. It felt confident in doing so, for, at the time, a majority of Australians supported the government's commitment of combat forces to Vietnam.[78] As Millar observes, "in Vietnam, Australia paid its overseas premiums to the American insurance policy. Some Australians disagreed on the premiums; few disagreed on the policy."[79] Such security challenges for Australia contrasted with Canada's more secure position at the side of the United States, which allowed it to focus instead on its NATO commitments and peacekeeping.

Beyond sending monitors for the ICSC, Canadians had no direct role in the Vietnam War other than supplying individual volunteers (who crossed the border to join the U.S. forces) and items such as green berets and napalm components. Canadian Prime Minister Lester Pearson visited the United States in 1965 and criticized its involvement in Vietnam. Meanwhile, Canadian peace organizations denounced U.S. policy on Vietnam, remained largely silent over the 1968 Soviet suppression of Czech democracy, and welcomed Vietnam War draft dodgers by the thousands. As Desmond Morton puts it, "no one trying to understand defence policy in Canada can ignore the organizing potential of a peace movement based on innocence, righteousness and Canada's remarkably long immunity from danger." While many Australians share Canadians' sense of righteousness, few identify with their feeling of immunity from security threats. As the Canadian diplomat John Holmes observed in 1969, "we have suffered for our independence, if not drastically. The official relationship [with the United States] has lost, for the present at least, the intimacy of close allies. We are less likely to be listened to than the Australians. These are consequences to be expected. They are bearable. Washington could turn nastier if our spokesmen became more critical. Whether we would be penalised economically is doubtful as long as the United States, being at war, needs our resources and products."[80] Holmes's remarks would have an uncanny echo during the period of the war in Iraq commencing in 2003.

In contrast to Canada, counter-insurgency operations, rather than peacekeeping, would remain the focus for the Australian Army for the subsequent decade. But Australians found U.S. military tactics in Vietnam to be inappropriate for them. Initially, in 1965, Australia committed an infantry battalion to fight alongside the 173rd U.S. Airborne Brigade in Bien Hoa province, just to the northeast of Saigon. The experience of working closely with U.S. forces disturbed Australian commanders, particularly with the American emphasis on "pile on" tactics that committed additional troops and equipment to those units in contact in order to ensure firepower superiority and enemy attrition.[81] In fact, firepower became the dominant characteristic of American operations. Manoeuvre was used primarily for locating and fixing the enemy, but even American officers conceded that this approach was "noisy, clumsy, awkward, and slow to catch the wary, elusive guerrilla."[82]

While impressed with American equipment and massive firepower, the Australians were concerned to reduce casualties and more effectively implement their British-influenced tactics of stealthy jungle patrols, frugal use of forces, and ambushing. By 1966, Australia had increased its deployed force to a combined-arms infantry brigade, in addition to its air and naval contributions. The dispatch of the self-supported brigade-group-sized "1st Australian Task Force" allowed the Australians to operate largely independently of U.S. forces, in Phuoc Tuy province, southeast of Bien Hoa and adjacent to the port city of Vung Tau.[83] Admittedly, the diplomatic effect of Australia's force contribution was partly muted by the far larger contribution of Korean forces (two army divisions and a Korean marine brigade) that coincided with the arrival of the Australians, but the deployment was popular with Australian voters. Barclay notes that Menzies's successor as prime minister, Harold Holt, "for his part could not doubt that he had a mandate for intervention in Vietnam."[84]

Eventually, despite the disbelief of many infantry officers in the operational efficiency and reliability of tanks in such terrain and climatic conditions, Australian-owned Centurion tanks (like those in the Canadian Army's inventory) would be deployed early in 1968 to work alongside the M113 armoured personnel carriers. There, the tanks would quickly gain the confidence of the infantry. Incidentally, the introduction of Centurions led to a drastic reduction in Australian casualties, much as the introduction of tanks had done in the jungles of New Guinea in the Second World War.[85] Michael Evans claims that the most important impact of Vietnam on Australian military doctrine "was the influence of combined arms warfare through the use of helicopters, close air support, artillery fire and armour."[86] But the use of tanks in "penny-packets" distributed to provide direct fire support to dismounted infantry proved equally significant for developing the Australian emphasis on individual initiative and soldier skills at the tactical level. The closest the Canadians came to this kind of combined-arms experience was on exercise with NATO forces on the plains of Germany. But there the emphasis was not so much on individual soldier skills and initiative as on the cohesive teamwork of the battle group in support of a massive defensive scheme against the Soviet threat.

Throughout the rest of the Vietnam War, Australian Army units would still continue to work with U.S. units, as did their navy and air force counterparts, with limited Australian interservice collaboration – once again, much like their Canadian counterparts in Europe and the North Atlantic. For the RAN, this meant carrying out naval-gunfire support and carrier-escort operations with the U.S. Seventh Fleet in the South China Sea and the Tonkin Gulf. For the RAAF, it included stationing Canberra bombers in Da Nang and "Huey" helicopters with the Army's 1st Australian Task Force, and using fixed-wing transport aircraft to conduct flights within Vietnam (the Canadian-built CC08 Caribou) and to and from Australia (the C130 Hercules). More than 50,000 Australians would serve in Vietnam and the army's peak contribution would be 8,300 soldiers in 1968. The experiences of the individual armed services helped foster robust and seasoned forces, including, in Australia's case, a well-honed special-forces capability.[87] However, for Australia and Canada (despite Canada's efforts towards integration), the lack of common joint (or interservice) experience also had the effect of delaying improvements in army-navy-air force cooperation and in the institutions that provided national-level military command and control. At the same time, the pervasive American influence on the Australian forces in Vietnam gradually transformed them from a predominantly British-influenced to a more hybrid structure, in a way similar to the experience of their Canadian "cousins" operating in NATO. The armed forces of Australia, like Canada's, were progressively gravitating to the United States. But in doing so they still remained part of the Anglo-Saxon family, although with the United States in effect acting as the lead "cousin."

BEYOND VIETNAM

While the 1st Australian Task Force was deployed as an all-arms independent brigade group on operations in Vietnam, the 4th Canadian Mechanized Brigade Group in Germany was developing into what was considered to be a "light division" of 6,700 troops – a number not dissimilar to the Australian Army's contribution to Vietnam. The Canadians also would work much more closely with their American counterparts, particularly once the Brigade Group relocated to Lahr in southern Germany in the mid-1970s. The move to Lahr also had the advantage of enabling the Canadians to work more closely with their German counterparts. But, whereas in northern Germany the Canadians compared themselves to the BAOR, in Lahr, they were working with elements of the U.S. Army that were suffering from the neglect and negative side-effects of the Vietnam War.[88] Also, while Canadians and Germans tended to adhere to NATO standardization agreements, the Canadians, like the Australians in Vietnam, found Americans replete with procedural and terminological peculiarities that they had not experienced with either the British or the Germans.[89]

By 1967, Britain had announced plans to withdraw its forces from Malaysia and Singapore, as well as from the remainder of its bases "East of Suez." Half of Britain's forces left by 1971 and the remainder left between 1973 and 1976. In the wake of this withdrawal, Britain, along with Australia and New Zealand, joined the Five Power Defence Arrangement (FPDA) in 1971, marking a permanent commitment to the defence of Malaysia and Singapore.[90] The forces of the three external powers formed a single combined force known as ANZUK, with naval, air, and ground components initially including an infantry battalion each from Britain, Australia, and New Zealand. The arrangement of permanently deployed ground forces would be short-lived, however, with Britain and Australia withdrawing their troops in 1973 (the New Zealand battalion would remain until the mid-1980s). Yet, as Millar states, "the change in the Anglo-Australian relationship is probably most noticeable in the pattern of trade." In 1948–49 Britain supplied 50 per cent (by value) of Australia's imports. But, by 1966–67, Japan had become Australia's biggest customer; British imports were down to 22 per cent by 1969–70 and the percentage continued to fall during the 1970s.[91] The reduced British presence that these figures represent left Australia without the equivalent of Canada's North Atlantic Triangle to complement its diplomatic manoeuvrings.

Also of concern to Australia was a parallel reduction in the U.S. will to remain engaged in southeast Asia. While Australia still had forces committed to the fight in Vietnam, in 1969 President Nixon enunciated his Guam Doctrine – stressing that the nations of the southeast Asian region should not assume automatic U.S. military support. Subsequently, Australian troop reductions matched those of U.S. forces in Vietnam, with the last Australian combat unit departing by the end of 1972. In 1973 the Australian government, under the newly elected Australian Labor Party prime minister, Gough Whitlam, took matters further. Uncomfortable with the apparently imperialist overtones of Australia's forward-deployed troops,

Whitlam ordered the withdrawal of permanently stationed Australian troops from Singapore and effectively abandoned the "forward defence" strategy.[92] Ironically, the reduction in Australia's military footprint (and hence also its public profile) in Asia occurred as the Australian government worked to increase trade with east Asia. Indeed, there was a view in government circles that Australian attitudes and policies prior to this juncture had alienated its Asian neighbours – despite the fact that the non-communist states in southeast Asia welcomed Australia's policy of forward defence. After all, as David Martin Jones observes, "these new states, born without the means of defending themselves, were profoundly insecure."[93] The effect of the Australian force reductions in southeast Asia would be much like the Canadian force reductions in Germany, which lowered Canada's profile and influence in Europe and threatened its European trade relations.[94]

The Whitlam government's approach was to strive towards a more independent Australian stance in international affairs and steer clear of a blind allegiance to the American alliance, emphasizing increased self-reliance instead. When it came to the United States facilities at Pine Gap and Nurrungar, for instance, Whitlam declared that Australia would honour existing obligations but did not favour the extension or prolongation of any of the existing ones. Whitlam's defence minister, Lance Barnard, would oversee the renegotiations to grant greater Australian access.[95] In addition, the Whitlam government developed a voting pattern in the United Nations that more closely resembled that of non-aligned countries and the "Third World," as well as of Canada under the prime ministership of Pierre Trudeau (discussed below).

Incidentally, it was in Whitlam's last year in office (1975) that a composite contingent of 150 soldiers from Australia's 3rd Task Force in Townsville conducted a six-week exchange exercise in Canada. The exercise was entitled WINTER SUN for the Australians and SUMMER HAZE for the Calgary-based soldiers from the 1st Battalion Princess Patricia's Canadian Light Infantry (1PPCLI), who deployed to Townsville in their place. For the Australians, the training included activities that would become more prominent in Australian Army exercises in the early 1990s, including tasks associated with aid to the civil power, such as establishing roadblocks and checkpoints, conducting vehicle searches, and riot control. Many of the instructors were French Canadians from the Canadian Airborne, but "the linguistic barrier did not prevent a very close bond from developing between the diggers and the French Canadians." Indeed, as the contingent commander said, "the most rewarding part of the visit to Canada was to discover how much there is between Australians and Canadians, and the relative positions both politically and geographically that each country holds ... The contingent was overwhelmed by the warmth of hospitality given by Canadians both civilian and military. There was no requirement to work to establish the relationship, it seemed as though the relationship already existed."[96] The ease of working together reflected on many of the common bonds referred to earlier. But few in the senior defence bureaucracy appreciated the merits of continuing such exchanges on a regular basis, particularly since the emphasis for defence planning increasingly revolved around the continental defence of Australia.

Even though Whitlam remained in office only until 1975, his strategic shift of defence priorities to self-reliance with a continental focus was set out in a 1976 Defence White Paper and would endure until the mid-1990s – although the Malcolm Fraser government would repudiate many of the diplomatic positions taken by its predecessor.[97] The emphasis on continental defence was a convenient response to the fact that, while uncertainties in the international environment were evident, no clear immediate threat to Australia could be identified. As part of the post-Vietnam experience, the Australian Army's regular forces shrank considerably, leaving six regular infantry battalions in three brigades, instead of the nine battalions required to maintain the Vietnam commitment. Still, the Soviets' overtures to gain access to island states in the South Pacific in 1976 and their agreement with Vietnam to have access to the former u.s. naval facility at Cam Ranh Bay provided the Australian government with an incentive to remain on good terms with its American allies – despite the hands-off approach followed by the United States since the enunciation of Nixon's Guam Doctrine.[98]

The post-Vietnam Australian policy reorientation echoed developments in Canada a few years earlier and matched that country's greater emphasis on aid to the civil power and domestic defence. The Canadian prime minister, Pierre Trudeau, who had come to office in 1968, strove to move Canadian foreign policy in a more autonomous and un-military direction. Trudeau's vision was of defence policy being driven by foreign policy, and not the other way around. With this in mind, his government issued a series of booklets partly in response to the Nixon Guam Doctrine entitled *Foreign Policy for Canadians* in 1970.[99] These booklets, which omitted discussion of Canada's relations with the United States, were followed in 1972 by the proposal of a "Third Option," which consisted of refocusing Canada's trade and international ties beyond North America in order to counterbalance predominant American influence. The intention was not to detract from u.s. trade but to expand trade elsewhere, thus making Canada less dependent on the United States. Despite the Third Option's political appeal in Ottawa, private industry did not see its value and indeed deemed it to be part of a larger industrial policy characterized by government intrusiveness.

Trudeau's outlook reflected in part a reduced confidence in U.S.-led military solutions as a consequence of the Vietnam War, a sentiment that was also shared south of the border by, among others, the 50,000 to 125,000 Americans (estimates vary) who moved north to avoid the draft. But there were other factors at work too. This period was also marked by the Nixon administration's announcement of the end of the so-called "special relationship" between Canada and the United States and its decision at about the same time to apply an interest surcharge on Canadian imports, which previously had been exempted (the surcharge was subsequently withdrawn). Trudeau's approach, then, was thus partly in reaction to the U.S.'s apparent retraction of trade and security guarantees for Canada. Thereafter, at least until the election of the Conservative government of Brian Mulroney in 1984, the concept of partnership enshrined at Hyde Park in 1941 and enlivened both by military cooperation and by the post-war foreign investment boom was no longer accepted unquestioningly. In addition, Trudeau's reconsideration of the traditional bases of Canadian foreign policy sprang from a strident new Canadian nationalism that demanded government action to stop the Americanization of Canada, while also reflecting the disenchantment with peacekeeping that became evident in Canada following the hasty evacuation of UNEF from the Sinai in 1967.[100]

On the latter score, David Last notes that "peacekeeping divorced from conflict resolution can be a dead end of pointless police actions in the end, an irritant."[101] Canada's unease with peacekeeping bore a striking resemblance to that of Australia during the Whitlam government. For instance, under Trudeau's direction in 1969, Canadian forces with NATO in Europe were almost halved, leaving what some have described as only a "token" presence in Europe, with a regional "reserve" role. Moreover, protection of the sovereignty of Canada's north was made the first defence priority – a task primarily assigned to the air and maritime elements. This isolationist or introspective tendency left little scope for the land forces' priorities.[102] As one writer states, the Trudeau government appeared to be acting on the premise that force readiness was a potential drawback. Thus, it was convenient to find ways to buy time to think or to have an excuse for not being able to provide troops to a United States looking for "more flags" for a future Vietnam.[103] Trudeau's attitude of giving moral equivalence to the United States and the Soviet Union left American political leaders resentful, dismissing him as a "leftist high on pot." As Canadian historian John

English maintains, Trudeau "enjoyed tweaking the eagle's beak" (not unlike his Australian political fellow traveller, Gough Whitlam) but would come to experience the difficulties of not being able to move beyond "the range of the eagle's talons."[104]

The peacekeeping difficulties of Canadian troops were compounded by numerous factors, including the growing malaise arising from budget and manpower cutbacks, careerism exacerbated by an arbitrarily administered policy of bilingualism, and a sense of political neglect and interference that is associated with the years of Trudeau's prime ministership, from 1968 to 1984. Indeed, Trudeau had little time for peacekeeping, seeing it as Pearsonian "do-goodism." Yet, paradoxically, Sean Maloney argues that the Trudeau government's "attempt to develop a post-colonial identity warmly embraced anti-militarism and it set about creating the myth that Canadians are morally superior to other people because they are peacemakers, not warfighters." In effect, this approach involved replacing the militia myth (which emphasized the intrinsic fighting qualities of the part-time soldiers) with the peacekeeping myth. Not surprisingly, the changeover still provided the government with a way to have defence on the cheap.[105] The peacekeeping mythology that stretched back to 1956 and beyond had become a central feature in Canadian public consciousness of its military, despite that military's record in two world wars and Korea.[106] In addition, the emphasis on peacekeeping was at odds with Australian defence doctrine and indicated to Australians that there was little utility in more closely considering the Canadian experience.

REVIEW AND REORGANIZATION

While the Trudeau administration was de-emphasizing NATO ties, Trudeau's defence minister, Donald S. Macdonald, instigated a Management Review Group (MRG) in 1971. Doug Bland argues that the MRG began as an attempt to redirect Defence Department decision making so as to free the minister from seeming dependence upon military advice.[107] After all, the MRG's findings commented unfavourably on "the development of adversary relationships and the compartmentalization in the various divisions of the headquarters of the Department of National Defence." The reorganization that followed in 1972 involved the integration of the civilian and military parts of the headquarters to form a single organization. Later, in 1974, in response to the MRG's recommendation that the civilian character of the Defence Department be enhanced, the deputy minister and the CDS became equals at the head of a "defence team" in National Defence Headquarters

(NDHQ) that included uniformed and civilian employees.[108] This change was similar to the reorganization that took place in Australia following the Tange Review (discussed below). Ironically, the cutbacks associated with the MRG and the force reductions in Europe also made Canada much more dependent on the American security umbrella, both nuclear and conventional. Charles Doran argues that "as a consequence of these changes in military defense, Canada experienced a decline in importance as a world power, from the security perspective, in about the same period that the United States rose to pre-eminence. The contrast in world roles, in responsibilities during crisis intervals, and in strategic planning was understandably felt deeply in Canada, yet this contrast was to some extent of Canada's own making ... in terms of overall relative national capability, especially in the context of the twentieth century, Canada's position in the world system is in reality far different from what many Canadians have perceived it to be."[109]

Nonetheless, the United States had not really listened to Canada in earlier years either. After all, there is little evidence of U.S. consultation with Canada in the 1950s and 1960s over issues of Cold War grand strategy. Indeed, Canada did contribute more in the 1950s and 1960s militarily, but, without a like-minded and similarly disposed strategic partner (like Australia) to bolster its position, this extra capacity provided little additional influence. Even U.S. foreign-policy literature that covers this period makes little if any reference to significant Pearsonian influence. Arguably, Pearsonian policies are invisible in the U.S. literature because Pearson acted in a manner essentially consistent with American foreign policy, leaving little of contention to draw attention. Even when Pearson chose to speak up, his influence was marginal – such as when, in a 1965 speech at Temple University, he asked for a bombing halt in Vietnam. In contrast to Pearson, Trudeau clearly tried to break out with some independent strategic thought, but, when his policies drifted too far from the "cousinhood's" mainstream, the inconsistencies of such policies developed their own momentum, which brought about another turnaround in Canadian foreign and defence policy – Trudeau's "pirouette."[110] This turnaround preceded a significant armament catch-up for Canada as obsolete and obsolescent equipment was replaced with U.S.-sourced CF-18 aircraft and CP-3 Aurora surveillance aircraft and, in the late 1970s, German-built Leopard I tanks.[111]

As just mentioned, Australia would undergo a review similar to the MRG. This review, conducted by Australia's secretary of the Department of Defence (from 1970 to 1979), Sir Arthur Tange, was completed in November 1973 and led to centralized control of Australian defence matters in the hands of the minister, his senior military adviser (the chairman of the Chiefs of Staff Committee, or, from 1976, the CDFS), and the secretary of the Department of Defence (equivalent to Canada's deputy minister). Under the Tange reorganization, which took effect between 1974 and 1976, service boards were abolished and the service and military functions more closely integrated with several committees established for oversight and co-ordination under a more powerful centralized Department of Defence that absorbed the single-service departments of Army, Navy, and Air. In addition, the title "Australian Defence Force" (ADF) was adopted to describe the three services and to suggest their unity under the CDFS. Australia's experience with high-level defence-machinery reform, according to Australian Lieutenant-Colonel Neil James, "marked a pendulum swing from inadequate inter-service and inter-departmental coordination to overcentralised and narrowly-experienced bureaucratic power ... by effect and perhaps design, the changes actually blocked and delayed the natural evolution towards ... a joint Service structure and culture."[112] James's comments reflect the parallel concerns aired concerning the changes introduced following the Canadian MRG.

Within the Australian Army itself, however, significant reform had taken place following a review completed in 1971 by Major-General F.G. Hassett and the Army Review Committee. Hassett's review led to the creation of functional, as opposed to regional, headquarters by November 1973. For instance, Headquarters Eastern Command in Sydney became Headquarters Field Force Command (later Land Headquarters), Headquarters Southern Command based in Melbourne became Logistics Command, Headquarters 1st Division in Sydney became Training Command, and Headquarters Northern Command in Brisbane became Headquarters 1st Division. This rearrangement preceded the 1974 amalgamation and disbandment of several CMF units and the renaming of the CMF as the Army Reserve following the report on the CMF prepared by Professor T.B. Millar.[113] The Australian Army's internal organizational restructuring in the mid-1970s resembled the Canadian restructuring of a few years earlier, where regional military commands were replaced by functional ones (including field force, training, and logistics commands). These changes were intended to enhance the operational capabilities of both armies, but, with declining defence budgets, significant atrophy in force capabilities ensued in Canada and Australia nonetheless.

The Australian Army had important limitations, but at least it had an operational focus that was intended to make it better prepared for operational commitments, wherever and whenever they might arise. In terms of tactical organizations, the six-battalion, three-brigade configuration determined upon the return from Vietnam in the early 1970s remained the basis for Australia's regular force structure until the mid-1990s. In 1980, however, each brigade (called "task forces" from the time of the Pentropic organization in the mid-1960s until the early 1980s) was given a specialization: 1st Task Force (Brigade) – mobile operations in conjunction with tanks; 3rd Task Force (Brigade) – light-scale air-mobile and air-portable operations; and 6th Task Force (Brigade) – conventional open-country infantry operations. From 1983, the regular forces would also include a battalion of paratroopers for the first time since the Second World War.[114] In contrast, throughout the late 1950s and until the end of the Cold War, Canada maintained its four regular-force army brigades, each with three infantry battalions, a battalion of tanks (first Centurions and then Leopard Mark I tanks, like Australia), and the battalion-sized Canadian Airborne Regiment.

Operational reforms like the ones carried out in Australia in the 1970s proved valuable and enduring and significantly transformed the way the Australian Army functioned. But the higher-level reforms, in both Australia and Canada, had only limited direct impact on the day-to-day running of the individual services and on their ability to conduct expeditionary operations abroad. In Canada's case, the navy's focus remained on the Atlantic, where, as Joel Sokolsky observes, NATO was "the political *raison d'être* of the RCN" – a fact that predisposed the RCN to think in terms of operations far removed from the Canadian homeland but rarely on Canada's west coast, facing the Pacific Ocean.[115] Indeed, virtually all the fleet remained on the Atlantic coast during the Cold War even though there was an equally close Soviet fleet across the Pacific at Vladivostok. In the meantime, in a departure from the focus on the Atlantic and Europe, the RCN participated in the U.S.-Navy's first Pacific Rim naval exercise (RIMPAC) in 1970 near Hawaii, alongside ships from the United States, Britain, and Australia, marking the commencement of Canada's regular participation in this major biennial international naval exercise in the Pacific Ocean. These regular exercises would provide the Australian and Canadian navies with the most substantive opportunities to work together since the Korean War. Following the end of the Cold War, the Canadian fleet would deploy a greater proportion of its ships on the Pacific coast, which thereafter would facilitate even greater involvement in the Asia-Pacific region.[116]

In the same year as the first RIMPAC exercise, the Canadian Armed Forces gained prominence for their handling of potentially explosive aid-to-the-civil-power tasks in Quebec during the so-called October Crisis of 1970.[117] The Canadian forces would later experience a similar challenge at the Oka stand-off with a group of Quebec aboriginal people in 1990, which helped provide impetus to refine NDHQ emergency planning procedures and capabilities.[118] Australia did not face the same degree of internal stress, despite resentment among the Australian aboriginal community. But the ADF was similarly called out for a Commonwealth Heads of Government meeting in the late 1970s, following the bombing of the Hilton Hotel in downtown Sydney.

In Australia, in the years after Vietnam, the focus on continental defence reflected an impulse similar to that experienced in Canada. Although, as Australian defence academic Hugh Smith observed, "it was recognized that while there existed 'substantial grounds for confidence' in American support in the event of a major threat to Australia, the U.S. could be unwilling or unable to act in other circumstances." For Australian Prime Minister (from December 1975 to March 1983) Malcolm Fraser, there would be no "all the way with LBJ," as his conservative predecessor, Harold E. Holt, had declared in 1966. The new mood, according to Glen Barclay, "was one of calculated and pragmatic national self-interest ... as far as possible, free of self-deception, self-delusion." As Fraser's foreign minister, Andrew Peacock, explained, "it is in Australia's interests that the U.S. not withdraw into itself. Indeed we would wish to see them confirm their role in such areas as the Indian Ocean. This is no betrayal of our national independence. It is a matter of our national interest and the security of the Australian people." But the real criticism of the Fraser government, according to Barclay, "was that its thinking was not military-oriented enough. It was doggedly insisting upon its fidelity to the American alliance, while at the same time [not unlike Canada at the time] deliberately reducing its capacity to make the main military effort in its own defence."[119]

The Australian continental approach was the strategic framework that allowed the government to take this hands-off attitude towards international obligations. The continental approach also emphasized northern defence, with a priority on air and maritime assets and a problematical role for ground forces, which would have little to do since the strategy focused on defeating enemy forces before they landed on Australian soil. The policy of self-reliance emerged with the increased prominence of continental defence. This policy sprang from a desire to be largely self-sustaining in a post-Guam Doctrine environment, where future Australian military operations conceivably would occur without U.S. support. The new emphasis had the effect of making interservice integration a higher priority than ever before. As a result, the ADF would emerge with a joint-command structure that bears an uncanny resemblance to Canada's – arguably, it was closer to the Canadian structure than to either the British or American equivalents – but that appears to surpass Canada's in terms of tri-service (that is, joint) capabilities.

Instrumental in this gradual evolution was a series of large scale KANGAROO exercises, starting in 1974, held in remote parts of Australia. In addition to Australian Army units, these exercises often involved traditional friends and allies. In 1976, for instance, the exercise was held in the Coral Sea (off the Queensland coast) and Shoalwater Bay Training Area in central Queensland. It involved 21 RAN ships, about 7,600 Australian Army troops, 58 RAAF aircraft, and elements of the U.S. Army and Marine Corps, the New Zealand Army, and even the Canadian Army. In Canada in the mid-1980s, under the direction of Lieutenant-General Charles Belzile, the commander of Mobile (land forces) Command, the Canadian forces also sought to exercise a field division with all the corps troops that would be required for mobilization. In all, 14,000 troops took part in Exercise "Rendezvous 85" – a six-week combined-arms training exercise.[120] But such costly large-scale field exercises were to be rarely repeated.

PEACEKEEPING'S RESURGENCE

Canadian and Australian involvement in several other international missions reflected a similar foreign- and defence-policy orientation marked by a willingness to contribute to peacekeeping. Missions that involved Canadians and Australians in varying numbers in the late Cold War years included the Multi-National Force and Observers (MFO) and the United Nations Emergency Force II (UNEF II) in Egypt, the United Nations Truce Supervision Organization (UNTSO) in Israel/Palestine and on the Golan Heights, the United Nations Iran-Iraq Military Observer Group (UNIIMOG), and the United Nations Force in Cyprus (UNFICYP). Generally speaking, Canada was more predisposed to contribute to operations in Africa. On one such mission in 1979, the British-led Commonwealth Monitoring Force in Zimbabwe, Canada committed some Buffalo aircraft and crews to transport election monitors. The mission also involved 152 Australians from January to March in 1980, the country's largest peacekeeping force to that time.[121]

With the onset of the Cold War thaw in 1988 and 1989, a peacekeeping mission also was launched in Namibia. There, Australia contributed a specialist contingent of three hundred engineers for the United Nations Transition Assistance Group (UNTAG) in 1989 and 1990. Canada similarly contributed a force of three hundred logisticians and one hundred policemen, as well as the chief of staff, Brigadier-General Mike Jeffery (later a lieutenant-general and chief of land staff from 2001 to 2003). UNTAG would prove to be the precursor of many more peacekeeping missions to follow with the end of the Cold War.[122] Many of these missions included both Australians and Canadians, yet, with little appreciation of the nascent reconvergence, most involved little if any combined Australian-Canadian planning in advance.

For Australia, prior to the end of the Cold War and even into the mid-1990s, such peacekeeping operations had little direct effect on force structures. Priority remained on war-fighting capabilities more attuned to the perceived threats in its region. In the meantime, Canada used its peacekeeping efforts to gain credit on the world stage – by the late 1980s, Canada had 2,300 soldiers on sixteen missions and one in ten of the world's peacekeepers were Canadians[123] – while its forces were being emasculated with reductions in troop strengths and only slow replacement of obsolescent and obsolete equipment. The decline of the forces continued through the 1970s, particularly following the cutbacks in the BAOR in Germany under the Trudeau government, the 1980s, and into the 1990s, to the point that Canada's acclaimed efforts in Egypt in 1956 – which involved the coordinated projection of largely self-reliant air, land, and sea forces – were beyond the capability of the force that would emerge by the end of the Cold War. During the same period, Australian forces continued to specialize in dismounted and jungle warfare – until the end of the Vietnam War at least. From then on, the two forces would start to reconverge to a significant degree, as both countries sought to develop and maintain a mixture of special, light, and mechanized forces.

RETHINKING DEFENCE STRATEGY

Reflecting a "diplomatic departure" from his predecessor's quasi-neutralist foreign and defence policy, the Conservative Canadian government of Brian Mulroney published a Defence White Paper in 1987 in an apparent effort to counter the deterioration of defence capabilities and to bolster Canada's support for NATO and the U.S. alliance.[124] Like its Australian equivalent, *Defence of Australia*, also released in 1987 under Labor Defence Minister Kim Beazley, it described Canada as a maritime nation with security and sovereignty issues in three oceans. The Canadian White Paper also outlined a plan to acquire new submarines, expand the reserve forces to 40,000 troops, and double Canada's NATO's commitment, from one to two mechanized brigades. But, like its Australian equivalent too, it suffered both from unrealistic projected expenditures and from its timing: it appeared shortly before the end of the Cold War – a development that

appeared to remove much of the existing rationale for Canada's maintenance of substantial and professional armed forces. One Canadian academic described the contrast between the 1987 Canadian White Paper
and its outcome as being like "big eyes and empty pockets" – symptomatic of what he described as the "two phases of Conservative defence policy." More damning is the verdict of Nelson Michaud, who argues that
"the 1987 White Paper was simply a matter of bad planning on the part
of engineers who wanted to be perceived as architects." In Australia's
case, the program outlined was predicated on a 3 per cent annual increase
in defence expenditure so as to reach allocation levels of between 2.6 and
3 per cent of GDP. Yet, by 1989, this figure had dropped to 2.3 per cent,
exposing the White Paper's unrealistic projections. It would drop even
lower throughout most of the 1990s. Moreover, for both Australia and
Canada, as David Twolan argues, the white papers were forced to serve
two purposes, a political and a military one, and in each instance it was
the political purpose that came first.[125]

Reflecting the enduring Cold War paradigm, the Canadian land forces
conducted a series of large-scale exercises during the late 1970s and 1980s.
In some of these "rendezvous" exercises, a Canadian battalion group
conducted amphibious operations alongside Alaskan-based U.S. Army brigades and Marines. From 1982 to 1989, the major annual exercises were
held at division or brigade level and were instrumental, according to one
participant, "in preventing the growth of disparate sub-armies (western,
Franco and NATO-oriented)," in helping units eager to fight off the designa-
tion as "peacekeeper," and in maintaining war-fighting skills in between
peacekeeping deployments.[126]

The Australian "continental defence" approach, which had emerged after the Vietnam War, featured motorized or mechanized operations and
peacekeeping, while not allowing peacekeeping to determine force structure. The 1987 Australian White Paper stressed a ground-forces role reliant
on continental task forces for single-scenario, "low-level" contingencies,
supported by RAAF Forward Operating Bases not unlike the Forward Operating Locations in Canada's far north outlined in 1985. For Australia,
this approach forced the army to modify its tactical organizations in order
to be more suitable for operations in remote and harsh conditions. The lack
of an identifiable threat led to the creation of the "core force" concept,
whereby residual capabilities would be retained to fend off "low-level"
military operations. More highly refined intelligence capabilities would, in
theory, enable the ADF to direct its light and mobile but meagre resources
onto specific targets. But the so-called "credible" scenarios of low-level

contingencies were never very credible, and the core force effectively became a hollow one, with most units below strength, inadequately equipped,
and poorly prepared.[127] Much the same was true of the Canadian forces in
the late 1990s and early twenty-first century.

The transformation process also resulted in the further erosion of critical
amphibious and other force-projection capabilities in the Australian Army
and Navy. For instance, in 1982 Australia's last aircraft carrier, HMAS
Melbourne, was decommissioned and sold for scrap, much like its sister
ship, Canada's HMCS *Bonaventure,* had been more than a decade before.
The justification was that the continental defence strategy did not require
such "offensive" capabilities (even though HMAS *Melbourne* had last seen
effective duty as a mobile platform for disaster relief in Darwin in 1974)
and that whatever air cover was required in Australia's immediate environs
could be provided with RAAF land-based aircraft.[128]

This approach reflected the rise to prominence of the "non-offensive defence" school of defence strategy. Championed by such Australian academics as Graeme Cheeseman, it argued that the creation of even a defensive
amphibious force should not be supported because of fears that such forces
might be destabilizing, historical evidence to the contrary. This view contended (by means of a curious logic) that, despite its utility for Australia's
own immediate defence and for prospective humanitarian-assistance operations, the acquisition of equipment such as amphibious vessels that could
conceivably be used to threaten neighbours was escalatory and therefore
dangerous. Yet, as one American exchange officer pointed out, the leaders
of numerous neighbouring states consider Australia an outsider in the region; it therefore "begs the question as to why anyone would consider a
'good neighbour' policy by Australia would sway potential aggressors from
attacking her. Indeed, even one week's review of regional news will show it
is resplendent with Asian Pacific nationalistic leaders verbally attacking the
West and Australia for their policies."[129] This non-offensive approach was
predicated on threats emerging from rationally "deter-able" sources – a
contention that has become increasingly questionable since the onset of the
War on Terror. The acceptance of the "non-offensive defence" school's
flawed rationale by senior defence and government policy makers in the
1980s and early 1990s left Australia with only a limited ability to project
any force beyond its shores.[130]

Still, efforts aimed at reform of Australia's defence organization continued. In 1984 the military component of the Department of Defence was organized as the Headquarters Australian Defence Force (HQADF) under the

command of the retitled chief of the defence force (CDF), General Sir Phillip Bennett, who was ascribed greater powers than his predecessors. These new arrangements were considered to be "an effective response to the changing nature of modern warfare in which joint operations – those involving more than one Service – are now commonplace." Unlike in Canada's unified higher-defence structure, the Australian model retained a diarchy between the departmental secretary and the CDF, both of whom reported to the minister of defence. In 1987 the Australian Parliamentary Joint Committee of Foreign Affairs Defence and Trade had tentatively argued that "a more unified higher defence structure similar to that in Canada offers the possibility of reducing [civil/military tensions] while reducing the overall size of the organisation and making it more efficient and effective. Such a possibility should not be lightly dismissed." Despite the committee's willingness to make such a recommendation, there was little support for replacing the diarchy with another administrative structure which Australian observers considered did not offer any advantage. Indeed, according to Australian defence scholar Allan Sheppard, anecdotal evidence indicated that civil/military divisions in Canada had been exacerbated by that country's unified system.[131]

In 1985 the minister of defence, Kim Beazley, authorized the creation of a joint force headquarters called Maritime Command. Land and Air Commands (formed from the respective Air and Land Headquarters) would follow, as well as the creation of a joint-force headquarters in Darwin titled Northern Command or NORCOM. The establishment of NORCOM would be the prelude to a significant shift in RAAF, army, and RAN assets to the Darwin area in the late 1980s and early 1990s. The army's 1st Brigade relocated to Darwin in 1993. These adjustments had the defence of Australia in mind, with forces prepositioned close to the purported likeliest landing areas in the north of the country and to vital assets that might need protection. But it would not be operations in continental Australia that would test these organizations. Rather, as any student of history could have predicted, the challenge would arise – as it always had in the past – from unexpected developments abroad.[132]

When a crisis arose in Fiji in May 1987, the Australian military response, Operation MORRISDANCE, was a scenario not envisaged in the one-year-old White Paper. The deployment of troops and helicopters on board HMAS *Tobruk* and then on three other RAN ships was intended to facilitate an evacuation of Australian nationals from Fiji.[133] In the end, such an evacuation proved unnecessary, but the operation demonstrated the extent of the ADF's lack of preparedness for crises beyond Australia's shores – despite the obvious geo-strategic and historical indicators of the need for such preparations. A political crisis in Vanuatu the following year saw Australian troops again placed on standby. Initially, Australian defence-policy makers were inclined to consider this incident largely as an aberration that did not have to be factored into defence-structure planning. But, over time, the effect of such experiences, combined with the major KANGAROO exercises, provided added incentive for reform of the operational command-and-control machinery that would facilitate more effective joint command of Australian forces. Operation MORRISDANCE gave still more impetus to this cause by allowing for great interservice cooperation.[134]

Coincidentally, the Fiji crisis occurred in the same year that Canada contemplated a non-combatant evacuation from Haiti in the wake of civil disturbances there. These efforts led Canada's force commanders to find several flaws in the national-crisis management machinery, as well as weaknesses in the ability of Canadian forces to plan and conduct a unilateral joint out-of-area operation.[135] The years ahead would demonstrate the limitations of the defence policies and strategies of both countries.

Even while the focus for Australians remained on continental defence, working with allies remained an important consideration. The KANGAROO series of exercises continued in the late 1980s and early 1990s as the Australian Army grappled with doctrinal concepts involving dispersed operations for continental defence in "low-level" or "escalated low-level" conflict. Working with New Zealand forces in such exercises became problematic because of New Zealand's effective abandonment of the ANZUS alliance in 1986 while Australia remained eager to continue exercising with the Americans. In Exercise KANGAROO 89, for instance, the largest peacetime joint and combined exercise since the Second World War was conducted from July to September 1989. The exercise provided significant opportunity to validate interoperability with U.S. forces – Australia's and Canada's most likely partners on expeditionary operations.[136]

Australia's northern exercises were paralled by the Canadian NEW VIKING series of exercises. These were regular and reserve company and battalion exercises in the high Arctic conducted throughout the mid-1970s and early 1980s, and were followed by the SOVEREIGN VIKING exercises. According to one participant, "the theory was that all operational battalions and regiments would have expertise in Arctic warfare."[137] Despite the divergence in force development and operational-deployment trajectories, the land forces of Canada and Australia would, indeed, continue to follow remarkably parallel paths.

CONCLUSION

By 1989, Canada's and Australia's force structures had changed significantly from those that fought alongside each other in Korea, yet significant similarities remained. For Australian military planners, relations with Britain had remained prominent until the early 1970s, particularly with forces stationed in Malaysia and Singapore. Canada likewise had kept close military ties with Britain until the early 1970s, maintaining mechanized forces in conjunction with the BAOR for a European war. The subsequent move of these forces to southern Germany meant that they became a reserve for American and German forces with which they developed a high degree of interoperability.[138] In addition, the Canadian forces continued to maintain a prominent role for peacekeepers.

The Australian and Canadian approaches to force structure and external security (including deploying forces overseas and relying on great and powerful friends) featured enduring parallels and several important differences. For instance, in both cases, for most of the Cold War period, they largely adhered to short-war, forces-in-being military doctrine. This approach, which corresponded to U.S. military doctrinal preferences, emphasized the need for operationally ready forces rather than the manpower- or industrial-mobilization potential that had been tapped into for the main industrial age wars encountered in the first half of the twentieth century. This meant that the regular forces would have preference for resources over the part-time forces.[139]

The forces of Canada and Australia would, again, become more alike in the years after the Cold War as globalization spawned numerous international collaborative military operations under the United Nations and other auspices. For Australia, this started with the Fiji crisis in 1988 and, shortly afterwards, the deployment of engineers with the United Nations to Namibia in 1989. Prior to that time, the Australian Army had maintained only a limited presence in UN military missions. Such developments were eventually followed by new command-and-control arrangements at the operational level that would be refined throughout the 1990s. These arrangements would involve the three Australian joint "two-star" commands – Maritime, Land, and Air – that were initially designated in 1987.[140]

Canada's greater focus on and much larger commitment to peacekeeping did not generate the same impulse to reform the command-and-control machinery much beyond the bureaucratic readjustments in NDHQ Ottawa. For Canada, the imperatives to be known as a "peacekeeper" had been evident since the 1956 Suez Crisis, but they would fade by the latter years of the

Cold War. For the Australian Army, the reasons to pursue a peacekeeping
métier would emerge only slowly, and were similar in rationale to those in
the Canadian case. But Australia's peacekeeping efforts became pronounced only in the post-Cold War years. Peacekeeping provided an operational outlet for a force with limited government funding. Particularly after
Vietnam, the Australian forces saw peacekeeping as a way to gain operational experience and maintain relevance and professionalism for the
troops involved – much like their Canadian counterparts did. In addition,
and also like Canada, the Australian government was looking for a simple
way to make limited contributions to United States- and United Nations-
led missions to further its own foreign policy interests.

Reflecting on the parallel experiences of the Canadian and Australian
forces during the period of Cold War divergence, one can easily discern the
similarities that still remained. Both countries made substantial overseas
commitments, on the one hand, while reducing their forces and budgets, on
the other. The Canadian government frequently shifted defence priorities
around, first from alliances then to peacekeeping and then to sovereignty
and territorial integrity. It did so in a manner that seemed to display dysfunctional policy choices not unlike those made in Australia, with its switch
from forward defence to a hollow continentalism.[141]

Both countries remained predominantly oriented towards expeditionary
operations with brigades and battalion groups alongside allies. Both also
remained similarly placed as junior partners alongside much larger and
more powerful allies, albeit with a predominantly mechanized Canadian
force with NATO in Europe and a predominantly dismounted Australian
force oriented towards operations in southeast Asia and northern Australia. In the end, however, the peacekeeping approaches of the two armies
would bear a remarkable resemblance, particularly after the end of the
Cold War.

7

Post–Cold War Reconvergence

The end of the Cold War altered the strategic dynamics for the Canadian and Australian forces in ways that could not have been fully imagined in 1989. As Australian military scholar Michael Evans observed, "war became at once modern (reflecting conventional warfare between states), post modern (reflecting the West's cosmopolitan political values of limited war, peace enforcement, and humanitarian military intervention), and premodern (reflecting a mix of substate and transstate warfare based on the age-old politics of identity, extremism and particularism)."[1] As the post–Cold War decade unfolded, it became increasingly apparent that the restrictive regional orientations of Canada and Australia would give way to more globally focused support of military alliances. For both countries, many of the military deployments that ensued tended to be driven by the United States. With its new-found freedom to focus on the moral character of regimes and to intervene for humanitarian reasons, the United States responded in Somalia to end hunger, in Haiti to restore order, and in Bosnia and Kosovo to limit Serbian excesses.[2] For Canada's NATO partners, the country's significance would diminish in light of the withdrawal of forces stationed in Germany, while, for Canada itself, NATO's significance would be affected by increased membership, eastward expansion, and a dilution of military interoperability. Still, Canada's NATO ties would keep its troops in the Balkans for over ten years.[3] In the meantime, for Australia, the focus on continental defence and the immediate geographic region beyond its shores also would no longer hold exclusive attention for defence- and foreign-policy makers. The changes and the shocks came more rapidly for Canada than for Australia – with the withdrawal of troops from Europe, after being stationed there for forty years, and the onset of decidedly non-traditional and varied peacekeeping missions.[4] Yet, before these changes fully came to pass, war broke out in the Persian Gulf.

THE GULF WAR

With the onset of the Gulf War, the Canadian and Australian political scenes revealed remarkable similarities as each country sought to secure a respectable place for itself in the post-Cold War order. Australia (with a centre-left Labor Party government under Prime Minister Bob Hawke) and Canada (under Progressive Conservative Prime Minister Brian Mulroney) were both supporters of u.s. multilateral efforts first to isolate Iraq and then to expel it from Kuwait by force of arms, despite the costs in trade which had run heavily in their countries' favour (with the sale of wheat and other primary products) prior to the war. The trade blockade was supported equally by Canada and Australia, in part as a useful means to ensure that, as one Australian official put it, "no other bastard takes over the trade" – the "other bastard" being Canada. However, they both made limited contributions and faced contentious debates at home over how and whether to contribute to the conflict's resolution, although, in both countries, opinion polls showed that 60 per cent or more of Australian and Canadian respondents approved of their government's actions. After all, this was the first war to which either Canada or Australia had contributed since the proclamation of multiculturalism as a policy goal, and large ethnic communities had links to several of the combatant states.[5] Like the United States, Canada and Australia face the challenge of reconciling disparate communities, languages, and cultures while avoiding what Arthur Schlesinger, Jr describes (in referring to the u.s. condition) as the potential "Balkanization" or "tribalization" of the national community.[6] Such concerns potentially affect where and to what kind of missions the governments of Canada and Australia are prepared to commit their expeditionary forces. They also affect the recruiting base for the armed forces, particularly since the armed forces of Canada and Australia have anglophile customs and institutions that some people from other immigrant communities find uncongenial.

The Gulf War also demonstrated that the Australian Labor Party had shaken its anti-Vietnam War (some would say anti-American) syndrome and was willing to send Australian forces to war overseas again. As Foreign Minister Gareth Evans pointed out, "Australia had a very strong interest in demonstrating both that acts of aggression of this kind were not tolerable, and that the international community had the means and the will to respond to them." Canada's actions reflected the same understanding of the war's broader significance, although the Liberal Opposition's foreign-affairs critic, Lloyd Axworthy, argued that the Canadian government was "betraying a fundamental principle of Canadian foreign policy by making a second unilateral commitment without pressing for overall United Nations command." Such remarks were symptomatic of a heated debate in Australia as well as in Canada. Yet, even though such objections were also heard from left-wing members of Australia's governing Labor Party, the Australian people would be more in favour of the United States, the ANZUS alliance, and the Joint Facilities at Pine Gap and Nurrungar by war's end than they were before it began. In this respect, Murray Goot claims that "the fashionable argument that Government action cannot change attitudes is invalid."[7]

As in the Korean War, Australia and Canada sent their navies early on, with both Mulroney and Hawke announcing a contribution in early August 1990 of two warships and a support ship to naval operations in the Gulf.[8] Canada even looked to Australia for an appropriate joint task force command-and-control model for its similarly configured deployed forces. The Canadian CDS, General John de Chastelain, ordered a senior NDHQ staff officer to visit the Australian High Commission in Ottawa and to obtain from the military attaché there as much detail as possible about how the Australians organized and conducted task-force operations. The Australian model was then used to manage the Canadian forces overseas. Indeed, the war provided the impetus needed for changes within NDHQ that many had long advocated, not unlike the experience of their Australian counterparts in ADF headquaters (HQADF). Afterwards, Australia committed a mine-clearance team and medical personnel as well as a small team of specialist intelligence-support staff. In contrast to Australia, Canada also sent eighteen CF-18 aircraft to Qatar, a 100-bed hospital unit, and some engineer mine clearers, along with infantry to guard the 450 Canadian support troops on the ground. Neither Canada nor Australia felt prepared to contribute substantial ground forces to battle, particularly given their lack of state-of-the-art tanks and the abundance of ground-forces support from other nations. But both the Mulroney and Hawke governments were impressed by the U.S. administration's efforts at multilateralism and were eager to encourage this behaviour. After the war, in 1991, Australia and Canada contributed to the humanitarian-assistance operation in support of the Kurds in northern Iraq.[9]

One particularly striking feature about the diplomatic approaches of Canada and Australia during the Gulf War was that, as Ronnie Miller notes, they "were almost identical." Both Canada and Australia walked a tightrope in attempting to balance domestic and international concerns as well as maintaining old friendships without making new enemies, while, in the end, they decided to contribute to the multinational force as a gesture of goodwill to the United States government of George H.W. Bush.[10] But the similarities between the two countries' approaches were not only diplomatic but also military, in terms of the forces contributed. These similarities could conceivably have been even greater had military planners and government leaders been prepared to contemplate a combined joint task force of Canadians and Australians. After all, the equipment, tactics, and procedures for the Canadian brigade group in Germany were remarkably similar to those in use by their Australian equivalents in the Sydney-based 1st Brigade, which also happened to be equipped with M113s and Leopard I tanks. Sean M. Maloney has written about the "missed opportunity" to deploy 4 Canadian Mechanized Brigade Group (4CMBG) to the Gulf War in 1990–91. He notes that the deployment of ground-combat forces was considered and British officers from the BAOR informally contacted their Canadian equivalents to see if Canada could provide a brigade under British control to form a Commonwealth Division, along the same lines as in the Korean War. But political timidity and Canada's predominant reliance on American equipment and spare parts made such an arrangement unappealing to the Canadians. The Americans also sounded out the Canadians about contributing as part of VII (U.S.) Corps,[11] but again unsuccessfully.

Possibly, however, a combined Canadian-Australian force could have been organized that would have been more tolerable politically and easier to put together logistically and procedurally, for both Canada and Australia, than a separate and self-supporting formation, such as 4CMBG. Indeed, it could have been as combat capable and as lethal as the French 6th Light Armoured Division, with its three mechanized infantry battalions in wheeled armoured personnel carriers. (While unsuited to frontal assault, the French forces proved instrumental in providing a flank guard of the main effort.[12]) Part of the problem was that, as in Australia, U.S. casualty estimates driven by an extremely pessimistic threat assessment made the deployment of ground-combat forces politically unpalatable for Canada as well as Australia. These concerns were compounded by fears about the vulnerability of the older Australian and Canadian armoured vehicles to the more modern anti-armour weapons available to the Iraqis – fears that were faced down by the French. After some analysis, Canadian land-force planners calculated that 4CMBG faced no serious impediment to deploying, apart from the availability of additional men to replace the wounded and killed – the number of whom, according to the threat assessment, would be large.[13]

But in Ottawa a different perspective emerged. As then assistant deputy minister (policy) Louis Delvoie noted, there were four reasons why Canada did not deploy ground combat forces: "(1) there was no military need and there were sufficient ground forces for the campaign without a Canadian contribution; (2) there was no [formal] request for such a commitment from the United States other than the other air, sea and ground elements offered; (3) Canada's contribution was "roughly right" for Canada's level of interest in the Middle East; and (4) even if the government had wanted to get there, they would have been unable to find the appropriate shipping to deploy the forces in sufficient time." In the end, Delvoie contends, "the United States was totally satisfied with our contribution to the Gulf War."[14] Ultimately, the decision was a political one and justifiable on the grounds Delvoie outlines. But the decision was made with little thought given to the option of joining up with another of Canada's wartime partners, Australia.

REDEFINING ROLES AFTER THE COLD WAR

While Canadian and Australian force contributions to the Gulf War in 1990–91 were relatively minor, the longer-term impact of the war on force structures was significant. The so-called Revolution in Military Affairs (RMA), which was facilitated by the information revolution and put on display for all to see during the Gulf War, demonstrated the wide application of high technology for modern warfare. In the years that followed, land-forces digitization and "information warfare" featured increasingly for military planners, with the United States often leading the way. Other countries' forces, including Canada's and Australia's, sought to stay "in the game," which was a challenge given the increasingly expensive technology required to maintain a qualitative edge in combat power and interoperability with U.S. forces. For many Canadians, however, such interoperability was contentious. Some saw it as a panacea while others considered it to be "perdition," making their forces dependent on an apparently fickle United States.[15]

For Australia, the RMA was seized as a way to retain a competitive edge over potential rivals, although there was recognition that "the RMA does not provide a 'silver bullet.'" Warfare, it was agreed, "would continue to be human endeavour that remains uncertain, chaotic, dangerous, and at times bloody."[16] In Canada, however, the preference for low-expense options for low-intensity ground operations provided the forces with less impetus to pursue the RMA – notwithstanding the CF-18 upgrades for the RCAF that enabled it to contribute to the Kosovo air campaign alongside the U.S. Air Force. Still, proximity and trade with the United States brought benefits with it, including sales for high-technology goods such as the sophisticated Canadian-built light armoured vehicles.

Meanwhile, the armies of Canada and Australia, having missed action in the Gulf War, subsequently would bear the brunt of their nations' involvement in international-security operations. For Canada, the heavy burden would strain its increasingly limited capabilities. By the early 1990s, over 4,000 Canadian military personnel were serving on multilateral operations abroad, 2,400 of them in the former Yugoslavia. The crisis in personnel would prompt the withdrawal of the 575 Canadian peacekeepers from Cyprus in 1993.[17] For Australia, during most of the 1990s at least, peacekeeping missions provided opportunities for units to gain operational experience and to test force capabilities abroad – an activity regarded favourably by Australian troops and their commanders. Indeed, this rationale closely paralleled that used by their Canadian cousins throughout the Cold War.

One consequence of the end of the Cold War and the significant increase in the number of such security operations was an attempt by the external affairs departments of Canada and Australia to redefine their missions in terms of "cooperative security." Cooperative security, they argued, relied on the United Nations and other multilateral security institutions that would obviate the need for large and expensive armed forces. Yet in both countries' cases, officials in the departments of defence resisted abandoning traditional concepts of security. They refused to concede that the diplomats were correct in their optimistic assessments of defence and security as being discretionary activities in the post-Cold War era.[18]

While this interdepartmental conceptual debate continued in both countries, in practice the foreign-affairs view appeared to be winning out as the two nations' defence forces – like those in many other countries, including Britain and the United States – were called upon to deliver post-Cold War dividends. There were "efficiency reviews" and major force reductions in Canada and Australia that resulted in organizational trauma for all three services in both countries. For Australia, these included the Force Structure Review, the Commercial Support Program, and the Defence Reform Program. As a consequence, by 2002, ADF strength would be reduced to 50,784, down from a post-Vietnam War high of 73,185 in 1982. (Despite ongoing recruiting campaigns, women and people from minority-ethnic or aboriginal backgrounds would remain under-represented in the ADF.) For Australia, the period included a multiple-Blackhawk helicopter accident in 1996 involving special forces that was largely attributable to poor aircraft serviceability and availability, combined with an excessive "can do" attitude that continued to prevail despite tight budget constraints.[19] This tragic accident paralleled numerous Canadian Navy "Sea King" helicopter accidents in the same period.

The story of the Sea Kings illustrated that Canada's forces experienced many of the same types of challenges as those faced by the ADF. For Canada, the initial post-Cold War years were marked by a significant national debt crisis that added momentum to the dramatic and demoralizing force reductions that accompanied the withdrawal of forces from Germany. This period also saw the fashioning of a new approach to security and force structure that stressed light deployable forces for operations in coalition, NATO, or UN contexts. No longer would the Canadian Army rely on Cold War NATO planning as its key force-structure determinant. The withdrawal of troops from Lahr in Germany saw one of the Canadian Army's four regular-force brigades dissolved, leaving three brigades remaining – the 1st Canadian Mechanized Brigade Group (1CMBG) based in Edmonton, Alberta, the 2CMBG based at Pettawawa, Ontario, and the French-speaking 5CMBG at Valcartier, Quebec. Each CMBG included three infantry battalions, armoured, artillery, and engineer regiments with combat support (including communications), and combat-service support elements (including logistics components). The Canadian Air Force's capability was similarly reduced. During this time, a renewed emphasis was placed on the defence of Canada; four air bases known as "Forward Operating Locations," equipped with upgraded radars designed to counter the threat of air-launched cruise missiles, were constructed across Canada. As mentioned earlier, Australia would follow suit with the construction of bases across Australia's north in support of similar strategic concepts of national defence. To observers like Canada's Douglas Bland, the period marked the culmination of the conversion of the Canadian Forces (CF) from their peak strengths and capabilities in the mid-1960s into what by 1998 he describes as a "sow's ear from a silk purse."[20] Bland's remarks were echoed by defence commentators in Australia concerning the state of the ADF in the mid-1990s.[21]

The 1990s also witnessed the Australian Army's ill-fated "Army-21" experimental concept, which reflected the high-water mark of the flawed post-Vietnam War continental-defence strategy set out in the 1987 Australian Defence White Paper. This 1987 strategy focused on the so-called "air-sea gap" to Australia's north but neglected the historical and geo-strategic significance of the "gap's" many islands. As in Canada, the Australian Army stressed the "total force" capability. This meant that the reserve forces would become an integral part of the force, being assigned specific vital asset-protection tasks in the favoured force-structure planning scenarios that centred on defence of remote northern facilities.[22] In addition, the concepts that emerged in the early 1990s remained grounded in the 1987 strategy and did not account effectively for the post-Cold War realities and growing pressure to provide forces for a wide range of "peacekeeping" missions well beyond Australia in Asia, Africa, and elsewhere.

The end of the Cold War also saw a shift from predominantly interpositional, or "first-generation," peacekeeping – at which Canadian troops had gained extensive experience during the preceding decades – to "second-generation peacekeeping," which proved much more difficult for the United Nations to manage.[23] This included more complex and challenging peace-support operations including "peace-making" or "peace- enforcement" operations – or what the Australian Army now calls "Military Operations Other Than Conventional Warfare."[24] The Canadian Forces came to realize that peace enforcement is an equally valid, albeit more challenging, form of "peacekeeping." As Andrew Cohen notes, "in reality, peacekeeping is no longer peaceful. It is often more like combat. As imagined by Lester Pearson, it no longer exists." However, politicians and the civil community have taken longer to recognize that a transition has taken place. The 1990s also featured Canada's more selective approach to "peacekeeping" or peace-support missions. The Canadian and Australian contributions to numerous UN missions to places such as Namibia, Cambodia, Somalia, Western Sahara, Haiti, Rwanda, and Yugoslavia made the complexity of such "second generation" peacekeeping missions or far-from-peaceful "stabilization operations" increasingly apparent. In addition, these deployments revealed shortcomings in the joint process, shortcomings that pointed, in Australia's case, to the value in having a headquarters that was separate from the strategic headquarters, HQADF, in Canberra, to plan, mount, and control such expeditionary forces deployed on operations abroad. The three commands of Land, Maritime, and Air were placed under an overall operational-level commander initially known as Commander Joint Forces Australia (CJFA) but eventually, from 1996 onwards, as the Headquarters Australian Theatre (HQAST) under a "two-star" Commander Australian Theatre (COMAST). In 2004 a new title, Joint Operations Command, would come into use.[25]

As these improvements were being made in Australia, a Force Structure Review in 1991 counteracted many of the advances made. The review, initiated under the Australian Labor Government of Prime Minister Bob Hawke, and his defence minister, Robert Ray, led to the loss of 10,500 uniformed and 4,000 civilian positions within the Department of Defence. For the army, the cut was 5,220 permanent-force personnel. To compensate for the loss and to maintain a readily deployable and sustainable capability, a Ready Reserve Scheme was introduced, whereby two infantry battalions of well-trained part-time troops would be available at considerably less cost than that required for permanent-force troops. Despite its merits and popularity, the scheme would not last beyond the next election, a victim of political party differences.[26]

Another review, conducted by a senior Canberra bureaucrat, Alan K. Wrigley, called for improved fiscal accountability by transferring much of the forces' administrative and maintenance tasks to private contractors. This review, entitled *The Defence Force and the Community: A Partnership in Australia's Defence*, essentially was based on the premise that Australian operations would be on Australian territory – not in an offshore environment bereft of facilities accessible to contractors. It reflected a superficial understanding of the ADF's strategic circumstances and led to the introduction of the Commercial Support Program (CSP) – which arguably marked the nadir of defence thinking about overall strategy and its implications for force structure.[27] Insiders reflecting on this difficult period of cutbacks and reorganization contend that the reforms "were as much a down loading of the Government's micro-economic reform agenda into Defence as much as anything else, as well as a bureaucratic attempt to develop policy and management rationales to avoid paying the 'peace dividend.'" The Australian CSP is remarkably similar to Canada's Alternate Source Delivery (ASD) Program, which has outsourced supply and other logistic functions to contractors, many of whom, according to one Canadian officer, "performed that function a year or two ago in uniform and who are now former service members hired as civilians."[28]

During this period, Australia's Headquarters 1st Division was reconfigured as a Deployable Joint Force Headquarters (DJFHQ). The view was taken that the Australian Army no longer needed a division on its establishment because operational requirements could be met by the various brigade headquarters. Brigades, it was argued, would be required to operate in a dispersed setting in the north of Australia. Hence, the required logistic and administrative elements previously attached to the division were required to be "brigaded" in the newly formed Brigade Administrative Support Battalions (BASB). This program was initiated in 1991. Eventually, the term BASB would be replaced with the Combat Service Support Battalion (CSSB) to reflect its function more accurately. Canada also had its divisional administrative-support elements co-located with its brigades. These elements were grouped together to form the Canadian Service Battalions, which were allocated one per brigade.[29] The Canadians also came to a similar decision regarding the need for a divisional headquarters. The Canadian Armed Forces restructured their Headquarters 1st Division in Kingston, Ontario, as the Canadian Forces Joint Task Force Headquarters in a way that was designed to perform a role similar to that of the Australian DJFHQ. For Australia, it would be some time before events farther afield, such as the increasing number of United Nations operations the country was committed to, acted to slow down and eventually reverse the rate of force reduction.

COMPLEX PEACEKEEPING

For Australia, the United Nations intervention in Cambodia was the most taxing peacekeeping commitment undertaken up to that point. Military command and a significant portion of the force was provided by Australia, under Lieutenant-General John Sanderson. Australia's foreign minister, Senator Gareth Evans, argued that "Australia's ability to talk comfortably to every country involved in the Cambodian dispute owed much to the fact that we were not carrying any great or major power baggage." Evans's assertion echoed similar sentiments expressed about Canadians. Nonetheless, the mission faced apparently insurmountable local challenges that constrained the implementation of the United Nations' mandate. Such constraints affected the UN's ability to act impartially, leading some to consider it an additional or "fifth faction" in the domestic Cambodian political scene for the duration of the mission. These constraints exposed the limited utility of Chapter VI mandates authorized under the United Nations Charter for such complex post-Cold War era peacekeeping missions.[30]

Further illustrating the limitations of Chapter VI mandates was the first United Nations mission to Rwanda (UNAMIR). In Rwanda, the Canadian government was willing to send a force commander and some staff officers, but it was not prepared to back up the commitment with substantive Canadian ground forces when the mission faced a crisis with insufficient force to resolve it. Canadian defence commentator Tom Axworthy suggests that the UN force commander, Canadian Brigadier-General Romeo Dallaire, could have used a Canadian brigade to stop the massacre. But such a move would have gone beyond the approach to peacekeeping that Canadians had practised since Suez in 1956,[31] and, for that reason, it required more political will than the Canadian government of the day was prepared to exercise. Canada's politicians would take some time to recognize the onset of what is sometimes referred to as "second generation" peacekeeping, or peace enforcement, which the Rwanda mission represented.

For several years, Canada was prepared to focus its efforts on structuring its forces for apparently benign peacekeeping missions, even at the expense of combat capabilities. By contrast, Australia, with its different geo-strategic concerns, continued to adhere firmly to the view that force structure was not to be driven by the requirements of peace-support missions. For Australia, peace-support endeavours could be considered only from the force in being – a force structured essentially for combat operations.

Yet, over the course of the decade following the fall of the Berlin Wall, a striking similarity emerged. Canada no longer focused on mechanized operations in Europe and Australia shifted from planning for implausible military attacks on continental Australia to contemplating more likely scenarios abroad. These scenarios required mounting remarkably similar expeditionary forces. In Australia's case, this also meant beefing up amphibious capabilities, something that became possible once the government recognized that such forces provided it with improved and more flexible policy options. Their so-called "offensive nature," according to a statement made by Defence Minister Kim Beazley in 1990, "makes them inappropriate for our force structure." But Beazley overlooked the fact that amphibious forces enable the government to plan, with a high degree of self-reliance, for a wide variety of options – ranging from humanitarian assistance and disaster relief in difficult-to-reach locations to peacekeeping aimed at maintaining order and even to options of last resort designed to restore order.[32] This was soon to be amply demonstrated by Australia's ability to deploy a battalion group to Somalia.

SOMALIA

Australia and Canada demonstrated a shared commitment to broader international stability and humanitarianism, contributing remarkably similar combat forces and supporting elements as part of the United States-led Unified Task Force (UNITAF) in Somalia between January and May 1993. These contributions included light-infantry battalion groups with mechanized and other support components and naval assistance (HMCS *Preserver* and HMAS *Tobruk*) and similarly arranged command elements assigned from their joint force headquarters staffs. (Australia's "robust approach to peace enforcement," according to Alan Ryan, "reflected the fact that

Australia's Army is based on a light-infantry force with a strong tactical focus."[33]) Yet, despite the comparable forces and tasks assigned, and the high regard in which Canadian and Australian forces were held by many aid organizations and military forces involved in Somalia, there are marked differences in the legacy of that operation for the two countries.[34]

Canada's forces had, for years, been on a tight budget and were increasingly asked to do more with less. As Ron Haycock observes, "they had that sycophantic attitude to politicians of 'can do.'" Moreover, their peacekeeping training, procedures, and handbooks were oriented towards relatively benign peacekeeping under Chapter VI of the United Nations Charter and not under the more warlike Chapter VII. Indeed, the Canadian Forces had anticipated going to Somalia under a Chapter VI mandate only to see that changed at short notice prior to deployment. The Canadians thus left for Somalia without clearly defined rules of engagement. With no clear mission or proper reconnaissance, the force under Colonel Serge Labbé tried to adjust the existing plan for different and more challenging circumstances. "Mission creep" was one result.[35]

The problems of an overstretched force, combined with political and budgetary neglect, reached a crisis following the deployment to Somalia with the shocking revelations of actions taken by members of the Canadian Airborne Regiment, including the torture and killing of a Somali teenager in March 1993. As a result, the Canadian Forces were stigmatized by the Somalia scandal as charges of cover-up and ill-conceived damage control unfolded. The report of the Commission of Enquiry into the Canadian deployment was revealingly entitled *Dishonoured Legacy: The Lessons of the Somalia Affair*. The report, written by two jurists and a senior journalist, lent credibility to public perceptions that the Canadian Forces in the 1990s were deficient and in danger of collapse, although the government wound up the commission just before it started scrutinizing the role played in the fiasco by the arguably more culpable politicians and the higher machinery of government. The result of the series of events related to the deployment was a casualty list from the scandal that included a minister of national defence, a deputy minister, three chiefs of the defence staff, and the Canadian Airborne Regiment itself. This, in turn, generated a malaise among the troops. For two years after the incident in Somalia, the media focus on this issue virtually obscured all other things happening in the Canadian Forces. The Canadian military historian John A. English summarizes the situation this way: "Constant buffeting by the cross-currents of unification, bilingualism, and peacekeeping had, in addition to the overt civilianization of NDHQ seriously eroded the professional foundations of army educational and training establishments set up after the war ... the only kind of experience that counted was one's own, preferably gained in officially approved usually highly bureaucratized slots." In addition, as Joseph Jockel declares, "since the Korean War in the early 1950s, all of [the Canadian Forces'] overseas deployments outside Europe were for peacekeeping. The Somalia deployment was therefore of a new kind for the CF, especially the army. Since the mission's goal was to restore order, it required a more robust capability, including combat capability, than the traditional peacekeeping missions. Yet the task was not to engage and defeat a clearly-defined foe ... Under these new circumstances, the CF bungled the deployment." As with the U.S. military after Vietnam, these events eventually triggered an internal demand for reform and for professional renewal that went beyond mere organizational change.[36]

Part of the problem appeared to be that Canada's NDHQ, established in 1972, had contributed significantly to dysfunction within the Canadian Forces. While democratic countries, as a rule, do not leave their militaries unfettered by civilian oversight, the Canadian experience arguably is an example of "civilianization" taken too far. For instance, the NDHQ power structure had civilianized the military's high command by allowing civilians the authority to make decisions at a high level and encouraging acquiescence by military commanders. This civilianization, according to Granatstein, entailed "the dominance of managers over the military, and of military bureaucrats over operational commanders ... Officers stayed in posts where civilians might have been more appropriate and, in some cases, the reverse was true." Indeed, there was an argument that the Somalia failure was about not just the civilianization of NDHQ in Ottawa but also the failure of commanders in the field. One Canadian staff officer observed that "when a real crisis occurs or things are not working well then the system's dysfunctional realities become apparent to even the most casual observer."[37] The Australian forces escaped unscathed from Somalia, perhaps by good fortune as much as by good training.[38] But, in Canada, Somalia spurred refinements in the higher command-and-control "architecture" in Ottawa's NDHQ.[39]

In contrast, for Australia, Somalia provided an opportunity to validate and refine force-structure concepts – including the requirement to maintain amphibious capabilities for the projection of such expeditionary forces. The experience reinforced the need for robust and well-rounded capabilities and validated the focus on individual soldier skills – so critical in the information age where the "strategic corporal" effect exists.[40] In addition, as Robert Patman has observed, in Baidoa, Australians demonstrated that it is possible to develop what might be termed a peace-enforcement strategy in a collapsed-state situation. The Australian troops sought to strike a balance between political reconstruction and a willingness to use force to obtain compliance with UN demands.[41]

THE BALKANS AND NEW DEFINITIONS

Unfortunately, Somalia was not the only peacekeeping disappointment faced by Canada. Under yet another UN "peacekeeping" mandate, this time in Croatia and Bosnia, Canada found itself in a quagmire with little peace to be kept. As early as April 1992, for instance, when Sarajevo erupted in violence, the Canadian chief of staff at the United Nations Provisional Force (UNPROFOR), Major-General Lewis MacKenzie, and his Australian senior military observer in Sarajevo, Colonel John Wilson, saw how inadequate a hamstrung but "impartial" UN mission could be in the face of the complexities of post-Cold War peacekeeping.[42]

As post-Cold War peacekeeping was becoming manifestly more complex, the Canadian government, under Defence Minister David Collenette, issued a new Defence White Paper in 1994 premised, according to Bland, largely on two certainties in the defence field – uncertainty and lower expenditures.[43] So-called peace groups had advocated the virtual abandonment of the Canadian Forces' combat capabilities, but the government specifically rejected this approach, explaining that to opt for "a constabulary force" specifically not designed for combat "would betray our history and diminish our future."[44] The key capability statement in the White Paper was that Canada would maintain "multi-purpose [not general purpose], combat-capable forces" that obviated the need to maintain specific capabilities like amphibious ships and medium-lift helicopters – widely considered critical capabilities for independent operations. Thus, "Canada was not obliged to take on a major portion of every operation or to contribute forces for longer than seems reasonable." (Canada's contingency planning has long been constrained to sea or air points of disembarkation secured by coalition partners. Thus, Canada has, since the 1970s at least, consistently chosen to make itself dependent on others to exercise its foreign and defence policy where the deployment of troops abroad is required – although Canada pays its own way, at least.[45]) The emphasis in the 1994 White Paper was on the United Nations, but not on expensive, open-ended commitments as earlier peacekeeping missions in the Suez or Cyprus had been. Like Australia, the Canadian government stipulated that its army would be "capable of conducting up to and including mid-level combat operations in a range of low to mid-intensity conflicts" at brigade level, although if a brigade was tasked to deploy, doing so would require the army's "entire focus." For Canada, this would be carried out by its "Sabre Brigade" – ostensibly the Canadian Forces' most readily deployable ground formation for low- to mid-level operational engagements which normally would have been expected to be ready for deployment within ninety days. This, in essence, is what the Australian 3rd Brigade did in East Timor. In Canada's case, however, the 1994 White Paper provided that, in place of the Sabre brigade, up to three Canadian battle groups of up to 1,000 troops might be deployed. Also like Australia, Canada set a nominal numerical "ceiling" or planning figure of 2,000 personnel for peacekeeping operations – although deployed numbers would surge to as high as 5,000 shortly after the White Paper's release. The numbers would remain high for the remainder of the decade as well, with 4,500 Canadian troops on operations abroad in 1999.[46]

In the next year, 1995, the Chrétien government issued an upbeat foreign-policy statement, *Canada in the World*, that seemed to take a leaf out of U.S. President Bill Clinton's "it's the economy, stupid" campaign slogan. It asserted that, while military capabilities might "remain important factors in the international system of the future, international affairs will be rooted increasingly in economic and trade relations between countries and regions."[47] This idealistic and contradictory statement, coming a year after the Defence White Paper, partly reflected the dysfunction between defence and foreign policy in Canada, whereby Canadian forces were committed to a level of international intervention inconsistent with its funding priority. But it also reflected an undue degree of optimism about international affairs that subsequent events, particularly since the onset of the "War on Terror," have shown to have been overdrawn.

The foreign-policy statement, coming at a time of economic dynamism in east Asia, also stressed the place for Canadians in the Asia-Pacific region. Canada's Foreign Minister under Prime Minister Mulroney, Joe Clark, attempted to launch a North Pacific Cooperative Security Dialogue (NPCSD) in order to broaden cooperative-security measures. But Canada's overtures were perceived in Washington as an attempt to use multilateralism to assert a Canadian presence in the region and circumvent American bilateral-security arrangements. While interest in this endeavour did not last,[48] other efforts, including the Asia-Pacific Economic Co-operation (APEC) forum, were sufficiently non-threatening to U.S. security interests that they received American endorsement and enthusiastic support from most Canadians, at least until the financial crisis of 1997 and 1998, when much of the dynamism of northeast and southeast Asia evaporated. In the meantime, the pull of Europe would significantly reduce the Canadian Forces' ability to follow up such economic- and foreign-policy initiatives in Asia with any significant redirection of military focus. This was particularly the case given the ongoing conflict in the Balkans.

Canadian troops stationed in Croatia were involved in a significant fire-fight in the Medak pocket in September 1993. Canadians were fired on by Croatians for fifteen hours, returned fire, and eventually secured the area but only after the Croatians had completed their grisly task of "ethnic cleansing." Canada's difficult role in Croatia continued until August 1995 when the Croats assaulted the ethnic Serb enclave in an all-out attack, by-passing or capturing Canadian military posts along the way. Canadian forces would remain engaged in neighbouring Bosnia with peacekeepers operating under UN and then NATO mandates for the remainder of the 1990s and beyond.[49] Canada's military involvement in Croatia and Bosnia was its most dangerous operation since the Korean War. Rempel notes that, between 1992 and 1995, 11 Canadians were killed, over 100 wounded, and 66 captured in the Balkans. However, little publicity was given to this obviously dangerous combat action by Canadian "peacekeepers." Factions in the government of the day, according to Maloney, apparently did not think that this "fit with the mythological image of the so-called peacekeep-ers." Indeed, Haycock contends that the government purposely down-played it, "lest Canadian voters get the impression that peacekeeping efforts were too dangerous and therefore object to the government using military force for politico-diplomatic purposes."[50]

Clearly, then, Canada's ability to maintain its stance on peacekeeping was severely challenged by its experience in the Balkans. What is more, the government apparently was not prepared to give the military any addi-tional resources to reduce the challenge or to even recognize it properly. Ca-nadians grew increasingly frustrated as troops were taken hostage and Canadian diplomats were excluded from the high-level contact group. As John Hillen observes, "UN military operations had their own grammar but not their own logic." By the mid-1990s, the United Nations, and strong supporters of it like Canada, would come to realize that the UN, lacking its own sovereign legitimacy and authority, could not provide the political and functional framework for significant military operations. Large, complex, and dangerous military operations required more legitimacy, authority, and systems of accountability than the United Nations could muster. Observers noted that "moral equivalency allows peacekeepers to pretend that they are dealing with two equal sides in a conflict, not with aggressors and victims." The United Nations had not yet found a way adequately to deal with such complexity; nor had the Canadian government been willing to admit this reality, and so one reinforced the other. However, eventually the United Nations would concede that the doctrine of moral equivalency was central to its failure in the Balkans. When NATO took over in the Balkans in 1995, Canada's contribution to UN operations diminished to only 900 peacekeepers – in the Golan Heights and in Haiti.[51] This trend continued as the century came to a close, with alternative "coalitions of the willing" becoming more prominent.

As the nadir of United Nations peacekeeping was approaching, considerable thought was given to the then UN Secretary General Boutros Boutros-Ghali's 1992 manifesto for second-generation peacekeeping, entitled *An Agenda for Peace*, which had optimistically championed robust UN peace-enforcement operations. The impetus for such a proposal reflected similar impulses that had been at work in Australia and that had led Australia's foreign minister, Senator Gareth Evans, to publish his own manifesto, entitled *Cooperating for Peace*, in 1993 – the same year that the ADF Peacekeeping Centre was established at the ADF Warfare Centre at RAAF Base Williamtown. Evans's paper enunciated a distinction between peacekeeping and "peacemaking." Both it and Boutros-Ghali's effort enjoyed only limited support at the time because the complex UN missions of the early to mid-1990s faced insurmountable difficulties which, in turn, damaged the United Nations' reputation.[52] But Canada took the matter further when it tabled a report at the United Nations in 1995 entitled *Towards a Rapid Reaction Capability for the United Nations*, which was not unlike the Canadian idea of a standby capability first raised in the late 1950s. The 1995 report was based upon the "Vanguard Concept" that called for a multinational standby force of up to 5,000 troops.[53]

Canada's proposed vanguard reflected a long-term Canadian search for foreign- and defence-policy distinctiveness from the United States. The proposal also complemented the UN secretary general's January 1995 "Supplement to an Agenda for Peace," which recommended the creation of a rapid-deployment force from a number of member states that would train and exercise together with interoperable equipment and procedures. This "supplement," along with Canada's proposal, laid the groundwork for the creation of a Multinational High Readiness Brigade. A letter of intent was signed in December 1996 to raise a force capable of independent operations under a UN mandate at short notice and for six months' duration. The Stand-By High Readiness Brigade (SHIRBRIG) would be declared available to the United Nations from the end of January 2000. Canada agreed to assign staff officers to the Denmark-based headquarters and to set aside a battalion group for short-notice operations with SHIRBRIG. That force would later successfully deploy to the UN mission in Ethiopia and Eritrea (UNMEE) in November 2000.[54] Conceivably, Australia also would have been an ideal candidate to join SHIRBRIG. But, with distractions closer to home and increased demands on the use of the ADF, calls for it to do so went unheeded.

Canada refrained from joining in the American invasion of Haiti in October 1994 as the newly elected Liberal prime minister, Jean Chrétien, sought to distinguish himself from his Conservative and more pro-U.S. predecessor, Brian Mulroney, and to assert national autonomy. Still, Chrétien's government appeared to be eager to appeal to a large Haitian community in Montreal and to enhance Canadian diplomatic credit in Washington. Canada therefore agreed subsequently to contribute over 600 troops to the UN Mission in Haiti (UNMIH) that was established following the U.S. intervention. Overall, Canada's contribution and willingness eventually to take the lead in Haiti demonstrated the compatibility of American and Canadian interests in the promotion of regional stability. Canada's role in 1996 reflected liberal foreign-policy orientations similar to those that would drive Australia to commit troops to East Timor in 1999 and to the Solomon Islands in 2003.[55]

After the Haiti mission, in 1997, Canada's foreign minister, Lloyd Axworthy, set out to reinvigorate the foreign-policy debate, arguing for a "Human Security Agenda." But his emphasis on "soft power" (stressing persuasion rather than coercion) served to bring even further attention to the limitations of Canadian military power to back up such grandiose ideals.[56] In addition, commitments along these lines potentially threatened to expose the "commitment-capability gap," whereby troops deployed with insufficient or inadequate support were unable to perform tasks assigned, thus exposing them to needless danger (à *la* Dieppe in 1942). As Andrew Cohen puts it, "soft power, however worthy, could be no substitute for hard power – a strong military, a generous aid program, and an able diplomatic corps." Moreover, this "soft power" approach, advocated by Lloyd Axworthy, stood in contrast to the approach Pearson had taken in 1956, when he had complemented diplomacy with the "hard power" of Canadian forces. This approach also reflected contrasting Foreign Affairs and Defence positions that, once again, marked an enduring trend for both Canada and Australia. This trend stretched back beyond such leading Department of External Affairs personalities as Loring Christie in Canada and "Doc" Evatt in Australia.[57]

During this period, the mid-1990s, the missions to Somalia, Haiti, and the Balkans highlighted what Sokolsky calls the "Americanization of Peacekeeping," whereby the United States took a more direct and robust role in deciding when, why, and how peacekeeping operations would be conducted. Peacekeeping, or peace "enforcement," under these circumstances still offered Canada an international role separate and distinctive from the United States and traditional u.s. policies of containment and deterrence. Moreover, "the Somalias, Haitis and Kosovos engaged America's security policy," as Sokolsky argues, "because they challenged America's values." At the same time, "realist" observers commented that Canada's contributions would give the United States, under the cover of supporting the United Nations, the kind of global commitment of expeditionary forces that Canada had ceased to give to the British Empire after the First World War.[58]

The increasingly complex nature of the domestic- and international-security challenges faced by the Canadian government stimulated the development of a special-forces capability in late 1992, based at Dwyer Hill, near Ottawa, that was more potent and specialized than the Canadian Airborne Regiment. This unit, known as Joint Task Force Two, or JTF2, was declared operational in April 1993 and became the very tip of the Canadian "sharp end." JTF2 was modelled on the British SAS, although its title has no special connection with any other force except that it was borrowed from an American military and law-enforcement body based in Florida, known as JTF4. It absorbed the Royal Canadian Mounted Police's Special Emergency Response Team (SERT), which had existed since May 1986. SERT's job had been hostage rescue, but the JTF2 would eventually develop capabilities for black (counter-terrorist) and green ("battlefield" special forces) roles. In the decade following its creation, JTF2 would deploy small teams on at least a dozen overseas operations – often as bodyguards for VIPs, as well as in support of troops on operations.[59] Australia's SAS Regiment, created in 1957 and actively involved in the early to mid-1960s in the "Confrontation" in Borneo and the Vietnam War, had become a more substantial and experienced organization by the mid-1990s. Indeed, its troops would develop capabilities similar to those of their Canadian equivalents (albeit on a larger scale) and deploy on similar tasks, including as a key component of Australia's mission to East Timor in 1999.[60]

Australia and Canada were facing similar imperatives and both were drawn into u.s.-influenced missions in the aftermath of the Cold War and the success of the Gulf War – Somalia being the most obvious example. Yet, even with Australia's more numerous opportunities to refine procedures and improve capabilities, the ADF would face significant challenges, with many of the lessons of Somalia apparently still unlearnt, when it sought to mount a South Pacific Peacekeeping Force to Bougainville in 1994. That mission was to protect a pan-Bougainvillean peace conference. Despite the smooth and efficient conduct of the military-controlled aspects of the operation, the mission was given insufficient lead time and subjected to overly stringent constraints on force size by its political masters. Consequently, peace in Bougainville would have to wait until a truce was negotiated more than three years later.[61] At that stage, a successful multinational truce- monitoring group (with contributions from New Zealand, Australia, Fiji, and Vanuatu) was inserted to help restore peace in Bougainville.

The surge in such operational requirements abroad contributed to the Australian government agreeing to conduct another strategic review, as the Canadians did, in 1994. The Australian White Paper, entitled *Defending Australia* and released in November 1994, was described as lacking the originality that should have been stimulated by the ending of the Cold War and the changing strategic circumstances in the Asia-Pacific region.[62] The White Paper reasserted the primacy of homeland defence but, like the Canadian report, acknowledged that other problems beyond its shores could produce an unstable and potentially dangerous situation that could affect its interests. Still, the defence of Australia would remain paramount, at least until the election of John Howard's Liberal (conservative) government in 1996.

Under Howard's new defence minister, Ian McLachlan, the Australian government initiated a series of reviews. In Canberra, HQADF was renamed Australian Defence Headquarters (ADHQ) in 1997, following a Defence Efficiency Review which reduced civilian staff by 3,100 and military staff by a further 4,700 by the year 2000. This cutback would bring service-personnel numbers down to just 50,000 while ostensibly increasing the combat strength of the ADF. While traumatic for members of the organization, the efficiency review further streamlined the Canberra staffs as a true strategic and joint headquarters. In addition, the review identified the need to rebalance and strengthen the capabilities of the ADF, while also creating and practising joint-force operations in peacetime. Although these were significant shortcomings that needed to be addressed, in essence, the key factor in shaping the army in the years leading up to and including the review had been the fiscal imperatives of the Department of Treasury. The theme of Australian reviews in the 1980s and 1990s had not been military effectiveness or capability. Rather, as in Canada, such reviews were motivated first and foremost by the desire for greater fiscal efficiency and economic rationalization, irrespective of the corrosive effects on the military or, indeed, how obvious it made the commitment-capability gap.[63]

Australia's "Restructuring the Army" (RTA) program had been part of this drive for increased efficiency; its trials commenced early in 1997 based largely on the work conducted for the Army-21 study. That study had reflected flaws similar to those exposed during the short-lived Australian Pentropic experiment of the early 1960s, including difficulties with interoperability among the countries of the ABCA forum – America, Britain, Canada, and Australia – which had been created as a quadripartite working group of the four nations' armies in 1947 (Australia was added as a full member in January 1963). But under the RTA program, Ian McLachlan presaged the forthcoming White Paper by stressing the need also to be capable of conducting offshore operations either unilaterally or as part of a coalition.[64] Like their Canadian equivalents, senior Australian Army leaders faced significant budgetary pressures. The RTA program appeared to offer a way to steal the limelight, and thus funding, from navy and air force projects that were more congruent with the rigid air-sea gap strategy outlined in the 1987 White Paper and retained in the 1994 White Paper.

Fortunately for the army, a new White Paper, released in 1997, reflected a more realistic assessment of prospective military missions and obviated the need to continue pursuing the single scenario-based RTA force structure. The 1997 White Paper, entitled *Australia's Strategic Policy* (ASP97), told planners to prepare for three broad requirements – defence of Australia, defence of regional interests, and defence of global interests. This remarkably broad statement of requirements led to a complex and growing menu of "military strategic objectives" and "military response options." But at least the focus was once again on the real-world requirements to prepare and deploy forces on expeditionary operations abroad. ASP97 was released in the same year as the Australian Department of Foreign Affairs and Trade issued its White Paper, entitled *In the National Interest*. These two 1997 white papers went beyond the single-minded focus of earlier reviews on efficiency and affirmed the importance of mainland defence, while also advocating greater capability for the ADF and emphasizing a greater regional role beyond Australia's shores.[65]

ASP97 paved the way for the Australian chief of army, Lieutenant-General Frank Hickling, to announce in October 1998 that the army "would embrace a maritime concept of strategy" – a significant departure from the twenty-five-year-old strategy of continental defence. Thereafter, more emphasis would be given to force-projection capabilities for operations beyond

Australia's shores in the immediate region and in support of global inter-ests.[66] These reports coincidentally were released only months before the east Asian economic meltdown that would trigger turbulence throughout the island chain to the north of Australia – turbulence that would generate a demand for ADF capabilities not put in use since the Vietnam War era.

Canada would not undertake another such strategic review for the remainder of Chrétien's term as prime minister, even though in 1995 the government budget slashed the appropriation for the Department of National Defence by 23 per cent, leaving it to close twenty-eight bases, stations, and units and without the funding required to carry out effectively the tasks stipulated in the one-year old White Paper.[67] Still, reflecting both obliviousness to the widening commitment-capability gap and an apparent resolve to follow up on the desire to buttress its support for the United Nations, Canada sought to take the lead, this time in a humanitarian-relief operation in the African Great Lakes region of Zaire in 1996. David Meren contends that "Prime Minister Chrétien was moved by the news on the TV and a sense that a mission in Zaire would play well with the missionary community in Quebec." But, with European lack of interest and only lukewarm American support for the mission, and lacking the ability to self-deploy a substantial force, the Canadian government faced an uphill battle to make the mission workable. The deployment relied on the Canadian deployable joint-force headquarters, not unlike its Australian equivalent organization that would be used in East Timor three years later. However, problems soon emerged which demonstrated Canada's inadequate ability to mount, deploy, and employ an autonomous joint task force. Not only was the mission virtually beyond the reach of its small, ageing, and occasionally unserviceable fleet of C-130 Hercules aircraft, but it was also remote from the coastal access points that were necessary for the deployment of a heavy force by sea transport. Clearly, a more challenging point of disembarkation for the limited deployment capabilities of the Canadian Forces could hardly have been found. The mission was made more difficult by Canada's lack of a strategic reconnaissance capability or of foreign intelligence about the situation on the ground. In addition, the failure to deploy combat troops in support of the mission put the government in Ottawa in a weak military and political position. At one stage, a Canadian officer observed, "we actually had troops 'interned' on arrival since they arrived armed and in uniform." As a result, the mission, which Rempel describes as "the bungle in the jungle," was short-lived. It stood in sharp contrast to the successful mission that Canada launched at Suez forty years earlier – and yet the government seemed still oblivious to the reality, or did not care enough to do anything about it.[68]

The Zaire mission further illustrated the Canadian Forces' lack of practice at operating above unit level. Long experienced at providing separate single-service contributions alongside u.s. forces or on peacekeeping missions, the CF lacked the experience of working together as their own tri-service expeditionary force, particularly at formation (brigade) level. The Canadian White Paper of 1994 had stipulated the requirement to maintain a high-readiness brigade group for rapid deployment that was designed to fight "alongside the best, against the best." But regular training did not feature at the brigade level until 2003. In fact, one private group's report in early 2001 indicated that "unfortunately, training in Canada is poor at battalion levels and almost non-existent at the brigade level, even as single service exercises. Full scale 'joint' exercises have almost ceased." As Sokolsky and Middlemiss maintain, the Canadian answer to the defence-planner's question "How much is enough?" has been "*just* enough."[69] But, by the end of the century, even that assertion was open to debate.

In late 1997 and early 1998, tensions over Kuwait led to deployments of u.s. and coalition forces to safeguard Kuwait. The United States deployed a mechanized brigade to augment the force there. Contributions also were made by Britain and several other European nations. Australian and New Zealand supplied elements from their respective SAS units, while Canada contributed two frigates, HMCS *Ottawa* and HMCS *Toronto*. Such force contributions, argues Maloney, were consistent with four aspects of the Canadian strategic tradition. These he identifies as forward security (deploying forces overseas to keep conflict as far from Canada as possible), coalition warfare (working with allies to compensate for Canada's inability to generate large standing forces), operational influence (to prevent the misuse of Canadian forces by coalition members), and saliency, or function (compensating for numerical limitations by offering unique or particularly effective capabilities).[70] His observations have a strong resemblance to the determinants affecting ADF decision makers and planners.

As the 1990s progressed, some efforts were made to improve Canada's joint capabilities, including the conduct of Maritime Command Operational Training (MARCOT) exercises. These exercises reflected the post-Cold War shift (experienced also by other navies, including the RAN) from traditional "blue-water" naval operations to "green water" operations in shallower and potentially more dangerous littorals.[71] In 1998, for instance, the east coast MARCOT, combined with the NATO exercise UNIFIED SPIRIT, was the largest joint and combined exercise ever held in Canada.[72] Yet the Canadian Forces' overall focus remained elsewhere for the duration of the 1990s. Canada continued to make significant main-force contributions to the UN and NATO-led missions to Bosnia and Kosovo. These involved Canadian troops in conflicts that were more warlike than any of the earlier Cold War peacekeeping missions. Force "sustainment" also became a key concern in Canada as the notion of "early in, early out" proved difficult to apply and the need for rotation units drained the forces.

In Kosovo, in 1999, Canada supported the U.S.-led NATO bombing campaign, despite the lack of authorization from the United Nations Security Council. It did so because it deemed the situation in Kosovo to be a sufficient threat to "human security" to justify extraordinary measures.[73] In Kosovo, Canada faced a "real war," particularly for the Canadian Air Force, which contributed to the bombing campaign with its CF-18 aircraft.[74] Indeed, Canada's stance over Kosovo was its most warlike one since the Korean War. Yet even here, despite the political fanfare, Canada's capabilities and influence were limited. Rempel observes that Canada had to borrow "Nite-hawk" forward-looking infra-red pods from Australia's FA-18 aircraft to enable it to deliver precision-guided munitions over Kosovo – an action that highlighted the low-key but important and enduring collaboration between the air forces of Canada and Australia. After the cease-fire, Canada also deployed an 800-person contingent of ground forces that was later reinforced by another 500-person contingent, including one troop of (four) Leopard tanks – providing a significant "presence" and morale boost for otherwise lightly armed Canadian forces with little else to fall back on should the situation have deteriorated further.[75]

In Kosovo, as Robert Kagan contends, "as in the Cold War, America fought in the Balkans ultimately to preserve 'the West.' And that goal determined military strategy." But the Kosovo war also "showed how difficult it was going to be for the United States and its European allies to fight any war together." For Canada, in contrast, the motivation for involvement in Kosovo appears to have been, at least in part, its desire for a continued "seat at the table" and its ongoing efforts to maintain its North Atlantic Triangle – whereby Canada sought to co-opt European influence to offset preponderant American power. Yet Canada's dispersed, or "penny-packeted," expeditionary peacekeeping forces appeared to be delivering reduced diplomatic leverage and political kudos to the Canadian government. Ironically, argued one Canadian officer, "the Europeans appeared to be counter-weighting all by themselves, leaving Canada out in the cold. The key Europeans dropped us before we really had a chance to shoot ourselves in the foot for them." Denis Stairs puts it sharply, arguing that Canadian policy in the 1990s was to "speak loudly and carry a bent twig."[76]

The Canadian experience in the Balkans and Africa stands in contrast to the experience of the Australians. For instance, Australia refrained from committing forces to the Balkans, seeing it as a primarily European concern (although New Zealand chose to contribute forces there). In addition, Australia saw its own "arc of instability" as requiring more urgent attention, with problems festering in Bougainville, the Solomon Islands, East Timor, and beyond.

EAST TIMOR AND ITS FALLOUT

In East Timor, the Australian command element, like its Canadian equivalent used in Africa in 1996, was based on the Deployable Joint Force Headquarters (also retaining its title for its dual role as Headquarters 1st Division). At its peak in late 1999, the East Timor mission involved over 7,500 ADF personnel (5,300 army personnel), either stationed in East Timor itself or providing support from the Australian base. Key to the success in East Timor, where a brigade-sized Australian force successfully deployed, was a unified and robust command structure and the deployment of balanced forces from all three services. Other important factors, in addition to brigade-level collective training, were individual soldier skills and the management of information and information technologies in an operational environment short of war with a "manoeuvrist" mindset. But, given the challenges, reviews, and cutbacks experienced in the years preceding the operation, the force commander, Major-General Peter Cosgrove, justifiably observed that the mission had proceeded smoothly *despite* the ADF's shortcomings up to that point, saying that "we were lucky and we were good."[77]

Just a few months before the operation, a command post exercise had been conducted based on DJFHQ using a scenario not unlike that of East Timor. This exercise involved members from the armies of the ABCA countries and certainly helped to ensure that techniques and procedures were well understood and practised in advance. The media featured prominently in this operation and was used as an effective supplement to the traditional "combat power" of the military forces that deployed on the operation. It was harnessed to assist in "shaping and influencing" events in a "non-kinetic" way to contain "collateral" damage, both physical and political in nature.[78]

The media message was buttressed by the contributions from twenty-two nations – including a Canadian ship (HMCS *Protecteur*), which provided critical support for the mission, Hercules aircraft, and a reinforced company from the French-speaking R22èR which was integrated into the Australian 3rd Brigade as part of the 1st Battalion, Royal New Zealand

Infantry Regiment (IRNZIR). Their inclusion served as an important re-
minder of how much Canada and Australia share a common heritage and
outlook, being prepared to face adversity together for the common good,
even in "remote" corners of the world. As Alan Hinge maintains, "Australia's material reliance on massive *allied* support was evident, especially in
terms of assistance required from the ABCA partners. British, US and Canadian forces played very important practical and political roles throughout
the crisis."[79]

Recognizing the limits of its military and financial capabilities, Australia
readily handed over command of administering the transition to independence in February 2000 to the United National Transitional Authority in
East Timor (UNTAET) and subsequently, in 2002, to its successor organization, the United Nations Mission in Support of East Timor (UNMISET).
Still, Australia maintained a strong interest, with the largest force contribution and the provision of key appointments such as the energetic Australian
deputy force commander of UNTAET, Major-General Mike Smith.[80]

The East Timor operation under the INTERFET mandate demonstrated
the merits of effective force-projection capabilities, including air and maritime elements that are critical to support and sustain land-force operations
away from the homeland. These capabilities are infrequently tested and are
even disparaged in peacetime because of their cost, but they were critical on
this operation. However, the mission exposed significant logistic shortfalls
and capability limitations that presented the ADF with an unprecedented
challenge, particularly following years of commercialization of administrative-support programs and logistic-capability cutbacks flowing from reviews of defence efficiency.[81] The mission also exposed the fallacy of
requiring only naval and air force assets to cross the "air-sea gap." After
all, only with ASP97 had the strategy of continental defence been effectively
shelved and priority on land forces increased. Arguably, the East Timor experience served to confirm categorically the shift in military strategy for
Australia, while also exposing limitations and areas where improvements
were needed.

In addition, the East Timor mission occurred when the efforts to improve
joint training and education were starting to bear fruit. In 1986 a tri-service
Australian Defence Force Academy (ADFA) had opened in Canberra and its
graduates were reaching the middle ranks of the officer corps of the respective services. Like Canada's Royal Military College, ADFA offered degrees in the liberal arts and sciences. Likewise, it provided an opportunity
for officer cadets from the three services to become friends before they became interservice rivals. Critics have argued that ADFA is an expensive and

wasteful institution, but this overlooks its profound benefits in terms of joint teamwork and effectiveness, even at the junior officer level, which were demonstrated in East Timor. There, what otherwise could have been a slow and tedious bureaucratic process for air support, for instance, was facilitated at least in part by familiarity and mutual friendship and respect.[82]

The East Timor operation further illustrated that the requirement for amphibious capabilities was one that was particularly significant for Australia. The East Timor operation made clear that forces are required for operations in the littorals and such commitments may include air and sea deployments. Consequently, such forces must be joint to take maximum advantage of the capabilities of each service in order to ensure success.[83]

Australia, like Canada, has had the option of deciding for itself what forces are necessary, albeit with a more persistent sense of concern over its geo-strategic isolation. Force structures designed for combat operations have been a key determinant of what Australia could contribute to such missions – hence the emphasis on ensuring the availability of balanced and rapidly deployable special, light, and mechanized forces by air and amphibious transport. This land-force focus has been complemented by the RAN's renewed interest in maintaining amphibious ships to provide "strategic lift" and to help sustain at least an independent battalion group.[84]

Shortly after the East Timor mission commenced, the Australian Department of Defence underwent another review, culminating in a White Paper released in 2000. This document, entitled *Defence 2000: Our Future Defence Force*, reversed the contraction of defence spending of the previous decade. Reflecting the implications of the East Timor operation, the role of the army was broadened to cater to a wider range of security contingencies, including a capacity to conduct expeditionary warfare, that is, to be able to deploy and sustain land forces away from home bases – be it in remote parts of Australia's north or abroad. Experience in East Timor and a succession of operations in the littorals of the Asia-Pacific region and beyond added impetus to the White Paper and led to the development of Australian doctrine for military operations in the littoral environment, or MOLE. As Australia's Lieutenant-General Peter Leahy observed, "the lesson is clear: the Army cannot work alone. In the future the ADF will need to be able to deploy and sustain itself as a joint force wherever it is directed to operate by the Government." The emphasis on expeditionary and amphibious warfare that is integral to MOLE generated the need to modify doctrine, structures, capabilities, equipment, and training. Given the nature of amphibious operations, joint operations became the hallmark of most foreseeable ADF deployments. Leahy argued that "this concept envisages that our land forces will be capable of achieving strategic reach through entry from the air or sea" – something that Canada last did in 1956. Furthermore, "the MOLE concept also embodies the notion of decisive action, followed by a transition to peacekeeping or support operations." The Australian Army's MOLE doctrine is complemented at the operational level by reference to ABCA doctrine. "To a certain extent," as Alan Ryan points out, "the need for operational-level coalition doctrine is filled by the ABCA *Coalition Operations Handbook*, which is widely consulted in relevant ADF operational-level headquarters."[85]

By the turn of the twenty-first century, Australia's force structure was being moulded for the defence of Australia and its immediate environs, whereas Canada's remained focused primarily to fit with NATO strategy – even though, following the end of the Cold War, NATO was becoming increasingly ill-defined militarily. Canada's commitment to an alliance strategy initially wavered as the Cold War ended and the withdrawal of troops from Lahr was initiated. But ultimately, even though Canada's strategic link with Europe became more tenuous as some European nations sought to stress their own distinctiveness at the expense of NATO, Canada's commitment to NATO endured – on account of the organization's increasing willingness to operate "out of area," that is, beyond Europe. With continuing demands for force contributions, however, the causal flow began to work in reverse for Australia. Force sustainment became a common issue as Australia's commitment to East Timor continued for several years and other commitments arose. Despite the rhetoric to the contrary, operational demands pressed Australia to follow Canada's lead to factor in military operations other than conventional war as a force-structure determinant. Reflecting on the last two decades of the twentieth century, Lieutenant-General Leahy claimed that "the Defence of Australia construct seriously eroded core land force capabilities and turned the Army into little more than a strategic goalkeeper ... During the 1980s and much of the 1990s, the strategic guidance given to the Army ultimately diminished land force capabilities. We gradually lost strategic agility; our units became hollow; and our ability to operate away from Australian support bases declined to a dangerous degree." Leahy's comments reveal an uncanny parallel with the experience of the Canadian Forces – an experience that has continued for longer than in Australia's case. For Australia, the East Timor experience provided the necessary cathartic experience that has so far eluded the Canadian Forces because of their government's lack of interest, despite the events in Zaire in 1996.[86]

The 1990s had witnessed Canadians and Australians deploying on many similar missions around the world, but often with starkly contrasting experiences. Canadians reflected on their own difficulties in the 1990s and saw how Australia managed to lead successfully an international force in East Timor. The contrast sparked a heightened awareness of the need for introspection and reinvigoration of the Canadian Forces. As one historian points out, two generations of Canadians had grown up without knowing, as three previous generations did, the experience of war. Yet "armed conflict continues to be one of the most enduring expressions of the human condition, and Canadian soldiers, while praying for peace, must prepare for war." Such increased self-awareness has prompted the Canadian Forces to promote more professional awareness through study (using, for instance, the *Canadian Army Reading List* as a guide) and through further tertiary education for all its officers.[87] These circumstances have also helped generate professional debate in the CF's military journals (the *Canadian Military Journal*, the *Army Doctrine and Training Bulletin*, and the latter's successor, the *Canadian Army Journal*). These fora have been used increasingly for discussions concerning the more complex peace support and war-fighting operations of recent years. One prominent figure in these discussions has been Brigadier-General Glenn Nordick, who, in an article on fighting in built-up areas, argued that "we can do this, so let's get on with it," and who, in another article, stressed the need to retain a focus on war-fighting (using NATO and ABCA standards) in order to develop officers with the ability to perform command and staff functions in war.[88]

The Canadian Army, some suggest, had never focused on education, preferring routine training instead, or, as Haycock contends, preferring to remain content with "the technical and tactical posture of the past, *sans* education."[89] Added to the lack of education was the lack of solid experience, with training capped at lower and lower levels. In particular, field exercises throughout the 1990s were infrequently force-on-force affairs, and opposing forces were seldom allowed free play. Brigade-group exercises rarely challenged the senior commanders and their staffs, and battle simulations tended to be repeats from past years. What is more, cutbacks curtailed collective training throughout the 1990s, and the army brigade-level exercise in early 2003 was the first in a decade.[90] One observer noted that "without a thinking and active enemy, few lessons are learned."[91]

Some progressive steps were taken. In 1996–97 the CF initiated planning for a Disaster Assistance Response Team (DART), a company-sized unit with 150–200 personnel including a headquarters and medical, engineer, logistics, and security platoons, with an advance party to move on forty-eight hours' notice from the deployment announcement (the main body being on seven days' notice). In June 2000 further improvements were made when the CF Joint Operations Group (CF JOG) was created, incorporating its component parts of the 1 Joint Signals Regiment and the Joint Task Force Headquarters – structures not unlike Australia's 1 Joint Support Unit and DJFHQ. In addition, a Joint Support Group was formed and assigned to the CF JOG. Concept development and experimentation also was fostered with the creation of the CF Experimentation Centre in May 2001. Like the ADF, with its CDF Preparedness Directives and Operational Preparedness Directives, the Canadian Forces developed a Canadian Joint Task List as a force-structure planning tool. Overall, it became evident that the CF was taking some clear, if sometimes tentative, steps towards improving its joint-command structure. Such efforts reflected the growing recognition that the CF would be required to conduct operations across a wide spectrum of conflict as part of a coalition. To this end, tactically self-sufficient units were being prepared that were capable of making a valuable contribution to joint (interservice) and combined (multinational) operations.[92] Such moves would prove prescient, given the events that unfolded after 11 September 2001.

CONCLUSION

This chapter has demonstrated that, in the post-Cold War years, the Canadian and Australian forces faced remarkably similar challenges often in the same places and usually far from their own shores around the world. In contrast to their experiences during the Cold War, the demands of the post-Cold War era had driven their respective forces to develop more flexible and rapidly deployable forces. These forces were required to be capable of responding to a wide variety of complex scenarios ranging from humanitarian assistance to interpositional peacekeeping, more complex peace-support operations, and occasionally even warlike situations. For Canada, many of these commitments took place alongside European partners in NATO. Indeed, as David Haglund points out, "by the latter half of the 1990s, Canada was more focused on Europe and NATO than it had been in the closing decades of the Cold War."[93] The European focus, however, obscured the growing convergence with Canada's non-NATO Australian "cousins." Clearly, in terms of defence policy and armed-forces development, the Canadian and Australian experiences demonstrated a significant reconvergence during this period, although, in Australia's case, the East

Timor mission provided the necessary impetus to reverse the atrophy of capabilities that would continue to plague the Canadian Forces.

Observers may caution against too closely comparing the Australian and Canadian experiences, arguing that defence-policy similarities often do not expand into foreign-policy and economic fields. One example is the Closer Economic Relations (CER) agreement reached between Australia and New Zealand that had its origins in the 1965 New Zealand-Australia Free Trade Agreement, covering about 60 per cent of trade between the two countries. In 1989 Australia rejected a proposal to extend the CER to include Canada, fearing that it would undermine attempts to develop stronger economic ties with the east Asian region, or even invite retaliatory trade discrimination. In hindsight, and with Australia eager for access to the North American Free Trade Agreement (NAFTA), perhaps closer cooperation with Canada through the CER would not have been as counter-productive as regional trade advocates, with their focus on the short term, had expected.

Another example sometimes referred to is the contrasting positions taken by the Australian and Canadian governments over trade negotiations as part of the Cairns Group, formed in the late 1980s and operative through most of the 1990s. Anne Capling and Kim Richard Nossal, for instance, declare that Australians' role as leaders of the Cairns Group from the mid-1980s onwards "was threatening Canada's traditional role of insider and interlocutor between the great powers." In addition, the Cairns Group's insistence on across-the-board liberalization in protectionist trade measures was not perceived to be in Canada's national interest owing to the handful of domestic political constituencies that objected to such moves. Capling and Nossal conclude that "there are limits to how far attributes as like-mindedness, friendliness, trust, and high comfort levels will go to mitigate the effects of divergent calculations of national interest."[94] Such sobering observations have significant ramifications for defence planners contemplating closer collaboration for the expeditionary forces of Australia and Canada. However, they also need to be considered in another light.

It could be argued that the divergent "tactical" positions taken by Canada and Australia in the Cairns Group negotiations betrayed a short-sighted understanding of their own longer-term and more fundamental or "enlightened" national interests. Such a short-sighted understanding has been an enduring feature of the conduct of Australian and Canadian officials for over a century, and it has been so at the expense of the alternate path less travelled – the path of enlightened self-interest where both nation's officials act together, with a greater strategic awareness of common bonds and interests. That kind of approach, conceivably, would further the interests of Australia and Canada alike by mutually reinforcing those of both. And it would be consistent with the notion of enlightened self-interest espoused by Joseph Nye, who argues that national interests are best understood holistically as a combination of economic, military, and transnational relations interests. Nye makes the point that "multilateralism involves costs, but in the larger picture, they are outweighed by the benefits." To date, tactical or short-term priorities have led to short-sighted and counter-productive positions and to no clear sustained national-security policy on the part of either Australia or Canada, which has weakened each country's place on the world stage. This weakening has resulted from the common lack of a strategic perspective – in other words, a lack of vision and a lack of awareness of the common interests at stake that have been shared by these cousins at opposite ends of the globe.[95]

Perhaps the most remarkable of such similar trajectories lies with their respective armed forces. This chapter has demonstrated how, in terms of their expeditionary-oriented force structures as well as the nature and location of their operational deployments, the Australian and Canadian forces largely reconverged in the post-Cold War years. This reconvergence has been to an extent not seen since the British Empire was at its height, and it points to renewed opportunities for closer and mutually beneficial collaboration.

The challenges and opportunities presented to the armed forces of Canada and Australia since the end of the Cold War have been further complicated by the onset of the War on Terror. The corresponding shift in national direction for defence and foreign policy in both Canada and Australia has continued to display enduring similarities, albeit with the same enduring differences at work, as the following chapter sets out to illustrate.

8

Responding to the Long War on Terrorism

On 11 September 2001 the World Trade Center Twin Towers were destroyed and the Pentagon was struck by the weapons of the newly "super-empowered" terrorists of the twenty-first century. As Australia's Michael Evans observes, post-modern conflict based on high-technology aerospace power had created its own antithesis, that is, "asymmetric warfare including the threat of weapons of mass destruction, waged against Western society."[1] But a more fundamental change was triggered in American self-consciousness as well. As the American scholar Victor Davis Hanson contends, "we went back to an appreciation of 19th century or classical values because when you have a crater in downtown Manhattan and two kilotonnes worth of explosive power and 3,000 dead, it makes an impression and questions received wisdom."[2] It was not only Americans who suffered at the terrorists' hands. Ten Australians and twenty-nine Canadians died in the Twin Towers, in addition to the hundreds from several other nations.

INITIAL RESPONSES

Countries around the world responded initially in shock and sympathy, and the NATO and ANZUS alliances' mutual-defence clauses were invoked by u.s. allies in support. But the greatest effect was to galvanize the will of the United States to respond with determination. Following that fateful day, the world was redefined for the United States, turning places beyond its borders from being vaguely irrelevant and largely harmless locations where good deeds could be performed – be it in Haiti, Somalia, or the Balkans – into something more deadly. The events of that day also created a focus for u.s. power not seen since the end of the Cold War: the incapacitation of militant

Islam as represented by al-Qaeda. Al-Qaeda was reported to be dispersed globally, from North America to Europe and even southeast Asia. American iconoclast and retired military officer Ralph Peters contends that apocalyptic Muslim warriors cannot be accommodated within the West's world-view, so "we must fight them, and we must destroy them."[3] His arguments sit uncomfortably with the West's postmodern cultural relativists but they reflect an imperative that drove the United States to act and to draw along a coalition of the willing to assist.

The United States began to hunt down and defeat al-Qaeda operatives wherever they were found. But the way such actions took place seriously affected the dynamics of the entire international system. For instance, the United Nations was partly marginalized and NATO at least temporarily rendered less militarily and diplomatically relevant than ever before. Such radical changes on the international stage have presented the governments of Australia and Canada with a range of significant challenges as they have sought to respond and adapt to the new geo-strategic environment – one dominated by an assertive and powerful United States seeking to dictate the terms of its international affairs. As one commentator states, "the United States has been a democratic republic, an anti-imperial power. Now it is an imperial power."[4] While such a position may be contentious, its ramifications have provided Canada and Australia with significant foreign- and defence-policy challenges.

Canada and Australia recognized the need to respond to the events of 9/11, beyond the initial expression of support and assistance to those stranded by the events of that fateful day. Consequently, both countries have contributed to the fight in the War on Terrorism, and this has affected their respective force structures. Their contributions rest on a fundamental alignment with and support for the United States as it faces an unprecedented challenge. As Australia's Lieutenant-General Leahy cautions, "in a world of borderless security, Australia cannot seek safety behind an Antipodean Maginot Line narrowly defined by a sea-air gap. That comfortable world of the 1980s has disappeared."[5]

For Canada, the incentive for keeping an open border for its vital cross-border trade has been the most obvious motivation.[6] This incentive became obvious when the U.S. border posts and airports were immediately closed in September 2001. Virtually overnight, the United States was once again concerned about homeland defence in a way not seen since the 1950s. As one scholar contends, scenarios of a fortress America with fortifications along the 49th parallel sent Canadians a frightening message that, after decades of pursuing an even deeper intermingling of the two systems, they now faced immediate and total (albeit temporary) exclusion.[7] Indeed, perceptions of the threat differed on the two sides of the Canada-United States border, with most Canadians not feeling as directly exposed. Still, the overwhelming imperatives associated with the border led both countries to sign a "Smart Border" Declaration to increase both security and efficiency along the shared border through expedited clearance programs and expanded information sharing and law enforcement.[8]

In contrast, for Australia, its isolation, sense of regional hostility, and perceived need to work harder at preserving its alliance with the United States spurred cooperation. As a writer for the u.s. Army's Strategic Studies Institute describes it, "Australia is a natural and effective partner for pursuing the war on terrorism in the Asia-Pacific, which is likely to be one of the major battlegrounds."[9] But, despite coming at the issue from different directions, as at so many times in the past, Canada and Australia ended up responding to the issues in similar ways.

For instance, reflecting the different nature of the threat posed by terrorism, homeland security featured more prominently for both Australia and Canada. As a consequence, the Australian and Canadian forces worked more closely with other domestic police, security, and emergency services, although both countries recognized that the responsibility for most of the domestic response to terrorism needed to fall on civilian agencies and not their departments of defence.[10]

Both countries faced pressure to demolish interagency barriers and improve information sharing and cooperation to advance the common goal. Both also faced similar constitutional and legal constraints affecting civil liberties as the lines between domestic police and military-security functions blurred. In addition, both have small defence industrial bases eager to tap into the high technology and industry associated with the RMA. In some ways, Australia was well placed to adjust to the post-9/11 world, given Australia's more substantial special forces and paramilitary police and the overhaul of domestic-security measures undertaken for the 2000 Sydney Olympics – an overhaul that involved state and federal police forces working closely with the ADF. (Australia's experience also echoed Canada's deployment of 16,000 troops for the Montreal Olympics in 1976.) By the time of the Sydney Olympics, Canada was once again showing enthusiasm for combating terrorism and similarly revamped and expanded its ability to respond to civil emergencies with its own younger and smaller special-forces group, reflecting at least in part a desire to minimize border problems with the United States.[11]

Such imperatives for closer Canadian collaboration and integration with the United States grew after Canada became a signatory to NAFTA in 1993. But, with increased globalization and the instant and widespread communications of the information era, the spread of terrorism was symptomatic of a large range of issues that have been global in cause and effect. This growth in international linkages suggests that a broader definition of national interests is necessary which takes account of the interests of others: an "enlightened self-interest," whereby mutual benefit can be accrued that is consistent with the national interest.[12]

AFGHANISTAN, 2002

Abroad, both Australia and Canada demonstrated that enlightened self-interest by playing important supportive roles alongside U.S. forces both in the Arabian Sea with their navies and in Afghanistan. Their contributions included elements of Canadian and Australian special forces – a 150-man Australian SAS team and a 40-man Canadian JTF2 team. Canada also deployed a light infantry battalion, the 3rd Battalion PPCLI, which was involved in operations aimed to "smoke-out" al-Qaeda operatives. The mission was Canada's largest ground offensive since the Korean War. The Canadian snipers attached to the battalion confirmed dozens killed and were recommended for the American Bronze Star of Valour.[13] The mission also pointed to the similar imperatives that had once again drawn Australians and Canadians to work with their major allies and alongside each other, yet with little forethought.

The 3PPCLI commanding officer, Lieutenant-Colonel Pat Stogran, happened to be a former exchange instructor in tactics with the Australian Army. Stogran's troops, as well as the JTF2, encountered issues with coordination and collaboration similar to those faced by the Australians. For both Canadians and Australians, the experience reinforced the need for lighter and more lethal, deployable, and networked joint forces capable of operating over vast distances.[14] Working as junior partners in a U.S.-controlled coalition drove renewed emphasis on interoperability and robust force-projection capabilities. Special forces, long-range precision "fires," and information operations also featured prominently. Both Australia and Canada were faced with rethinking the force-structure mix, as they grappled with the implications of this apparently new style of warfare and sought to find a less expensive middle course. Admittedly, Australia's experience in East Timor stood it in good stead for such events, while Canada's experience in the Balkans also was of value.

ADAPTING TO THE NEW STRATEGIC SETTING

Despite the experience in the Balkans, argues Andrew Cohen, Canada's ability to make such commitments had been reduced throughout the 1990s. Cohen suggests that "by three principal measures – the power of the military, the generosity of its foreign aid, the quality of its foreign service – it [Canada] is less effective than a generation ago." Cohen further contends that Canada made the mistake of assuming that "we could have sovereignty without substantial military expenditure. That illusion is over." Indeed, the lament comes from many quarters, with over a dozen major military studies since 2001 all reaching similar conclusions about the Canadian Forces being under-funded, under-staffed, and ill-equipped, to the extent that, as one American diplomat indicated, "Canada effectively has surrendered its military defence to the United States." In late 2002 even the minister for national defence, John McCallum, made a public plea to his own government for more money – a step usually reserved for closed-door cabinet meetings. Outgoing Prime Minister Jean Chrétien, known for his aversion to military affairs, played down McCallum's overtures. But, following McCallum's lead, the CDS, General Ray Henault, also appealed in his annual report for the government to focus on the military's shortfalls. "Now is not the time to pause in our resolve to reposition Canada's military as a relevant, combat-capable player in the new defence and security environment. We must move forward with determination, commitment and unity of purpose and we must capitalize on this opportunity. The time to act is now."[15]

Such sentiment reflects concerns similar to the ones that were aired in Australia in the mid-1990s, when defence spending and personnel strengths reached a post-Vietnam War low point. But Australia's policy response since September 2001, although in substance quite similar to Canada's, was more visibly robust. For Australia, the effect of the events of 9/11 and the Bali bombing in October 2002, which killed nearly 100 vacationing Australian citizens, led the government to prepare and issue a *Defence Update 2003*. Released by the defence minister, Senator Robert Hill, on 26 February 2003, it argued that, while the threat of direct military attack on Australia remained small, "geography does not protect Australia from rogue states armed with weapons of mass destruction and ballistic missiles or from terrorism" – including from al-Qaeda and its regional offshoots and affiliates. The paper stressed that "Australia's immediate region continues to face major challenges, making it more vulnerable to transnational security threats." The global security environment had changed and there was an "increasing likelihood that Australian national interests could be affected by events outside our immediate neighbourhood." As a consequence of this rethinking of Australia's security environment, a rebalancing was required – although this would "not fundamentally alter the size, structure and role of the Australian Defence Force." Yet it would "ensure a more flexible and mobile force, with sufficient levels of readiness, sustainability and interoperability to perform the increased range of tasks it is likely to have to play in our current strategic environment."[16]

Underlying the concerns expressed in Australia's *Defence Update 2003* and *Defence Update 2005* (including the willingness to deploy "further afield") was an apparent understanding of the unique geo-strategic environment faced by Australia. This understanding appears to have prompted a desire to address the Middle Eastern sources of southeast Asian terrorist training and funding that some linked to weapons of mass destruction and the Bali bombing. In essence, the Bali bombing illustrated for Australians that geographic isolation was no longer a guarantee of safety from the world's security problems. Consequently, the Australian government took the view in 2003 that it was "unrealistic to think that Australia's security interests are not directly engaged by the threat of proliferation of [weapons of mass destruction] through Iraq."[17]

Australia's Department of Foreign Affairs and Trade also issued a White Paper in 2003 entitled *Advancing the National Interest*. This White Paper focused largely on Australia's need to fight terrorism and global threats to its security, including the proliferation of weapons of mass destruction. The paper stressed the value of collaborating with the United Nations and other multilateral groupings to facilitate Australia's national security.[18]

Australia's Defence and Foreign Affairs and Trade white papers were based on a significant reassessment of the dynamics at work in the United States. By 2003, the United States had become, according to an Australian defence policy adviser, "a strategic reality as present and pervasive as geography" – and geography has been a factor that has always dominated strategic thinking in Australia and Canada to an equal extent. Consequently, "defence policy needs to rethink the relationship between its two fundamental shaping influences – geography on one hand, and the Alliance on the other. In a globalised world, geography is less of a strategic asset. Conversely ... the potential strategic value of the US Alliance is increased."[19] Similarly, one Canadian military officer contends that "in the global interconnected Western world, the house under threat is no longer geographic, but geopolitical – no longer physical, but perceptual and cultural. In this sense, one can argue that the importance of Canada's geography as one of the primary 'invariants' of defence policy is much diminished and is being superseded by such elements as geopolitical alignment, historical alliances, and national political and public character."[20] For Australia, this increase in strategic value also manifested itself in the nation's growing importance to u.s. strategic plans in the Asia-Pacific. u.s. Deputy Secretary of Defense Paul Wolfowitz indicated that, in conjunction with Japan, Australia acts as the foundation of a u.s. strategic triangle in the Pacific. This may result in a greater u.s. military presence in Australia, with increased military exercises and greater sharing of Australian naval and air facilities.[21]

Unlike Australia, and despite the observations made above, Canada under the Chrétien government showed little enthusiasm for significantly reworking its defence policy or significantly increasing defence spending in the light of new and greater demands on the use of its forces. For instance, in contrast to the periodic reviews conducted in Australia, Canada waited for a decade after 1994 to initiate a new white paper on defence, despite the calls for a significant and public reconsideration of Canadian defence strategy in the post-9/11 era. Some Defence officials defended the lack of another review, arguing that the issues addressed and conclusions reached in the 1994 White Paper remained pertinent for the post-9/11 world.[22] In fact, the Canadian government did conduct a security review (a defence review would have to wait until 2005) after the events of 11 September that resulted, as already noted, in the "Smart Border" Agreement with the United States to facilitate the trade flow between their two countries. For Canada, like Australia, bilateralism has always been viewed as an attractive means to achieve broad foreign-policy objectives, including the tempering of u.s. whims and excesses. But, in contrast to Australia, most cases of regional conflict or instability have, for many years, not even indirectly affected Canada's economic or security interests. As Sokolsky observed in 1997, "Ottawa may still believe that Washington is 'bound to lead,' but it does not always hold that it [Canada] is necessarily bound to follow." Frank Harvey explains this as being in part due to Canada's search for "foreign policy distinctiveness," to its desire that it not be seen to be towing the Washington line. Yet, as Sokolsky notes, despite this search for distinctiveness, in the 1990s at least, "Canada followed the us lead pretty closely."[23]

Given Canada's search for distinctiveness, the robust stance taken by Australia, particularly following the East Timor intervention in 1999, made some Canadian defence-policy analysts and other observers increasingly envious. For instance, one Canadian journalist wrote in August 2003 about "how Australia's plucky military does more with less." He argued:

There was a time when Canada and Australia both punched above their weight. Each country made immense contributions at great cost in lives and money ... The reality today, as can be seen in Afghanistan, Timor and the Solomons, is entirely different ... In addition to tough talk, pledging to increase its defence budget by three per cent annually to 2011, Australia intends to spend $14.37 billion Cdn this year, compared to Canada's $13 billion ... Furthermore, since the Chrétien government chose not to join the war against Iraq, Canada has been excluded for the first time from the tight intelligence circle that it developed with Washington, London and Canberra ... it is another damning indicator of where Canada finds itself in this turbulent world. Australia shows Canada that a plucky country with limited financial resources can have a military that has teeth, confidence and purpose.[24]

In response to this article, the executive director of the Canadian Conference of Defence Associations, Alain Pellerin, "encouraged the Government of Canada to address these important issues." Indeed, following the selection of Paul Martin, Jr as prime minister after Chrétien's retirement in December 2003, an International Policy Review, incorporating defence- and foreign-policy matters, was undertaken early in 2004.[25] Such policy steps suggest that the continuities between Australian and Canadian defence policy observed so far – particularly as they pertain to the use of expeditionary forces – will endure for the foreseeable future as well.

The Australian comparison aside, Canada's geography and circumstances point to ongoing security cooperation with the United States as a tremendous economic imperative. The country's overwhelming trade ties with the United States mean that American security priorities have a significant impact on the security and foreign-policy priorities that Canada sets for itself. As Canada's Department of Foreign Affairs and International Trade's policy statement, A Dialogue on Foreign Policy, indicated in January 2003 (echoing sentiments expressed in Australian policy circles), no international relationship "is more important than the one we share with the United States." Indeed, "we will continue to work with the u.s. and other allies to protect the values that we hold in common, such as freedom, tolerance and respect for cultural diversity."[26]

In the face of the new post-9/11 security climate, defence-policy priorities changed and pressure grew for closer Canadian cooperation with the United States. Indeed, Canada and Australia both saw their security interests largely aligned with the United States, and interoperability featured prominently as an issue critical to enhanced collaboration. At the same time, both countries faced the need to reconcile popular opinion and idealism with the dynamics of realpolitik.

The events of 11 September 2001 suddenly made North American defence of vital importance to the United States. Yet, while defence overseas had always been seen as discretionary for Canada, the litmus test of loyalty to the United States after 9/11 may be not what is done in North America but what is done in support of U.S. objectives abroad.[27] This requirement for support overseas has had a significant effect on the formulation of Canadian defence and security policy – both by encouraging conformity and cooperation and by fostering a desire for Canadian distinctiveness and protection of sovereignty, however ill-defined those goals may be.

Canada, like several of its European NATO partners, believes that radical Islamic extremism does not necessarily force the West to prove itself unified and coherent, as Soviet communism once did. In contrast, Australia, once again concerned about its more volatile region, has felt greater certainty in backing U.S.-led efforts to extend the "War on Terror" to Iraq. Nonetheless, both Canadians and Australians do struggle with reconciling their liberal-internationalist predispositions with the often harder-nosed American reckoning of power politics in international affairs.[28] For Canada, comfortable in its secure and benign environment under the largely U.S.-provided security umbrella, the apparent absence of direct and imminent threat also means being able to pick and choose which international military missions it supports.

WAR IN IRAQ

After 11 September 2001, Canada was prepared to strengthen some of its military links with the United States, but it was not willing to go as far in support of American military actions as Australia was. For instance, in early 2003, 2,000 Australian troops deployed as part of the "coalition of the willing" to the Gulf region and participated in the U.S.-led war against Iraq. In addition, lead elements of the Australian special forces deployed into Iraq two days before the opening salvo of the war to track key military targets and destroy them as well as capture the Al Asad air base west of Baghdad, with the support of Australian FA-18 aircraft.[29] The Australian task group included members of the SAS Regiment, a force-protection team from 4RAR (Commando), members of the Incident Response Regiment, Chinook helicopters, transport and surveillance aircraft, naval ships, and headquarters elements attached to the U.S. forces. The Australians played a significant role in neutralizing the missile threat to Israel in the opening days of the war. Moreover, the Australian FA-18 aircraft performed roles similar to those of Canada's CF-18s in the Kosovo campaign in 1999 and the Gulf War of 1990–91.[30] The FA-18s conducted strike missions and close air support with precision weapons and with no civilian casualties

observed. This was the first time that Australian aircraft had dropped
bombs in a war zone since the Vietnam War more than thirty years previously.[31] It was also the first time that Australia conducted aerial resupply
for its own troops in combat since the Vietnam War.[32] After the war in Iraq
initially subsided in May, Australia maintained a force of nearly nine
hundred troops in the region.[33] Australian Major-General Jim Molan,
commenting on the interservice teamwork displayed by the Australian
forces in Iraq in 2003, observed that "it is our ability to 'do jointery' that
makes us different from most of our neighbours and many other armies in
the world."[34]

Conceivably, Canada and Australia could have collaborated to form a
combined joint task force, had there been a greater awareness of the two
countries' military compatibilities as well as the political will to take such
action. After all, Canada also maintained ships in the Gulf and deployed a
comparable number of staff officers to the same U.S. headquarters. Indeed,
Canadian military planners had contemplated joining Australians in a
"Commonwealth Brigade" that would be part of a British Army division.
Instead, and in contrast to Australia, Canada sought to avoid participating
in what some described as the "coalition of the coerced" and therefore
committed 1,900 troops to relieve U.S. forces in Afghanistan instead. By so
doing, the Canadian government cunningly attempted to sidestep the issue
of direct military support to the U.S. campaign in Iraq, largely for what has
been described as short-term domestic political reasons.[35] Some observers
suggested that Canada's reluctance had more to do with concerns about being too closely positioned with English-speaking countries, something that
a majority of Quebeckers (facing a provincial election, which was to be
held during the war) were eager to avoid[36] – an argument that points to the
enduring preoccupation in Canada with national unity. Others speculated
that Canadian oil interests associated with a relative of Prime Minister
Chrétien may also have been a factor in the government's decision.[37]

The contrasting positions between Australia's Howard and Canada's
Chrétien underline a frequent difference in political orientation between the
federal government often of the two nations, with Canada's Liberal (progressive) government often at variance with Australia under its Liberal (conservative) government (as indicated in appendix 1). But, in fact, such positions
reflect more a certain hard-nosed yet short-term-focused "realism" than
any fundamental or permanent differences in values that would prevent
closer cooperation in the future. This has become more evident following
the federal election of January 2006, which returned a Conservative government led by Stephen Harper.[38]

As reports now indicate, the military contributions to Iraq in early 2003 could have been otherwise. For instance, if Australia and Canada had previously scheduled exercises between their two countries' forces for a combined joint task force, and if the Quebec provincial elections of April 2003 had preceded the start of the war in Iraq, Australia and Canada might have operated alongside each other – as a team, even – and gained greater diplomatic leverage than they did otherwise. After all, Canadian forces remained in the Gulf region throughout the war in Iraq despite the Canadian government's public opposition to the war. For the sake of its ties with the United States, the Canadian government could have been convinced to side with the United States in this conflict. Had Canada done so, a combined Australian-Canadian force may have been able to make a significant contribution and retain considerable influence. As it turned out, with only 2,000 troops involved, Australia's contribution remained relatively minor, not unlike Canada's contribution to the International Security Assistance Force (ISAF) in Kabul, Afghanistan.[39]

In responding to the Iraq issue in the way they did, Australia and Canada were reversing the roles that they had played in the Suez Crisis of 1956: then Australia sided with Britain and France against the United States, while Canada acted as the American proxy. The reversal points to a distinction that reflects a continuing difference in the foreign-policy dynamics of Australia and Canada. For Canada, distinctiveness, or at least a stance different from that taken by more powerful "cousins," sometimes trumps alliance cooperation. The same is not true of Australia.

In light of the pressures to align with the United States, Paul Martin, prior to becoming prime minister of Canada, outlined his view of Canada's future foreign and defence policy, arguing in May 2003 that "the time for multilateral initiative has never been greater" and yet "fixing multilateralism is not just a matter of strengthening the UN. It also means identifying – and using – new arrangements and rules outside of the UN ... We have our interests too. We have joined alliances to preserve and protect them. We have fought wars to defend them. And we have worked diplomatically for an international system that embodies and extends them."[40] Voicing similar concerns, the historian Margaret MacMillan laments what she considers the loss of a clear sense of Canada's mission in the world. She points to the long preoccupation with Quebec's place in Canada and claims that "a lot of our best minds were turned inwards." The superpower polarity of the Cold War reinforced the sense that there was not much Canadians could do about it. But, with the Cold War over, Canadians, MacMillan argues, "show signs of being ready to reengage with the world."[41] Martin's and MacMillan's comments hint at the prospects of closer collaboration between Canadians and their "cousins down under"– two peoples equidistant from the prospective emerging powers of the twenty-first century and the potential "hot spots" of northeast Asia.

BEYOND THE WAR IN IRAQ

Statements about Canada's readiness to re-engage in international defence and security affairs augur well for the prospects of collaboration between the Australian and Canadian forces. Indeed, despite Canada's reluctance to join the coalition in Iraq in 2003, its interests are intrinsically aligned with the United States and its key allies.[42] In this respect, there is no doubt that the contrasting positions over the war in Iraq tend to obscure the fundamental but often unnoticed similarities in outlook shared by Canadians and Australians (outlined in chart 1). These similarities are enduring – having lasted for more than a century – and numerous, even taking into account the occasional differences of opinion.

Still, Canada's unwillingness to join its traditional allies in Iraq early in 2003 left Canadian policy makers with a significant challenge. As Victor Davis Hanson argued in mid-2003 concerning the mood in the United States, "it's stunning how much goodwill there is towards Britain and Australia, but not necessarily for Canada and New Zealand. It goes deeper than just historical ties or the English language. It has more to do with the idea that certain countries have not become post-modern yet. They're still muscular, they still have values and see the world as still a dangerous and tragic place. We in America don't necessarily always care what the exact material contribution of those countries is. It's got more to do with a shared kindred spirit."[43] That lack of demonstrated Canadian "kindred spirit" over Iraq in 2003 left Australian policy makers wary, in the short term at least, of closer engagement with Canada. Overcoming such wariness will require a re-examination of each other's national interests to see how much is shared in common – a move that may be facilitated by the Conservative election victory of 2006.

Australian policy makers recognized the value of placing interests and hard-headedness first, and, for the ADF, this also meant enhancing its warfighting capabilities. In 2003 the ADF published a position paper entitled *Future Warfighting Concept*, touted as a "stake in the ground" for ADF strategic thinking. The concept known as "Multidimensional Manoeuvre" incorporates three components that reveal a strong American influence – "the Seamless Force, effects-based operations and network-centric warfare." Like Canada, Australia faces significant pressures and incentives to enhance military interoperability with the United States and these are reflected in the "Multidimensional Manoeuvre" concept. Yet, regardless of what changes may occur, the same kinds of requirements remain extant for Australian and Canadian soldiers. The ADF's paper acknowledges that "only a disciplined armed force capable of warfighting has the necessary skills and equipment to contribute to the full range of possible operational contingencies and peacetime tasks. Warfighting must therefore remain at the core of our preparation and training because it will remain a dangerous and difficult task that requires specialist training to master and significant personal risk to apply."[44] Michael Evans takes this further, arguing that the ability to combine fire, protection, and movement by different arms of the military has been critical to success in close combat. This combination, as Lieutenant-General Monash once argued, is like an orchestra. It "represents an important measure of an army's professional effectiveness. In close combat, no one single arm or weapons system can succeed alone: infantry must be teamed with tanks and both must be linked to artillery."[45]

Beyond the acknowledgment of the centrality of war-fighting skills for soldiers, and the need for the maintenance of combined-arms skills, there remains some vexed issues for modern Western armed forces like Canada's and Australia's to consider. As both countries look ahead to prospective operations, they may ponder what Michael Evans has said about the future of conflict. In his view, "as every good operational commander knows, in the military art one can 'trade down' but one can never 'trade up' ... In the West we must reconcile how we would like to fight with how we might *have* to fight ... A military force may now be required to conduct intervention operations in conditions that correspond to neither classical warfare nor traditional peace-support operations ... To meet the challenges of tomorrow's wars, Western countries will need highly mobile, well equipped, and versatile forces capable of multidimensional coalition missions and 'mastery of violence' across a complex spectrum of conflict."[46]

A new term has come into vogue that reflects the complex nature of the forces considered necessary to handle the challenges of the future. That term is Joint, Inter-agency and Multi-lateral (JIM) operations. These operations involve all armed services (joint), international organizations, non-government organizations, other government aid, security, and intelligence agencies (interagency), and multiple nations (multilateral). The conflict and post-conflict challenges in Afghanistan and Iraq in 2002, 2003, and beyond suggest that this likely will be a continuing trend. For the Canadian forces with the ISAF in Kabul, Afghanistan, for instance, as one journalist noted, "it's a far cry from the classic peacekeeping formula." The multilevel approach evident there has involved a cooperative effort among Defence, Foreign Affairs, and the Canadian International Development Agency as well as the forces from other nations. Canada's redeployment to Afghanistan since 2003 represents Canada's most conspicuous contribution to the U.S. "war on terror – and Ottawa's main calling card when it comes to rebuilding credibility with Washington after sitting out the invasion in Iraq."[47]

These Canadian commitments, however, have come at a price, particularly given financial constraints that have resulted in operational costs eating into the funding required for capability development. In 2002–03, for instance, the Canadian Forces deployed nearly 10,000 personnel on 14 missions throughout the world.[48] As in Australia, however, the numbers of personnel and units deployed overseas in the "War on Terror" were reduced significantly in 2004, thus allowing for a respite in operational tempo. (Subsequently, in 2005 and 2006, Australia's commitments surged again, with a task group operating in southern Iraq, special forces reinserted into Afghanistan, and a provincial reconstruction team working close by to the Canadian forces in Afghanistan.)

Australia's experience in the Regional Assistance Mission Solomon Islands (RAMSI), launched in 2003, demonstrates the high operational tempo that has affected both countries' forces. In the Solomon Islands, initially 1,500 Australian navy, army, and air force personnel, alongside military personnel from Fiji, Tonga, New Zealand, and Papua New Guinea, provided security for police who were assisting the local government to restore law and order. The experience in the Solomon Islands, while not involving Canadian forces, is an example of the kind of international activism that Canada has long embraced, as it seeks to restore stability beyond its own shores out of enlightened self-interest. Indeed, that activism saw both Australia and Canada commit specialist support elements following the Asian Tsunami in December 2004 and to Sudan in 2005 and 2006 in response to similar impulses.

Desmond Morton is correct when he observes that investment in sealift and airlift, better communications, precision-guided munitions, and light but robust military vehicles are exactly what will be needed in the future. Similarly, other Canadian defence-policy papers note that "amphibious or littoral warfare capability is vital for any nation that wishes to deploy self-supporting military forces on operations overseas."[49] By the early 2000s, a gap had emerged between the realization of the strategic-lift capabilities that Morton refers to and the apparently entrenched but rosy views in Canadian defence circles. Nonetheless, Canada has subsequently made a considerable effort towards acquiring two multi-role joint-support ships and is considering the acquisition of a dedicated amphibious ship as well. In addition, steps are being taken to increase the size of the forces by 5,000 people, to expand the special forces' capabilities, and to continue the process of transforming the Canadian military into a "modern combat-capable medium-weight force" (as outlined in the 2005 Canadian Defence White Paper). These measures closely match those articulated in the Australian Army's "Hardened and Networked Army" paper, endorsed by the Australian government late in 2005.[50]

All of this further indicates that Australia and Canada face similar challenges as they seek to reconcile their approaches to peacekeeping and warfighting in light of the "War on Terror." As Australia's Lieutenant-General Peter Leahy observes, "in a borderless world in which many security challenges transcend nation-states, we cannot afford to close off any conflict scenario."[51] How collaboration between the forces of Canada and Australia may take shape as the two countries face such scenarios is discussed in the concluding chapter.

Overview and Prospects

This work has compared Canada and Australia, focusing particularly on the experiences of their respective armed forces. It has shown that there are many remarkable similarities, as well as substantial differences, between the two countries' armed forces and the policies of their governments towards the use of such forces. By making the comparison, this book provides students of Australian and Canadian defence and foreign policy, military history, and international relations with a unique perspective from which to understand their own idiosyncrasies in light of each others' distinguishing features – particularly as they pertain to the use of expeditionary forces. This work also provides observers with a frame of reference for understanding how and why Australian and Canadian expeditionary forces have been deployed on alliance and coalition operations for over a century, and how they have contributed to the world order represented by the British and American "Empires" over the same period.

Perhaps there are broader lessons that can be drawn from this book, too. In particular, there appears to be scope to move away from narrow nationalistic – at times even jingoistic – interpretations of events by examining them from a broader comparative perspective. This work sets out to do that in the context of one of the most remarkable international parallels – between Canada and Australia. Nonetheless, the intention has not been to suggest that Canadian and Australian defence and foreign policies are totally congruent or that their forces are predestined always to work together. Clearly, they have different geo-strategic priorities.

The argument has been made that Australians and Canadians and their key allies should better understand the significance of this unique relationship in terms of foreign-policy and defence matters, not least because of the missed opportunities to enhance their national interests through common efforts. By making the comparison, this work also has highlighted several foreign- and defence-policy dynamics that help explain how the armed forces of these two nations, with their predisposition for expeditionary operations, have developed, as well as the enduring constraints on and incentives for future development. Two countries facing the "tyranny of distance" from each other, naturally enough, have several differences, but the similarities are striking and point to areas of mutual benefit through closer cooperation, particularly given the likelihood of their encountering each other again on future military operations in remote locations around the world – much as they have done, repeatedly, for more than a century, most recently in Afghanistan in 2006.

ENDURING DIFFERENCES

Important and enduring differences separate Australia and Canada, particularly in terms of foreign and defence policy and their force-development trajectories, and these differences have long discouraged closer cross-examination of the two countries. But, for such an examination to be most fruitful, the differences must be kept firmly in mind. The most important of these is the different geo-strategic setting that has made Australians more anxious about their place in the world. For much of the twentieth century, Australia had its own mandated territory to administer in Papua (1906–75) and in New Guinea as well (1914–75). This helped provide Australia with an incentive to be at least partly outward-looking. By contrast, Canada's proximity to and protection by the United States helped to justify not taking defence as seriously as the more remote, isolated, and nervous Australians did. In addition, proximity to the United States has led Canada to pursue distinctiveness itself as a foreign-policy priority. Yet, at the same time, the search for distinctiveness has in part been negated by the military priority placed on interoperability with u.s. forces. For example, the Canadian Navy prides itself on its ability to integrate seamlessly into a u.s. naval task force. But the same level of priority does not appear to be placed on tri-service teamwork and interoperability between Canada's own services that would enable Canada to take a largely self-reliant lead role in a multinational joint-force operation – as it did in Egypt in 1956.

Some may argue that the apparent foreign- and defence-policy dysfunction that these tensions represent is a part of a deliberate policy of ambiguity over prospective military commitments. For instance, such ambiguities enabled Prime Minister Mackenzie King to argue for "conscription if necessary, but not necessarily conscription" during the Second World War.

Similarly, early in 2003, Prime Minister Chrétien maintained an ambiguous position on the war in Iraq until the last moment, in the hope that a United Nations Security Council resolution would obviate the need for him to take a political stand that was popular in certain domestic constituencies but unpopular with Canada's major ally and trading partner, the United States. Canadian policy clearly has been strongly influenced by United States actions, but it also has sought to retain robust links with its European partners in NATO, as a kind of "third leg" in the North Atlantic Triangle, at least in part to counter-balance the preponderance of American influence. Yet events since the end of the Cold War point to the diminishing reliability of this "third leg" of Canadian diplomacy.[1]

By contrast, Australia's location predisposes it to more diversified trade links and a greater security focus on Asia. The Asian focus particularly involves southeast Asia (vulnerable to the operations of militant Islamist networks) and its immediate Pacific environs – where several island nations with only rudimentary facilities and points of access struggle to function effectively.[2] The Asian Tsunami of December 2004, for example, triggered a robust response from Australia – with unprecedented financial aid and substantial ADF assistance, especially to neighbouring Indonesia. (That response once again capitalized on the ADF's expeditionary-oriented capabilities to respond to crises.) Canada responded similarly, particularly in Sri Lanka, although its proportionately smaller financial and military contribution is largely explained by its remoteness from the disaster-affected region.

Australia's location also inclines it to worry less about national distinctiveness and more about providing support for U.S. military action that is perceived to be congruent with its own long-term national interests. As a result, Australia has maintained a more forthright military stance (such as in Vietnam and more recently in Iraq) than its safer and more comfortable northern "cousin." As well, particularly since the late 1990s, the ADF has placed greater emphasis on a maritime strategy that focuses on the littoral environment, where the operational domains of land, sea, and air merge.[3] Paradoxically, while on one level appearing to be more compliant (or interoperable) with U.S. interests than their Canadian equivalent, the Australian forces have developed a degree of distinctiveness or self-reliance that seems more in line with declared Canadian foreign-policy priorities. This self-reliance has been developed by maintaining a high degree of interservice operability through major periodic army-navy-air force KANGAROO, CROCODILE, and TANDEM THRUST exercises. It also has been enhanced by the retention of an amphibious orientation in the RAN that allows the army and other services to work as a team – without necessarily having to call for major support from an ally to make it work. Steps are being taken to rectify shortfalls, but Canada still lags behind Australia in some respects as a consequence of not maintaining these skills, which are so critical for self-reliance. Indeed, not only is there a lag, but Canada's lack of self-reliance makes it more dependent on the United States when it needs these services, for it is usually the United States that supplies them for Canada.[4] As the United States-based Canadian scholar Michael Ignatieff contends, "to be a serious peacekeeper in a modern world you have to have tanks, helicopters, military lift – expensive."[5]

The second key distinguishing feature is the unique French Canadian influence on Canadian foreign and defence policy. Ultimately, the criteria by which any Canadian policy has had to be judged revolves around the preservation of national unity. As Sokolsky argues, this balancing act led Canada for most of the twentieth century to find its own comfort zone. In the second half of the century, it meant that Canadian troops remained in NATO and Canada stayed in NORAD but avoided being entangled in foreign wars like Vietnam. In the meantime, Canada contributed to the Cold War through more politically acceptable peacekeeping – including to francophone countries that Australians have been more (but not entirely) reluctant to be involved with. Still, as Sean Maloney points out, the Canadian altruist "peacekeeping" mantra was also useful in terms of the Cold War calculus.[6] This formula allowed the Canadian Forces' political masters to pay little attention to military affairs beyond the peacekeeping threshold, at least until 11 September 2001.[7] But, as Andrew Cohen and Doug Bland argue, peacekeeping is one of Canada's "great national myths," with Canadians maintaining "the rhetoric of peacekeeping but not the capability."[8] This peacekeeping rhetoric was most credible prior to the end of the Cold War, when United Nations missions were often interpositional and mandated under the more benign rules of Chapter VI of the UN Charter. In contrast, the post-Cold War "peacekeeping" missions that Canada joined tended to be more complicated, mandated sometimes under the more robust rules of Chapter VII of the UN Charter and more demanding in terms of Canada's military resources.

ENDURING COMMON TIES AND RECONVERGENCE

Since the fateful day in September 2001, the basis on which this Canadian strategic calculus was formed has altered significantly. For instance, the links with NATO have become less reliable as the sought-after diplomatic

counterweight to the United States. Arguably, Canada can no longer rely on
the North Atlantic Alliance as its key counterbalance. Some have suggested
that the ABCA forum may have become more important, at least conceptu-
ally, for the Canadian Army, as that elusive but still sought-after ballast.[9]
There also appears to be scope for an interservice or joint version of ABCA
that extends beyond the respective armies to include the navies, air forces,
and, in the case of Britain and the United States, Marines. Such views point
to the need for Canadians and Australians to look more closely at relations
with each other. They also point to potential benefits from using each
other's capabilities for diplomatic and military leverage.

Both Australia and Canada retain a common concern about security
developments in the Middle East and the prominent states of Asia, particularly in light of forecasts that Asian states will gain in prominence in the
twenty-first century. Australia and Canada also have a propensity to offer
humanitarian assistance in places such as Africa as need dictates. In addition, Canada's track record suggests a similar interest in being able to
project and sustain expeditionary forces – for "peacekeeping" and complex humanitarian-assistance operations as well as war-fighting – across
air-sea gaps.

The point made here is that, despite the distance between them and their
different geographic locations, the two countries, and particularly their
armed forces, have an amazing resemblance. They both have an enduring
requirement for similarly organized and equipped expeditionary forces,
each with their own distinctive yet similar traditions and ethos. The requirement for expeditionary forces springs from different national interests
yet has remarkably similar results. In the case of Canada, it is in its national
interest to defend itself against unwanted help from its southern neighbour.
This leads Canadians to want to work closely with the United States to
ensure that American security concerns over the "strategic depth" to its
north are sufficiently looked after. Canada addresses this concern through
NORAD and homeland-security measures, which are largely designed to ensure that the U.S. border remains unthreatened and open – a vital goal
given Canada's overwhelming economic dependence on the United States.
It also does so through its deployment of expeditionary forces in support of
shared military endeavours. Such actions have repeatedly helped to ensure
that, if fighting is necessary, it will happen far away from the North American homeland, thereby calling to mind the British adage in the First World
War that "it is better to fight for your freedom on the fields of Flanders
than the fields of Sussex," or, in C.P. Stacey's words, "it was clearly
better to defend Canada on the beaches of Britain than in the suburbs of

Halifax."[10] Stacey's remarks are perhaps even more apt today, particularly given the potential effects of ballistic missiles and weapons of mass destruction in the wrong hands, which result in an even stronger imperative to deal with such threats before they become more threatening closer to home.

A further spur to the maintenance of Canada's expeditionary forces is the fact that, as already noted, Canadian national interests centre largely on the need to maintain national unity. This leads Canadians to want to project their values abroad in order to demonstrate to themselves, as much as anyone else, that what they have in common is more important than what divides them. David Last puts it this way: "Managing big wars abroad and small wars at home helps keep the country together." In other words, what Canadians do abroad can act as a distraction from the narcissism of minor differences that they otherwise find so debilitating. Nonetheless, as others have made clear, "peacekeeping, although one of the longest standing roles of the Canadian Forces since 1945, has been of only marginal importance in the formulation of defence policy and the shaping of the military's posture. It has been something that the forces are expected to be able to do along with their other tasks."[11]

In contrast, while Australia has a greater sense of nervousness about its place in the world, it also has a greater degree of internal self-confidence, lacking as it does Canada's concerns over internal unity. Consequently, Australia regularly and often promptly seeks to ingratiate itself with its major ally in times of conflict far from its shores as an "insurance policy" against potential hard times closer to home in the future. However, the end result of these two sets of contrasting national interests is the same type of commitment of expeditionary armed forces, repeatedly, alongside the same major ally in military operations and often in the same places abroad (as illustrated in appendix 4).

In effect, the contrast between the contributions of the Canadian and Australian armed forces to international stability over more than a century has been principally apparent at the political level. Yet parallels in the scope and nature of Australian and Canadian military contributions to UK- and then U.S.-led, as well as UN-mandated, efforts to maintain world order have endured. The uniqueness of the Canadian and Australian experiences cannot be denied. But this has been stressed too much to date. The focus on uniqueness has obscured the significant Canadian parallels with Australia and hampered increased collaboration as both countries have, in their own interests, sought to contribute to alliances and other international-security endeavours while still maintaining their own identities.

The historical review undertaken in this work demonstrates that there are durable peacetime and wartime force-structure determinants that are similar for both countries. In peacetime, domestic politics, budgetary constraints, and bureaucratic infighting have taken centre stage as threats to national security have receded. But in wartime, budgetary constraints have tended to be reduced, national resources have been pooled for the common cause, and the imperatives of new tactics and war-fighting technology have gained attention, affecting force structures. Such factors are common to many countries. But, in the case of Canada and Australia, they have led both countries to develop and retain similarly organized professional and deployable ground forces in the years since the Second World War (see appendix 2).

As events since the end of the Cold War have shown, the difference between ground forces designed for war-fighting and those designed primarily for peace-support operations or "second-generation peacekeeping" has narrowed significantly. And both Australian and Canadian force-structure planners recognize this fact. Moreover, in the age of instant and global news, the deployment of ground forces denotes commitment in a more visible and politically valuable way to achieve foreign-policy goals than transitory air and naval forces. Such ground commitments offer greater potential for shaping the opinion of allies, in part because deployed ground forces remain the ultimate measure of national resolve. This is particularly the case given the increased risk of casualties, the drain on scarce manpower resources, and the high media profile of such commitments – where media access is often easier than it is with inaccessible air and sea platforms. Both the Canadian and Australian governments understand that they cannot easily afford large, readily deployable forces, but they can, and do, pursue quality force structures that yield strategic leverage.[12]

Canada and Australia are considered post-modern and post-industrial middle powers with democratic ideals and parallel constitutional, sociological, and legal circumstances that are distinct from those of the United States and Europe. Hence the focus in this book has been on these two nations in relation to each other, rather than the more frequently considered alternatives of the United States and Britain. After all, Canada and Australia face similar issues and pursue policies that reflect the same enlightened self-interest, supporting cooperative international-security measures. They both also continue to contribute to the fight against terrorism. They have a similar defence and intelligence partnership with the United States, share membership in the ABCA forum, and are both widely respected internationally for their military, humanitarian, and diplomatic initiatives and capabilities.

For both Canada and Australia, an important legacy flows from the informal, bilateral, consultative, and collaborative arrangements associated with ANZUS, NORAD, and NATO. For Canada, security ties with the United States stretch back to the Ogdensburg Agreement, the Permanent Joint Board of Defence, the post-war Basic Security Plan for North American Defence, and the Joint Statement on Defence Collaboration. For Australia, the ties go back to the wartime alliance under General MacArthur, the Radford-Collins naval agreement, the ANZUS alliance, and the consultative arrangements concerning the Joint Facilities at Pine Gap.[13] For both countries, the ties still also include intimate intelligence links shared with few others. These enduring parallels stand in opposition to the obvious contrasts at the political level between Canada and Australia and demonstrate the uncanny similarity in the nature and orientation of their defence policies and their armed forces.

In addition, Canada and Australia have struggled with tension between opposing defence strategies at home and the projection of expeditionary forces overseas. This tension has manifested itself in "nationalist" versus "imperialist" debates that have ebbed and flowed between military commanders and their civilian masters since the founding of both countries. As the Australian defence scholar Graeme Cheeseman notes, "in spite of their different interests and strategic locations, the overall trajectories of defence in the two countries have followed remarkably similar paths."[14]

Australia's experience at balancing force structures for self-reliant and amphibious operations, as demonstrated in East Timor, parallels the acclaimed Canadian lead role with UNEF in 1956 – Canada's last successful attempt at projecting military force as the lead nation. In 1956 Canada had forces that were at high readiness, with their own force-projection capabilities, and that were able to operate virtually independently of a politically constrained United States. In addition, while Australia spends more per capita on defence, overall it spends about the same amount as Canada (see appendix 6), but, in terms of its own integral and stand-alone military capabilities, it seems to get more "bang for its buck." Australia's similarly sized and funded defence force has emerged as distinctive and largely self-reliant, and also able to act as a lead nation with an interoperable tri-service team, a bit like Canada in 1956.

Some may argue that Canada has little choice but to push for interoperability or face irrelevance on the world stage, particularly as the option of independent operations appears to be beyond the budgetary will-power of the government. However, the example of the Australian experience in East Timor provides a useful alternative model should Canada seek to do more than strive only for interoperability – that is, if it wishes to match its distinctive internationalist foreign-policy rhetoric with its defence-policy priorities by reinvigorating its force structures with an infusion of greater autonomy (or self-reliance), distinctiveness, joint teamwork, coalition interoperability, and strategic relevance. Andrew Cohen contends that "to rearm the army ... is to be a good ally and a good citizen of the world. It is to do what we can, where we must, in good conscience, in war and peace, as we did before" – much like the functionalism of old. Canadian journalist Michael Elliott, looking at the Australian model, makes the following appeal: "If Canadians are going to rethink their foreign policy, then – please – take a leaf out of the Australians' book, and do it with a bit of enthusiasm and fun." Such efforts may enable Canada to play a lead (but not necessarily solo) role in "second-generation peacekeeping," complex humanitarian-assistance missions, and even – if necessary – war-fighting without being restrained by an over-reliance on support from its preoccupied neighbour. A recent Canadian report puts it more forcefully: "The CF must be shaped into a joint, combat ready force, capable of defending Canada and its surrounding oceans, and capable of rapidly deploying within Canada and abroad ... [with] amphibious forces capable of transporting and deploying a well-armed battle group to overseas locations." The report further observes that, while "not glamorous," amphibious operations "are essential for future deployments and guarding Canada's sovereignty."[15] Recent Australian operational experience both in the Middle East and in its immediate region in East Timor, the Solomon Islands, and Aceh, Indonesia, supports this contention.

In the meantime, for Australia, Canada's advantage of proximity to and trade with the United States, its vast experience with NATO and complex multilateral military operations other than conventional war, and remarkably similar force structure, equipment, and military doctrine make it truly worthy of closer examination. For instance, there are opportunities for Australia to benefit from Canada's efforts to adapt concepts and lessons from the United States and Europe. Roy Rempel contends that, in the demise of the Canadian-German security relationship following the end of the Cold War, "one was able to witness the final failure of Canada's post-war search for counterweights."[16] But Canada would have been hard-pressed to maintain a presence in Germany, the Balkans, and Afghanistan at the same time, and, in any event, Rempel overlooks the one key and remarkably comparable nation which might serve as Canada's long-sought-after "counterweight" – Australia.

The similarities stretch back over a century and reveal a closeness that overrides the ebb and flow of political and strategic differences. Such differences led Australia and Canada to take divergent paths with their military organizations, particularly during the Cold War. Events in the post-Cold War years, however, point to a reconvergence in the development of their respective armed forces. For instance, both Canada and Australia produced noteworthy generals that would feature prominently in international "peacekeeping" missions. Following in the footsteps of Canada's original peacekeeping commander, Major-General E.L.M Burns (UNEF), were Canadian generals such as J.A. Dextraze (UNOC), Clive Milner (UNFICYP), Romeo Dallaire (UNAMIR), and Lewis Mackenzie (UNPROFOR); and Australia's R.H. Nimmo (UNMOGIP chief UNMO, 1950–56), John Sanderson (UNTAC), David Ferguson (MFO), Peter Cosgrove (INTERFET), Tim Ford (UNTSO and UN headquarters), and Mike Smith (UNTAET).

In addition to the senior leaders, these countries' troops have deployed alongside each other in recent years with similar organizations and equipment in places such as Somalia, Western Sahara, Cambodia, Rwanda, East Timor, Sierra Leone, and Afghanistan – much as they did under British direction in earlier times, while rarely pausing to consider one another. These similarities point to a greater convergence than a superficial glance at the inherent differences between Australia and Canada would indicate. Moreover, as the Canadian scholar Charles Pentland has observed, Canada and Australia together "are of European great power proportions." This suggests that, if "Americans are from Mars and Europeans are from Venus," as Robert Kagan puts it, then perhaps, in between those two groups here on earth, Australians and Canadians can use their combined gravitational pull to influence both these "planets" and help reduce the prospects of interplanetary turbulence.[17] If, as some believe, "size does matter"[18] when it comes to military deployments in support of alliances, then Australia and Canada, out of enlightened self-interest, should seek ways to pool their resources to contribute to their common national interests in support of world peace and stability. As the Canadian scholar David Mutimer states, "there are walls other than the American military into which the Canadian Forces can be fitted, which produce roles that are no more or less 'niche' than the one produced by interoperability [with the United States]."[19]

Yet such other walls have only infrequently included Australia and Canada at the same time. The reader may contend that there must be good reasons why this state of affairs has been so enduring. What follows, therefore, is an attempt to address such concerns. For instance, those who are sceptical of closer collaboration between Canada and Australia may argue that Canada has little interest in becoming more involved militarily with a Pacific power. Yet Canada has a long history of military involvement in the Pacific which requires a significant degree of Pacific-phobia or Europhilia to obscure. Canada deployed forces to Vladivostok (in 1919); Hong Kong, India, Burma, the Aleutians, and Australia (during the Second World War); South Korea (1950–57); West New Guinea (1962–63); Cambodia (1993); and East Timor (1999–2000). Canada also sent ICSC monitors to Laos, Cambodia, and Vietnam (1954–65 and 1973). In addition, Canada's trade with the Pacific region grew dramatically in the latter years of the twentieth century and has continued to expand in this century. Indeed, if the twenty-first century is to be the Asian Century, then Australia and Canada may be drawn together, even more so than during the last century.

Having been reluctant to concede the merits of the argument expounded here thus far, critics of closer cooperation between Australian and Canadian forces may stress the contrasts inherent in the two nations' geography and economies. After all, the United States completely dominates Canadian defence and security consciousness. Such critics would argue this domination is so compelling that, despite the range of issues that Canada has in common with Australia, Canadian military and social consciousness is absorbed by its enormous southern neighbour – making concerns about relations with Australia of little consequence.[20] However, virtually the same could be said of Australia and almost every country in the world that looks to the United States with rapt attention. Even so, the allure of all things "American" does not mean that both Canada and Australia cannot make more out of their relationship than they have done so far. As Sokolsky argues, "there has been a persistent duality in Canadian foreign and defence policy: the desire to play a more independent and distinct role through the UN and a strongly held instinct to join the US and other traditional allies when unified western action was organized."[21]

Critics may further argue that Australia has enough on its hands worrying about the "arc of instability" to its north without concerning itself about closer collaboration with Canada, and indeed it is true that events such as the Bali bombing in October 2002 and the Tsunami in December 2004 have helped focus Australia's attention on its immediate region, including several Pacific island nations. Such critics may additionally posit that close comparisons are of restricted value because Canada has demonstrated only a limited interest in security affairs in Asia, and Australia did not participate in the various operations in the Balkans, where much of Canada's experience has been gained in the post-Cold War years. Yet, as this book has demonstrated (and as appendix 4 illustrates), holding this view requires a particularly short-range perspective on the two countries' shared histories and priorities.

Critics may also argue that the combined effects of the cousins' rivalry, their different geo-strategic settings, and the cultural disparities between them are such enduring features that they cannot easily be circumvented or overcome. Yet such critics must weigh the more numerous things that Canada and Australia have in common, as argued throughout this book (and as summarized in chart 1). Then there is the argument that the ADF has nothing to learn from the CF, given the latter's parlous financial condition in recent years and its traumatic experiences in such places as Somalia and the Balkans. The CF certainly has to address significant issues, but it has gained a remarkable amount of valuable experience, particularly since the end of the Cold War, and its leadership has demonstrated a determination to achieve renewal and transformation. Yet this still misses the point: Australia and Canada, as I have said, have much to gain by working more closely together to use each other's limited diplomatic and military strength for leverage on the world stage. After all, both countries' forces are having similar experiences in attempting to meet asymmetric threats. Both face the challenge of recruiting a defence force from relatively small populations and a shrinking but very similar demographic pool. These constraints necessitate smarter, smaller, and more adaptable force structures that can be tailored to counter varied threats. In addition, time and again, Australians and Canadians have made similar contributions to multinational military operations beyond their shores that are consistent with their mutual self-interest. As a consequence, more frequently than ever, Australians and Canadians are bumping into each other in remote corners of the globe on multilateral military operations.

With so many issues associated with globalization and the information era generating linkages between national and international interests, there is a clear incentive for enhanced collaboration between these distant but so similar middle powers. As in the past, Australia and Canada are well placed to support common goals out of enlightened self-interest. But in doing so, their interests may best be served by collaborating with each other along the way in order to improve their own limited diplomatic leverage. Such collaboration can only be helped by raising awareness of the commonalities between the experiences, structures, and capabilities of the forces of Canada and Australia – which is the very purpose of this book.

The information era is indeed breaking down the tyranny of distance and facilitating opportunities for cross-pollination. The Australian political scientist Coral Bell describes this as a "normative shift," a social process of changing domestic and international rules, that is facilitating "a form of trans-regional international action" or a "global grouping" of shared interests whereby international military interventions (she cites Kosovo and East Timor as examples) are norm-driven and not just interest-driven.[22] The reader would find it difficult to identify two countries with more obvious similarities in standards or "norms" than Australia and Canada (as reflected in charts 1 and 2).

Armed with this understanding, both countries could learn from each other in order to make the best use of limited resources, to increase flexibility, and to improve efficiency. Moreover, from a U.S. perspective, understanding the nature and limitations of these two close and enduring allies may help in formulating ways to improve collaboration with them both. Besides, as Joel Sokolsky contends, "the United States does not want Canada necessarily to lead. When it wants Canadian involvement, it does not want a serious departure from US foreign policy." And so Canadian actions in the field of defence policy "are not about being anti-American, but about making an identifiable contribution."[23] Such a contribution, this study maintains, has on occasion been successfully carried out alongside Australian forces and quite likely will be again.

"It isn't conceited to believe," says Andrew Cohen, "that Canada has something to contribute to the peace, progress, life and letters of this world."[24] Arguably, the "more independent and distinct" roles sought by both Canada and Australia can be complemented – even enhanced – by increased cooperation between them. With a reconvergence in outlooks and structures, and with renewed common experiences, the armies – as well as the navies and air forces, to say nothing of the foreign-assistance and development agencies – of such remarkable and similar countries may have much to gain from strengthening the bonds between them by working together more closely. They could do this, for instance, through increased exchanges of members of headquarters staffs, unit personnel, and students at training establishments. They also could increase their reciprocal attaché staff, sponsor shared military exercises, and support an annual or biannual (and relatively cost-neutral) individual exchange of military personnel along the lines of the extant annual three-month "Long Look" exchange arrangement among the armed forces of Australia, New Zealand, and Britain. In addition, they could share munitions research and production, particularly given the remarkably similar equipment in their inventories. Of course, interoperability has more to do with shared language and culture than with common and compatible skills, let alone the nuts and bolts of the shared command-and-control architecture. With this in mind, as well as the commonalities between Canada and Australia outlined earlier, there appears to be significant scope for such exchange arrangements to be implemented with relatively little effort or cost.

As Australia's Alan Ryan notes in relation to the Australian Army's relations with the United States land forces, "experience has shown that, when cooperating with a superpower in a military context, the junior partner must work hardest if it to exercise any influence over coalition strategy and objectives ... In the future, Australia's Army will have to think beyond merely establishing tactical interoperability with its major partners. It will have to position itself to take advantage of the combat multiplier effect of multinational forces in an ever expanding range of contingencies ... [This includes] international officer exchange programs, combined training and attendance at each other's military educational institutions."[25] Ryan's remarks appropriately focus on Australia's principal ally. But his remarks appear to apply equally to the Canadian Forces, and they support the conclusions reached in this study.

PROSPECTS OF CLOSER COLLABORATION

Perhaps in future, these two nations with such similar strategic interests will not only accidentally end up working together militarily, as they have done on many occasions before, but will do so after having, in advance, strengthened ties and improved mutual awareness, understanding, and interoperability. As Joseph Nye observes, the world's only superpower faces the paradox of American power, in that it cannot afford to go it alone. Robert Kagan argues that this assertion is "facile" because the "fact remains that the United States can act unilaterally and has done so many times." But, as Ron Haycock contends, "the situation in Iraq in late 2003 suggests the United States cannot 'go it alone,' even if it can 'act alone.'" Even Kagan and others concede that "Americans certainly prefer to act together with others, and American actions stand a better chance of success if the United States has allies." Indeed, Joel Sokolsky points out that "America can fight alone, but can't run its 'empire' on its own. That is, it can't bring stability on its own. That is where Australia and Canada make a contribution." Australia and Canada, as liberal Western capitalist democracies with a tradition of expeditionary forces, often have a vested interest in participating in u.s.-led or u.s.-supported multilateral operations. Their main political objective likely will remain to influence u.s. behaviour (particularly behaviour perceived to be "extreme" by their politicians) in a crisis and to have a "seat at the table" in the subsequent settlement. Yet, on their own, Canada and Australia often find themselves sitting in the corner and with little substantive influence; it is only by operating together that their influence can be out of proportion to their size – making them truly able to "punch above their weight." Canada's Foreign Affairs officials recognized in 2003 that "the coming years are likely to see high demand for military forces with varied capabilities." They argued that "Canadians need to consider how our military can best support our foreign policy."[26] Australian military practitioners and their Foreign Affairs officials likely would echo those sentiments.

On the South African plains at the dawn of the twentieth century, at Versailles in 1919 following the monumental combined efforts at the Battle of Amiens in 1918, at the battle of Kapyong in 1951, on peace-support operations in East Timor in 1999, and also in the mountains of Afghanistan in 2002 and again in 2005 and 2006, along with the countless other occasions when Canadians and Australians have worked together on peace-keeping and observer missions in the Middle East, Africa, and Asia, their combined efforts have proven more noteworthy than their sometimes scattered individual contributions. This remarkable historical parallel suggests that similar benefits may be gained by working more closely together in future. But, in order to do so, a vehicle needs to be found to enable the two countries to cooperate with each other in advance of an event occurring in order to prevent the circumstances of the event from overwhelming the prospects for cooperative teamwork. For instance, the two countries could formalize a Canadian Australian Defence Arrangement (CASDA?) along similar lines to the Five Power Defence Arrangement (FPDA) that facilitates cooperation and shared exercises among Malaysia, Singapore, Australia, Britain, and New Zealand. By creating such a cooperative vehicle, Canada and Australia conceivably could develop plans and contingencies in advance that capitalize on each other's military capabilities and limitations while recognizing the limits of their own national interests.

To date, such national interests and short-term, introspective political concerns have prevented Australians and Canadians from rising above their circumstances to see the value of closer mutual cooperation. Perhaps the greatest "enemy" of such mutual collaboration is not the unworkability of the relationship but the continued focus on short-term, local political concerns rather than on longer-term, or strategic, shared interests. Greater mutual awareness and understanding of the closeness of this imagined community, however, could change perspectives on the utility of closer collaboration. With an increased level of mutual understanding, contingency plans could be developed and short-term domestic political priorities could be managed, thus allowing the two countries' forces to pursue cooperation. Such measures, taking advantage of the strengths of both nations, likely would generate greater effect than either country could generate on its own, and in a way that suits their different but often complementary interests.

Critics may still offer resistance, arguing that political "sine waves" – like the oscillations of a radio wave – leave Australia and Canada predominantly at odds politically, with conservatives in office in one country and liberal-progressives in office in the other (see appendix 1). Certainly, the historical trend supports this contention. For Canada and Australia to make more out of their relationship, their politicians will need to come to an appreciation of the benefits of collaboration, which may in fact be at hand following the Conservative 2006 election victory. The two nations' political leaders will have to encourage recognition and articulation of the shared desires and needs. So far, admittedly, neither country's leaders has done so, but perhaps this lack has been due to ignorance of what is shared more than anything else.[27] All the same, that is no reason why more effort cannot be made one level down from the political level, for instance, to effect coordination and collaboration between senior policy and decision makers in the two countries' departments of defence and foreign affairs.

Kagan observes that "those who cannot act unilaterally themselves naturally want to have a mechanism for controlling those who can." "They want to control the behemoth [the United States] by appealing to its conscience." As Rear-Admiral Fred W. Crickard points out, "this is classic, middle power, alliance behaviour." Australian defence-policy adviser Brendan Sargeant suggests that it is by engagement with the United States armed forces on force structure and disposition, through action or cooperation (burden sharing), that friends and allies have the most capacity to influence U.S. strategic decision making.[28] In this respect, Australia and Canada, more so than any other two countries, are well placed to join hands – out of enlightened self-interest – in using their armed forces, thereby furthering their own interests while also working in such a way that not only suits the interests of the United States but even augments their utility to the United States as the lead "cousin" and benefactor of the West and its system of world order.

The Canadian scholar Andrew Cooper, commenting on Australian-Canadian diplomatic relations, states that the relevance and value of like-minded diplomatic activity should not be underestimated since it reinforces many of the positive attributes of Australian and Canadian diplomacy.[29] As with diplomatic approaches that have often complemented one another, so it has been on occasion with the Canadian and Australian forces – and potentially this may be an increasingly common phenomenon as they look to closer cooperation and collaboration to exploit complementary military capabilities for greater combined effect. Similarly, Margaret MacMillan and Francine McKenzie conclude their 2002 review of Australian-Canadian relations, a review entitled *Parties Long Estranged*, with an upbeat prognosis. They cogently argue that cooperation is not always possible, and rarely uncomplicated, but the commitment to try to work together and the belief that an effort towards cooperation is worthwhile is more evident now than ever before.[30] The reasoning outlined here supports this contention with historical evidence as well as plausible alternative scenarios to actual historical events, all of which points to the enduring utility of such a cooperative approach.

It is true that strategists have rarely predicted with much certainty when or where the next military conflagration is likely to take place, let alone how it will unfold – and Australia, as much as Canada, is justified in being distracted by its own neighbourhood. But the increase in frequency of coalition military operations abroad in the post-Cold War years suggests that past experience is worth considering in order to recognize emerging patterns. After all, while history does not repeat itself and future events cannot be predicted with confidence, the past does appear to have echoes that help in understanding the present and in preparing for what lies ahead. Moreover, history often begs tough questions such as "Why?" and "How?" as well as "What?" and the answers are frequently revealing.[31] This, too, suggests that Australian and Canadian policy makers may well find value in considering the cause-and-effect linkage between Canadian and Australian combined military feats and the diplomatic consequences of such achievements. For instance, the question may be asked: When will be the next Amiens and its Versailles, or the next Kapyong and its ANZUS? The argument here is that cooperative efforts between the forces of Canada and Australia should be made in anticipation of future coalition military operations. Such a partnership could yield benefits that would, together, be greater than the sum of its parts. There is a niche that Canada and Australia can fill together, as they have done, virtually by accident, on numerous occasions before.

I am not suggesting that the way ahead is for Australia and Canada to reduce their military ties with the United States, to say nothing of their other allies and partners. Clearly, the United States will continue to play the dominant geo-strategic and military role as Canada's and Australia's main security alliance partner. Interoperability and cooperation with the United States will remain important for both countries. Instead, what I am arguing is that, when Australia and Canada have combined forces, their actions have complemented the goals of their major allies as well. At the same time, such military actions have also helped further their national interests and enhanced their strategic leverage in a world where Australia and Canada appear to have few natural strategic partners, let alone "counterweights."

Canada and, to a certain extent, Australia have long sought counterweights, first to the British Empire and then to the United States. But these counterweights really never amounted to much because they were being played off against Canada's and Australia's allies – countries with which they did not have serious and irreconcilable strategic differences. For Canada and Australia, throughout their histories, their basic strategic interests have been bound up with those of their "cousins." For instance, when real danger loomed, whether from imperial Germany, Nazi Germany, and Japan, or the Soviet Union, the iron logic of realpolitik placed Canada and Australia firmly within the "family" – that is, in the Anglo-American-led world of "the West." While this world tended to revolve around the roles played by Britain and the United States, the extended family included the Empire/Commonwealth, including New Zealand, Australia, and Canada. While older powers of Europe and Asia also became allies, they did so effectively under British and American leadership. They "married into the family," into the "cousinhood," and accepted its rules and ways of doing business with each other. To be sure, Canada also likes to operate within the United Nations framework. But, as its experiences in Cold War and post-Cold War peacekeeping shows, even in this supposedly signature Canadian activity, Canada has invariably worked with and for the old Anglo-American alliance.

The focus on the "cousins" in this work is done with an awareness of the unease expressed about anglophone domination in Canada, particularly by the inhabitants of the province of Quebec. Certainly, French Canada has had difficulties with the "Anglo" orientation of Canada in the past. But, here too, the reality of Canada as part of the Anglo-American world could only be hidden temporarily by short-term political compromises made in wartime. Canadian unity has always depended upon domestic adjustments which have been largely successful. This success has been achieved, in part, because Canada belongs to a "cousinhood" that guarantees the kind of peaceful and prosperous world within which Ottawa can focus most of its attention on domestic problems. Indeed, without the benign environment of that world, Canada would not have been sufficiently free from external distractions to prosper and hold itself together.

While arguing that Canada and Australia have had numerous important ties in the past and can develop others in the future, this book is not calling for a dramatic reorientation of Canadian foreign and defence policy. Rather, I am suggesting that, in a world where the threat of terrorism now challenges Canada's cousins, Canada itself has a great deal in common with one of those cousins, Australia. This commonality applies not only to basic strategic objectives but also to how the two countries go about their military business – particularly as "junior partners" with limited yet useful assets to contribute. Canada and Australia have been strategic cousins in war and peace for over a century. The issue now before them is whether or not Ottawa and Canberra can finally recognize that, at the start of the twenty-first century, history, technology, common heritage, and self-interest have done much to shorten the distance between them. During the "War on Terror," Canada, for all its pretensions to even-handedness, remains deeply rooted in the West. So it is not just that Canada and Australia have specific reasons for collaboration, but also that they are on the same side in this current global conflict. [32]

Strategy is as much about choices as about history and geography, and the foundations and arguments are there if Canadians and Australians want to pursue a closer relationship. There may well be convergence in the future, built around the Asia-Pacific region and the security challenges likely to emerge in this century. Such convergence probably will continue as the utility of a closer Australia-Canada strategic relationship increases and becomes more visible. But, as Brendan Sergeant contends, the convergence between Canada and Australia postulated here "is not certain, and identity insecurities in both countries are a formidable inhibiter. For Canada it seems like it is [the issue of separatism linked with] Quebec. For us [Australians] it is our insecurities [and hence preoccupations] about Asia."[33] Furthermore, cousins can choose to ignore each other. For domestic political consumption, Canada may wish to continue to stress values over interests and opportunistic anti-Americanism. But, as I have argued, there is a real alternative path that may be chosen – particularly if these two nations, out of enlightened and mutually beneficial self-interest, choose to work more closely together.

For over a century, Australia and Canada have sought to rise above their tactical or short-term perceptions of their own national interests. But only on occasion have they succeeded in combining their military forces and in generating a political momentum that furthers their own national interests in addition to the interests that they both share with the broader "cousinhood" as part of the Anglo-American-led West. Usually, their military concerns have not gone beyond tactical and technical issues and only rarely have their combined efforts had strategic ramifications.

Often, their ignorance or at least limited understanding of the profound degree of commonality that they share has prevented them from seeing beyond short-term obstacles and envisaging the exponential strategic benefits of cooperation and collaboration. Yet I believe that, in an ever shrinking global village, and with the blinkers removed, Australian and Canadian officials and military planners, and even the United States, the United Kingdom, and other like-minded countries, are now well placed to gain from closer collaboration between the expedition-oriented forces of these "strategic cousins."

APPENDICES

Appendix One
Canadian (CA) and Australian (AU) Political "Sine Waves"

Year	Canadian Prime Minister	CA Min of Nat Defence	Australian Prime Minister	AUS Minister for Defence	Selected Events
1900	W. Laurier (96–11)	F.W. Borden (96–11)	E. Barton (01–03)	J. Dickson/J. Forrest (01–03)	Boer War (99–02)
			A. Deakin (03–04)	J. Drake/A. Chapman (03–04)	
			J.C. Watson (04)	A. Dawson (04)	
			G.H. Reid (04–05)	J. McCay (04–05)	
				T. Playford/T. Ewing/	
			A. Deakin/A. Fisher (05–09)	G. Pearce (–09)	
1910			A. Deakin (09–10)	J. Cook (09–10)	
	R.L. Borden (11–20)	S. Hughes (11–16)/E. Kemp (16–17)/ S.C. Mewburn (17–20)/ J.A. Calder (20)	A. Fisher (10–13)	G. Pearce (10–13)	WWI (14–18)
			J. Cook (13–14)	E. Millen (13–14)	
			A. Fisher/W. Hughes (14-16)	G. Pearce (14–21)	
1920	A. Meighen (20–21)	H. Guthrie (20–21)	W.M. Hughes (16–23)	G. Pearce (14–21)/ W.M. Greene (21–23)	Treaty of Versailles (19)
	W.L. Mackenzie King (21–30)	G.P. Graham (21–23)/ E.M. Macdonald (23–26)/ J.L. Ralston (26–30)	S.M. Bruce (23–29)	E. Bowden (23–25)/ N. Howse, (25–27)/ T. Glasgow (27–29)	Chanak Crisis (22)
1930	R.B. Bennett (30–35)	D.M. Sutherland (30–34)/ G. Stirling (34–35)	J.H. Scullin (29–32)	A. Green (29–31)/J. Daly (31)/ J.B. Chifley (31–32)	Great Depression
			J.A. Lyons (32–39)	G. Pearce (32–34)/ A. Parkhill (34–37)/J.A. Lyons (37)/ H. Thorby (37–38)	
1940	W.L. Mackenzie King (35–48)	I.A. MacKenzie (35–39)/ N.M. Rogers, (39–40)/ J.L. Ralston (40–44)/ A.G.L. McNaughton (44–45)/ D.C. Abbott (45–46)	E.C.G. Page (39)	J. Fairbairn (39–40)	WWII (39–45)
			R. Menzies/A. Fadden (39–41)	R.G. Menzies (39–41)	
			J.J. Curtin (41–45)	J.J. Curtin (41–45)	
			F.M. Forde (45)	J. Beasley (45–46)/F.M. Forde (46)	
			J.B. Chifley (45–49)	J. Dedman (46–49)	

Appendix One
Canadian (CA) and Australian (AU) Political "Sine Waves" (*continued*)

Year	Canadian Prime Minister	CA Min of Nat Defence	Australian Prime Minister	AS Minister for Defence	Selected Events
1950	L.S. St. Laurent (48–57)	B. Claxton (46–54)/			Korean War (50–53)
		R.O. Campney (54–57)	R.G. Menzies (49–66)	E. Harrison (1949–50)/	
				P. McBride (50–58)/	Dien Bien Phu (54)
	J.G. Diefenbaker (57–63)	G.R. Pearkes (57–60)/		A. Townley (58–63)/	Suez Crisis (56)
1960		G. Churchill (63)		P. Hasluck (63–64)/	Congo (60–63)
				S. Pattridge (64–66)	Vietnam advisers (AS: 62–72)
	L.B. Pearson (63–68)	P.T. Hellyer (63–67)			Cyprus (64–94)/CA 64 White Paper
			H.E. Holt (66–67)	A. Fairhall (66–69)	Vietnam War/CA 71 White Paper
			J. McEwen (67–68)	A. Fairhall (66–69)	
1970	P.E. Trudeau (68–79)	L.A.J. Cadieux (67–70)/	J.G. Gorton (68–71)	J.M. Fraser (69–71)/J.G. Gorton (71)	
		D.S. Macdonald (70–72)/	W. McMahon (71–72)	D. Fairbairn (71–72)	
		E.J. Benson (72)/		L. Barnard (72–75)/	
		J.A. Richardson (72–76)/	E.G. Whitlam (72–75)	W. Morrison (75)	
		B.J. Danson (76–79)			AS 76 White Paper
1980	C.J. Clark (79–80)	A.B. McKinnon (79–80)	J.M. Fraser (75–83)	D.J. Killen (75–82)/	Afghanistan (79)
	P.E. Trudeau (80–84)	G. Lamontagne (80–83)/		I. Sinclair (82–83)	
		J.J. Blais (83–84)			
		R.C. Coates (84–85)/E. Nielsen,			CA & AS 87 White Papers
	M.B. Mulroney (84–93)	(1985–86)/P. Beatty (86–88)/	R.L. Hawke (83–91)	K. Beazley (84–90)	Namibia (UNTAG –'89)
		W. McKnight (89–91)/			Gulf War (90–91)
1990		M. Masse (91–93)			
	K. Campbell (93)	M. Masse (91–93)	P. Keating (91–96)	R. Ray (90–96)	Cambodia (92–93)/UNPROFOR (92–95)
		D. Collenette (94)/D. Young			Somalia/Rwanda/Bougainville (93–94)
	J. Chrétien (93–03)/	(95–97)/A. Eggleton (2000–92)/			AS 93/CA 94 White Paper
	P. Martin (03–06)	MacCallum (2002–03)/	J.W. Howard (96–)	I. McLachlan (96–98)/	Bougainville (98–)
2000		W. Graham (03–06)		R. Hill (99–06)/	Kosovo (99–)/East Timor (99–)
	S. Harper (06–)	G. O'Connor (06–)		B. Nelson (06–)	Afghanistan (02–)/Iraq (03–)

Appendix Two
Canadian and Australian Deployable Ground Combat Forces (full-time)

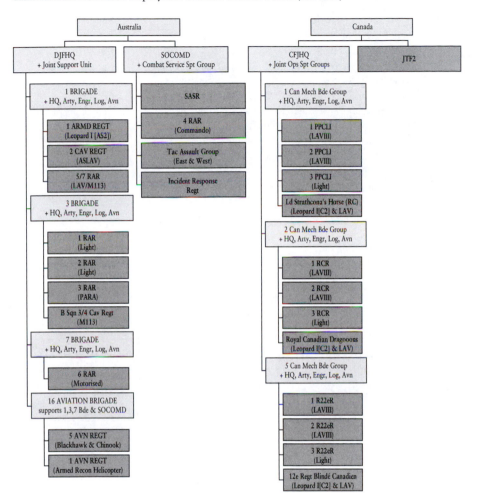

Appendix Three
Military Hierarchy Terminology

Level	Command Rank
Section/Squad: 10 troops	Corporal/Sergeant
Platoon (2–4 sections) (PL): 30–40 troops	Lieutenant
Company/Squadron/Battery (2–4 platoons): 800–2,200 troops	Captain/Major
Battalion/Regiment (3–5 companies): 600–1,000 troops	Lieutenant-Colonel
Regiment (U.S. Army) (2–3 battalions): 2,000–3,000 troops	Colonel
Task Force (Australia) (1–3 battalions): 1,000–4,000 troops	Colonel or Brigadier
Brigade (Canada) (3–4 battalions): 3,000–5,000 troops	Colonel
Brigade (AS/US/NZ) (2–4 battalions): 3,000–5,000 troops	Brigadier
Division (2–4 brigades): 8,000–15,000 troops	Major-General
Corps (2–5 divisions): 20,000 + troops	Lieutenant-General
Army Group (2 or more corps)	General

Military Branch or Specialization Identity Terminology

Corps   branch of the Army (e.g., Signals Corps, Infantry Corps, Engineers Corps)
Regiment   battalion affiliation within a Corps (e.g., Royal Australian Regiment, in the Royal Australian Infantry Corps)

Ranks of the Armed Forces

Land Forces (Army)	Air Forces	Maritime Forces (Navy)
General	Admiral	Air Chief Marshal
Lieutenant-General	Vice-Admiral	Air Marshal
Major-General	Rear-Admiral	Air Vice-Marshal
Brigadier (General)	Commodore	Air Commodore
Colonel	Captain	Group Captain
Lieutenant-Colonel	Commander	Wing Commander
Major	Lieutenant-Commander	Squadron Leader
Captain	Lieutenant	Flight Lieutenant
Lieutenant	Sub-Lieutenant	Flying Officer
Second Lieutenant	Midshipman	Pilot Officer
Regimental Sergeant Major	Chief Petty Officer	Warrant Officer I
Company Sergeant-Major	Chief Petty Officer II	Warrant Officer II
Staff Sergeant	Petty Officer I	Flight Sergeant
Sergeant	Petty Officer	Sergeant
Corporal/Bombardier	Leading Seaman	Corporal
Lance Corporal	Able Seaman	Leading Aircraftsman
Private	Ordinary Seaman	Aircraftsman

Appendix Four
Post–Second World War Operational Deployments

Operation	Mission Location	When	Australian Involvement Pers Strength	Role	When	Canadian Involvement Pers Strength	Role
BCOF	Japan	45–52	13,500 (max)	Occupation duties			
UNGOC/UNCI	Indonesia	47–49/49–51	15 (max)	UNMO			
UNTCOK	Korea				47–48	2	UNMO
UNCOK	Korea	49–50	2	UNMO			
UNMOGIP	India/Pakistan	50–85	18 Army/177 RAAF	UNMO & air tpt	49–96	39 (max)	UNMO/air transport
UNC-K	Korea	50–53	6000 (approx)	Combat & Logistics	50–53	6100	Combat
NATO	Germany				51–93	8000 (max)	Brigade Group & Air Division
BCC-K	Korea	53–57	1500 (approx)	Amistice tasks	53–57	1500 (approx)	Armistice tasks
BCFESR	Malaysia	55–72	1200 (approx)	Counter-insurgency/training			
UNTSO	Israel/sorrounds	56–today	12	UNMO	54–today	11	UNMO
UNCMAC	Korea	56–today	1	Cease-fire monitor	56–today	1	Cease-fire monitor
ICSC	Indochina				54–65	220 (approx max)	Observers
UNEF	Egypt-Sinai				56–67	1007 (max)	UNMO & support
UNOGIL	Lebanon				58	77	UNMO
ONUC	Congo	60–61	3	Medical team	60–64	421 (max)	Aircrew, staff, comms
UNTEA	West Irian	62	11	HA support + air transport	62–63	13 RCAF	Otter aircrew
UNYOM	Yemen	63	2	UNMO	63–64	36 (max)	Aircrew & UNMO
Confrontation	Borneo-Malaya	63–66	1500 (approx)	Counter-insurgency			
UNFICYP	Cyprus	64–95	16–50 police	Law & order	64–93	800 (approx)	Battalion UNMOs
FWMAO	South Vietnam	65–72	8000 (approx)	Counter-insurgency			
DOMREP	Dominican Repub				65–66	1	UNMO
UNIPOM	India/Pakistan	65–66	4	UNMO	65–66	112 (nax)	Aircrew & UNMO
OTN	Nigeria				68–69	2	UNMO
ICSC	Vietnam				73	19	Mil Observers
UNDOF	Syria	74–today	a few	UNMO	74–today	194	Logistic & comms
UNEF II	Sinai	76–79	46 RAAF	Cease-fire monitor	73–79	1145 (max)	Aircrew/sigs/Mps/HQ staff
UNIFIL	Lebanon	78	a few	UNMO	78	117	Comms & movements
CMF	Zimbabwe-Rhodesia	79–80	152	Monitor & canton	79–80	a few	Buffalo acft and logistic support
MFO	Sinai	82–86/93–now	110/25	Monitor withdrawal	81–today	29	Helicopters (86–90), staff
CMTTU	Uganda	82–84	20	Training			

Appendix Four

Post–Second World War Operational Deployments (*continued*)

Mission		Australian Involvement			Canadian Involvement		
Operation	Location	When	Pers Strength	Role	When	Pers Strength	Role
UNGOMAP	Afghan-Pakistan				88–90	5	UNMO
OSGAP	Afghan-Pakistan				90–92	1	Mil advisor
UNMCTT	Afghan-Pakistan	89–93	13	Mine clearance & training			
UNIIMOG	Iran-Iraq	88–90	15	Mil observer	88–91	525 (max)	UNMO & comms
UNBRO	Cambodia	89	2 police	Law & order			
UNTAG	Namibia	89–90	300 (approx)	Enginer support	89–90	301 (+ RCMP)	Logistics, elections, police
ONUCA	Central America				89–92	174 (max)	UNMO & helicopters
UNOVEH	Haiti				90–91	11	UNMO & elections
MIF	Persian Gulf	90–03	3 RAN ships	UN sanction enforcement	91–03	1 RCN ship	UN sanction enforcement
UNIKOM	Kuwait				91–03	4	UNMO
Op Habitat	Nth Iraq/Kurds	91	75	HA delivery			
UNSCOM	Iraq	91–98	5 (approx)	NBCW inspection	91–98	12 (max)	NBCW inspections
MINURSO	Western Sahara	91–94	45	Communications	91–94	35 (max)	UNMO
UNAVEM II	Angola				91–93	15 (max)	UNMO
ONUSAL	El Salvador				91–95	55 (max)	UNMO
UNAMIC	Cambodia	91–92	65	Communications	91–92	7	UNMO
UNTAC	Cambodia	92–93	500 (approx)	Comms/transport/elections	92–93	240 mil/121 civil	UNMO/elections/transport
UNOSOM I	Somalia	92–93	30	Movement Control etc	92–93	a few	Advance party
UNITAF	Somalia	92–93	1200	HA protection	92–93	1410 (max)	HA protection
CMAC	Cambodia	93–00	a few	Demining training	93–00	60 (approx)	Demining training
UNOSOM II	Somalia	93–95	40 (approx)	Movement Control etc	93–95	9 (max)	HQ staff
UNPROFOR	ex-Yugoslavia	92–93	a few	UNMO & liaison	92–95	over 2000	UNMOs, logistics
UNOMUR	Uganda-Rwanda				93	3	UNMO
UNAMIR	Rwanda	94–95	300 (approx)	Medical, infantry, logistics	93–96	112 (max)	Logistics & HQ staff
ONUMOZ	Mozambique	94–95	20 (max)	Police, mine clearance	93–94	4	UNMO
SPPKF	Bougainville	94	220/2 RAN ships	Logistics & support			
UNMIH/UNSMIH	Haiti	94–95	30	Police monitors	94–97	750 mil/100 Police	Monitors
IFOR/SFOR	Bosnia-Herzegovina	95–today	a few	With UK, US & CA forces	95–today	1227	Battalion-group monitors
UNPREDEP	Macedonia				95–today	1	UNMO

Appendix Four

Post–Second World War Operational Deployments (*continued*)

Mission		Australian Involvement			Canadian Involvement		
Operation	Location	When	Pers Strength	Role	When	Pers Strength	Role
UNMOP	Prevlaka				96–01	1	UNMO
	Zaire				96	354	Medical and Infantry
MINUGUA	Guatemala				97	15	UNMO
MINURCA	Central African Rep				98	61 (max)	HQ staff/logistics/comms
TMG/PMG	Bougainville	98–03	300 (max)	ADF-wide truce monitoring			
INTERFET	East Timor	99–00	5500	ADF-led peace restoration	99–00	400	Monitors
UNTAET	East timor	00–today	1500 (approx)	ADF-wide peace restoration	00–01	3	UNMO
UNMIK/KFOR	Kosovo	99–01	a few	With UK forces	99–01	1300 (max)	Battle group & CF support
IMATT	Sierra Leone	00–03	2	Training	00–today	11	Training
UNMEE	Eritrea-Ethiopia	00–03	2	UNMO	00–01	450 (max in 01)	Company group & UNMO
IPMT	Solomon Islands	00–01	300 (approx)	Evacuation & protection			
OEF	Afghanistan	01–02 & 05–06	1500 (approx)	SAS/air/logistics/HQ staff	01–02	887	Air/SF/infantry/logistics/HQ staff
OIF	Iraq	03	2000	SAS/air/logistics/HQ staff			
MONUC	Congo				03	63	Air transport/HQ staff
ISAF/UNAMA	Afghanistan	03	1	UNMO	03–	1800	Battle group & Brigade HQ
Op Solitude	Senegal				03	1	Senior Mil Liaison Officer
RAMSI	Solomon Islands	03	2000	ADF-Police peace restore			
UNMIS	Sudan	05–06	9	UNMO and air staff	05–06	40	Military Police
Op Tsunami Assist	Thailand	04–05	12	Health & logistics advisers			
Op Tsunami Assist	Indonesia	04–05	1000 (+)	ADF Joint Task Force			
Op STRUCTURE	Sri Lanka	05			05	17	DART

Sources: David Horner, "Chronicling the Peacekeepers: Report on the Feasibility of an Official History of Australian Peacekeeping Operations," prepared for the AWM by David Horner, 27 May 2003; James, "A Brief History of Peacekeeping"; Granatstein, *Canada's Army*; Last "Almost a Legacy," in Horn, ed., *Forging a Nation*.

Appendix Five
Economics and Demographics Compared

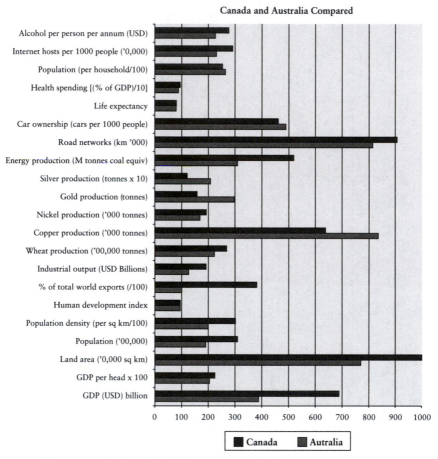

Canada and Australia Compared

Alcohol per person per annum (USD)	
Internet hosts per 1000 people ('0,000)	
Population (per household/100)	
Health spending [(% of GDP)/10]	
Life expectancy	
Car ownership (cars per 1000 people)	
Road networks (km '000)	
Energy production (M tonnes coal equiv)	
Silver production (tonnes x 10)	
Gold production (tonnes)	
Nickel production ('000 tonnes)	
Copper production ('000 tonnes)	
Wheat production ('00,000 tonnes)	
Industrial output (USD Billions)	
% of total world exports (/100)	
Human development index	
Population density (per sq km/100)	
Population ('00,000)	
Land area ('0,000 sq km)	
GDP per head x 100	
GDP (USD) billion	

■ Canada   ■ Autralia

Source: The Economist, Pocket World in Figures 2003 Edition

Appendix Six
Army Strengths Compared

Australian Army Strengths (excluding WWI & WWII)

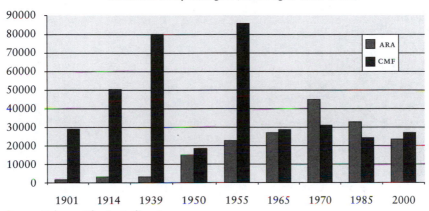

Source: Palazzo, *The Australian Army*.
ARA = Australian Regular Army/Permanent Force.
CMF = Citizen Military Forces/Part Time.

Canadian Army Strengths (excluding WWI & WWII)

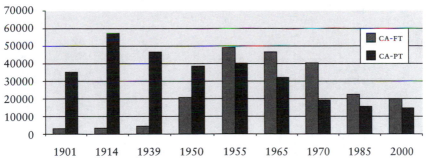

Source: Granatstein, *Canada's Army*.
CA-PT = Canadian Army-Part Time.
CA-FT = Canadian Army-Full Time.

Regular ground forces compared

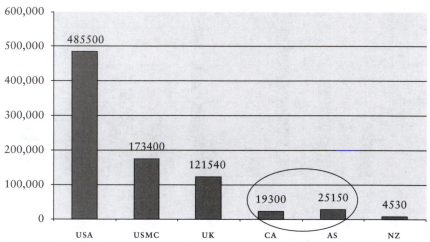

Source: Military Balance 2002–2003 (London: IISS 2002). United Kingdom figures include Royal Marines.

Defence expenditure compared, UK-CA-AS-NZ (USD billions)

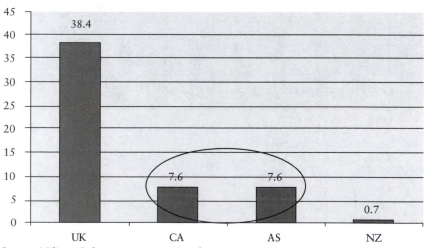

Source: Military Balance 2002–2003 (London: IISS, 2002).

**Total troops (regular and reserve force)
and per person defence expenditure**

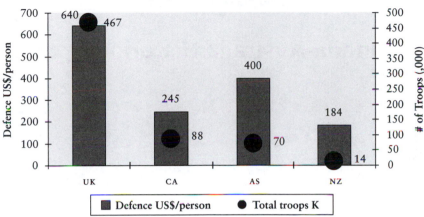

Source: Military Balance 2002–2003 (London: IISS 2002).

Comparing AS-NZ-CA ground forces

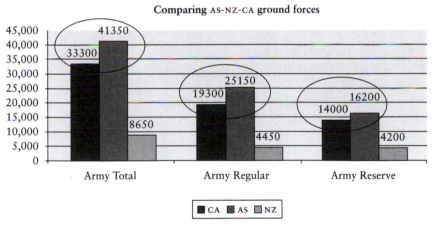

Source: Military Balance 2002–2003 (London: ISIS 2002).

Canada-Australia Historiography

The predominant focus in Canadian and Australian foreign and defence policy is on the United States and Europe, but "folk wisdom" in military circles reflects the sense of a wider imagined community, which suggests that the peoples of the two countries indeed have many things in common. While little effort has been made to substantiate or debunk the prevailing focus in the context of the two countries' respective armed forces, several academic studies have recognized the vast array of similarities between Canada and Australia and have ventured into directly comparing the Canadian and Australian experience in various fields. In particular, though military affairs have been neglected, other fields – literature, foreign policy, and public policy (including constitutional, economic, educational, health, social, cultural, agricultural, and environmental matters) have been compared in several books and journals.[1] This eclectic array of works, spanning decades, illustrates how frequently, at least in academic and policy circles, the comparison between Canada and Australia has been made, with varying degrees of success and differing results. For instance, even among these varied comparative studies, some have argued that "there are as many differences as similarities, separate paths taken as well as shared."[2] Similarly the Canadian scholar Andrew Cooper observes that "not only have the structural, situational and psychological locations of Australia and Canada set them apart in the post-1945 period, but their pattern of political development has differed appreciably."[3] Such views reinforce the inclination not to dig further to explore the value of cross-examination and mutual cooperation. In addition, these studies have tended to be largely edited compilations of works by disparate Australian and Canadian scholars, with only limited effort made to synthesize and derive greater meaning out of their collective efforts. Nevertheless, the breadth of subjects covered in such works suggests that Canada and Australia are virtually "secret alter-egos," with a surprising number of infrequently recognized similarities.[4]

The following brief review of the extant works covering the armed forces of Canada and Australia is intended show how this book fits into the broad span of military historiography and comparative Canadian-Australian studies. To begin with, Galen Roger Perras has contributed some excellent essays on specific periods in Australian-Canadian military historiography, including one entitled "'She Should Have Thought of Herself First': Canada and Military Aid to Australia, 1939–1945," in Margaret MacMillan and Francine McKenzie's edited collection, *Parties Long Estranged: Canada and Australia in the Twentieth Century.* Perras's work provides a detailed snapshot of the discussions over Canadian military aid to Australia during the Second World War and proved extremely useful for this study. One of Canada's foremost historians, Desmond Morton, has also contributed a chapter entitled "Canada and Australia: An Ocean of Difference in Threat Perception" to Linda Cardinal and David Headon's *Shaping Nations.* Morton's short essay covers the topic in a fashion a mile wide and an inch deep, while also overstating the differences in threats faced by Canada and Australia – for in fact the threats have been rare for both countries.[5] Richard A. Preston and Ian Wards come to similar (and superseded) conclusions in their late Cold War article "Military and Defence Development in Canada, Australia and New Zealand: A Three-Way Comparison," in *War & Society.*[6] Their conclusions are not only sensible but understandable, given that the post-Cold War reconvergence of the Australian and Canadian militaries had not yet become apparent when their work was published. Ronald G. Haycock's "The 'Myth' of Imperial Defence: Australian-Canadian Bilateral Military Co-operation, 1942," also in *War and Society*[7] explores one of the missed opportunities for cooperation between Australia and Canada during the Second World War. Haycock's work has helped to add colour to an otherwise dimly lit corner of military historiography. J.F. Hilliker's "Distant Ally – Canadian Relations with Australia during the Second World War," in *Journal of Imperial and Commonwealth History,*[8] is often referred to as a useful overview of Canadian-Australian relations during the Second World War.

Other broader comparative studies include Richard A. Preston's *Canada and "Imperial Defense": A Study of the Origins of the British Commonwealth's Defense Organization, 1867–1919.*[9] This is a helpful work but it is Canada-United Kingdom-centric and does little to compare the Australian and Canadian experience directly. F.W. Perry, in *The Commonwealth Armies: Manpower and Organisation in Two World Wars,*[10] includes chapters on the armies of Canada and Australia but also stops short of drawing many parallels. Jeffrey Grey's *The Commonwealth Armies and the Korean War: An Alliance Study*[11] makes deeper comparisons. But the focus in Grey's work is on the broader Commonwealth and the time period covered is restricted to a few years in the middle of the twentieth century. Nicholas Mansergh's *Survey of British Commonwealth Affairs*[12] makes an important contribution but is focused on higher defence policy and strategy issues. Graeme Cheeseman's short monograph, *Canada's Post-Cold-War Military Blues and Its Lessons for Australia*,[13] does not consider the historical parallels in any depth, and his conclusions are based on events in the mid- to late 1990s, when the reconvergence between the experiences of the armies of Canada and Australia was harder to discern. Elinor C. Sloan, in *The Revolution in Military Affairs*[14] discusses the RMA in Australia and Canada in separate chapters but makes little direct comparison between the developments in the two countries' forces.

In terms of unpublished dissertations, a few works stand out for consideration. Bruce Faraday's PHD thesis, "Half the Battle: The Administration and Higher Organisation of the AIF, 1914–1918,"[15] compares administrative aspects of the Canadian and Australian forces in the First World War. His work demonstrates many of the "nuts and bolts" similarities in the way the forces were administered in that conflict. It also begs the question of what might have occurred if they had collaborated more closely. A helpful comparison of the Australian and Canadian navies has been written by Rear-Admiral Fred W. Crickard, RCN (ret'd), "A Tale of Two Navies: United States Security and Canadian and Australian Naval Policy during the Cold War."[16] Crickard's work alludes to the armies of the two countries but focuses more on the key similarities in their navies. In addition, Crickard's interest is more the navies per se and their compatibility with the U.S. Navy. His intention is not to step back to reflect in depth on what it is that brings the two countries together and what has kept them apart.

At first glance, this list of published and unpublished works may appear long, but, given that it covers two countries and spans more than a century, it is almost infinitesimal. In fact, it demonstrates how limited the coverage of Canada-Australia military affairs is and how open that field is for the kind of analysis embarked upon in this book.

Exploring the Parallels between Australia and Canada

WHY COMPARE AUSTRALIA AND CANADA?

Australians and Canadians have compared various aspects of their military experiences with the military experiences of Britain and the United States, and this interest has been encouraged, for instance, by numerous personnel exchanges between their armed forces. Britain and the United States, after all, have been both Canada's and Australia's most significant allies and military partners throughout the last century to the present, and both also maintain forces that are expeditionary in nature. However, Canadian and Australian comparisons with either the United States or the United Kingdom are between substantially different kinds of nations – that is, between relatively small states, or "middle powers," armed only with "medium-weight" conventional forces, on the one hand, and nuclear and global or once global powers, on the other.[1] In military terms, middle-power status is reflected in the fact that Australia, like Canada, is prepared only to "develop combat weight needed to achieve its missions as a medium-weight defence force, no more, no less."[2]

Comparing Canada's and Australia's military forces and capabilities with those of the United States or even Britain, then, is like comparing apples and oranges (see appendix 6). In the case of the United States, a possible exception is the United States Marine Corps (USMC) – the only U.S. force remotely comparable in size and modus operandi to the Canadian and Australian forces when the latter are viewed as joint army-navy-air force teams. Yet even the USMC – an almost exclusively expeditionary force – operates with its own distinctive ethos and in a league of its own. This scale of operations is beyond the capacity or aspirations of the joint forces of either Canada or Australia, and the USMC operates as only one of several arms of the u.s. armed forces. Even on relatively small operations in Grenada and Panama in the 1980s, the American armed forces have tended to rely on overwhelming quantity to overcome shortcomings in quality and to avoid casualties.[3] This is an approach that the economically and demographically far smaller countries of Canada and Australia have never been able to afford. Consequently, a fixation on the lessons that the American experience may hold for these middle powers is fraught with potential difficulties.

The British forces are also frequently considered for comparison with those of Canada and Australia. Arguably, Britain is the most important security ally of the United States, but, in many ways, Australia is its closest ally[4] and Canada has usually been nearby as well, particularly because of its predominant trading relationship with its southern neighbour.[5] In any case, they are all remarkably close in many ways. Comparisons with Britain's forces, however, also have their limitations. Britain's forces are about three times the size of the forces of Australia and Canada (see appendix 6). Britain was also the focus of Canadian and Australian imperialist affection in many quarters in the late nineteenth and early twentieth centuries. But Canadians, Australians, and New Zealanders appeared to have had a far stronger emotional attachment to Britain than what was returned. Indeed, as the Canadian historian Carl Berger has observed, the vision of imperial unity "had turned out to be an illusion, their sacrifice and exile were rewarded with contempt, and their hopes were betrayed by Englishmen who identified the Empire with the United Kingdom."[6] Such responses triggered anxiety and resentment.

In a sense, like their American cousins, Australians and Canadians had to establish for themselves their own identity and nationhood, and this sprang in large part from their wartime experiences. In forging their own identity, however, the psychological, religious, and idealistic commonalities between them had to be denied or downplayed, while imperialism had to be explained away, primarily as an expression of realpolitik. During the adolescence of Canadian and Australian nationalism, what the two countries had in common was often overlooked, in part because of the focus on the "mother country." That focus on Britain reflected the centripetal nature of the British Empire and predisposed Canadians and Australians to overlook the common ties between them – ties that this work argues has made them more like each other than either was ever like the stratified society of Old World and imperial Britain.

All that said, this work is not intended to diminish the significance either of the differences between Canada and Australia or of their strong and enduring military ties with Britain and the United States. Rather, I contend that the comparison between the Australian and Canadian experience adds to the broader understanding of how Canada and Australia have fitted in as part of grand alliances for more than a century.

Canada has also compared itself and sought to conform to many of the practices of other NATO countries.[7] However, with the exception of France and Britain and, to a lesser extent, the Netherlands, these nations have focused mostly on home-based armed forces rather than the expeditionary ones common to the New World nations.[8] For NATO, "back-filling" (that is, relieving American "war-fighters" of "peacekeeping" responsibilities) became "the name of the game" in the Balkans and Afghanistan as U.S. forces redeployed from peacekeeping to more active missions and for rest at home. In addition, the terrorist threat did not provide the "new magical glue that could fix the cracks in the Atlantic building" and the political divide has been accompanied by "a widening gap in military technology between the two sides of the Atlantic."[9] From the Canadian perspective, the Atlantic has metaphorically "got wider, colder and deeper" in recent years.[10] This phenomenon has occurred despite the fact that Canadians have been predisposed to working with NATO. Yet Canada's actions at home and deployments abroad since 9/11 have demonstrated that these changed dynamics are largely understood in Ottawa, where strategic interests, concepts of world order, and shared values have usually kept Canada "firmly fixed to its seat at the table of the American-led and dominated western alliance."[11] Canada's focus on NATO reflects, as well, the commonalities between it and several of the European "middle powers" with which Canada and Australia are sometimes compared. Small European states like the Nordic countries and the Netherlands also maintain a strong interest in international security and economic cooperation. But, as Andrew Cooper notes, "despite these similarities, these countries lack many of the defining features shared by Canada and Australia."[12]

When seeking comparisons, Australia often looks at its smaller neighbour, New Zealand, as the most similar to it in terms of geography and military culture and organization. New Zealand, however, is a much smaller nation, with a population under four million, and with even smaller forces. It is also a unitary state, unlike the federations of Canada and Australia.[13] Admittedly, in some ways, New Zealand's army is more similar to that of Australia than Canada's is, partly because the New Zealand Defence Force has sought to maintain a high degree of interoperability with the Australian Defence Force to enable it to operate in coalition with

Australia and as an economy measure. Yet, in terms of scale as well as the nature and breadth of issues affecting the development and employment of their armies, the New Zealand-Australia comparison has limitations not found when comparing Canada and Australia. Some would draw a comparison between New Zealand and Canada, since both have the luxury of optional force structures, a preference for peacekeeping, and populist foreign-policy positions because of the protection offered by more powerful neighbouring friends. After all, New Zealand, like Canada, tied its stance to the 2003 war in Iraq to an imprimatur from the United Nations Security Council. But this parallel, while valid, once again is limited by the differences in scale between Canada and New Zealand, much like the limitations inherent in comparing either Australia or Canada with the United States.[14]

Culturally, Australia and Canada are often seen as closely linked to the United States, and, to some extent, of course, this is true. Yet the differences are also pronounced. For instance, the United States has about nine times Canada's population (fifteen times Australia's) and also has major African-American and Latino populations not common to Canada or Australia. In addition, divergent beginnings distinguish their nationalities, with a strong Revolutionary War and Civil War heritage and much heavier checks and balances in government. To a far greater extent than in Canada or Australia, the diffusion of authority in the American system tends to dissipate power between the presidential executive and the congressional legislative arms – which also lack the party discipline, let alone the concentration of power in the hands of the prime minister, evident in the Westminster parliamentary counterparts in places like Canada and Australia. For the respective armed forces, these differences result in markedly different approaches to civil-military relations in the U.S. system compared to Australia and Canada. At the same time, the values and attitudes of the predominantly English-speaking nations are surprisingly pervasive, despite their institutional differences and even though they may be "separated by a common language," as often has been said.

One comparison rarely made in Canada or Australia is between the armies of these countries – which is surprising, given that their armies are more alike than the other prime candidates commonly used for comparison or emulation. Several books have been written comparing specific defence aspects of British Commonwealth relations, but only a few have ventured into reviewing directly the military experiences of Canada and Australia and their enduring parallels. Yet the parallels are striking. For instance, neither Australia nor Canada fought a revolutionary war,[15] had their own global empires, or faced a major civil war; although some would argue that they both fought a "war" against their indigenous populations. "In the particular sense," argues Australian historian Richard Broome, there was enough "armed fighting" to make the conflicts with aboriginal peoples truly wars, although such views have been contested.[16] In Canada, military forces were employed in the Northwest Rebellion led by Louis Riel and his Metis supporters. But beyond this (and in stark contrast to the U.S. experience), neither the Canadian aboriginal peoples nor those of Australia presented a sufficient threat to the colonies to compel the employment of military force, particularly after the United States War of Independence. In both cases, this type of "war" against aboriginals reflected what could be described as "settler imperialism," which resulted in continual pressure to extend the boundaries of colonized land.[17]

With their nations secured, Canadian and Australian governments and their defence planners tended to look to the use of power abroad, linked with their trade interests. Indeed, for both Canada and Australia, economic prosperity and security have been heavily dependent on international trade. That trade, in turn, has underlined the importance of overseas influence and thus reinforced the strategic tradition of "forward security." Canada, like Australia, has long been part of a cultural and economic bloc and has derived substantial security benefits from such ties. As one Canadian politician contends, "a healthy trading environment needs global stability and prosperity. Our military is essential to maintain this stability."[18]

A historical review demonstrates that the armed forces of Canada and Australia have, for more than a century, performed similar yet distinctive roles as the ultimate instruments of national resolve in international affairs.[19] But, before I explore these parallel historical experiences, the reader may benefit from having a clearer picture of what the distinctive features of the two countries are, what sets them apart, what has prevented closer military cooperation thus far, and what it is that they and their armed forces have in common at the beginning of the twenty-first century.

WHAT DO THEY HAVE IN COMMON?

Broad Similarities

Canada and Australia have many general points of similarity. Indeed, if the model used by the University of Michigan's study of world values is to be believed (and as chart 2 indicates), Canada and Australia have similar and distinctive values that set them apart from other countries and place them closer to each other than to any other country. The study also places them closer than any others to the United States.

To begin with, Canada and Australia (along with New Zealand and the United States) are New World countries that share common Anglo-Celtic and European roots, as well as a shared colonial heritage, although both still retain Britain's monarch as their head of state.[20] Both, naturally enough, are also members of the Commonwealth of Nations – the successor of the British Empire. Membership in the Commonwealth offers a wide range of opportunities for Australian and Canadian politicians and diplomats to meet informally in various fora, including the periodic Commonwealth Heads of Government Meetings.[21]

The Commonwealth is only one of many ties that make comparisons between Canada and Australia valuable. For instance, as a consequence of their European roots, Canada and Australia were both derivative societies, being "among the first by-products of the American Revolution." Loyalists fled north and, arriving as they did after the original French settlers, helped to set the pattern of anglophone and francophone spheres of influence in what would become Canada. Shortly thereafter, Australia became a new repository for felons of the type that had earlier been sent to the southern colonies of the future United States.[22] Clearly, however, the founding "myths" were in contrast. Australia's featured convicts (with their tendency to irreverence and questioning of authority) while the Canadian "myth" featured Loyalists (at least in the predominantly Anglo-Canadian Maritime provinces and the province of Ontario).

The process of becoming recognizable as distinct nations rather than as British appendages was a drawn-out one for both Canada and Australia. It took Canadians and Australians a long time to cast off the "apron strings" of colonialism, partly because the British, having learned their lessons from the American struggle for independence, had ameliorated their colonial practices in the nineteenth century.[23] On the way to nationhood, both Canada and Australia experienced gold rushes (Yukon and Ballarat). They also experienced surges in immigration (including European and, more recently, non-European) and late-twentieth-century multiculturalism (following a long period of similar assimilationist policies). In both countries, too, multiculturalism has been matched by a tendency on the part of recent immigrants to remain politically active. As Kim Nossal observes, "ethnic groups will frequently press the government in Canberra and Ottawa to play an activist role in the politics of their *patria* ... a pressure to which the politicians in Canberra and Ottawa are not insensitive."[24]

Both Canada and Australia also share a widespread use of the English language,[25] Judaeo-Christian values, and similar "post-modern" influences, but not the legally pedantic separation of church and state evident in the United States. Canada and Australia are both open societies, with democratic practices and a capitalist economic system reliant on a meritocracy rather than European-style hereditary titles. Both countries once had but then discarded the British system of honours (Canada earlier than Australia). They have similar gross domestic product per capita and share equal ranking in the United Nations Development Program's human-development index (see appendix 5).[26] While distinct from Europe, Canada and Australia (as well as New Zealand) also belong to the "Western Europe and Others Group" (WEOG) in the United Nations. As the abbreviation WEOG suggests, Australia and Canada share a perception that "they are not attached to a single regional home, but straddle regions."[27]

In addition, despite the demise of the British Empire, Canadians and Australians remain part of an "imagined community." Both countries have chosen to seek national security in alliance with more powerful nations.[28] In foreign-policy matters, this manifests itself through a sense of familiarity vis-à-vis their operational habits and world-views that allows them to work together on a range of issues. The low-key or "quiet" Canadian way in diplomacy is often in contrast to the Australian reputation as the loudest, most demanding, and least diplomatic of the older former British dominions.[29] But, as Cooper suggests, the contrasting diplomatic styles of Australia and Canada can be seen as complementary rather than at odds with one another. Moreover, "despite the implicit claim of moral superiority, neither Canada nor Australia has an unblemished record with respect to international issues."[30]

They also are signatories to the 1989 Canada-Australia Consular Sharing Agreement, which has led to them share embassy premises in places like Cambodia and Barbados. At the bureaucratic level, the main focus for contact has been the Canada-Australia Senior Officials Consultations (SOC). This informal network has also tapped into the Canada-Australia-New Zealand (CANZ) ministerial and senior officials' meetings. What these wide-ranging ties point to is what has been described as "a commonality in Australian and Canadian diplomatic approaches to matters of substance but a disjuncture in matters of style."[31]

Today, both countries face a comparable set of challenges. Each has industrialized (or "post-industrial') economies with a large service sector but also display a substantial reliance on exportable primary products, and each is heavily dependent on trade with other industrialized powers.

Additionally, through well-educated workforces, both have diversified into a range of high-technology industries.

These two countries' governments also grapple with similar aboriginal issues –although, in Canada, as in the United States, natives' rights and land ownership have been recognized through treaties. In Australia, the treaty process was resisted and, until recently, the land was in effect treated as *terra nullius* (the land of no one). The Canadian experience, with an indigenous population that accounts for just under 3 per cent of the population, contrasts with Australia's, where the aboriginal population is slightly below 2 per cent of the total population. Still, despite their differences, the political struggle of indigenous peoples in both places – a struggle that is increasingly a global phenomenon – has put Canada and Australia on converging paths,[32] particularly with respect to issues such as the management of Defence-controlled land and inclusive recruiting policies.

Canada and Australia are alike in other ways too. In both countries there has been some anti-British sentiment: in Australia this was primarily associated with the Irish Catholic diaspora, while in Canada it was associated most commonly with the opposition of French-speaking Canadians to involvement in the wars of the British Empire.[33] Their policies on gun control, gender issues, and public health care are similar and in contrast to those of the United States. Both Canada and Australia maintain extensive state-sponsored health, welfare, and education programs, and the standards of these programs are similar in the two countries. Both countries have comparable national broadcasting networks, known respectively as the CBC and the ABC, and their political systems bear remarkable similarities as well. Canada and Australia are the only two countries that share common, albeit distinctive, federal and bicameral Westminster-style parliamentary and legal systems, having inherited the same body of legislative tradition and policy instruments from Britain.[34] At the same time, both the Canadian and Australian models were influenced strongly by the American experience of representative and bicameral federal democracy. Canadian constitutional principles, with their emphasis on peace, order, and good (that is, active) government, have been a major influence on Australia.[35] Yet there are distinctions between the two countries' approaches, as centrifugal and centripetal regional powers (of the Canadian provinces and Australian states) and national ones have waxed and waned.[36] In addition, as Cooper points out, "Australian politics in the main revolves around non-territorial debates based on class, ideology and religion. In complete contrast, territoriality has long assumed a commanding position in politics and policy making in Canada." In Canada, regional divisions are based on the distinctiveness of Quebec, the sense of isolation of Atlantic Canada, and the "western alienation" of the prairie provinces and the Pacific coast.[37]

These two countries have tended to gravitate towards one another on the world stage and have often found opportunity for contact, if not always co-operation. Despite their occasional acrimony and rivalry, they constitute a special international relationship that brings out essential differences and enduring compatibilities.[38] In military terms, this means that Canadians and Australians often find themselves on United Nations or coalition operations working alongside each other, taking similar positions, and contributing similar forces.

One of the key commonalities between Canada and Australia is the broadly similar perception (despite their geographical dissimilarities) about the international role of the United States. Neither Canada nor Australia has usually played a crucial role in u.s. global strategy but neither have they presented any particularly challenging dilemma for the United States, unlike France in the mid-1960s, when it pulled its forces out of NATO. In addition, Canada, like Australia, has avoided the domestic political liability (experienced by most NATO countries, and the east Asian allies of the United States, for instance) of having substantial numbers of u.s. combat forces stationed on its soil.

Partly in reaction to the concentration of power in American hands, there remain varying degrees of latent anti-Americanism in Canada and Australia. As a classified official Canadian report observed as early as 1951, this "means on the one hand that a Canadian administration is subject to the temptation to pull the Eagle's feathers in order to get more support in Canada, and ... if it goes too far in deferring to the United States, it would lose a substantial measure of support in Canada." Yet, as the report also pointed out, the "differences are largely of emphasis and timing, but these can be very important." While Australia tends to be more averse to "pulling" such "feathers," a similar sentiment is evident there – particularly in media, academic, and left-wing political circles.[39]

Despite such latent anti-Americanism, Canada and Australia share unique compatibilities with the United States, since all are cosmopolitan states built on predominantly Anglo foundations that fuel a strong sense of common identity. Both countries are culturally and intellectually aligned with the United States on key issues, including support for democracy, free enterprise, and globalization – being beneficiaries of the spread of the English language (despite intermittent misgivings in francophone Quebec) as well as the Internet and other such technologies. Both also have flourished under the security umbrella provided by Anglo-American global domination over the last century, which has provided the framework in which their trade and prosperity has flourished. Both have a vested interest in seeing that protection continue, along with the stability and economic prosperity it fosters. Those same interests have driven the need for both countries to maintain what in essence amounts to expeditionary forces that are able to be deployed far from their native shores.

Walter Mead has indicated that power is not the only factor that binds in international affairs. He points out that "the United States and Great Britain have a special relationship that goes beyond their common language, heritage and democratic values."[40] Australia and Canada share many of the values of the United States and Britain, receive the benefits – and experience the consequences – of the Anglo-American relationship, and, in each case, have clearly shifted into the American security orbit since the demise of Britain's Empire. But, beyond that submissive relationship, Canada and Australia failed to feature prominently in u.s. consciousness for most of the twentieth century – despite the inherent commonalities of these New World nations. This was in part because, for many years, they were seen as an adjunct of the British Empire, and also because of their relatively less consequential military and economic clout.

In recent decades, both Australia and Canada have sought security in collective defence and have played constructive global middle-power roles in foreign, trade, environmental, and security issues, agreeing on a range of bilateral matters.[41] They have tried to make their mark in international-security affairs, in part, to assert – without unduly compromising – sovereignty in unequal relationships with more powerful allies. This approach is illustrated by their common membership in the Asia Pacific Economic Co-operation Forum, alongside the United States and other Pacific-rim nations. They also participate in the Council for Security Co-operation in the Asia Pacific (CSCAP), the Pacific Economic Co-operation Conference (PECC), and the Pacific Basin Economic Conference (PBEC)[42] and exercise foreign-policy assertiveness in other multilateral fora.[43]

In terms of the socio-economic issues often associated with great disruptions, the world is commonly divided into two broad camps known as "North" and "South." Canada and Australia fall clearly within the "North" camp, being relatively wealthy, content, and demographically stagnant societies, reliant on immigration for population growth. In contrast, some argue, the "South" has a large number of poverty-stricken, resource-depleted nations with populations that are doubling every twenty-five years or so. This growing divide points, it is said, to increased prospects of mass migration from "South" to "North" and of the instability that radiates from collapsing states.[44] Australia and Canada both recognize the gulf that divides their wealthy societies from the many less fortunate ones and both have sought to respond, at least in part, with humanitarian assistance that is frequently delivered and protected by their armed forces on expeditionary operations.

Canada and Australia are beneficiaries of globalization and the digital or information age, with similarly high standards of living and national economic productivity (see appendix 5). Both have high levels of Internet connectivity – Canada is ranked eighth and Australia tenth (the United States ranks first) in the world – in terms of per-capita Internet hosts.[45] Both Canada and Australia have little in common with reactionary and traditionalist societies resistant to the Western influences associated with the Internet.

Canadians, like Australians, accept that their country is highly "globalized," being penetrated by peoples, ideas, finance, capital, technology, and culture from around the world. Arguably, both countries always have been globalized, since, from the beginning, they have been so heavily reliant on international trade and immigration. As David Dewitt observes about Canada (but his remarks also apply to Australia), its sense of identity within the global community has become linked with a compelling need to "do something" that drives its engagement in international affairs. Consequently, Canada, like Australia, maintains professionally trained and equipped armed forces able to conduct expeditionary military operations with like-minded partners in support of United Nations and allied objectives.[46]

Clearly, both Canada and Australia remain part of the Anglo-American "club" or "extended family," having ready access to shared educational institutions and standards among professional elites. In addition, Australian and Canadian universities maintain a number of exchanges to foster cross-fertilization of ideas in such fields as the humanities and social sciences, as they also both do with the United States and Britain.[47] In military terms, this means ready recognition of each other's procedures and military "cultures" as well as trade and professional military qualifications and standards. Such compatibilities make for relatively easy and rapid cooperation and collaboration on military operations, even when these operations are put together at short notice, such as the Australian-led mission to East Timor in 1999.

Military Culture Similarities

Both Australian and Canadian government officials and military planners face a latent anti-militarist element in society which needs to be taken into account when seeking to structure forces for and then deploying them on expeditionary operations. Every Canadian and Australian federal government must consider the ramifications of this sentiment (which waxes and wanes as views of the United States change) for their policies towards the world's sole remaining superpower. Indeed, how the armed forces of Canada and Australia are structured and used is in part a reflection of how their governments envisage their forces interacting with and relying on the United States.

Both Canada and Australia have similarly sized armed forces and spend virtually the same amount on defence (see appendix 6). Both have historically relied on their respective allies for protection, and both celebrate the exploits of their part-time and largely citizen-based armies.[48] Their small but professional forces provide what Sean Maloney (referring to Canadians) describes as saliency and a degree of operational influence that is well suited to coalition warfare.[49] Reflecting this outlook, Canada's CDS, General J.M.G. Baril, together with Canada's deputy minister of national defence, Jim Judd, issued in June 1999 *A Strategy for 2020* which stressed interoperability and deployability. The strategy "sought to position the force structure of the CF to provide Canada with modern, task-tailored, and globally deployable combat–capable forces that can respond to crises at home and abroad, in joint or combined operations. The force structure must be viable, achievable and affordable."[50] The Australians illustrated a similar mindset when they led the mission to East Timor in 1999 and subsequently deployed to Afghanistan in 2002 and again in 2005–06 as well as Iraq and the Solomon Islands in 2003.

The Canadian scholar Douglas Bland, commenting on Canada's enduring tendency to work with successive major allies (the British and Americans), points out that "interoperability is as Canadian as a beaver." He could just as easily say that interoperability is as Australian as a kangaroo. What is more, Australian efforts aimed at interoperability with U.S. forces has led to a de facto high level of interoperability between Canadian and Australian forces as well. As Canadian Major-General H. Cameron Ross and Nigel R. Thalakada observe, "there is a converging point for interoperability efforts. Such convergence allows middle powers, like Canada, Australia and the Netherlands, to mount missions in which the United States may only play a limited supporting role." In Canada's case, however, as Bland notes, interoperability "may become a substitute for political direction of national strategy."[51]

Interoperability, particularly for the armies of Canada and Australia, is facilitated through the quadripartite America-Britain-Canada-Australia armies working-group forum known as ABCA.[52] ABCA has facilitated enhanced interoperability, particularly through its policy-formulating body, known as TEAL,[53] and through the various quadripartite working groups. But these groups' findings are not binding and the program has little profile outside senior army circles. For Canada, as for Australia, ABCA remains relevant because it facilitates doctrinal and *matériel* standardization and interoperability, opportunities to participate in occasional field exercises at formation level and above, and access to innovations and lessons learned by partner armies at low cost.[54] As one British officer observes, "the benefits of common language, shared heritage and less formal association [than NATO] permit greater flexibility in the working of the ABCA Programme."[55] The standardization fora include such bodies as the Combined Communications-Electronics Board (CCEB) and the Technical Co-operation Program (TTCP). Still, standardization has the drawback of tending to produce a kind of logistical dependence for the lesser allies, Canada and Australia (and, to a lesser extent, New Zealand). Even when collaboration on *matériel* projects has been considered, the United States has dominated, leaving little room for the smaller ABCA partners. In the 1960s, for instance, Project Mallard was intended to facilitate a quadrilateral trunk-communications project, with shared component manufacture. But the project failed to "get off the ground" largely because of excessive U.S. business and congressional demands for control. Despite such occasional setbacks on the road to enhanced interoperability, periodic combined exercises have been conducted. But, with the United States in the lead, the focus has not been necessarily on maximizing collaboration between the two smaller partners, Canada and Australia.[56]

Canada and Australia also cooperate with the United States and Britain in intelligence matters. They are both co-signatories of the agreements signed in 1947–48 and collectively known as the UKUSA agreement.[57] This agreement helped create what Australian scholars Desmond Ball and David Horner describe as "the most important secret intelligence co-operation regime ever organised."[58] Consistent with these commitments, both countries also contribute to the U.S.-based Space Detection and Tracking System (SPADATS) through Canada's stations at Cold Lake, Alberta, and St Margarets, New Brunswick, and Australia's equivalent, the communications intercept station at Pine Gap.[59] Beyond these measures, and several personnel exchanges, Canada and Australia do not share in any formal military alliances.

Reflecting on this interoperability, American political scientists such as Jon B. McLin suggest that Canada maintains its armed forces as "club dues" for five reasons: to secure the alliance with the United States, to promote the Canadian defence industry, to support Canadian diplomacy, to preserve the right to be consulted, and to promote solidarity between the United States and Western Europe.[60] Similar dynamics have been at work in Australia, albeit with a more acute sense of geo-strategic isolation and vulnerability and a focus on Asia rather than Europe.

In terms of geography – usually an important force-structure determinant – Canada and Australia cover large and often dry land masses. Both the Canadian Arctic and the remote Australian outback are vast areas of inhospitable, predominantly arid, and difficult-to-traverse terrains, with small populations living along relatively narrow corridors of fertile land on the rim of vast expanses of largely uninhabitable territory.[61] In both countries' cases, war and the airplane have driven home the importance of their north for strategy, resources, and communications. Their parallel circumstances have spawned popular rugged "frontier" cultures that are distinctive from the Old World as well as from the United States. This geographic circumstance has presented similar logistic challenges to both Australian and Canadian military planners assigned to prepare northern-defence contingencies against unlikely and largely implausible prospects of ground offensives.[62]

As the superimposed maps of Australia and Canada (on page xxxi) illustrate, they are similarly sized nations with significant ocean frontages and strikingly similar population dispersal. In contrast to most other countries in the "West," Canada and Australia are sparsely populated.[63] The regional concentration of electorates (and hence political power) is in the southeastern extremities of both countries. For Australia, it is centred on the Sydney-Canberra-Melbourne axis, stretching to Adelaide and Brisbane; for Canada, it is centred on the Montreal-Ottawa-Toronto corridor, stretching to south-central Ontario and Quebec City. This leaves Tasmania and the Canadian Maritime provinces on the margins and the "wests" of the two countries faced with similar balance-of-power disparities vis-á-vis their eastern counterparts. The comparable geographic circumstances led to similar demands in each country for air-transport networks – served by Air Canada and Qantas respectively.[64] For both countries and in similar ways, these dynamics also affect the imperatives for air power as well as the distribution of military infrastructure and concerns about homeland defence. The freedom from concern over immediate local defence has enabled both countries to focus on developing forces that can operate remote from their shores, either to prevent a threat from getting closer to home or to fulfil secondary foreign- and defence-policy priorities beyond protection of the homeland itself.

Naturally enough, the two countries have placed priority on developing transportation, industrial infrastructure, and social and health services for the populations clustered in a few densely populated urban centres. In terms of government funding, these important national priorities offer competition to military defence in both countries. Similarly, the vast uninhabited expanses that presented such substantial infrastructure and transportation challenges also prompted the creation of extensive surveillance systems in the north of both countries, which also led, in Canada's case, to the enlistment of aboriginals in the five Canadian Ranger Patrol Groups, and, in Australia's, to the Australian Army's three northern regional-surveillance units.[65] Such units were raised in response to domestic attempts to formulate grand national strategies that took account of geography, but, preoccupied as they are with allies, grand strategy has never been a forté for Canadians or Australians.

Canada and Australia have a propensity to rely on others to develop grand strategy – particularly in war, where neither country has had much opportunity to excel militarily beyond the tactical level. For instance, both the Australian and Canadian armies have worked well up to a certain level because of the limited opportunities provided and the limitations of their training, but higher allied strategy has rarely been a domain that welcomes the participation of Canadian and Australian commanders and politicians. That said, both Canada and Australia, early in their histories as nations, sought to foster military thought and established their own military colleges. Today, both countries' forces are similarly refining their national-level military command-and-control structures, as well as their entry-level military colleges and staff-level and senior defence colleges. But their organizations have yet to mature intellectually beyond the realm of tactics to the point where either can comfortably operate at the strategic level.[66]

Force-Structure Similarities

Both countries have faced tension over whether defence at home or military operations overseas should take priority. While home defence ostensibly always has remained the top priority, in practice it has been otherwise. In Australia after federation, the force-structure priority was homeland defence alone, despite calls from London to structure forces for imperial contingencies. Thus, Australian militia forces were legally constrained under the Defence Act from being used for expeditionary operations beyond Australia's shores. This predicament led to the ad hoc raising of the Australian Imperial Force in 1914 to circumvent the ill-conceived legislation that excluded service abroad. Canada found itself in a similar quandary. One report observed that "Canadians have thus been caught flatfooted by the outbreak of war, but never fainthearted, often unprepared but never unwilling. They have more than 100,000 dead buried in foreign fields to prove it."[67] Virtually the same is true for Australia.[68] Interestingly, close to 100,000 U.S. citizens lost their lives in the battles to contain communism in Korea and Vietnam. In contrast, Australian and Canadian killed in action in Korea (and, for Australia, in Vietnam as well) were only in the hundreds.[69]

Both countries' armies still retain a residual influence from inherited British military traditions, tactics, and ethos. Both also use capability-based planning for force structure and contingency planning. Even their military force structures and equipment inventories, at the time of writing, bear a remarkable resemblance. Both have been equipped with German-built Leopard tanks, Canadian-built light armoured vehicles, modified U.S.-sourced M113 armoured personnel carrier variants, and a three-brigade regular land-force structure[70] supported by special forces and similarly sized, regionally based volunteer militia (or reserve) forces (see appendices 2 and 6). They both have maintained up to a battalion of airborne forces.[71] Their tactical command-and-control systems also bear a high degree of commonality. Australia's battlefield command-support system (BCSS) and Canada's land forces command-and-control system (LFC2) allow for a high degree of interoperability. This interoperability is due in part to the shared membership in the multilateral interoperability program (MIP).[72]

Their air forces also both use the FA/CF-18 (Hornet),[73] C130 (Hercules), and P3 (Orion/Aurora) aircraft and both joined the Joint Strike Fighter Program as third-tier international partners with a view to purchasing it as the next-generation combat-aircraft platform. They also have explored the prospect of acquiring larger strategic transport aircraft (Australia still uses the versatile Canadian-built CC08 Caribou short-take-off-and-landing transport aircraft. It also maintains a fleet of upgraded F-111 strategic strike aircraft). Their navies have similar two-ocean fleet configurations, with the Australian fleets based in Fremantle, on the west coast facing the Indian Ocean, and Sydney on the east coast, facing the Pacific Ocean, while Canada's fleets are based in Halifax on the Atlantic coast and Esquimalt on the Pacific. They both have virtually the same degree of interoperability with the United States Navy. They also have a similar number of helicopter-equipped frigates, replenishment ships, conventionally powered submarines, and coastal defence vessels.[74] As Canadian Rear-Admiral (ret'd) Fred W. Crickard notes, by the beginning of the twenty-first century, the

Australian and the Canadian navies were both small, ocean-going, balanced naval fleets completely interoperable with the u.s. Navy. In addition, they were "close to being fleet units" of the u.s. Navy, just as the British Admiralty had wished the new Dominion navies to be part of the Royal Navy at the beginning of the twentieth century.[75] However, unlike Australia, Canada has a smaller fleet of patrol boats and no amphibious shipping.[76]

Clearly, then, there are many points of similarity (encapsulated in chart 1). In one sense, the similarities between the navy, army, and air force equipment and organizations are merely coincidental. But the remarkable parallels over such a long period of time also point to a series of parallel geo-strategic fundamentals that have driven Canadians and Australians to develop forces and acquire weapons and equipment from similar sources and with comparable capabilities to perform like functions. These underlying fundamentals include large land masses, small populations, relative security, "Western" values, and enduring and close security and defence ties with British and American "cousins," including shared production agreements. Still, there remain several points of difference which help explain their distinctiveness and these are explored below.

WHAT MAKES THEM DIFFERENT?

To a non-Canadian, a striking difference between Australia and Canada is the distinct culture of the French majority in Quebec and its influence on Canadian foreign and defence policies – especially during wartime. This Canadian concern about national unity reflects a nervous introspection that appears to be an enduring part of the Canadian condition, and that is in contrast to the easygoing Australian approach which takes its own national coherence for granted. For Canadian policy makers, preoccupation with French-speaking Quebec has usually seemed fully warranted, particularly given Canada's "near death experience" in 1995 when a vote for Quebec secession was only narrowly defeated.[77] Yet the cost of conciliating French Canadian nationalism has been a forty-year "stalemate at the heart of the nation's institutions."[78] Australian and Canadian contrasting attitudes towards national coherence are among the most prominent distinguishing factors that influence the development of their distinctive national defence and security strategies.

To understand the significance of national coherence for Canada, an understanding of the concerns of French Canadians is required. To start with, Canada's historical turning point was the defeat by the British under

General Wolfe of the French forces under General Montcalm on the Plains of Abraham outside Quebec City in 1759 and the subsequent cession of the country by France to Britain in 1763 – considered by many as a long-remembered point of betrayal of Quebec by France. Particularly for French Canadians, this event has remained a point of national disunity, not solidarity. Ever since, French Canadians in Quebec, as one American scholar has observed, "have been inculcated with a version of history stressing the plight of the French and the sturdiness of their defense against waves of English-Protestant influence. Outside Quebec, Canadian children have been served a very different ideological diet. Again, no counterpart problem exists in Australia."[79] The inculcation of this distinctive history has led French Canadians to seek to safeguard provincial rights and to protect French-speaking Canadians from social and linguistic absorption in predominantly English-speaking North America.[80] Yet even here there are similarities with the influence of Irish Catholic and Labor Party nationalism in Australia, which sought to distance Australia from the imperial clutches of Britain[81] and then reinforced an anti-communist sentiment during the Cold War that was similar to that found in Catholic Quebec.[82] Unlike Australia, however, Canada's greatest threat has been internal – that of national disunity, particularly along linguistic lines.[83] As the Canadian historian Francine McKenzie says, "Australian leaders assumed that support would beget support and so have consistently participated in US military interventions around the world." She further notes that Australia's usual stance is "in contrast to Canada, where participation in war has often had a divisive effect." For Canada, as David Last points out, the real threat to Canadian security and identity came not from the Boers, the Kaiser, or the Nazis but from the wars themselves – which pitted anglophone against francophone on matters of policy and principle.[84]

Consequently, one of the Canadian Forces' main *raisons d'être* appears to be not necessarily to fight but to reinforce national unity, acting as an institution in which all Canadians can feel a sense of ownership – particularly if they are aware of the forces' inclusiveness. Given their major role in promoting national unity, the Canadian Forces also are required to reflect the bilingual and bicultural nature of the country.[85] But maintaining national unity, in a setting of divergent regional interests and loyalties, has often come at the expense of coherent Canadian foreign and defence policies – particularly during the world wars and even in recent times. Consequently, while Canadians and Australians have often gone to the same wars and deployed on the same peacekeeping missions, Canada has been, on occasion, conspicuously absent, especially during the more divisive wars in Vietnam and in Iraq since 2003. Meanwhile, as McKenzie points out, Australia has tended to work on the sound basic assumption that "you don't get something for nothing."[86]

The contrast manifests itself in public monuments as well. In Canada, a Korean War memorial portrays a Canadian soldier holding a girl in his right arm and with his left hand on the shoulder of a boy. One newspaper editorial criticized this sanitized view of soldiering, stating that "to sentimentalize the reality leaves a nation psychologically ill-prepared for the real thing."[87] A lack of psychological preparedness is complemented by the absence of a significant genre of Canadian war movies. Canadians speak glowingly about well-known Australian movies including *Breaker Morant, Gallipoli, The Light Horsemen,* and *The Odd Angry Shot.* Such movies certainly have contributed to a robust Australian self-image, and few could point to any substantive Canadian equivalents.

Along with national unity, Canada's place next door to the United States seems to be an ever-present concern for many Canadians. For instance, Canadian Prime Minister Pierre Trudeau told American interlocutors in 1969 that "living next to you is in some ways like sleeping with an elephant. One is affected by every twitch and grunt."[88] Particularly since the middle of the twentieth century, that proximity has had a more profound ideological, cultural, and economic influence on Canadians than the United States has had on Australians. In some parts of Canada, north-south ties (between Canadian provinces and adjacent regions in the United States) are almost as strong as east-west ties among the Canadian provinces. In contrast, Australians are arguably more homogenous than Canadians, with no culturally distinct province like Canada's Quebec.

The fundamental fact that cannot be ignored is that Canada lives directly beside its major trading partner and ally.[89] The vast majority of the Canadian population lives within close proximity of the United States border and Canada's largest cities are an hour or two by car from the border. Thus, Canada, qualitatively as well as quantitatively, has more of an American "branch plant" economic structure than Australia.[90] Being so overshadowed by the United States on the international stage has certainly added to Canadian angst.

Proximity to the United States has led to Canada being described as a "regional power without a region."[91] But, as Annette Fox stated even before the advent of the Internet age, the "technological revolution renders doubtful the very notion of regionalism." Proximity between the two countries appears to have driven the Americans to make an implicit bargain with Canada. As Charles F. Doran maintains, "that bargain involved the extension of certain trade and financial concessions plus strategic security, on the one hand, in return for a relatively open investment and trading situation, on the other. The United States would provide security for Canada, as for itself, without attempting to exact proportionate payment, and would grant Canada exemptions from u.s. trade and commercial policies not granted to other states."[92] Australia was never in such a favourable bargaining position and never offered the United States such a significant quid pro quo. Consequently, Australia has long felt more concerned to ingratiate itself with the United States.

Australians are also more British-like, with cultural ties reinforced until the end of the 1960s by economic ties through membership in Britain's sterling bloc. For many years, Australia had no other option, particularly since there were no real alternatives emerging from Europe, the United States, or Japan. For instance, for Australians, the United States Congress has been regarded as a hindrance (more so than the executive branch) to better access to American markets – once again, a concern shared by Canadians as well. American special interests in Congress tend to be adversarial towards Australia, competing with Australian interests. In contrast, according to Annette Fox, Canada was "rather easily weaned away from most imperial preference arrangements as the United States market loomed more important, and with the easing of barriers, trade between the two countries grew rapidly." Thus, Canada has emerged as the country with the most extensive American direct investment.[93] As one American scholar states, "apart from the socio-psychological and security value to the United States of the relationship with Canada, that relationship's economic value is matched by no other."[94]

Canada's well-founded sense of external security is without parallel in Australia. But this confidence has bred what could be described as "complacency" and, at times, enhanced the appeal of limiting foreign interventions that could demand the use of military force as a realistic policy. Confidence in the protection inherent in being close to the United States has allowed Canadian leaders, according to Canadian military scholar Douglas Bland, to "talk loudly, while carrying a small stick and to feel superior about it." In addition, these circumstances have encouraged a military culture that "habitually accepts strategic direction from other states and international organisations as 'natural.'" According to Bland, designing or managing a national strategy and controlling civil-military relations in Canada are "activities foreign to Canada's political culture."[95] Another observer comments that one of the primary purposes of the Canadian armed forces in the North American theatre is to provide "defence against help," that is, to ensure that the United States will not feel the need, out of self-interest, to defend Canada whether Canadians like it or not and to intrude on Canada's sovereignty in the process.[96] On the other hand, as Jon McLin notes, "Canada's security interests are so closely identified with those of the U.S. that it is assured of American protection. Such reasoning calls into question the very basis for the maintenance of a defense establishment in Canada."[97] This rationale has made it difficult for advocates of a reinvigoration of defence to make an effective argument for extra funding. Still, while assured of American protection, Canada's long land border with the United States has been an issue of concern. With 425 border crossings and the vast majority of Canada's trade traversing the border largely by truck, the border has caused Canada acute anxiety about its economic security. On the other hand, unlike Australia, Canada has presented a special internal-security concern to Washington.[98] Canada's politicians have been aware of the significance of this trade-and-security nexus.

At the same time, Canadian defence and foreign policy has tended to apply the principle of functionalism, which was used to determine when Canadian interests really mattered.[99] The Canadian diplomat Hume Wrong, the architect of functionalism during the Second World War, argued that in those areas in which Canada was pulling its weight or more, the country should have a seat at the table with the other powers.[100] After all, as middle powers, and with relatively small populations, Canada and Australia are not in a position to aspire to "great power" pretensions. Instead, these two nations have preferred to exercise what former Australian Foreign Minister, Gareth Evans, called "niche-diplomacy," acting as catalysts, facilitators, and managers of international initiatives while remaining aligned with the United States. The exercise of such "middle power" has meant a tendency to pursue multilateral solutions, compromise positions, and notions of "good international citizenship" in diplomatic endeavours.

Particularly for Canada, however, functionalism allowed for a certain tolerance of dysfunction between the stated priorities of foreign and defence policies. This has occurred because policy ambiguity and constrained (let alone joint) military capability has often served Canada's perceived national interests, allowing Canada not to have to commit military forces in circumstances not considered favourable. This approach to international affairs has given Canada only niche capabilities to support foreign-policy objectives, with little scope for independent or even Canadian-led military action.[101]

Beyond the limited capabilities, one major difference between Canada and Australia is that Canada is a member of NATO. Canada retains NATO

membership largely because of its tendency to look to Europe and its eagerness to bind the United States into a transatlantic alliance – an eagerness
that is compatible with U.S. imperatives for the alliance to be transatlantic
and not just European. The NATO connection draws Canadian military
practitioners in a transatlantic rather than trans-Pacific direction. In NATO,
Canadians participate in a wide range of functions ranging from headquarters staffs to participation in "Partnership for Peace" arrangements with
former Eastern European nations.[102] The longevity and enormity of the
NATO experience also has tended to prevent Australia (a non-NATO country) from being considered more prominently by Canadian defence and
strategic planners.

For Canadians, more so than their distant and more idiosyncratic Australian "cousins," to be seen not to be American also has often informed
foreign and security policies, even at times to the detriment of Canadian interests.[103] Concerns over perceived encroachments on sovereignty by their
giant southern neighbour are regularly featured in Canadian media. Unlike
Canada, Australia is geographically remote from its European roots and
other New World neo-European offshoots (like the United States), leaving
it with a sense of relative isolation and perceived vulnerability – a perception that has, for much of the twentieth century, included fears of the Asian
"Yellow Peril." The Australian diplomatic historian W.J. Hudson considers
that "survival is what Australian foreign policy has been all about, virtually
to the exclusion of all else." Thus, the principal motive for possession of
New Guinea, for instance, was that "if we possessed it, a potential enemy
did not."[104]

Australia's closest neighbour, Papua New Guinea, is an important country in the "land bridge" to Asia and to the island nations of Melanesia.
Some 10,000 Australian citizens live there and Australia retains strong
historic and emotional links to Papua New Guinea. After all, Papua New
Guinea has played a key role in Australian defence and security over the
last century and it is still a focus for Australian humanitarian assistance and
disaster relief, with a significant presence of Australian personnel in
exchange and assistance positions alongside members of the Papua New
Guinea Defence Force. Similarly, Australia is the de facto leader of the
South Pacific Conference of Nations, which carries with it security responsibilities, as demonstrated by the Australian-led Regional Assistance Mission in the Solomon Islands in 2003.[105] Canada has no territory over which
it has any comparable long-term obligations.[106]

Beyond the South Pacific, Australia has been concerned to develop and
maintain good relations with its southeast Asian neighbours. Consequently,

many citizens of neighbouring southeast Asian nations (particularly Indonesia, Malaysia, Singapore, the Philippines, and Thailand) have been encouraged to study at Australia's universities. Australian schools also feature Asian-language programs, notably Indonesian and Japanese. Australia also maintains a series of active multidisciplinary bilateral exchanges with universities and organizations in southeast Asia. (In Canada, only the westernmost province, British Columbia, and more particularly the city of Vancouver, has a comparable Asian orientation.) Reflecting this trend, the ADF places priority on regional engagement with its southeast Asian and South Pacific neighbours through exchanges at its military-officer training institutions, armed forces staff college, and higher defence college, as well as through a variety of bilateral military exercises. This focus on the nearer region, it could be argued, has prevented Australian policy makers from seeing the value of closer cooperation with their more distant but in many ways closer Canadian "cousins."

On the subject of Australia's preoccupation with its neighbourhood, Andrew Cooper, Richard Higgott, and Kim Nossal observe that Australian foreign policy has a long-standing tradition of the search for "threats" and "protectors" that predisposed its diplomacy to favour a more "heroic" style. Such "heroics" have meant that Australian initiatives have tended to be ambitious exercises involving greater risks, and more effort, than comparable Canadian ventures.[107] Australian fears peaked during the Second World War, when the Japanese advanced into New Guinea. The events of 1942, when the United States came to Australia's aid in fending off the Japanese, became Australia's defining historical moment, generating academic and policy interest in military strategy. Symptomatic of the significance of the United States to Australia's security is the Australian-American Memorial – an impressive centrepiece around which is built Australia's Defence Headquarters in Canberra. The memorial commemorates U.S. assistance to Australia during the Second World War.

Concerns over threats to Australia have been more subdued since 1945, particularly following Australia's military withdrawal from Vietnam in 1972 and subsequent U.S. partial disengagement from southeast Asia, when an Australian defence policy of self-reliance was implemented. Yet fears about domestic security have revived recently, in part because of illegal immigration, drug smuggling, illegal-arms shipments, and terrorism. Some increasingly see Australia as vulnerable because of its proximity to a so-called fault-line between civilizations. Concerns have been expressed about the threat of a resurgent China and the prospects of future conflict in the archipelago to Australia's north and among the smaller, virtually bankrupt states of the southwest Pacific (sometimes referred to as the "arc of instability"). As the Australian strategist Hugh White states: "Things that no longer seem credible in Europe are still possible here." Not surprisingly, therefore, Australia has maintained a separate and distinct overseas secret intelligence service, modelled on the British equivalent, MI6, while Canada has not felt the need to do so.[108]

For Canada, as Joel Sokolsky argues, its security relationship with the United States is different from Australia's because it is in the U.S. interest to prevent Canada from becoming a strategic liability. "The United States doesn't help Canada defend Canada. It helps Canada defend the United States."[109] While American security interests do not affect Australia nearly as directly as they do Canada, many in Australia have felt that, like Canada, their nation faces no readily identifiable conventional military threat to their national security, despite the sense of vulnerability that others express. For such Australians, concerns about China or Indonesia are minor and hypothetical. Similarly, for many in Canada, a more important consideration than perceived threats in their country's geographic environs has been Canada's ability to assert its own sense of sovereignty and maintain its credibility and reputation with the United States and other allies.[110] Such themes are also present in Australian strategic discourse, but they feature less prominently there, given the greater unease over Australia's location adjacent to Asia and the world's largest Muslim nation, Indonesia. Despite the usually vague threat, Australia's sense of isolation has been matched with a difference in the way people perceive the place of their armed forces in society.

Canadians have been described as "an unmilitary people," although, as the former Canadian CDS, General J.M.G. Baril, points out, "the truth of the matter is that conflict has shaped Canadians and this nation more than we like to admit."[111] Yet Canada has no coming-of-age national celebration comparable to Anzac Day[112] and the 2002 Bali bombing, arguably, holds the same significance for Australians as 11 September 2001 does for Americans. Australians also have a greater willingness than Canadians to see their armed forces as central to their national purpose, though both Canada and Australia have had their share of promoters of jingoistic myths about national military prowess.

For instance, Canada's Max Aitken (who became the British media baron Lord Beaverbrook) and Australia's C.E.W. Bean and Keith (later media magnate Sir Keith) Murdoch carefully nurtured the "digger"[113] myth during the First World War with grand rhetoric and romanticized imagery.[114] Since then, the myth has endowed the Australian armed forces with what the Australian historian Jane Ross calls "a special sensitivity and sacredness." "Unlike the efficient German or the can-do American marines," argues Ross, "the rowdy, laconic" Australian digger is different. "He is very much a soldier rather than an officer ... Other nations make films about their generals, we have films about our privates."[115]

For Australia, at least, this digger myth and the "Anzac legend," created at Gallipoli, of a natural fighting quality among Australian and New Zealand men complemented the sense of vulnerability that has driven military planners to develop a more self-reliant and well-rounded "general purpose" capability, adaptable for the wide variety of circumstances that can arise at short notice. The digger mythology is in stark contrast with the Canadian experience, where no such figure helps promote a military consciousness in Canadian society. The only comparable figure is a "Mountie" – a policeman. Such a defender of the establishment would win little popularity among irreverent Australians, many of whom are descended from convicts. Coincidentally, Canadian force-structure imperatives are also less outwardly muscular than their Australian equivalents. Despite the warlike operations the government of Canada commits its troops to, Canada retains a "multipurpose" capability, adaptable for combat operations if required but without the wider spectrum of capabilities necessary for independent or self-reliant operations. In other words, the expression "multipurpose" rather than "general purpose" capability signals that, while certain military roles may be assumed, others cannot be.[116] By the same token, both countries have, at times, tended to downplay the ability of their forces to operate overseas, yet strategic realities have repeatedly reinforced the need to be able to raise and deploy expeditionary forces – a contingency that remains by far their likeliest employment.

A key military corollary of these economic and geo-strategic determinants for Australia has been a low-key retention of amphibious military capabilities, particularly since the Second World War.[117] Australia's long and remote northern coastline, its defence obligations in the region, including Papua New Guinea, and its regional-leadership aspirations in the South Pacific have pointed to the need for such capabilities to enable its military to operate in areas with only rudimentary port facilities and airstrips. In support of this capability, Australia has acquired more military helicopters than Canada.

Canada has shown a sporadic interest in security issues in the West Indies, having independently deployed naval forces to the Caribbean more than sixteen times since 1956 to support Canadian foreign-policy and economic objectives. In some respects, the West Indies is a region not unlike the "East Indies"[118] in Australia's neighbourhood, which spurred the creation and maintenance of an Australian amphibious capability. Canada's interests conceivably could have stimulated a requirement for amphibious forces and a more integrated joint-force capability.[119] Cynics could argue that the Canadian government has chosen not take this route because of its reluctance to have its forces too readily deployable and therefore liable to be too readily called upon by allies.[120]

Other notable differences between the armed forces of Canada and Australia include Australia's more substantial and growing Special Operations Command,[121] its more robust intelligence capabilities, its army parachute forces, and its air force's F-111 strategic strike aircraft.[122] These differences reflect Australia's greater sense of vulnerability and its sense that it requires a self-reliant yet interoperable force to protect the country's national interests in a geo-strategic setting vastly different from that of Canada.

The differences outlined so far are significant. But, given the counterbalancing similarities between the two countries, a reader may well ask why the mutual ties are so restrained.

LIMITED MUTUAL TIES

Several factors have held back progress towards greater cooperation between the Canadian and Australian armed forces. For both countries, the "bright lights" of more powerful friends have long absorbed attention. As one observer notes, "Australia and Canada don't register on each other's public horizons: Both are transfixed by the United States."[123] "Perception is reality" is a frequently cited slogan, and Canada and Australia barely feature in each other's perceptions because of the strong media and other cultural influences emanating from the United States and, to a lesser extent, Britain. Such overwhelming media and cultural influences leave little space for greater awareness of Canada by Australians or vice versa, and the mutual inattentiveness is reinforced, for instance, by the lack of strong trade ties and competition over markets to which both countries export similar goods (including wheat, beef, uranium, and diamonds). In the meantime, the military focus on powerful friends has often led to the introduction of British and American defence equipment, structures, and policies that have required significant modification or reinterpretation before being applied on a smaller domestic scale. As Australian defence-policy official Brendan Sargeant observes:

We both are dominated by the US relationship. We see ourselves responding to that and we position other relationships within a competitive, rather than cooperative framework. Part of this is cultural immaturity, but part of it is the inability of a small country (so to speak) to create enough psychic energy to diversify its focus. We tend to see things in relation to the US, not in relation to ourselves. So Canada becomes a function of the US relationship. When Canada is different (in the 70/80s with its unified force and peacekeeping focus) it is the alternative, the path not taken. When it gets close, it is invisible. My sense is that neither Canada nor Australia is confident enough to make the jump into a different conceptualisation.[124]

There is considerable evidence to support this notion of a common lack of confidence. But the historical review (in the main part of this book) also points to the opportunity to shape these parallel "perceptions" in a way that generates a greater self-confidence, thus enabling both countries to be more willing to fashion their "realities" in tandem. This is something that few historical works have ventured to attempt.

The existing literature in Canadian military history tends to search for the cultural and political factors that explain how the Canadian armed forces have developed. In this regard, the focus has been on shared interests and experiences with Britain and the United States, which have been more important than those with any other country; the Australian parallels have not been strong enough to counter the pull of the North Atlantic Triangle among Canada, the United States, and Britain (later Europe, through NATO, as well). As a consequence, Canada has had no pressing incentive to examine closely the Australian experience, and, once Canada recognized that the United States and Britain were prepared to provide most of the security in the North Atlantic, there remained little incentive for massive Canadian expenditure on defence matters. At the same time, Canada's military planners realized that interoperability was easier to achieve than self-sufficiency, both in political and in budgetary terms. (Arguably, Australia, unlike Canada, can neither become complacent nor worry more about fulfilling a niche role in an alliance than about being self-sufficient, because it remains geo-strategically exposed in a way that Canada is not.) Canada's strategic position has also tended to make it a complacent ally that Australians have not considered worth pursuing vigorously as a close security partner, beyond their shared membership in quadripartite (United States, United Kingdom, Australia, and Canada) and other U.S.-led fora.[125]

Although threats to Canadian security have generally appeared less severe than those confronting Australia, the American scholar Stephen Walt's observations remain true: threat remains a stronger determinant of how a nation identifies enemies and selects allies than either culture or ideology.[126] Consequently, Canada's experiences in the Second World War, predominantly in Italy, Normandy, and Holland, and its membership in NATO predisposed its military planners to look towards Europe for examples of how to structure their forces and for prospective partners and allies. Canada's contribution of forces in the Pacific, including the Aleutians and Hong Kong, do not feature highly in Canadian public consciousness.[127] Thus, Canada's concerns over interoperability have remained primarily focused on Britain and the United States rather than on its smaller and more distant ABCA partner, Australia. By contrast, in the Second World War, Australia's ground forces were mainly sent to North Africa, the eastern Mediterranean, and the Pacific. These divergent orientations endured at least until the end of the Cold War, despite both countries having a coastline facing Asia and the Pacific Ocean (see map 1).

Political preferences have often been at odds as well, reducing the prospect of high-level collaboration and often masking grass-roots similarities (see appendix 1). Australia often has elected Conservatives to federal government when Canada has elected Liberals (progressives) and vice versa.[128] Reflecting this disparity, and in contrast to his Australian counterpart, John Howard, Canada's prime minister at the time, Jean Chrétien, avoided committing troops or even offering support to U.S.-led military efforts in Iraq in March and April 2003. "Strategic convergence," argues Brendan Sargeant, "in an arena of choice is partly governed by ideological compatibility. The political compatibility between Australia and Canada has been out of phase (until 2006 at least). So there is no political incentive to get closer."[129] Yet the different stances obscure the fundamental parallels.

For generally unilingual Australians, the French linguistic and cultural influence in Canada has further masked the commonalities. This masking of commonalities occurs despite the parallels (in broad terms) between the stereotypical image of the outgoing Québécois *bonhomme* and that of the gregarious, rough-edged, and hard-drinking Australian. At the same time, for many Canadians, Australia's remoteness and its warm climate, combined with the proximity and scale of American, British, and European influences, have tended to hinder closer collaboration with Australia. These differences are reinforced by sentimental perceptions of other contrasts between the two countries, such as diverse sporting preferences (ice hockey, American football, and baseball versus rugby, "Aussie rules" football, and cricket), which have resulted in limited mutual exposure and awareness through athletics – particularly on television. Also, only a few military officers have worked with their counterparts at the opposite extremities of the globe.[130]

Perhaps of equal significance is the quest for a distinctive national identity that is associated with a certain intellectual parochialism in both

Canada and Australia. In 1919, at the Versailles Peace Conference, the secretary to the British war cabinet, Sir Maurice Hankey, remarked that "the Dominions are as jealous of each other as cats." This comment captures what is perhaps the essence of the rivalry. Similarly, Canada's Desmond Morton states that "we envy Australians for their image of 'wild colonial boys' in South Africa and the First World War. How dull to discover that Canadians won victories only after they became efficient and disciplined soldiers."[131] Meanwhile, as some scholars have noted, "Australians do not wish to be told that they can learn from Canada's experience, possibly because it is too close to their own ... possibly because they feel ... competitive with the Canadians."[132] As a consequence of such sentiments, some observers may have resisted analysis of similarities that would challenge each country's sense of uniqueness. The struggle for a national identity has encouraged the obscuration of commonality, relying on sentiment or even jingoism rather than hard evidence.

Michael Ignatieff, building on a Freudian argument, refers to the "narcissism of minor difference" whereby the smaller the real difference between two peoples, the larger it is bound to loom in their imagination.[133] Australia and Canada have faced similar struggles with their own identities and therefore have tended to be dismissive of each other – much like cousins who do not concern themselves with what they have in common, seeing it more important to impress "Mother" England or their big "Uncle" Sam with their differences. In addition, Canada, as the "senior" Dominion in the Commonwealth and, unlike Australia, a member of the Group of Eight (G8) leading world economies, has an understandable inclination to disregard the experience of its younger and smaller fellow Commonwealth member. Simultaneously, Australian military practitioners have tended to be dismissive of the Canadian military experience, given Canada's greater emphasis on its apparently less muscular peacekeeping ethos, the terrible reports arising from the events in Somalia in 1993, and the country's reluctance to commit ground forces, alongside u.s. and Australians ones, in North Africa during the Second World War, in Vietnam, and, most recently, in Iraq.

Prominent in Canadians' imagination has been the idea that their northern climate – a climate alien to most Australians, who are used to a comfortable, subtropical existence – imparted a high degree of energy, vigour, and strenuousness to their national character. Perhaps it is time to leave such simplistic stereotypes – and comparable ones on the Australian side – behind. While the circumstances of the two countries are different in many ways, there are also a surprising number of continuing parallels that point to benefits of more closely working together in order to respond and adapt to a changed global security environment and the ongoing Revolution in Military Affairs.[134] To understand the extent and limitations of the parallels, and the prospects for cooperation that they may engender, the historical review undertaken in this book is useful.[135]

Notes

INTRODUCTION

1 The focus on Britain is reflected in such excellent studies as Preston, *Canada and "Imperial Defense"*; Mansergh, *Survey of British Commonwealth Affairs*; and Hancock, *Survey of British Commonwealth Affairs*.

2 Kendle, *The Colonial Imperial Conferences 1887–1911*, ix, 1.

3 Saul, *Voltaire's Bastards*, 13, 33.

4 Rempel, *Counterweights*.

5 The term "middle power" is contentious for some, but it captures the sense of identity in Australian and Canadian foreign- and defence-policy consciousness and thus is a valid term for our purposes.

6 Cooper, *In Between Countries*, 9–10, 22.

7 See Bermant, *The Cousinhood*.

8 Jordan, Taylor, Jr, and Mazarr, *American National Security*, 270.

9 Ryan, *Australian Army Cooperation with the Land Forces of the United States*, 1–2.

10 See, for instance, Scowen, *Rogue Nation*; and Broinowski, *Howard's War*.

11 Bacevich, *American Empire*, 3; and Mandelbaum, *The Ideas That Conquered the World*.

12 Capling, *Australia and the Global Trade System*, 3–4.

13 The Nationality and Citizenship Act of 1948 created the status of Australian citizen, but until 1973 Australians technically remained British subjects.

14 See "Howard Backs Away from 'Anglosphere' Alliance," Sydney *Morning Herald*, 6 May 2003, downloaded from www.smh.com.au, 10 May 2003; and Owen Harries, "Understanding America," Centre for Independent Studies lecture, downloaded 18 October 2002 from http://www.cis.org.au/Events/CISlectures/2002/Harries030402.htm.

15 This is the approach taken in Albinksi, *Canadian and Australian Politics in Comparative Perspective*.

16 Post-modernism encompasses a relativist philosophical view of culture and values.

17 Deconstructionist theory is often associated with Friedrich Nietzsche and is considered to be a radical refutation of Platonism. Deconstructionists deny the traditional divide between the world of reality and the world of appearance.

18 See, for instance, Granatstein, *Canada's Army*; Grey, *A Military History of Australia*; McNeill, *The Pursuit of Power*; Keegan, *A History of Warfare*; and LaFeber, *The American Age*.

19 For a further discussion of the two planes, see Dominick Graham, "Stress Lines and Gray Areas: The Utility of the Historical Method to the Military Profession," in Charters et al., ed., *Military History and the Military Professions*, 147–58.

20 Australian, Canadian, and NATO glossaries do not define the term. See http://www.dtic.mil/doctrine/jel/doddict/data/e/01957.html, downloaded 22 April 2003, and the UK Joint Warfare Publication definition.

21 Prominent Australian and Canadian works in the field of military history include Palazzo's *The Australian Army*; Grey, *The Australian Army*; Morton, *Understanding Canadian Defence*; Granatstein, *Canada's Army*; Morton, *A Military History of Canada*; Hunt and Haycock, ed., *Canada's Defence*; Hillmer and Granatstein, *Empire to Umpire*; and Marteinson, *We Stand on Guard*. For a detailed and useful reference work on Australian military history in general, see Dennis et al., ed., *Oxford Companion to Australian Military History*. A similar but more condensed Canadian equivalent is Bercuson and Granatstein's *Dictionary of Canadian Military History*.

22 See Barrett, "No Straw Man"; and Robson, "Beyond a Pale Horse."

23 The use of this deliberately ambiguous term suggests that the dual meaning of the word "forged" is retained to convey a sense that both meanings apply here. See Cook, "Documenting War and Forging Reputations."

24 Cited by Ignatieff, *Blood and Belonging*, 109. But the term "imagined community" belongs to Benedict Anderson.

25 That is, to challenge traditional beliefs, stereotypes, and preconceived notions.

CHAPTER ONE

1 This was despite the fact that several thousand men from Upper Canada joined the Union forces to fight against the Confederacy. Some estimates place the number much higher.

2 Harris, *Canadian Brass*, 12–17, 44; Winks, *Canada and the United States*; and Grimshaw, "On Guard," 5.

3 Jordan, Taylor, Jr, and Mazarr, *American National Security*, 57; and Granatstein, *Canada's Army*, 4–23.

4 "New Zealand Wars," in Dennis et al., ed., *Oxford Companion to Australian Military History*, 435.

5 People of mixed aboriginal and non-aboriginal ancestry whose sense of national identity was forged through resistance to Canada's western expansion.

6 Graves, ed., *Fighting for Canada*, 187; Morton, *Understanding Canadian Defence*, 33; and Stanley, "British Army in Australia," in Dennis et. al., ed., *Oxford Companion to Australian Military History*, 123.

7 A.A. Dorion (leader of the Rouge opposition) in Canada, *Confederation Debates*, repr. (Ottawa: Queens Printer 1951), 257, cited in Grimshaw, "On Guard," 4.

8 The confrontation between Britain and Russia over the integrity of Turkey in 1877–78 triggered rumours that Russian steamers planned to bombard Canadian and Australian ports. Both Canada and the colonies of Australia reacted by fortifying key coastal ports and by raising their first permanent army troops in coastal artillery units. They also reacted by laying the foundation for munitions industries that would play critical roles during both world wars of the twentieth century.

9 Hadly and Sarty, *Tin-Pots & Pirate Ships*, 5; Haycock, "The Clash of Imperatives," in Horn, ed., *Forging a Nation*, 236; Barratt, *Russian Shadows*; and Preston, *Canada's RMC*, 10.

10 Faraday, "Half the Battle," 11; and Harris, *Canadian Brass*, 47–8, 51.

11 See MacLaren, *Canadians on the Nile*, 126; Stacey, *Canada and the Age of Conflict, Volume I*, 42; and Inglis, *The Rehearsal*.

12 See Russell, "Colonization of Indigenous Peoples," in MacMillan and McKenzie, *Parties Long Estranged*, 74.

13 Harris, *Canadian Brass*, chapter 2; and Preston, *Canada and "Imperial Defence,"* chapters 2 and 5 and p. 179.

14 Preston, *Canada and "Imperial Defence,"* 211; and Harris, *Canadian Brass*, 22–32.

15 Royal Military College (Kingston, Ont.), Massey Library, Bridges Papers, G.H. Knowles to Colonel Bridges, Melbourne, 21 October 1907.

16 Preston, *Canada and "Imperial Defence,"* 230–1.

17 "Boxer rebellion," in Dennis et al., ed., *Oxford Companion to Australian Military History*, 117. This reference cites Bob Nicholls, *Bluejackets and Boxers: Australia's Naval Expedition to the Boxer Uprising* (Sydney: Allen and Unwin). See also Millar, *Australia in Peace and War*, 63–4.

18 "Report on the Department of Defence for the period 1st March 1901 to 30th June 1906," *Commonwealth Parliamentary Papers*, vol.2 (1906), cited in Palazzo, *The Australian Army*, 16.

19 For specific Australian and Canadian accounts of the Boer War, see Field, *The Forgotten War*; Wilcox, *Australia's Boer War*; and Miller, *Painting the Map Red*, 224–300.

20 Morton, *A Military History of Canada*, 117; and Dennis et. al., ed., *Oxford Companion to Australian Military History*, 109.

21 For instance, Canada's Sir Donald Smith, benefactor of the cavalry regiment known as Lord Strathcona's Horse.

22 Author's correspondence with Dr Galen Perras, 29 September 2003.

23 Berton, *Marching as to War*, 18, 20–1; Miller, *The Canadian Career of the Fourth Earl of Minto*, 70, 108–13; Morton, *Ministers and Generals*, 134; and Morton, *Understanding Canadian Defence*, 38.

24 See Hill, *Chauvel of the Light Horse*, 22–3, 28–9; Wilcox, *Australia's Boer War*, 78–9, 299; and Miller, *Painting the Map Red*, 224–30.

25 *Tommy Cornstalk*, cited in Brian A. Reid, "'F or God's sake … save your guns!': Action at Liliefontein 7 November 1900," in Graves, ed., *Fighting for Canada*, 198.

26 Field, *The Forgotten War*, vi; and Hill, *Chauvel of the Light Horse*, 19.

27 Miller, *Painting the Map Red*, xi–xiv, 15–30, 438.

28 Preston, *Canada and "Imperial Defence,"* 239, 243, 277, 349; and Berger, *The Sense of Power*, 234.

29 Desmond Morton, "'Junior but Sovereign Allies': The Transformation of the Canadian Expeditionary Force, 1914–1918," in Hunt and Haycock, ed., *Canada's Defence*, 33; Miller, "Borden," in ibid., 13–15. See also John Mordike, *An Army for a Nation*, 112–22; and Preston, *Canada and "Imperial Defence,"* 260.

30 American troops had advanced into Canada during the War of 1812 and the so-called Fenian raids were launched with tacit American support from upstate New York in 1866, although Generals Grant and Sherman denounced the Fenians' actions. The Fenians were Irish immigrant veterans of the American Civil War with logic-defying plans to free Ireland by attacking Canada. The last, and least effective, Fenian raid occurred in 1870.

31 Senior, *The Last Invasion of Canada*, 191; Granatstein, *Canada's Army*, 45; Berger, *The Sense of Power*, 236; and Morton, *A Military History of Canada*, 117.

32 Preston, *Canada and "Imperial Defence,"* 228; Dennis et. al., ed., *Oxford Companion to Australian Military History*, 108; and Field, *The Forgotten War*, chapter 1.

33 Frederic M. Cutlack, *Breaker Morant: A Horseman Who Made History* (Sydney: Ure Smith 1962), cited in Preston, *Canada and "Imperial Defence,"* 275. See also Field, *The Forgotten War*, 170–4; and Wilcox, *Australia's Boer War*, 276, 292–3.

34 For coverage on Hughes's exploits in South Africa, see Haycock, *Sam Hughes*, 83–94.

35 Morton, *A Military History of Canada*, 118.

36 Stacey, *Canada and the Age of Conflict, Volume I*, 70; Preston, *Canada and "Imperial Defence*," 284; and Harris, *Canadian Brass*, 64.

37 The Ross Rifle was modified to fire the British standard .303-calibre ammunition but became a controversial choice that would eventually be replaced mid-war by the British Lee-Enfield .303 rifle.

38 Haycock, "Early Canadian Weapons Acquisition"; Miller, "Borden," in Hunt and Haycock, ed., *Canada's Defence*, 9–11; and Preston, *Canada and "Imperial Defence*," 324.

39 Craig Wilcox, "Lieutenant General Edward Thomas Henry 'Curly' Hutton,'" in Dennis et. al., ed., *Oxford Companion to Australian Military History*, 303–4; Palazzo, *The Australian Army*, 20; and Grey, *The Australian Army*, 11–12, 15.

40 Australian colonies had paid a subsidy since 1887 and in 1903 this was extended, increasing the amount from £106,000 to £200,000.

41 Palazzo, *The Australian Army*, 20–3; and Mordike, *An Army for a Nation*, 113.

42 Palazzo, *The Australian Army*, 35–48; Hitsman, *Inspection Services in Canada*, 18; Preston, *Canada and "Imperial* Defence," 318; Mordike, *An Army for a Nation*, chapter 6; and Grey, *The Australian Army*, 22–3.

43 Travers, *The Killing Ground*, 6, 26, 111, 144; Miller, "Borden," in Hunt and Haycock, ed., *Canada's Defence*, 12–13; Harris, *Canadian Brass*, 71–2; and Bezeau, "The Role and Organization of Canadian Militia Staff," 34.

44 Miller, "Borden," in Hunt and Haycock, ed., *Canada's Defence*, 15–16; and Morton, *A Military History of Canada*, 127.

45 Preston, *Canada and "Imperial Defence*," 302–3, 379; Mansergh, *Survey of British Commonwealth Affairs*, 138; and Palazzo, *The Australian Army*, 40.

46 Bezeau, "The Role and Organization of Canadian Military Staffs."See also Bradford, "The Modern Field General Staff."

47 Preston, *Canada and "Imperial Defence*," 357, 376.

48 Ibid., 361; Faraday, "Half the Battle," 16; Bezeau, "The Role and Organization of Canadian Militia Staff," 39; Wigley, *Canada and the Transition to Commonwealth*, 9; Mansergh, *Survey of British Commonwealth Affairs*, 137; and Palazzo, *The Australian Army*, 41–3.

49 Revisionists in Canada and Australia have argued that they both could have remained neutral or disengaged in 1914, 1939, and 1950. This discounts the economic imperatives as well as the emotional ties that left the governments of the day with little option but to fight alongside Britain. Robertson, in *Anzac and Empire*, argues that for Australia, at least, the awareness of the

severity of the situation and growing fears of an expansionist Japan made a commitment to Britain's cause unavoidable.

50 Preston, *Canada and "Imperial* Defence,*"* 384; Barclay, *Friends in High Places,* 1; and author's correspondence with Dr Galen Perras, 29 September 2003.

51 Following an arbitration hearing by a panel of three judges (one British, one American, and one Canadian), the u.s. and uk judges voted in favour of the United States and Britain acknowledged u.s. sovereignty over the Alaskan Panhandle. Observers could see that, despite Canadian objections, Britain needed to improve relations with the United States at a time when Germany was rapidly arming and building a battle fleet.

52 Mansergh, *Survey of British Commonwealth Affairs,* 73.

53 The fleet included the flagship *Australia* (18,800 tons, eight 12-inch guns), three light cruisers (5,400 tons, 6-inch guns), and three destroyers (700 tons). Within a few months, the new 725-ton submarines *AE1* and *AE2* also joined the fleet.

54 Hadly and Sarty, *Tin-Pots & Pirate Ships,* 19; Tom Frame, "The Royal Australian Navy," in Dennis et. al., ed., *Oxford Companion to Australian Military History,* 515–20; Preston, *Canada and "Imperial Defence,"* 390, 415; and Robertson, *ANZAC and Empire,* 12–13.

55 The ships acquired were hmcs *Niobe* and *Rainbow* as well as the navy's two submarines (purchased from Chile early in the First World War).

56 Order-in-council, 4 August 1914, Department of External Affairs, in *Documents on Canadian External Relations* (hereafter as dea, dcer), vol.1, 1909–18, 40; Hadly and Sarty, *Tin-Pots & Pirate Ships,* xi, 24–6; telegram, acting high commissioner (Perley) to prime minister, London, 10 October 1914, in ibid., 52; and Eayrs, *In Defence of Canada, Vol. I,* 150.

57 Grey, *The Australian Army,* 26; Preston, *Canada and "Imperial Defence,"* 406, 442; and Palazzo, *The Australian Army,* 47.

58 "Defence in Australia Memorandum by Field Marshall Viscount Kitchener of Khartoum," in *Commonwealth Parliamentary Papers,* vol. 2: 11, cited in Palazzo, *The Australian Army,* 50.

59 Kitchener's proposal included plans for an army of 80,000 troops with twenty-one brigades of infantry (each with four battalions), twenty-eight regiments of light horse, fifty-six artillery batteries (with 224 guns), and additional engineers, communications. and support elements.

60 Hill, *Chauvel of the Light Horse,* 39–40, 54; Palazzo, *The Australian Army,* 50–1; and Grey, *The Australian Army,* 27.

61 The college in Kingston opened in 1876. See the letter from Colonel Davidson, commander Corps Troops, 1st Army Corps, Bloemfontein, Orange River Colony, 29 May 1900, in Bridges Papers.

62 Coulthard-Clark, *Duntroon*, 14; Preston, *Canada's RMC*, 61; and Hill, *Chauvel of the Light Horse*, 40.

63 Harris, *Canadian Brass*, 38, 79.

64 The Australian graduates would include future senior Second World commanders John Lavarack and Thomas Blamey.

65 Preston, *Canada and "Imperial Defence,"* 215–18, 353–5, 410–14; Faraday, "Half the Battle," 24, 27; and Harris, *Canadian Brass*, 75, 83–4. See also the Bridges Papers for examples of correspondence concerning Australian efforts to match British and Canadian officer-promotion standards and practices.

66 Author's correspondence with Dr Galen Perras, 29 September 2003. Perras cites evidence in the Governor General's Papers (RG7, G21) in the Library and Archives Canada (LAC), Ottawa.

67 Haycock's *Sam Hughes* is the authoritative biography. See also Harris, *Canadian Brass*, 83–91, and Ronald G. Haycock, "Sir Sam Hughes: A Canadian General – Why Bother!" in Horn and Harris, ed., *Warrior Chiefs*, 17–36.

68 Public Record Office (PRO), London, War Office (WO) 33/682, 4, 10–14, "Returns of the Land Forces of British Dominions Beyond the Seas," cited in Faraday, "Half the Battle," 26.

69 MacMillan, "Sibling Rivalry," in MacMillan and McKenzie, ed., *Parties Long Estranged*, 18.

CHAPTER TWO

1 Fisher was leader of the opposition Federal Labor Party when he said this on the campaign trail on 31 July 1914, but he was soon voted into office, replacing Cook as prime minister.

2 Morton, "Junior but Sovereign Allies," in Hunt and Haycock, ed., *Canada's Defence* 34; Morton, *A Military History of Canada*, 130; author's correspondence with Dr Galen Perras, 29 September 2003; and Morton and Granatstein, *Marching to Armageddon*, 134.

3 Pay arrangements are detailed in Faraday, "Half the Battle," chapter 4. Faraday indicates that the financial burden placed on the dominions was much less than the actual cost of the supplies and ammunition they received.

4 Robertson makes the point that a defeated Britain would have left Australia at the mercy of German-Japanese rivalry and that this would have extracted as great if not greater concessions and reparations than were imposed on Germany at Versailles in 1919. See *Anzac and Empire*, 259–67.

5 The request was for two infantry, one cavalry, and one artillery brigade.

6 Robertson, *Anzac and Empire*, 22.

7 Faraday, "Half the Battle," 34, 98–100; and Grey, *The Australian Army*, 51.

8 Robertson, in *Anzac and Empire*, meticulously reviews the perspectives of strategists, politicians, observers, military officers, and ordinary fighting men and argues that the legend was created not so much by the official Australian historian of the campaign, C.E. W. Bean, as by the deeds of the Anzacs themselves.

9 Robertson, *Anzac and Empire*; Morton and Granatstein, *Marching to Armageddon*, 52. The major Australian study on this subject is Robson, *The First A.I.F.*, although Robson's conclusions have been challenged by Jeffrey Grey.

10 Palazzo, *The Australian Army*, 66–76.

11 Hill, *Chauvel of the Light Horse*, 44; and Coulthard-Clark, *A Heritage of Spirit*, and *Duntroon*, 14; and Preston, *Canada's RMC*, 61.

12 For a discussion of the different British and Australian assessments of Australian fighting prowess on 25 April 1915, see, for instance, Thomson, "'The Vilest Libel of the War?'"

13 For a detailed account of the wartime experiences of General Sir John Monash, see Pedersen, *Monash as Military Commander*.

14 Incidentally, Lester B. Pearson, Canada's prime minister from 1963 to 1968, served during the Gallipoli campaign as a medical orderly in Salonika.

15 Hill, *Chauvel of the Light Horse*, 82–3, 119–20, 156. For a broader view of the Palestine Arabian campaigns and where the Australian contribution fitted into the overall campaign, see Bullock, *Allenby's War*.

16 Canadian cavalry saw action at Moreil Wood in March 1918, but this instance stands in stark contrast with most of the Canadian experience of war from 1914 to 1918.

17 Major-General Monash was appointed to the 3rd Division and Major-General James McCay to the 5th Division, while British Major-General H.V. Cox, who had commanded an Indian brigade in Gallipoli, was given command of the 4th Division.

18 Grey, *The Australian Army*, 44–5.

19 Eventually the CEF would recruit 619,636 men, of whom 228,174 were immigrants from the United Kingdom.

20 Goodspeed, *The Road Past Vimy*, 13; and Haycock, *Sam Hughes*, 5.

21 See Harris, *Canadian Brass*, 93–104; Goodspeed, *The Road Past Vimy*, 11; Haycock, *Sam Hughes*, 177–97; and telegram, governor general to colonial secretary, Ottawa, 6 October 1914, in DEA, DCER, vol.1: 51.

22 Morton and Granatstein, *Marching to Armageddon*, 107; Preston, *Canada and "Imperial Defence,"* 469, 476; Faraday, "Half the Battle," 78; Harris, *Canadian Brass*, 106; and English, *Failure in High Command*, 15. Currie biographies include Urquhart, *Arthur Currie*; and Hyatt, *General Sir Arthur Currie*.

23 Morton, *A Military History of Canada*, 144; Harris, *Canadian Brass*, 123–4; Preston, *Canada and "Imperial Defence,"* 490–4; Morton, *Understanding*

Canadian Defence, 139; Griffith, *Battle Tactics of the Western Front*, 86; and Monash, *The Australian Victories in France in 1918*, 5.

24 Griffith, *Battle Tactics of the Western Front*, 10–11; and Prior and Wilson, *Passchendaele*, 57.

25 Harris, *Canadian Brass*, 106, 131–3.

26 Preston, *Canada and "Imperial Defence*," 469; Morton, "Junior but Sovereign Allies," in Hunt and Haycock, ed., *Canada's Defence*, 36–9; Morton, *A Military History of Canada*, 137–43, 150; and Harris, *Canadian Brass*, 132.

27 Prime Minister Borden to George Perley, acting high commissioner to the United Kingdom, Ottawa, 24 February 1916, in *DEA, DCER*, vol.1: 115; and Preston, *Canada and "Imperial Defence*," 470–1. On Godley, see Dennis et. al., ed., *Oxford Companion to Australian Military History*, 270–1, with citations from Alexander Godley's *Life of an Irish Soldier* (London: John Murray 1939).

28 Grey, *The Australian Army*, 47, 66–7; Faraday, "Half the Battle," 191; Mallett, "The Interplay between Technology, Tactics and Organisation in the First AIF"; Pulsifer, "Canada's First Armoured Unit," 44–57; McCulloch, "The 'Fighting Seventh'"; and Horner, *The Gunners*.

29 Grey, *The Australian Army*, 47; and McCulloch, "The "Fighting Seventh,'" 8–11.

30 Prior and Wilson, *Passchendaele*, xiv, 159, 200; Monash, *Australian Victories*, 7; Bean, *Anzac to Amiens*, 375; and author's correspondence with Dr Galen Perras, 29 September 2003.

31 Prior and Wilson, *Passchendaele*, xv.

32 This view has been put forward by a former Australian defence minister, Kim Beazley. He argued that in this instance Australia was affecting the global strategic balance.

33 Morton and Granatstein, *Marching to Armageddon*, 196; Bean, *Anzac to Amiens*, 444; Granatstein, *Canada's Army*, 135; and David Bercuson and J.L. Granatstein, "Raymond Brutinel," *Dictionary of Canadian Military History*, 27.

34 Comment by General Von der Marwitz (commander of the German Second Army in 1918), cited in Blaxland, *Amiens*, 144.

35 Cited in Bean, *Anzac to Amiens*, 469–70.

36 Granatstein cites Sandra Gwyn's claim in *The Tapestry of War* (Toronto: HarperCollins 1992), 143–6, that trench raids were an invention of the PPCLI, which had launched the first such attack at the end of February 1915. However, Rawlings points out that Indians and British Worcesters had conducted such raids as early as November 1914.

37 Granatstein, *Canada's Army*, 82; Rawling, *Surviving Trench Warfare*, 47, 102; and Griffith, *Battle Tactics of the Western Front*, 57, 195.

38 Granatstein, *Canada's Army*, 136.

39 Popular Australian folklore would have the British staff officers and commanders blamed for most of the Australians' woes, but many of the early mistakes in
battle experienced by the Australians were at the hands of inexperienced and
inept Australian officers.

40 Stacey, *Canada and the Age of Conflict, Volume I*, 198.

41 Bashow, "Who Killed von Richtofen?" 59.

42 Australia had five divisions in Europe, as well as a large portion of the desert
Mounted Corps in Palestine, as compared to Canada's four divisions.

43 For a discussion of the effects of the conscription plebiscites in Australia,
see Robson, *The First* AIF. See also Morton and Granatstein, *Marching to
Armageddon*, 145, 173; and Bean, *Anzac to Amiens*, 290–6.

44 Author's correspondence with Dr Galen Perras, 29 September 2003.

45 Quebec electoral returns decidedly favoured the Liberals throughout the 1920s,
the Conservatives' association with conscription being not soon forgotten.

46 Morton, *A Military History of Canada*, 151–8, 165; Dexter, *The Conscription
Debates of 1914 and 1944* (Winnipeg *Free Press*), 6, cited in de Chastelain,
"The Canadian Contribution and the Conscription Crisis 1914–1918," iii;
O.D. Skelton, *Life and Times of Sir Wilfrid Laurier* (Toronto: Oxford Univer-
sity Press 1921), 429, cited in ibid; and Eayrs, *In Defence of Canada, Vol. II*, 7.

47 de Chastelain, "The Canadian Contribution and the Conscription Crisis 1914–
1918," 138–9; McGibbon, ed., *Oxford Companion to New Zealand Military
History*, 117–19, 173–5; Alan D. Gilbert and Ann-Marie Jordens, "Traditions
of Dissent," in McKernan and Browne, ed., *Australia: Two Centuries of War
and Peace*, 338–65; Morton and Granatstein, *Marching to Armageddon*, 24,
100; Morton, *A Military History of Canada*, 159; and McLachlan, *Waiting for
the Revolution*, 175. Canadian women gained the right to vote in federal
elections in 1918 and the extension of the provincial franchise to them occurred
in stages: Manitoba, Saskatchewan, and Alberta, 1916; British Columbia and
Ontario, 1917; Nova Scotia, 1918; New Brunswick, 1919; Prince Edward
Island, 1922; Quebec, 1940.

48 Gammage, *The Broken Years*, 31; Godefroy, *For Freedom and Honour?* 2; and
Faraday, "Half the Battle," 245–9.

49 Granatstein, *Canada's Army*, 89.

50 Preston, *Canada and "Imperial Defence,"* 482, 510.

51 Palazzo argues that the British Empire forces waged war without a doctrine
(correspondence with author, 7 January 2003). Tim Travers likewise suggests in
The Killing Ground, 48 and 254, that the British Army, like the French Army,
lacked a doctrine of war as late as 1914. Travers points to the "cult of the
offensive" as the key doctrinal concept in British pre-war thought. Still, Griffith

cogently argues that the British did begin the war with a single set of centralized tactics. Moreover, following the battle of the Somme, the British Army began publishing and promulgating tactical manuals and training notes that captured many of the lessons learned. The new techniques and procedures found in the manuals were then applied in subsequent battles, albeit with varying degrees of success until late in 1917 and the summer of 1918, when the British Army reached a peak in performance. See Griffith, *Battle Tactics of the Western Front*, chapters 4, 5, and 10.

52 Ibid., chapters 4, 5, 10; and Travers, *The Killing Ground*, 48, 254.

53 Monash, *Australian Victories*, 1; Morton, *A Military History of Canada*, 161; Rawlings, *Surviving Trench Warfare*, 225; and Harris, *Canadian Brass*, 124–5.

54 Grey, *The Australian Army*, 94; Morton, *A Military History of Canada*, 481–2; Harris, *Canadian Brass*, 107–9; and Haycock, *Sam Hughes*, 277–8.

55 Morton, *A Military History of Canada*, 146–7; Preston, *Canada and "Imperial Defence,"* 466–7; and Faraday, "Half the Battle," 124–5.

56 Griffith, *Battle Tactics of the Western Front*, 62; Blaxland, *Amiens: 1918*, 21–2, 140, 144–7; Monash, *Australian Victories*, 44; Prior and Wilson, *Command on the Western Front*, 295; and United States, *United States Army in the World War 1917–1919*, 186.

57 Monash, *Australian Victories*, 57; and Rawling, *Surviving Trench Warfare*, 65–6, 125, 148, 167, 184, 189, 203–4.

58 Griffith, *Battle Tactics of the Western Front*, 92.

59 On 8 August the u.s. 33rd Infantry Division was assigned in reserve as part of the III British Corps on the left flank of the Australian Corps, although their troops were not committed to the attack until after the opening day of the battle.

60 Morton and Granatstein, *Marching to Armageddon*, 200.

61 On Rawlinson, see Prior and Wilson, *Command on the Western Front*. See also Blaxland, *Amiens*, ix.

62 Blaxland, *Amiens*, 159, 163, 191; Morton, *A Military History of Canada*, 163; Pedersen, *Monash as Military Commander*, 235–48; Monash, *Australian Victories*, 107; Rawling, *Surviving Trench Warfare*, 6, 205; Morton and Granatstein, *Marching to Armageddon*, 202; Bean, *Anzac to Amiens*, 473; Travers, *The Killing Ground*, 250; Griffith, *Battle Tactics of the Western Front*, 156, 166; and Prior and Wilson, *Command on the Western Front*, 309–10.

63 Blaxland, *Amiens*, 170, 173, 199.

64 Morton, *A Military History of Canada*, 164. For an account of Canada's crucial role during the last 100 days of the war, see also Schreiber, *Shock Army of the British Empire*.

65 Monash, *Australian Victories*, 169, 223, 236, 240–5. For details on the American contributions, see United States, *United States Army in the World War 1917–1919*.

66 By late 1918, the Australian Corps' effectiveness had been damaged by high losses and shortages of reinforcements. Arguably, however, had the men known that the end of the war was only a few days away, they may have stayed in the line, regrouping to compensate for troop shortfalls. Indeed, the troops fully anticipated being placed back in the front line in early 1919 since the commonly held view was that the war would continue well into the next year. The high morale and *esprit de corps* of such troops is hard to explain or capture in writing.

67 Preston, *Canada and "Imperial Defence,"* 480, 494; Morton and Granatstein, *Marching to Armageddon*, 219; and Grey, *The Australian Army*, 50.

68 Lloyd George, *Memoirs*, vol.6: 356, cited in Preston, *Canada and "Imperial Defence,"* 495; Morton and Granatstein, *Marching to Armageddon*, 238; Granatstein, *Canada's Army*, 98; and author's correspondence with Dr Galen Perras, 29 September 2003.

69 Jeffrey Grey, "'A Pathetic Sideshow,'" 12–17; Wigmore and Harding, *They Dared Mightily*, 133–5; LaFeber, *The American Age*, 311; Swettenham, *Allied Intervention in Russia 1918–1919*; Hunt, "Canada and Armed Intervention in Russia 1918–1919"; and Eayrs, *In Defence of Canada, Vol. I*, chapter 1.

70 "Extract from Minutes of Forty-Second Meeting of Imperial War Cabinet, 'Retention of Dominion Troops in Our Army of Occupation,'" 12 December 1918, in *DEA, DCER*, vol. 2: 11–13.

71 English, *Lament for an Army*, 19; LaFeber, *The American Age*, 306; Haglund "Are *we* the Isolationists?" 10, with extract from Jean-Baptiste Duroselle, *La Grand Guerre des Français: L'Incompréhensible* (Paris: Perrin 1994), 7.

72 Morton, "Junior but Sovereign Allies," in Hunt and Haycock, ed., *Canada's Defence* 31.

73 Preston, *Canada and "Imperial Defence,"* 496, 523; and telegram from Prime Minister Borden, Ottawa, 29 October 1918, in *DEA, DCER*, vol. 2: viii.

74 Stacey, *Canada and the Age of Conflict, Volume I*, 270–7; MacMillan, *Paris 1919*, 15, 48, 93.

75 C.E.W. Bean, cited in Ross, *The Myth of the Digger*, 107.

CHAPTER THREE

1 Margaret MacMillan, "Sibling Rivalry: Australia and Canada from the Boer War to the Great War," in MacMillan and McKenzie, ed., *Parties Long Estranged*, 24, 26, 29–30.

2 Granatstein, *Canada's Army*, 152; Stacey, *Six Years of War*, 6, 18–22, and *Canada and the Age of Conflict: Volume 2*, 61; and Harris, *Canadian Brass*, 138, 160.

3 Francine McKenzie, "New Best Friend," *Globe and Mail*, 2 May 2003; Morton, *Understanding Canadian Defence*, 109; Mansergh, *Survey of British Commonwealth Affairs*, 54; Eayrs, *In Defence of Canada, Volume 1*, 19, 73; Palazzo, *The Australian Army*, 81–2; telegram, governor general to colonial secretary, Ottawa, 15 February 1921, and "Extracts from Meeting of Representatives of the United Kingdom, the Dominions and India," 21 and 29 June and 1 July 1921, in *DEA, DCER*, vol. 3: 162–94; "The Washington Conference and Its Effect upon Empire Naval Policy and Co-operation," 28 July 1922, and "Empire Naval Policy and Co-operation," Admiralty, 11 June 1923, in ibid., vol. 3: 329–38.

4 See Galen Roger Perras, "Parties Long Estranged: The Initiation of Australian-Canadian Diplomatic Relations, 1935–1940," in Cardinal and Headon, ed., *Shaping Nations*, 135–45; and McKenzie and MacMillan , "Introduction," in MacMillan and McKenzie, ed., *Parties Long Estranged*, 6.

5 McCarthy, "The Once and Future Army," xviii.

6 Granatstein, *Canada's Army*, 157; Harris, *Canadian Brass*, 142–4; Hill, *Chauvel of the Light Horse*, 200–3.

7 Stacey, *Six Years of War*, 4–5; and DHH report no. 22: C.P. Stacey, "The Reorganization of the Canadian Militia 1919–20 (31 January 1949), 37–47; Harris, *Canadian Brass*, 145–51; and English, *Failure in High Command*, 19.

8 The Canadian chief of the general staff, Major-General A.G.L. McNaughton, proposed the cut in 1933. His Australian counterpart, Lieutenant-General Sir Henry Chauvel, made a similar proposal in 1930.

9 See Albert Palazzo, "Failure to Obey"; and James Eayrs, *In Defence of Canada, Volume 1*, 275.

10 Japan seized the Mariana, Caroline, and Marshall Islands from Germany and issued its "Twenty-One Demands" to China in 1915. These demands were an attempt to reduce Chinese independence.

11 Some would argue that the call for help to Canada was not a mistake but an attempt to shame Mackenzie King into backing Britain.

12 Eayrs, *In Defence of Canada Volume 1*, 20; Hillmer and Granatstein, *Empire to Umpire*, 87–90; and Morton, *A Military History of Canada*, 168.

13 Mansergh, *The Commonwealth Experience*, 11.

14 Wigley, *Canada and the Transition to Commonwealth*, 282; Palazzo, *The Australian Army*, 133; Eayrs, *In Defence of Canada, Volume I*, 22; Grey, *The Australian Army*, 79; Harris, "The Canadian General Staff," 70, Harris, *Canadian Brass*, 177; and author's correspondence with Dr Galen Perras, 29 September 2003.

15 Haycock, "The Clash of Imperatives: Canadian Munitions Development in the Inter-war Years, 1919–1939," in Horn, ed., *Forging a Nation*, 235–70.

16 Under the Defence Act, the AIF existed "in time of war." On the force's return to Australia, the government issued a proclamation ending the "time of war," which legally terminated the AIF.

17 Grey, *The Australian Army*, 78; and Palazzo, *The Australian Army*, 94–5.

18 This history includes the wars of conquest of French Canada in the seventeenth century, the "wars" against the Indians, the War of 1812 against the United States, and also the Fenian Raids of the 1860s.

19 According to an Ipsos-Reid survey, Canadians have only a sketchy knowledge of the battle of Vimy Ridge. See *Globe and Mail*, 9 April 2002.

20 Adam-Smith, *The ANZACS*, ix; Austin, *The White Gurkhas*, ix; Beck, *Pendulum of Power*; and author's discussions with Kim Richard Nossal, March 2002. Jeffrey Keshen explores the divisive aspect of the war for Canada in "The Great War Soldier as 'Nation Builder' in Canada and Australia," in Cardinal and Headon, ed., *Shaping Nations*, 195.

21 British Staff College exercises at Camberley from the early 1920s onwards demonstrated that the Japanese could land a force of over 100,000 troops and enough supplies for three months and capture the island of Singapore from the landward side even before the British fleet could have time to sail to the rescue from Britain.

22 Telegram, colonial secretary to governor general, London, 17 March 1924, in *DEA, DCER*, vol.3: 356; Hill, *Chauvel of the Light Horse*, 211; and Palazzo, *The Australian Army*, 82–4.

23 Ross, *Armed and Ready*, 36; and Stacey, *Six Years of War*, 4.

24 Mackenzie King's attitude is explored in G.F.G. Stanley, *Canada's Soldiers: The Military History of an Unmilitary People* (Toronto: Macmillan 1974), cited in Haycock, "The Clash of Imperatives"; Lang is cited in MacKirdy, "Canadian and Australian Self-interest, the American Fact, and the Development of the Commonwealth Idea," in Dyck and Krosby, ed., *Empire and Nations*, 121; Eayrs, *In Defence of Canada, Volume 1*, 3–4, 168–73.

25 Eayrs, *In Defence of Canada, Volume I*, 17; Douglas and Greenhous, *Out of the Shadows*, 15; Stacey, *Canada and the Age of Conflict, Volume 2*, 71, 79; and Mansergh, *The Commonwealth Experience*, 19.

26 Telegram, colonial secretary to governor general, London, 26 May 1920, and Paper by the Admiralty for the Committee of Imperial Defence, E-61, Admiralty, 18 July 1923, in *DEA, DCER*, vol.3: 325–6, 338–48; Eayrs, *In Defence of Canada, Volume 1*, 178; Archives of the League of Nations (Geneva), "Canada 8/21328/20397, box R218, cited in Haycock, "The Clash of Imperatives."

27 Eayrs, *In Defence of Canada Volume 1*, 185, 199; Morton and Granatstein, *Marching to Armageddon*, 56; C.D.Coulthard-Clark, "Royal Australian Air Force," in Dennis et al., ed., *Oxford Companion to Australian Military History*, 507–8; "Extracts from Minutes of Imperial Conference," 15 November 1926, in DEA, DCER, vol. 4: 160–1; Eayrs, *In Defence of Canada Volume 1*, 201–5; and Morton, *A Military History of Canada*, 168–9.

28 Wigley, *Canada and the Transition to Commonwealth*; *Imperial Conference, 1926, Summary of Proceedings*, 14, cited in Mansergh, *Survey of British Commonwealth Affairs*, 11. See also Stacey, *Canada and the Age of Conflict, Volume 2*, 85–8, 102, 134–6; McKenzie, *Redefining the Bonds of Commonwealth*, 4–5.

29 Millar, *Australia in Peace and War*.

30 Mansergh, *Survey of British Commonwealth Affairs*, 45; McKenzie, *Redefining the Bonds of Commonwealth*, 63, 21–3; Millar, *Australia in Peace and War*, 73, 82, 111; LaFeber, *The American Age*, 351; and Stacey, *Canada and the Age of Conflict, Volume 2*, 16, 119–20, 177, 203.

31 David Varey provides a useful explanation of the challenges Britain faced in its relations with an expansionist Japan in the 1930s. He articulates the problems involved in pushing too hard for closer relations with Japan, which arguably would have come at the expense of poorer relations with the United States and other European powers as well as the USSR. See Varey, "Clash of Strategies," 3, 138–40.

32 Ross, *Armed and Ready*, 44, 110–13, 137. For a biography of Pearce, see Heydon's *Quiet Decision*.

33 Defence expenditure in Australia rose from £5,400,000 in 1934–35 to £8,800,000 in 1936–37.

34 Grey, *The Australian Army*, 95–7; and Hill, *Chauvel of the Light Horse*.

35 Dennis, et. al., ed., *Oxford Companion to Australian Military History*, 546; Horner, *Defence Supremo*, 30–55; Evans, "From Deakin to Dibb"; and Ross, *Armed and Ready*, 138.

36 Ross, *Armed and Ready*, 144; Horner, *High Command*, 12; and Horner, *Defence Supremo*, 34–6.

37 English, *Lament for an Army*, 22; Perras, *Franklin Roosevelt*, 20–1; and Eayrs, *In Defence of Canada, Volume 1*, 287.

38 Evans, "From Deakin to Dibb"; and Ross, *Armed and Ready*, 285, 291–4.

39 Eayrs, *In Defence of Canada, Volume 1*, 13–14.

40 Norman Hillmer, "Defence and Ideology: The Anglo–Canadian Military 'Alliance' in the 1930s," in Hunt and Haycock, ed., *Canada's Defence*, 86–93, with citation from M.A. Pope, *Soldiers and Politicians: The Memoirs of Lt.–Gen. Maurice AS. Pope, C.B., M.C.* (Toronto: University of Toronto Press 1962), 53; Harris, *Canadian Brass*, chapter 10; and Eayrs, *In Defence of Canada, Volume 1*, 91.

41 Between 1932 and 1936, the Canadian Army employed over 170,000 men on over 140 projects including road and airfield construction and forestry.

42 Adrian W. Preston, "Canada and the Higher Direction of the Second World War 1939–1945," in Hunt and Haycock, ed., *Canada's Defence*, 101; and Eayrs, *In Defence of Canada Volume 1*, 119–36, 148.

43 Stacey, *Canada and the Age of Conflict, Volume 2*, 17; Harris, "The Canadian General Staff," 75–6; Canada, *House of Commons Debates*, 1937, vol. 1: 894–5, cited in Mansergh, *Survey of British Commonwealth Affairs*, 123; and Eayrs, *In Defence of Canada, Volume 1*, 136.

44 There were four Canadian plans: Defence Scheme No. 1 – War against the United States; Defence Scheme No. 2 – Canadian Neutrality in a War between the United States and Japan; Defence Scheme No. 3 – Expeditionary Forces and Home Defence in a Major War; and Defence Scheme No. 4 – Minor Empire Crisis. See Stacey, *Six Years of War*, 30–3; Stacey, *Canada and the Age of Conflict 1921–48*, 156–8; Granatstein, *Canada's Army*, 170; and Perras, *Franklin Roosevelt*, 13–16.

45 Hooker, "Serving Two Masters," 44; and Harris, *Canadian Brass*, 183–4.

46 Mansergh, *Survey of British Commonwealth Affairs*, 52; and Hillmer, "Defence and Ideology," 82.

47 Lyons and his successor conservative leaders, Page and Menzies, remained in power in Australia from 1932 to 1941.

48 Mansergh, *Survey of British Commonwealth Affairs*, 142.

49 Ross, *Armed and Ready*, 112.

50 This case is argued in Perras, *Franklin Roosevelt*.

51 Mansergh, *Survey of British Commonwealth Affairs*, 268, 366–7; Eayrs, *In Defence of Canada, Volume 2*, 73–80, 88, 117–19; Stacey, *Arms, Men and Government*, 7–8; Hillmer and Granatstein, *Empire to Umpire*, 149; Douglas and Greenhous, *Out of the Shadows*, 17–21, 39; Hillmer, "Defence and Ideology," 87; Ronald Haycock, "The Clash of Imperatives"; Stacey, *Six Years of War*, 34–7; and Hitsman, *Inspection Services in Canada*, 40–1.

52 Harris, "The Canadian General Staff," 75–6; DEA, DCER, vol. 6: xiii; and Harris, *Canadian Brass*, 160–1.

53 Horner, *Defence Supremo*, 1–7, 11.

54 Harris, "The Canadian General Staff," 77–9, and *Canadian Brass*, 160.

55 Roosevelt, cited in Dziuban, *Military Relations*, 3; Mackenzie King cited in Eayrs, *In Defence of Canada, Volume 2*, 183; Dziuban, *Military Relations*, 5; Perras, *Franklin Roosevelt*, x; and Stacey, *Canada in the Age of Conflict, Volume 2*, 6; Haycock, "The Clash of Imperatives," 235; author's correspondence with Dr Galen Perras, 29 September 2003, and discussions with Dr Joel Sokolsky, August 2002.

56 Speech by prime minister to the House of Commons, 30 March 1939, in DEA, DCER, vol.6: 609; and Mansergh, *Survey of British Commonwealth Affairs*, 129.

57 Eayrs, *In Defence of Canada, Volume 2*, 10, 81; Perras, *Franklin Roosevelt*, xi, 17; Holmes, *The Shaping of Peace, Volume 1*, 7, 13; Mansergh, *Survey of British Commonwealth Affairs*, 127, 150–6; and Millar, *Australia in Peace and War*, 87–8.

58 Palazzo, *The Australian Army*, 126–30; and Grey, *The Australian Army*, 105.

59 Preston, *Canada and "Imperial Defence,"* 529.

60 Eayrs, *In Defence of Canada Volume 2*, 90.

61 Millar, *Australia in Peace and War*, 132. Leacock cited in J.L. Granatstein, "Why Go to War? Because We Have to," *National Post*, 20 February 2003.

CHAPTER FOUR

1 Robertson, *Australia at War*, 5; Stacey, *Arms, Men and Government*, 120–3; Horner, *High Command*, 107; Stacey, *Arms, Men and Government*, 48; Bryant, *The Turn of the Tide*, 658.

2 Robertson, *Australia at War*, 2.

3 This phrase is taken from the title of Australian historian Geoffrey Blainey's seminal work, *The Tyranny of Distance*.

4 Long, *The Six Years War*, 12; Robertson, *Australia at War*, 10; and Watt, *The Evolution of Australian Foreign Policy*, 24, 27, 29.

5 A memorandum makes clear that the government recognized that "the weight of traditional opinion favours the assumption that legally Canada is at war when the United Kingdom is," but it had also pledged by explicit statements to leave the decision on the issue of war to Parliament.

6 "Most Secret Memorandum," 29 August 1939, in DEA, DCER, vol. 6: 1263–7. Also, see Granatstein and Neary, *The Good Fight*, 2; Stacey, *Canada and the Age of Conflict, Volume 2*, 269; and McFarlane, *Ernest Lapointe*.

7 A total of 8,000 troops were mobilized on 3 September for sixteen days and on 16 September eight garrison battalions were raised for immediate home-defence tasks, but, by early 1940, only Darwin, Newcastle, and Port Kembla's coastal defences were fully manned.

8 In 1939 the fleet included two heavy cruisers (*Australia* and *Canberra*), four light cruisers (*Perth, Hobart, Sydney*, and *Adelaide*), five old destroyers (*Stuart, Waterhen, Vampire, Vendetta*, and *Voyager*), and two sloops. Additional ships were ordered and, by July 1941, seven shipyards were rapidly producing additional ships.

9 Stacey, *Arms, Men and Government*, 32; Stacey, *Canada and the Age of Conflict, Volume 2*, 355; Douglas and Greenhous, *Out of the Shadows*, 30; Long,

The Six Years War, 18–19, 26; and Marc Milner, "Royal Canadian Navy Participation in the Battle of the Atlantic Crisis of 1943," in Granatstein and Neary, *The Good Fight*, 65–81.

10 Robertson, *Australia at War*, 16, 39; and Douglas and Greenhous, *Out of the Shadows*, 36.

11 Several biographies of Blamey exist. The most recent and comprehensive is David Horner's *Blamey*. See also Carlyon (a former aide-de-camp), *I Remember Blamey*; and Hetherington, *Blamey Controversial Soldier*.

12 Hooker, "Serving Two Masters," 52–5; and Haycock, "Clash of Imperatives: Canadian Munitions Development in the Inter-war Years, 1919–1939," in Horn, ed., *Forging a Nation*, 257.

13 However, "Canadianization" in the RAF had its effect. For instance. No. 6 (RCAF) Bomber Group was commanded by an RCAF air vice-marshall by 1 January 1943. Australia lacked even this level of representation in the air force chain of command in Britain.

14 Robertson, *Australia at War*, 17.

15 Robertson, *Australia at War*, 29; Long, *The Six Years War*, 22; and Grey, *The Australian Army*, 108–13, 120–1.

16 By 1945, Canada's Army, Corps, and most divisional commanders as well as the four wartime chiefs of general staff were graduates of Canada's RMC, whereas in 1939 no RMC Duntroon graduate held rank higher than lieutenant-colonel. By 1945, however, Duntroon graduates had been commanding corps and divisions for some years. Three were even lieutenant-generals.

17 The 7th Division was raised on 28 February 1940, the 8th Division on 22 May 1940, the 9th Division in early June 1940, and the 1st Armoured Division on 1 January 1941.

18 Ross, *Armed and Ready*, 200–1.

19 Palazzo, *The Australian Army*, 146.

20 Over 68,000 had applied for enlistment in the RAAF by March 1940, of whom only a fraction could be accepted.

21 Long, *The Six Years War*, 30–1, 34, 43.

22 Stacey, *Six Years of War*, 151; Robertson, *Australia at War*, 19; and Long, *The Six Years War*, 172.

23 Stacey, *Arms, Men and Government*, 13; Stacey, *Canada in the Age of Conflict*, Volume 2, 259; Stacey, *Six Years of War*, 48–51, 63, 182–3; and DHH report no.57: C.P. Stacey, "A Summary of Major Changes in Army Organization, 1939–1945 (22 December 1952), 22.

24 Dr Galen Perras contends that McNaughton was chosen by Mackenzie King for three reasons: (1) he was a Tory and thus Mackenzie King could not be accused of patronage; (2) McNaughton was a Canadian nationalist who had been

criticized in the inter-war period by Colonel Sutherland Brown as an anti-imperial "little Canadian"; and (3) McNaughton believed in mechanized war and its hoped-for corollary: fewer casualties.

25 McNaughton cited in Bezeau, "The Role and Organization of Canadian Militia Staff," 110; Granatstein, *Canada's Army*, 185; author's correspondence with Dr Galen Perras, 29 September 2003; Harris, *Canadian Brass*, 190; English, *Failure in High Command*, 67; Stacey, *Canada and the Age of Conflict, Volume 2*, 289, 291; secret telegram 1790, high commissioner in Great Britain to secretary of state for external affairs, London, 7 July 1942, and "Secret Extract from Minutes of Cabinet War Committee," Ottawa, 8 July 1942, in *DEA, DCER*, vol. 9: 307–9.

26 Robertson, *Australia at War*, 18; Morton, *A Military History of Canada*, 188; Granatstein and Neary, *The Good Fight*, 7–9; Douglas and Greenhous, *Out of the Shadows*, 247; F.R. Scott, "What Did 'No' Mean?" in Granatstein and Neary, *The Good Fight*, 233; Byers, "Mobilizing Canada."

27 Hillmer and Granatstein, *Empire to Umpire*, 86; Mansergh, *The Commonwealth Experience*, 13; and Cohen, *While Canada Slept*, 105.

28 Churchill was upset over Ogdensburg because he felt that Mackenzie King was selling out Britain. His comments stung Mackenzie King because, although Canada was acting independently, it was doing so with Britain's interests in mind. Indeed, the fact that Canada was taking its own initiative rankled Churchill, even though he himself repeatedly ignored the dominions when making decisions.

29 Cordell Hull's remarks cited in Perras, "She Should Have Thought of Herself First," in MacMillan and McKenzie, ed., *Parties Long Estranged*, 126; Hillmer and Granatstein, *Empire to Umpire*, 141, 159–61; Eayrs, *In Defence of Canada, Volume 2*, 181–4.

30 "Secret Memorandum from Air Mission of Australia to Air Mission of Great Britain," Ottawa, 22 November 1939, in *DEA, DCER*, vol. 6: 608–9; Granatstein and Neary, *The Good Fight*, 9–10; Douglas and Greenhous, *Out of the Shadows*, 47; Stacey, *Canada and the Age of Conflict, Volume 2*, 315; Eayrs, *In Defence of Canada, Volume 2*, 41, 177; LaFeber, *The American Age*, 417–18; and McKenzie, *Redefining the Bonds of Commonwealth*, 28.

31 *DEA, DCER*, vol. 6: xiv; McKenzie, *Redefining the Bonds of Commonwealth*, 8; Perras, *Franklin Roosevelt*, xii, 1.

32 Watt, *The Evolution of Australian Foreign Policy*, 20–1, 293; Millar, *Australia in Peace and War*, 81–2, 86; McKenzie, "Coming of Age," in MacMillan and McKenzie, ed., *Parties Long Estranged*, 49–50.

33 Melbourne *Herald*, 27 December 1941, cited in Millar, *Australia in Peace and War*, 146–7; Long, *The Six Years War*, 137; and Watt, *The Evolution of Australian Foreign Policy*, 55.

34 McKenzie, *Redefining the Bonds of Commonwealth*, 65; Barclay, *Friends in High Places*, 11; and Watt, *The Evolution of Australian Foreign Policy*, 50. Churchill cited in ibid., 58.

35 Ibid., 41; and Barclay, *Friends in High Places*, 12.

36 Dwight D. Eisenhower, *Crusade in Europe*, cited in Watt, *The Evolution of Australian Foreign Policy*, 68; and Millar, *Australia in Peace and War*, 161.

37 See O'Brien, "Empire v. National Interests in Australian-British Relations."

38 For example, the arbitrary split of the South Pacific prevented Australia from operating closely with its traditional Pacific partner, New Zealand.

39 By July 1943, Australia had eight CMF divisions, three AIF infantry divisions (the 6th, 7th, and 9th, with the 8th already in captivity), and three armoured or motorized divisions. The United States had the 41st and 32nd infantry divisions in Australia.

40 David M. Horner is the pre-eminent historian and biographer in this field. The relationships and tensions among Blamey, Shedden, MacArthur, and Curtin are explored in two key works: *Defence Supremo* and *Blamey*.

41 The difficult relationship between Australia's high command, under Blamey and Curtin, and MacArthur and his staff is covered in detail in Horner, *High Command*.

42 Stacey, *Canada and the Age of Conflict, Volume 2*, 328–9; Palazzo, *The Australian Army*, 172; Bell, *Unequal Allies*, 87–106; Robertson, *Australia at War*, 82; and author's correspondence with Dr Galen Perras, 29 September 2003.

43 Nonetheless, MacArthur's decision to commit elements of the 9th AIF Division against the far larger Japanese forces at Finschhaffen, New Guinea, in 1943 placed Australians in a similarly unenviable position. In fact, his generalship also placed U.S. generals, including Wainwright and Eichelberger, in invidious positions.

44 Horner, *High Command*, 438–42; Bell, *Unequal Allies*, 101–2; Robertson, *Australia at War*, 26; and Long, *The Six Years War*, 176–7.

45 Bland, *Chiefs of Defence*, 10–11.

46 Preston, "Canada and the Second World War," in Hunt and Haycock, *Canada's Defence* 114–17.

47 Australia's share of Lend Lease was U.S.$1,570 million. This was mostly in the form of consumer goods for American troops under MacArthur's command. In addition, it was offset by Australian reciprocal aid estimated at U.S.$1,041 million – approximately 70 per cent of the material provided to Australia by the United States.

48 The hiatus in Australian-American security ties is explained in Bell, *Unequal Allies*.

49 Singleton and Robertson, *Economic Relations between Britain and Australasia,* 1, 214, 217; Thompson and Randall, *Canada and the United States,* 110, 112; and Doran, *Forgotten Partnership,* 79.

50 Five divisions were raised as part of the 2nd AIF (6th to 9th, and the 1st Armoured Division) and seven divisions from the militia (1st to 5th, plus 11th and 12th), together with another armoured and a motor division (2nd Motor and 3rd Armoured).

51 Author's correspondence with Dr Galen Perras, 29 September 2003. Perras cites the Rogers Papers at Queen's University Archives. DHH report no. 57: C.P. Stacey, "A Summary of Major Changes in Army Organization, 1939–1945," 22 December 1952, 22. Stacey, *Six Years of War,* 20, 82, 118–19.

52 For instance, the AIF's 1st Brigade was raised in New South Wales, the 2nd in Victoria, and the 3rd from the remaining states. Canada's 1st Brigade was raised in Ontario, the 2nd from the western and Maritime provinces, and the 3rd predominantly from Quebec.

53 These included the 1st, 2nd, and 3rd divisions, two armoured divisions (the 4th and 5th), and the 1st and 2nd armoured brigades.

54 Palazzo, *The Australian Army,* 146.

55 For detailed operational-level accounts of these campaigns in the official histories, see Long, *To Benghazi,* and *Greece, Crete and Syria.* These histories avoid detailed discussion of Australia's higher-defence arrangements, but the gap is addressed in Horner, *High Command.* See also Johnston and Stanley, *Alamein.*

56 Some 350 Canadian officers and NCOs were sent to serve with British units in North Africa for three-month periods from early 1943 onwards. Granatstein, *Canada's Army,* 214.

57 For an account of Australian armoured forces in the Second World War, see Hopkins, *Australian Armour.*

58 For an excellent single-volume operational overview of Australia's military campaigns in the Second World War, see Long, *The Six Years War.* For the role of Canada's Army in Britain and the Pacific War, see Stacey's similarly titled *Six Years of War.*

59 Perras, "She Should Have Thought of Herself First," 126; Stacey, *Canada and the Age of Conflict, Volume 2,* 339; telegram 162, Dominion secretary to secretary of state for external affairs, London, 19 September 1941, in DEA, DCER, vol. 6: 807; and Morton, *A Military History of Canada,* 188. For a detailed official account of Canadian forces in defence of Hong Kong, see Stacey, *Six Years of War,* chapter 14. See also Patricia E. Roy, J.L. Granatstein, Masako Iino, and Hiroko Takamura, "The Hong Kong Disaster," in Granatstein and Neary, *The Good Fight,* 82–96.

60 Mackenzie King cited in Perras, "She Should Have Thought of Herself First," 127. Throughout the war, Mackenzie King referred in his diary to Menzies's fall from power in August 1941. Author's correspondence with Dr Galen Perras, 29 September 2003; Perras, *Franklin Roosevelt*, 106–9; Robertson, *Australia at War*, 13; Stacey, *Canada and the Age of Conflict, Volume 2*, 317; and B.J.C. McKercher, "The Canadian Way of War," in Horn, ed., *Forging a Nation*, 128.

61 German U-boats also operated off the Atlantic coast of Canada and a Japanese submarine shelled the lighthouse at Estevan Point in British Columbia.

62 Charles J. Burchell arrived in Australia in December 1939 as Canada's first high commissioner to Australia. Australia's first high commissioner to Canada was former general and politician William Glasgow, who landed in Ottawa in March 1940.

63 See, for instance, Library and Archives Canada (LAC), RG 24, vol.3900, NSS 1037–1–20, "Most Secret Cypher No.20," Canberra, 24 January 1942; and "Cypher No 44," Canberra, 14 February 1942, from high commissioner for Canada in Australia to the secretary of state for external affairs, Canada.

64 Robertson, *Australia at War*, 107, 124, 128.

65 See "Chiefs of Staff Paper No.4," 29 January 1942: "Australian-Canadian Co-operation in the Pacific – Appreciation of Defence of Australia and Adjacent Areas." Printed in Robertson and McCarthy, *Australian War Strategy*, 257–60.

66 The draft wording of the original response shifted from "should" be submitted to the combined chiefs of staff to "must' be submitted, suggesting perhaps, a desire simply to wash their hands of the issue.

67 LAC, RG 24, vol.3900, NSS 1037–1–20, "Most Secret Cypher No. 21," Ottawa, 29 January 1942. Compare this to RG 24, vol. 3900 NSS 1037–1– 20, HQ.S, 5199, vol. 11, "Secret Ministerial," 4 March 1942 (signed by the three service chiefs).

68 "Most Secret Telegram 5," high commissioner in Australia to secretary of state for external affairs, Canberra, 10 January 1942 (and subsequent correspondence on 12, 24, and 29 January), in *DEA, DCER*, vol. 9: 1032–5; Hanson cited in Perras, "She Should Have Thought of Herself First," 130, 134. Also, Nossal, "Chunking Prism"; and Haycock, "The 'Myth' of Imperial Defence," 79.

69 LAC, RG 25, vol. 3116, telegram, secretary of state for external affairs, Ottawa, to high commissioner for Canada in Australia, 16 October 1942; RG 25, vol. 3116, telegram, high commissioner for Canada, T.C. Davis, to secretary of state for external affairs, Ottawa, 4 June 1945; Robertson, *Australia at War*, 111; and Perras, "She Should Have Thought of Herself First," 142–3.

70 Haycock, "The 'myth' of imperial defence"; and Haycock's correspondence with author, 8 October 2003.

71 The council met weekly for the rest of 1942 and about twice a month in 1943. It last met on 11 January 1944. Robertson, *Australia at War*, 113.

72 Eayrs, *In Defence of Canada, Volume 2*, 186.

73 Long, *The Six Years War*, 128.

74 Grey, *The Australian Army*, 134, 136.

75 By September 1943, the AIF would include over 265,000 members while the CMF would include 117,000. By the end of the war, over 206,000 personnel opted to transfer from the militia to the AIF.

76 These included: Headquarters 1st Army in New South Wales and Queensland, raised from the returning 1st Australian Corps and including 1st and 2nd Australian Corps; Headquarters 2nd Army, based in Victoria, South Australia, and Tasmania; Headquarters III Corps in Western Australia; Headquarters Northern Territory Force in Darwin; Headquarters New Guinea Force in Port Moresby; and the 1st Armoured Division.

77 These included substantial special operations (for reconnaissance, subversion, and sabotage), secret intelligence (spying), field intelligence (including coast watchers), military propaganda, censorship, translation, and foreign broadcasting.

78 Horner, *High Command*, 224–46, 445.

79 DHH 112.1009, "Recruiting and Use of Cdn Tps for Australia," 1945, Memorandum HQC, 8023–90–9, 21 July 1945. See also DHH 322.009, "Japanese Personnel Enlistment and Discharge, Secret Memorandum," HQS 8932–8 FD 44, 4 May 1945, "Enlistment and Att CF Cdn Nissei to Australia." See also Ballard, *On ULTRA Secret Service*, 197–8, 278–9; and Horner, *High Command*, 243.

80 By 1945, when the scheme was wound up, it had produced 131,553 trained aircrew – including 72,835 for the RCAF, 42,110 for the RAF, 9,606 for the RAAF, and 7,002 for the RNZAF In all, 16,000 Australian airmen were in Europe by the end of the war.

81 McCarthy, *Last Call of Empire*; Perras, "She Should Have Thought of Herself First," 125; Long, *The Six Years War*, 101; Douglas and Greenhous, *Out of the Shadows*, 42; Stacey, *Arms, Men and Government*, 17, 29; Stacey, *Canada and the Age of Conflict, Volume 2*, 287, 296; Hooker, "Serving Two Masters," 48; Robertson, *Australia at War*, 52, 55; and Morton, *Understanding Canadian Defence*, 58.

82 Australian Archives CRS, A5954/1, item 309/4, "The Maintenance of a Balanced Australian War Effort While Providing for United States and United Kingdom Needs," January 1945, cited in Palazzo, *The Australian Army*, 177–8. See also Barclay, *Friends in High Places*, 19; Grey, *The Australian Army*, 140; Robertson, *Australia at War*, 195; Stacey, *Arms, Men and Government*, 51; and Long, *The Six Years War*, 37.

83 By contrast, New Zealand (population of 1.5 million) had one division overseas and South Africa (two million Europeans) had two divisions serving in North Africa.

84 Ross, *Armed and Ready*, chapter 13; Grey, *The Australian Army*, 149–53; and Palazzo, *The Australian Army*, 184.

85 Broad, "'Not Competent to Produce Tanks'"; Hopkins, *Australian Armour*, 72; and Ross, *Armed and Ready*, 414.

86 For a discussion of doctrinal development in the immediate post-war years in Australia, see Welburn, *The Development of Australian Army Doctrine*.

87 For an examination of these amphibious operations, see Wahlert, ed., *Australian Army Amphibious Operations in the South Pacific: 1942–45*.

88 "Secret Extract of Minutes of a Meeting of Cabinet War Committee and War Cabinet of Great Britain," Quebec, 11 August 1943, in DEA, DCER, vol. 9: 347–8; Coates, *Bravery above Blunder*, 146; Douglas and Greenhous, *Out of the Shadows*, 124; and author's correspondence with Lieutenant-Colonel Casey Haskins, 14 October 2003.

89 The 1st Brigade's deployment was brief and it saw no action, but it returned to Britain missing most of its vehicles.

90 Greenhous, *Dieppe, Dieppe*; Granatstein, *Canada's Army*, 205–6; Bryant, *The Turn of the Tide*, 596; Stacey, *Six Years of War*, chapters 10 to 12; and Douglas and Greenhous, *Out of the Shadows*, 109–21.

91 For a description of their experiences and the effect on Canadians, see Stacey and Wilson, *The Half-Million*.

92 The 2nd Canadian Infantry Division was raised in early 1940, with some elements initially dispatched temporarily to defend Iceland. The 3rd and 4th Canadian Infantry divisions were raised after the fall of France in May 1940, along with the 1st Canadian Armoured Brigade in August 1940 (later expanded to become the 1st Canadian Armoured Division and then redesignated as the 5th Canadian Armoured Division in July 1941). The 4th Canadian Infantry Division was converted into the 4th Canadian Armoured Division in 1942. The 1st Canadian Corps was raised in 1940 and the 2nd in 1941. The 1st Canadian Army, a composite of both Canadian corps, was raised in April 1942.

93 To some degree, the United States faced similar alliance pressures. The joint chiefs of staff objected to the campaigns in North Africa, Sicily, and Italy as diversions that would delay and weaken the main effort – the decisive invasion of Western Europe and the drive into Germany.

94 "Most Secret – 'Memorandum from Assistant Under-Secretary for External Affairs [H. Wrong] to Under-Secretary of State for External Affairs,'" Ottawa, 28 January 1943, in DEA, DCER, vol.9: 326–9; Stacey, *Canada and the Age of*

Conflict, Volume 2, 349–50; English, *Lament for an Army,* 32; and author's correspondence with Dr Galen Perras, 29 September 2003.

95 Douglas and Greenhous, *Out of the Shadows,* 144–5; and Nicholson, *The Official History of the Canadian Army in the Second World War.*

96 Granatstein, *Canada's Army,* 255; Douglas Delaney, "The Soldiers' General"; Douglas and Greenhous, *Out of the Shadows,* 142; Granatstein, *The Generals,* 189–203; Stacey, *Six Years of War,* 253, chapter 12; English, *Failure in High Command;* Douglas and Greenhous, *Out of the Shadows,* 218; and Donald E. Graves, "On the Left Flank: Normandy to the Maas, June 1944 to January 1945," in Graves, ed., *Fighting for Canada,* 317.

97 Coates, *Bravery above Blunder,* 219, 252, 256; and United States Army Center for Military History, *New Guinea,* 29–31.

98 For an account of Simonds's performance as corps commander and his clash with the commander of 1st Canadian Army, General Crerar, see Granatstein, *The Generals,* 145–78.

99 Granatstein, *Canada's Army,* 278–9; and Delaney "The Soldiers' General."

100 For accounts of McNaughton's generalship, see Granatstein, *The Generals;* and Bill Rawling, "The Generalship of Andrew McNaughton: A Study in Failure," in Horn and Harris, ed., *Warrior Chiefs,* 73–88.

101 Harris, *Canadian Brass,* 206–8; English, *Failure in High Command,* 308; and author's correspondence with Dr Galen Perras, 29 September 2003.

102 Of the 90 allied divisions in Western Europe, 61 were American, 14 British, 8 French, 5 Canadian and 1 Polish. The Soviet Union fielded 158 divisions against the Germans' 180 divisions in 1942. Over 24 German divisions faced the Allied invasion at Normandy.

103 Horner, *SAS,* 19–32; Stacey, *Six Years of War,* 104–8; and Horn, *Bastard Sons.*

104 In 1942 a British Special Operations executive officer helped establish the Inter-Allied Services Department, or Services Reconnaissance Department, in Australia, which was the precursor organization to Special Operations Australia. It closed at war's end and special forces were not revived until 1957 with the formation of the Australian SAS.

105 U.S. divisions also served under command of the First Canadian Army at various points in northwest Europe in 1944 and 1945.

106 Galen Perras's chapter in Donaghy, ed., *Uncertain Horizons;* Pope, *Soldiers and Politicians;* War Cabinet Minute 3065, Canberra, 1 October 1943, printed in Robertson and McCarthy, *Australian War Strategy,* 390; DHH 171.009 Jungle Warfare Liaison Letters (General Liaison letters were also distributed around the Empire); DHH 314.009, "Canadian Army Observers – S & SW Pacific Theatres – Corresp, msgs, nominal rolls, instructors,

memoranda etc.," May 1943–November 1944; "Secret," R–1–1, 24 May
1943, "S & SW Pacific Theatres, Memo from Major General Maurice Pope,
Washington, to Chief of the General Staff," Ottawa.

107 DHH report no. 16: C.P. Stacey, "The Canadian Army Pacific Force, 1944–
1945, 7 January 1953 [15 July 1947], 30, 33, 37, 54; Holmes, *The Shaping of
Peace*, 22–3.

108 This question was brought to the author's attention in discussions with
Dr Ron Haycock, 8 October 2003.

109 The Canadian Special Wireless Group operated in Australia from February
1945 to the end of the war.

110 Stacey, *Six Years of War*, 510. See also DHH report no.16: C.P. Stacey, "The
Canadian Army Pacific Force, 1944–1945," 7 January 1953 [15 July 1947];
DHH 322.009, "Secret," "Cdn Offrs Attached to Australians –1944/45:
Interim Report No. 1, Canadian Officers Aust Attachment," 26 April–26 May
1944; DHH 314.009 "Australian Personnel on Loan to Canada –Msgs, cor-
resp, etc.," 16 June 1944–28 September 1945; "Confidential Message to
Canadian Military Attaché Canberra," 16 June 1944.

111 Prime Minister Mackenzie King, cited in Stacey, *Arms, Men and Government*, 54.

112 Arguably, this was more of MacArthur's empire-building as well. He was in a
tug-of-war for influence in southeast Asia with Britain's Field Marshall
Sir William Slim and Admiral Mountbatten.

113 See Horner, *High Command*, 384–7; and Stacey, *Arms, Men and Government*,
62.

114 Desmond Morton, "Interoperability and Its Consequences," in Griffiths, ed.,
The Canadian Forces and Interoperability, 160.

115 Holmes, *The Shaping of Peace*, 126–7; Stacey, *Six Years of War*, 513–19; and
Stacey, *Arms, Men and Government*, 65.

116 See Doug Owram, "The Dominion-Provincial Conference on Reconstruction:
The Limits of Success," in Granatstein and Neary, *The Good Fight*, 98–100.

117 Bassett, *Guns and Brooches*; Grey, *The Australian Army*, 144–5; Palazzo, *The
Australian Army*, 176, 190, 213, 334. Peter Neary and Shaun Brown, "The
Veterans' Charter and Canadian Women Veterans of World War II," in
Granatstein and Neary, *The Good Fight*, 393, 400. For an example of the
post-war integration of women into the Australian Army, see Blaxland, *Signals
Swift and Sure*.

118 Matloff, *United States Army in World War II*, 7–9.

119 Ritchie, *Diplomatic Passport*, 8; Holmes, *The Shaping of Peace*, 43–4;
McKenzie, "Coming of Age," in MacMillan and McKenzie, ed., *Parties Long
Estranged*, 51–3; Reynolds, *Australia's Bid for the Atomic Bomb*, 32, and
"In the Wake of Canada," in MacMillan and McKenzie, ed., *Parties Long*

Estranged, 164; Reid, *On Duty*, xi-xii, 34; Andrew F. Cooper, "Keeping in Touch: Patterns of Networking in the Canadian-Australian Diplomatic Relationship," in MacMillan and McKenzie, ed., *Parties Long Estranged*, 253; and Perras, "She Should Have Thought of Herself First," 144.

120　Bland, *Chiefs of Defence*, 43; and Horner, *High Command*, 444–5.

121　Author's discussions with Dr Charles Pentland, 24 April 2003.

122　Horner, *High Command*, xix, 435, 446.

123　McKenzie, "Coming of Age," in MacMillan and McKenzie, ed., *Parties Long Estranged*, 47.

124　Holmes, *The Shaping of Peace*, 304.

CHAPTER FIVE

1　By comparison, the key roles for the Canadian Forces in 2003 were to "defend Canada, contribute to the defence of North America in cooperation with the United States, and contribute to international peace and security."

2　Major Graeme Sligo, "The Development of the Australian Regular Army, 1944–1952," in Grey and Dennis, ed., *The Second Fifty Years*, 36; and Holmes, *The Shaping of Peace*, 153–4.

3　Reynolds, *Australia's Bid for the Atomic Bomb*, 21, 29, 31, 38, 47.

4　Sligo, "The Development of the Australian Regular Army," 30; Millar, *Australia in Peace and War*, 175; "British Commonwealth Occupation Force," in Dennis et al., ed., *Oxford Companion to Australian Military History*, 124–6; and author's correspondence with Dr Galen Perras, 29 September 2003.

5　*Canada's Defence, 1947*, cited in Bland, *Canada's National Defence, Volume 1*, 21; McKenzie, "Coming of Age," in MacMillan and McKenzie, ed., *Parties Long Estranged*, 48; Andrew F. Cooper, "Keeping in Touch: Patterns of Networking in the Canadian-Australian Diplomatic Relationship," in MacMillan and McKenzie, ed., *Parties Long Estranged*, 249–50; Ball and Horner, *Breaking the Codes*, 154.

6　Barclay, *Friends in High Places*, 26; Watt, *The Evolution of Australian Foreign Policy*, 102, 105; Millar, *Australia in Peace and War*, 200–5; and Reynolds, *Australia's Bid for the Atomic Bomb*, 39.

7　Palazzo, *the Australian Army*, 203–13; and Doughty, *The Evolution of US Army Tactical Doctrine*, 2.

8　Canadian *House of Commons Debates*, 4 September 1950 and 8 June 1950, cited in Crickard, "A Tale of Two Navies," 88–9.

9　For an elaboration of this debate, see Ann Capling and Kim R. Nossal, "The Limits of Like-Mindedness," in MacMillan and McKenzie, ed., *Parties Long*

Estranged, 229–39. See also Singleton and Robertson, *Economic Relations between Britain and Australasia*; and McKenzie, *Redefining the Bonds of Commonwealth*, 68.

10 Albert Palazzo lists frequent changes in the direction of national-security policy as one of the three major national characteristics of the Australian Army. His observations appear to apply equally to Canada.

11 See Granatstein and Stafford, *Spy Wars*, 47–75.

12 Horner, *Defence Supremo*, 264.

13 This view about Soviet intentions is challenged by Frank Cain (see, for instance, "Governments and Defectors: Responses to the Defections of Gouzenko in Canada and Petrov in Australia," in MacMillan and McKenzie, ed., *Parties Long Estranged*), but he does not take into account (let alone even refer to) the detailed analysis and exposition outlined in Horner and Ball's *Breaking the Codes*.

14 Defence Signals Branch subsequently was renamed the Defence Signals Directorate (DSD). The Joint Intelligence Bureau subsequently became the Joint Intelligence Organisation (JIO) and is now called the Defence Intelligence Organisation (DIO).

15 Ball and Horner, *Breaking the Codes*, 163–4, 186, 340; Horner, *Shedden*, 247–9, 261; Anderson, "The Evolution of the Canadian Intelligence Establishment"; Granatstein and Stafford, *Spy Wars*, x-xi; and Rudner, "Canada's Communications Security Establishment."

16 Watt, *The Evolution of Australian Foreign Policy*, 106. Churchill cited in McDougall, *Promised Land*, 161.

17 Reynolds, *Australia's Bid for the Atomic Bomb*, 75–85, 89.

18 Eayrs, *In Defence of Canada, Volume 3*, 47–51; and author's correspondence with Dr Galen Perras, 29 September 2003.

19 Eayrs, *In Defence of Canada, Volume 3*, 60, 75–6.

20 For an account of Australia's involvement, see Londey, *Other People's Wars*, 40–57.

21 The invasion was witnessed by the two Australian officers attached to the UN Commission on Korea (UNCOK). The evidence cited in their report proved instrumental in swaying UN members to support the United States in countering the invasion.

22 A useful overview of the Commonwealth countries' military contributions to the Korean War is Grey's *The Commonwealth Armies and the Korean War*. More recently, he, along with Dennis, edited *The Korean War: The Chief of Army's Military History Conference 2000*. The official and authoritative Australian account is O'Neill's two- volume work, *Australia in the Korean War*. Canada's is Wood, *Strange Battleground*, although, unlike O'Neill's work, this is army-centric. More recent and detailed is Bercuson, *Blood on the Hills*.

23 Eayrs, *In Defence of Canada, Volume 3,* 62; Sligo, "Australian Regular Army," 40, 44– 5; Privy Council Office, "Survey of Relations between Canada and the United States," dated 20 June 1951 (copy in possession of author); Eayrs, *In Defence of Canada, Volume 3,* 62; Stairs, *The Diplomacy of Constraint,* x-xi; and author's correspondence with Dr Galen Perras, 29 September 2003.

24 Palazzo, *the Australian Army,* 218; Barclay, *Friends in High Places,* 40, 45; Odgers, *Across the Parallel,* 28, 57, 90; Crickard, "A Tale of Two Navies," 14; and Wood, *Strange Battleground,* 13.

25 Wood, *Strange Battleground,* 22–7, 34.

26 Ibid., 37.

27 This later formation would include two Australian infantry battalions, a New Zealand infantry battalion, a reinforced company of British Gurkhas, a reinforced company of Canadian "Van Doos," and a platoon of Irish Rangers.

28 Wood, *Strange Battleground,* 78.

29 For engaging tactical accounts of the battalion battles fought by the Australians and Canadians, see Gray, *Beyond the Danger;* Breen, *The Battle of Kapyong;* and O'Neill, *Australia in the Korean War, Volume 2,* 31–60.

30 For a gripping account of the Gloucester's battle, see Farrar-Hockley, *The Edge of the Sword.*

31 Technically, with a separation of three kilometres between the 3RAR and 2PPCLI positions, the two battalions could not provide "mutual support" with their direct-fire weapons (machine guns). But, essentially, the Chinese could not pass through the gap between their positions, considered crucial for their advance, without clearing the hills held by both battalions.

32 Grey, *The Commonwealth Armies and the Korean War,* 92; Stairs, *The Diplomacy of Constraint,* 198, 203; Wood, *Strange Battleground,* 14, 113, 117–18, 179; and Blaxland, *Signals Swift and Sure,* 67–9.

33 Grey, *The Commonwealth Armies and the Korean War,* 103–5; Bercuson, *Blood on the Hills,* 37–40; and Wood, *Strange Battleground,* 181–211.

34 O'Neill, *Australia in the Korean War, Volume 2,* 253; Bercuson, *Blood on the Hills,* 193, 210.

35 The Canadians suffered eighteen killed and thirty-five wounded from the incident.

36 For an excellent synopsis of the techniques used at Tobruk, see Coates, *Bravery above Blunder,* 11–43.

37 Grey, *The Commonwealth Armies and the Korean War,* 150–3; Bercuson, *Blood on the Hills,* 160, 182, 212, 224–5.

38 Blaxland, *The Regiments Depart,* 190.

39 McLin, *Canada's Changing Defense Policy,* 172; and Wood, *Strange Battleground,* 215–16, 232.

40 Grey, *The Commonwealth Armies and the Korean War*, 139–40, 144; Bercuson, *Blood on the Hills*, 83; and Wood, "Employment of ... Commonwealth and U.S. Field Artillery."

41 Grey, *The Commonwealth Armies and the Korean War*, 111–12; and Wood, *Strange Battleground*, 112.

42 Bercuson, *Blood on the Hills*, 199–202; Wood, *Strange Battleground*, 191–6; and Grey, *The Commonwealth Armies and the Korean War*, 114, 131.

43 Grey, *The Commonwealth Armies and the Korean War*, 172; and Stairs, *The Diplomacy of Constraint*, 201.

44 Wood, *Strange Battleground*, 244, 250; Bercuson and Granatstein, *Dictionary of Canadian Military History*, 111; and Dennis et. al., ed., *The Oxford Companion to Australian Military History*, 336.

45 Stairs, *The Diplomacy of Constraint*, 138–9; and Stairs, "Canada and the Korean War Fifty Years On," 52–3, 58.

46 Eayrs, *In Defence of Canada, Volume 4*, 47; O'Neill, *Australia in the Korean War, Volume 2*, 409; Barclay, *Friends in High Places*, 49; Horner, *Shedden*, 307; Watt, *The Evolution of Australian Foreign Policy*, 120–1, 125–7; and Bercuson, *Blood on the Hills*, 221.

47 Wood, *Strange Battleground*, 258.

48 Nossal, *The Politics of Canadian Foreign Policy*.

49 Granatstein, *Canada's Army*, 3.

50 Granatstein, *The Generals*, 264.

51 See Australian Army, *The Fundamentals of Land Warfare*, chapter 4.

CHAPTER SIX

1 Cited in Crickard, "A Tale of Two Navies," 82.

2 Christopher Waters, "Diplomacy in Easy Chairs: Casey, Pearson, and Australian-Canadian Relations, 1951–7," in MacMillan and McKenzie, ed., *Parties Long Estranged*, 207–9. Indeed, Richard Casey's diaries prominently feature exchanges with his Canadian counterpart, Lester Pearson, and Pearson's papers in Canada's Library and Archives in Ottawa do likewise with Casey. Millar, ed., *Australian Foreign Minister*, 63, 83, 208, 226; and author's correspondence with Dr Galen Perras, 29 September 2003.

3 Eayrs, *In Defence of Canada, Volume 3*, 213–14; Maloney, *War without Battles*, 27; Hopkins, *Australian Armour*, 148–9, 202; Maloney, *War without Battles*, 27, 33; and author's correspondence with Lieutenant-Colonel Casey Haskins, 14 October 2003.

4 Eayrs, *In Defence of Canada, Volume 3*, 220, 278; Rempel, *Counterweights*, 5; Barclay, *A Very Small Insurance Policy*; and author's correspondence with Lieutenant-Colonel Casey Haskins, 14 October 2003.

5 NORAD's name was changed to North American Aerospace Defense Command in 1981.

6 Eayrs, *In Defence of Canada, Volume 3*, 279–80, 283; Millar, ed., *Australian Foreign Minister*, 53; and correspondence with Dr Joel Sokolsky, August 2002.

7 Arguably, however, Canada could not afford a balanced self-reliant force, nor did it even want one. In addition, had it not been for NATO, Canada may not have had a navy at all. According to this view, the Canadian forces used NATO as leverage to get Mackenzie King to spend on the RCN, when he would have preferred not to. Indeed, the antisubmarine warfare function suited Canada well in this period, since the ships could be based in Canada most of the time.

8 Crickard, "A Tale of Two Navies," 2, 9, 33.

9 The agreement was signed between the Australian chief of naval staff, Vice-Admiral Sir John Collins, and the United States commander-in-chief Pacific, Admiral Arthur Radford.

10 Reynolds, *Australia's Bid for the Atomic Bomb*, 151; and LaFeber, *The American Age*, 519.

11 John Foster Dulles, cited in Sokolsky, "Glued to Its Seat," in Pentland, ed., *The Transatlantic Link in Evolution*, 44.

12 Ibid., 46–7.

13 Bland, *Chiefs of Defence*, 226.

14 Wayne Reynolds, "In the Wake of Canada: Australia's Middle-Power Diplomacy and the Attempt to Join the Atomic Special Relationship, 1943–1957," in MacMillan and McKenzie, ed., *Parties Long Estranged*, 156, 162; Wayne Reynolds, "In the Footsteps of Manhattan: Australian Defence Science and the Quest for the Atomic Bomb, 1946–1960," in Cain, ed., *Arming the Nation*, chapter 4; Peter Morton, *Fire Across the Desert*.

15 Watt, *The Evolution of Australian Foreign Policy*, 115–16; Millar, *Australia in Peace and War*, 371; Cohen, *While Canada Slept*, 73–7; and Munro and Inglis, ed., *Mike, Volume 2*, 108–11.

16 Waters, "Diplomacy in Easy Chairs," 222; and Eayrs, *In Defence of Canada, Volume 4*, 186, 219, 272, 283.

17 Munro and Inglis, ed., *Mike, Volume 2*, 231; Barclay, *Friends in High Places*, 62–3; Kagan, *Of Paradise and Power*, 72; Mansergh, *The Commonwealth Experience, Volume Two*, 172; and John W. Holmes, "Canada and the Pax Americana," in Dyck and Krosby, ed., *Empire and Nations*, 75.

18 Citation from Hillmer and Granatstein, *Empire to Umpire*.

19 B.J.C. McKercher and Lawrence Aronsen, "Afterword," in McKercher and Aronsen, ed., *The North Atlantic Triangle*, 264; LaFeber, *The American Age*, 559–60; Millar, ed., *Australian Foreign Minister*, 252, 299; and author's correspondence with Dr Galen Perras, 29 September 2003.

20 Gregory Blaxland, *Egypt and Sinai*, 289; Jordan, Taylor, Jr, and Mazarr, *American National Security*, 511; Chaim Herzog, "The Suez-Sinai Campaign: Background," in Troen and Shemesh, ed., *The Suez-Sinai Crisis 1956*, 13; Londey, *Other People's Wars*, 69; and Rosner, *The United Nations Emergency Force*, 120–4.

21 Burns, *Between Arab and Israeli*; Findlay, *The Use of Force in UN Peace Operations*, chapter 2; Doug Bland, presentation, 21 February 2002; Rempel, *The Chatter Box*, 118; and Cohen, *While Canada Slept*, 44, 69.

22 Hudson, *Blind Loyalty*, 6, 14, 141, 142; and Reynolds, *Australia's Bid for the Atomic Bomb*, 168.

23 Author's discussions with Dr Joel Sokolsky, 16 October 2003.

24 Reynolds, "In the Wake of Canada," 174–7, and *Australia's Bid for the Atomic Bomb*, 174, 183.

25 McLin, *Canada's Changing Defense Policy*, 124.

26 Ball, "The Strategic Essence" and *Australia's Secret Space Programs*.

27 Eayrs, *In Defence of Canada, Volume 3*, 252.

28 This case is well argued by Maloney in *Canada and UN Peacekeeping*. The Trudeau era saw Canada's pro-NATO orientation diminish, making the case less convincing from 1970 onwards.

29 Jett, *Why Peacekeeping Fails*, 25; Granatstein, *Canada's Army*, 391–3; Jordan, Taylor, Jr, and Mazarr, *American National Security*, 516; LaFeber, *The American Age*, 620; Sean M. Maloney, "'Mad Jimmy' Dextraze: The Tightrope of UN Command in the Congo," in Horn and Harris, *Warrior Chiefs*; and Delvoie, "Canada and International Security Operations," 16.

30 For instance, UNMOGIP (1949–78), UNTSO (over fifty years), and UNDOF in the Golan Heights from 1974 onwards. Canadians also served in UNEF from 1956 to 1967 but without an Australian contribution.

31 Some claim that Johnson thanked Canada for its role in Cyprus by agreeing to the 1965 Autopact.

32 Delvoie, in "Canada and International security Operations," cites the "Sharp Principles" as the basic criteria for Canadian participation in peacekeeping missions. These include: the existence of a threat to international security; the existence of a political settlement; the responsibility of a political authority, preferably the United Nations; a clear mandate; acceptance by the parties involved of the presence of peacekeepers and of Canadian participation; and equitable financial arrangements.

33 Ibid., 13–17; John Rixon, "The Role of Australian Police in Peace Support Operations," in Smith, ed., *International Peacekeeping*, chapter 11; Crickard, "A Tale of Two Navies," 57, 131; Stairs, "Canada in the 1990s," 43; "HMCS *Bonaventure*," in Bercuson and Granatstein, *Dictionary of Canadian Military History*, 20; and author's correspondence with Dr Galen Perras, 29 September 2003.

34 Off, *The Lion, The Fox and the Eagle*, 363.

35 Sokolsky, *The Americanization of Peacekeeping*, 38; and Cohen, *While Canada Slept*, 70.

36 Granatstein cited in Sokolsky, *The Americanization of Peacekeeping*, 62.

37 Cited in Rod Byers, "Peacekeeping and Canadian Defence Policy," in Hunt and Haycock, ed., *Canada's Defence*, 192.

38 This was certainly the experience of the Canadian Airborne Regiment as detailed in Horn, *Bastard Sons*, 143–84.

39 See Blaxland, *Organising an Army*; and Palazzo, *The Australian Army*, 240–80.

40 See Bacevich, *The Pentomic Era*.

41 Singleton and Robertson, *Economic Relations between Britain and Australasia*, 169; and Reynolds, *Australia's Bid for the Atomic Bomb*, 216.

42 See Fox, *The Politics of Attraction*, 71–2.

43 Blaxland, *Organising an Army*, 83.

44 Grimshaw, "On Guard," 162.

45 Reynolds, *Australia's Bid for the Atomic Bomb*, 83, 86; Horner, *Shedden*, 288, 323; Palazzo, *The Australian Army*, 236; and Watt, *The Evolution of Australian Foreign Policy*, 104, 163–70.

46 Horner, *Shedden*, 319; Watt, *The Evolution of Australian Foreign Policy*, 143–63; and LaFeber, *The American Age*, 551–2.

47 Cited in Barclay, *Friends in High Places*, 79.

48 Ibid., 80; Watt, *The Evolution of Australian Foreign Policy*, 178; and Millar, *Australia in Peace and War*, 245–6. For a detailed history of these events, see Dennis and Grey, *Emergency and Confrontation*.

49 McLin, *Canada's Changing Defense Policy*, 7.

50 An indigenously designed and built Canadian advanced jet aircraft, but with no prospect of international sales, that was scrapped in 1959. This led to the immediate loss of 15,000 jobs and a significant contraction of the Canadian defence industry.

51 Prime Minister Diefenbaker's government acquired Bomarc missiles, but he was unwilling to place nuclear warheads on them, so they sat there. This prompted a no-confidence motion that resulted in an election which Lester Pearson won. Pearson acquired the nuclear warheads but they, in turn, were removed under Pearson's successor, Pierre Trudeau.

52 Canadian forces commanders deployed assets in support of the United States at the height of the crisis, prior to receiving prime ministerial approval. The Americans wanted to go to DFCON 3 (Defence Readiness Condition level 3 – a heightened state of alert in the face of imminent threat) and Prime Minister Diefenbaker could not come to a decision. Secretly, the minister of national defence put Canadian forces on the same alert as the United States without Diefenbaker knowing, a Canadian admiral ordered RCN warships to fill gaps

left by American ships, and RCAF fighters staged their own standby. This led to a crisis, since Diefenbaker resented the apparent erosion of Canadian sovereignty.

53 McLin, *Canada's Changing Defense Policy*, 7, 214, 217; and Haydon, *The 1962 Cuban Missile Crisis*, 1–3, 10.

54 See, for instance, Minifie, *Peacemaker or Powder-Monkey*.

55 Richter, *Avoiding Armageddon*, 9, 150.

56 Reynolds, *Australia's Bid for the Atomic Bomb*, 208–10.

57 Haydon, *The 1962 Cuban Missile Crisis*, 221; Hellyer, *Damn The Torpedoes*; Morton, *Understanding Canadian Defence*, 181; and Kronenberg, "All To-gether Now," 2, 24.

58 Morton, *Understanding Canadian Defence*, 174.

59 Bland, *Canada's National Defence, Volume II*, xvi–xvii.

60 Horner, *Making the Australian Defence Force*, 43, 47.

61 W. Harriet Critchley, "Civilianization and the Canadian Military," in Hunt and Haycock, ed., *Canada's Defence*, 233–7.

62 Author's discussions with Dr Joel Sokolsky, 16 October 2003.

63 Lieutenant-Colonel Graeme Sligo, "The Staff College at Armour Heights 1943–2003."

64 J.L. Granatstein, "The American Influence on the Canadian Military," in Hunt and Haycock, ed., *Canada's Defence*, 137; and New York *Times,* 20 February 1967, cited in Kronenberg, "All Together Now," 168.

65 Kronenberg, "All Together Now," 168, 174–7; and Gowans, "Canadian De-fence Integration," 19–26, 170–1.

66 Author's correspondence with Dr Ron Haycock, 8 October 2003.

67 Australian defence chiefs received regular updates through the defence attaché staff in Ottawa on Canada's progress towards unification and integration. The author has had informal discussions (not for attribution) with senior retired Australian military officers who, while interested in developments in Canada, were dismissive of the radical and traumatic approach taken in the mid-1960s.

68 Horner, *Making the Australian Defence Force*, 42.

69 John C. Holmes, "Canada and the Pax Americana," in Dyck and Krosby, ed., *Empire and Nations*, 87.

70 Australia committed two infantry battalions in succession to operations in Borneo, in addition to two squadrons of the Special Air Service Regiment (SASR), several artillery batteries, engineer teams, signals-intercept teams, air force transport aircraft, and naval ships.

71 For a detailed account of the work of these advisers, see McNeill, *The Team.*

72 LaFeber, *The American Age*, 563.

73 See Pemberton, *All the Way,* 254–67.

74 Millar, *Australia in Peace and War*, 214–15.

75 Barclay, *Friends in High Places*, 125.

76 See Pemberton, *All the Way*; and Edwards and Pemberton, *Crises and Commitments*.

77 Barclay, *Friends in High Places*, 126.

78 Even conspiracy theorists acknowledge that Australian public opinion in 1965 was strongly supportive of the government's moves in Vietnam. See, for instance, Sexton, *War for the Asking*.

79 Millar, *Australia in Peace and War*, 217; and Palazzo, *The Australian Army*, 267.

80 Holmes, "Canada and the Pax Americana," 81; LaFeber, *The American Age*, 662; and Morton, *Understanding Canadian Defence*, 117, 121.

81 Australia's experience with the 173rd Airborne is explored in detail in Breen, *First to Fight*.

82 Doughty, *The Evolution of US Army Tactical Doctrine*, 36, 38.

83 See, for instance, Frost, *Australia's War in Vietnam*; and, for the official account of the ground campaign, see Ian McNeill, *To Long Tan*; and McNeil and Ekins, *On the Offensive*.

84 Barclay, *Friends in High Places*, 154, 158.

85 Rigorous analysis in Australia in 2002 indicated that tanks remained pivotal to the combat power and survival of assaulting forces.

86 Evans, *Forward form the Past*, 7.

87 See Grey, *Up Top*; Coulthard-Clark, *The RAAF in Vietnam*; and McNeil and Ekins, *On the Offensive*. For a detailed account of Australian Special Air Service (SAS) troops on operations in Borneo and Vietnam, see Horner, *SAS: Phantoms of the Jungle*.

88 English, *Lament for an Army*, 57.

89 While most NATO partners felt constrained to comply with NATO standardization agreements, the U.S. forces were prepared to maintain procedures and protocols unique to them.

90 Permanently stationed Australian troops were withdrawn from Malaya and Singapore in 1973 but an ADF presence has been maintained in the region ever since – including rotational deployments of aircraft and an infantry company to the Malaysian air force base at Butterworth, as well as regular ship visits and combined exercises as part of the FPDA.

91 Millar, *Australia in Peace and War*, 189, 246–7, 272.

92 Barclay, *Friends in High Places*, 170–1; and Millar, *Australia in Peace and War*, 409.

93 Jones, "Regional Illusion and Its Aftermath," 42.

94 This case is cogently argued in Canada's case in Rempel, *Counterweights*.

95 Barclay, *Friends in High Places*, 191; and Millar, *Australia in Peace and War*, 405, 409.

96 Major R.D. Letts, Royal Australian Regiment, "Exercise Winter Sun."

97 Ralph Harry, "Australian Multilateral Diplomacy," in Boyce and Angel, ed., *Independence and Alliance*, 81.

98 Hugh Smith, "Defence Policy," in ibid., 41–3; Palazzo, *The Australian Army*, 285, 310–12; and R.A. Herr, "Australia and the South-West Pacific," in Boyce and Angel, ed., *Independence and* Alliance, 279–92.

99 Canada, Department of External Affairs, *Foreign Policy for Canadians*.

100 Thompson and Randall, *Canada and the United States*, 244, 246, 249, 252; Doran, *Forgotten Partnership*, 2, 24, 28; and author's discussions with Mr Louis Delvoie, 7 October 2003, and with Dr Ron Haycock, 8 October 2003.

101 David Last, "Almost a Legacy," in Horn, ed., *Forging a Nation*, 375.

102 Maloney argues that, despite the force cutbacks, the Canadian forces deployed in Germany remained more than just a symbolic commitment after the 1969 reductions. See Maloney, *War without Battles*. Grimshaw, in "On Guard," 189, makes the point that with NATO and peacekeeping roles designated to third and fourth priority respectively, the Canadian army's role was problematical during this period.

103 Peters, "Club Dues?" 52.

104 Cited in Thompson and Randall, *Canada and the United States*, 273.

105 English, *Lament for an Army*, 58; Sean M. Maloney, "The Canadian Tao of Conflict," in Horn, ed., *Forging a Nation*, 271; and correspondence with Dr Ron Haycock, 8 October 2003.

106 This is strikingly evident in the prominent place given to the Peacekeeping Monument in Ottawa.

107 Bland, *Canada's National Defence, Volume I*, 115.

108 Morton, *Understanding Canadian Defence*, 184; Critchley, "Civilianization and the Canadian Military," 235; and English, *Lament for an Army*, 55–6.

109 Doran, *Forgotten Partnership*, 33.

110 This argument is developed in Granatstein and Bothwell, *Pirouette*.

111 Author's discussions with Dr Joel Sokolsky, 16 October 2003.

112 Lieutenant-Colonel Neil James, cited in Horner, *Making the Australian Defence Force*, 59; Palazzo, *The Australian Army*, 316. A detailed account of the Australian evolution into a joint force is found in Horner, *Making the Australian Defence Force*. See also Dennis et al., ed., *Oxford Companion to Australian Military History*, 584.

113 Palazzo, *The Australian Army*, 286–92, 298–302.

114 Ibid., 310–12, 328.

115 Sokolsky cited in Crickard, "A Tale of Two Navies," 138.

116 Ibid., 122; and author's discussions with Mr Louis Delvoie, 7 October 2003.

117 The separatist terrorist group Front de Libération du Québec (FLQ) called for the violent overthrow of government and for Quebec independence. But the FLQ resorted to kidnapping and murder, triggering a government backlash (that included the use of Canadian armed forces) and discrediting the group.

118 Mohawk aboriginals faced a challenge from the Oka municipal government over land rights and illegal smuggling in 1990, triggering a Mohawk-led armed blockade and a call-out of armed forces in response.

119 Glen Barclay, "Australia and North America," in Boyce and Angel, ed., *Independence and Alliance*, 146, 151; Peacock cited in Barclay, *Friends in High Places*, 195; and Hugh Smith, "Defence Policy," in Boyce and Angel, ed., *Independence and Alliance*, 50.

120 Horner, *Making the Australian Defence Force*, 66; and Granatstein, *Canada's Army*, 378.

121 James, "A Brief History of Peacekeeping," 3–18; Londey, *Other People's Wars*, 7, 126–32; and author's correspondence with Mr David Elder, 15 August 2003.

122 Last, "Almost a Legacy," 372; Jordan, Taylor, Jr, and Mazarr, *American National Security*, 437; and James, "A Brief History of Peacekeeping," 10–11.

123 Cohen, *While Canada Slept*, 60.

124 Nelson Michaud and Kim Richard Nossal, "The Conservative Era in Canadian Foreign Policy, 1984–93," in Michaud and Nossal, ed., *Diplomatic Departures*, 13–14.

125 Canada, Department of National Defence, *Challenge and Commitment*; Morton, *Understanding Canadian Defence*, 85; Norrin M. Ripsman, "Big Eyes and Empty Pockets: The Two Phases of Conservative Defence Policy," in Michaud and Nossal, *Diplomatic Departures*, 100–12; Nelson Michaud, "The Making of the 1987 Defence White Paper," in ibid., 272; and Twolan, "Defence Policy Making in Canada."

126 Author's correspondence with Lieutenant-Colonel Terry Loveridge, 22 October 2003.

127 Middlemiss and Sokolsky, *Canadian Defence*, 47; and Palazzo, *The Australian Army*, 332, 327.

128 Evans, *The Role of the Australian Army*; and Horner, *Making the Australian Defence Force*, 55, 226–7.

129 Roggeveen, "Amphibious Warfare in the ADF," 35–7; and Richert, "An Essay on the Vulnerability of Australia's Centers of Gravity to Asymmetric Attack."

130 The rationale is flawed because it is predicated on an unproven direct cause-and-effect linkage between Australian defence acquisitions and regional stability. If anything, Australia's experience in the Second World War, when it

was insufficiently capable of adequately responding to the Japanese threat, points to the contrary. In addition, Australia's most "offensive" strategic strike asset, the F-111 aircraft, had been in the ADF inventory for many years by the time the issue of the replacement of HMAS *Melbourne* or the acquisition of additional amphibious ships were considered, yet without causing any deterioration in regional stability.

131 Sheppard, *Trends in Australian Defence*, 23, 26, 28.

132 Palazzo, *The Australian Army*, 321, 336–42.

133 During this period, an inadequately equipped and prepared infantry company was embarked for possible protection or evacuation operations in Fiji.

134 Gubb, *The Australian Military Response to the Fiji Coup*; Hinge, *Australian Defence Preparedness*, 31–3; and Horner, *Making the Australian Defence Force*, 62, 108, 227.

135 Maloney, "Domestic operations"; and Bland, *Chiefs of Defence*, 192–8.

136 See Australia, Department of Defence, *Defence Report 1989–90*.

137 Author's correspondence with Lieutenant-Colonel Terry Loveridge, 22 October 2003.

138 Maloney, *War without Battles*, 426.

139 Dan Middlemiss, "Canada and Defence Industrial Preparedness: A Return to Basics," in Hunt and Haycock, ed., *Canada's Defence*, 248.

140 Horner, *Making the Australian Defence Force*, 115.

141 Author's correspondence with Dr Ron Haycock, 8 October 2003.

CHAPTER SEVEN

1 Evans, "From Kadesh to Kandahar," 135.

2 Stratfor, "American Empire," downloaded http://www.stratfor.com, 20 April 2003.

3 Throughout most of this period, Australia also contributed ten military officers to the staffs and units of the British forces deployed to the Balkans.

4 Horn and Harris, *Warrior Chiefs*, 12; and correspondence with Colonel Mike Cessford (CF), 12 May 2003.

5 Miller, *Following the Americans to the Persian Gulf*, 21–2; Cooper, Higgott, and Nossal, *Relocating Middle Powers*, 122, 127, 134; Goot and Tiffen, ed., *Australia's Gulf War*.

6 Schlesinger, Jr, *The Disuniting of America*, 70.

7 Bob Howard, "Labor and the United Nations," in Goot and Tiffen, *Australia's Gulf War*, 216; Gareth Evans, "The Case for Australian Participation," in ibid., 9; Miller, *Following the Americans to the Persian Gulf*, 128; and Murray Goot, "The Polls," in Goot and Tiffen, *Australia's Gulf War*, 180–1.

8 For a discussion of the defence-policy aspects of the conflicts from Australia's and Canada's perspective respectively, see Horner, *The Gulf Commitment*; and Maloney and Llambias, *War with Iraq*. See also Crickard, "A Tale of Two Navies," 254–6.

9 Fitzgerald and Hennessy, "An Expedient Reorganization," 28; Cooper, Higgott, and Nossal, *Relocating Middle Powers*, 137; Bland, *Chiefs of Defence*, 200–3; James, "A Brief History of Australian Peacekeeping," 11; Horner, *The Gulf Commitment* and *Making the Australian Defence Force*, 231–7; and Maloney, *War without Battles*, 460.

10 Miller, *Following the Americans to the Persian Gulf*, 156–7.

11 Maloney, "Missed Opportunity."

12 The French Army interpreted its effort in the Gulf War as being insufficiently "lethal," thus warranting subsequent greater emphasis on heavier armoured forces.

13 Maloney, "Missed Opportunity."

14 Delvoie cites a need for 52 supply ships and 220 Hercules "chalks" to deploy the brigade. Author's discussions with Mr Louis Delvoie, 7 October 2003.

15 See Griffiths, ed., *The Canadian Forces and Interoperability*.

16 Blackburn, Cordner, and Swan, "'Not the size of the dog in the fight ...,'" 66.

17 Jockel, *The Canadian Forces*, 25.

18 Nossal, "Seeing Things?"

19 Schindlmayr and Ong, "Attaining 54,000?" 6; and Hinge, *Australian Defence Preparedness*, 39–40.

20 Jockel, *The Canadian Forces*, 16, 38; and Bland, "A sow's ear from a silk purse."

21 One of the most articulate defence critics of this period was Michael O'Connor, a retired naval officer who headed up a private lobby group called the Australian Defence Association.

22 Bland, *Canada's National Defence, Volume I*, 252, 257.

23 John Hillen defines second-generation peacekeeping as being distinguished from first-generation peacekeeping by the more bellicose and complex environment and, usually, the lack of a definitive and reliable peace settlement. See Hillen, *Blue Helmets*, 140–1.

24 See Australian Army, *The Fundamentals of Land Warfare*, 27. In the u.s. military, the term is Military Operations Other Than War.

25 Cohen, *While Canada Slept*, 61; author's correspondence with Dr Ron Haycock, August 2002 and 8 October 2003; and Horner, *Making the Australian Defence Force*, 128, 139.

26 Sheppard, *Trends in Australian Defence*, 109–11.

27 Palazzo, *The Australian Army*, 348; and Sheppard, *Trends in Australian Defence*, 136–7.

28 Author's correspondence with Brendan Sargeant, 20 October 2003, and with Lieutenant-Colonel Terry Loveridge 22 October 2003.

29 Palazzo, *The Australian Army*, 349, 355; and author's correspondence with Lieutenant-Colonel Terry Loveridge, 22 October 2003.

30 Senator Gareth Evans, "Cambodia – The Political Settlement," in Smith, ed., *International Peacekeeping*, 10; Bartu, "'The Fifth Faction'"; and author's correspondence with Dr Ron Haycock, 8 October 2003. Under a Chapter VI mandate, peacekeepers are not authorized to enforce an agreement, only to monitor compliance with it. In many cases, missions mandated under Chapter VI involve deploying unarmed troops or, at most, troops armed for personal protection only. In contrast, Chapter VII of the UN Charter provides warlike mandates under which enforcement of agreements is authorized, with lethal force if need be. The Korean War was conducted under Chapter VII, as was the mission to East Timor in 1999.

31 Dr Tom Axworthy, presentation, 27 February 2003.

32 Evans, *The Role of the Australian Army in a Maritime Concept of Strategy*, 12–15.

33 Discussion with Brigadier W.J.A. Mellor (commander of the Australian force in Somalia), June 2002. See also Breen, *A Little Bit of Hope*; Hillen, *Blue Helmets*, chapter 7; and Ryan, *Australian Army Cooperation with the Land Forces of the United States*, 19.

34 Lieutenant-Colonel Bernd Horn argues that, because of the obsessive focus on the death of a local Somali at the hands of Canadians, the excellent overall performance of the Canadians through most of their tour in Somalia has been ignored. See Horn, *Bastard Sons*.

35 Bercuson, *Significant Incident*, 230; Douglas Bland cited in Wood, ed., *Talking Heads*, 15; and author's correspondence with Dr Ron Haycock, 8 October 2003.

36 Windsor, "Professionalism under Fire," 20; English, *Lament for an Army*, xiii, 3, 64; Rempel, *Chatter Box*, 163; Jockel, *The Canadian Forces*, 29; and Horn and Harris, ed., *Generalship and the Art of the Admiral*, xii.

37 Taylor and Nolan, *Tarnished Brass*, 8–9; Granatstein, *Canada's Army*, 373; Loomis, *The Somalia Affair*, 552; and author's discussions with Dr Joel Sokolsky, 16 October 2003.

38 Australian soldiers in Somalia also confronted serious challenges and there were several incidents where soldiers' frustrations conceivably could have resulted in fiascos similar to those involving the Canadians. More recently, in East Timor, Australian soldiers, like their Canadian counterparts in Somalia, faced allegations of grave misconduct.

39 The different command approaches of company commanders – majors Anthony Blumer and Doug Fraser – reflect these tensions. See Breen, *A Little Bit of Hope*, 153–88. Also, see Australia, Department of Defence Media Release PACC 95/03.

40 That is, the actions of a corporal on today's battlefield can have strategic effects, particularly given the media's pervasiveness.

41 See Patman, "Beyond the 'Mogadishu Line.'"

42 See MacKenzie, *Peacekeeper*; Wood, ed., *The Chance of War*; and Brigadier J.B. Wilson, "Observations on Peacekeeping and Peacemaking in the Former Yugoslavia," in Smith, ed., *International Peacekeeping*, chapter 18.

43 Bland, *Canada's National Defence, Volume I*, 281.

44 Citation in Jockel, *The Canadian Forces*, 32–3; and Canada 21 Council, *Canada 21*, 53.

45 The reliance on coalition-secured points of disembarkation remains the official view at the time of writing, but the acquisition of an amphibious ship has been mooted.

46 Richter, "Strategic Ambitions and Fiscal Realities"; Jockel, *The Canadian Forces*, 44, 57; Bland, *Canada's National Defence, Volume I*, 283–4, 311; and Granatstein, *Canada's Army*, 414.

47 Cited in Rempel, *Counterweights*, 197.

48 See Doran, et. al., *Pacific Partners*, xii–xviii.

49 See Snider and Maloney, "Firefight at the Medak Pocket"; Rempel, *Chatter Box*, 154–5; and Maloney and Llambias, *Chances for Peace*. See also MacKenzie, *Peacekeeper*; and Cohen, *While Canada Slept*, 64.

50 Rempel, *The Chatter Box*, 158–60; Sean Maloney cited in Cohen, *While Canada Slept*, 65; and author's correspondence with Dr Ron Haycock, 8 October 2003.

51 Author's correspondence with Dr Ron Haycock, 8 October 2003; Hillen, *Blue Helmets*, 238–40, 243–4, 250; Off, *The Lion, The Fox and the Eagle*, 165–7, 222; and Sokolsky, *The Americanization of Peacekeeping*, 41.

52 Hillen observes that the United States played a key role in launching complex UN missions because it did not want to be principally responsible for difficult and protracted military operations. But such assertive U.S. diplomatic multilateralism left the UN with inadequate support to carry out such missions effectively.

53 Hillen, *Blue Helmets*, 252–5; Boutros-Ghali, *An Agenda for Peace*; Evans, *Co-operating for Peace*; Canada, *Towards a Rapid Reaction Capability for the United Nations* (Ottawa: Minister of Supply and Services 1995), cited in Sokolsky, *The Americanization of Peacekeeping*, 44; and author's correspondence with Dr Ron Haycock, 8 October 2003.

54 United Nations, "SHIRBRIG Multi-National Standby High Readiness Brigade for United Nations Operations." Canada, along with Austria, Denmark, the Netherlands, Norway, Poland, and Sweden, signed the letter of intent in December 1996. Since then, others have joined, including Argentina, Italy, Portugal, Romania, and Slovenia.

55 Delvoie, "Canada and International Security Operations," 20; and James A. Helis, "Haiti: A Study in Canadian American Security Cooperation in the Western Hemisphere," in Haglund, ed., *Over Here and Over There*, 113–44.

56 Axworthy, "Canada and Human Security," 192–3; and Jockel, *The Canadian Forces*, 5.

57 Rempel, *Chatter Box*, 119; Cohen, *While Canada Slept*, 155; Sokolsky, "The Politics of Defence Decisions at Century's End," in Horn and Harris, ed., *Generalship and the Art of the Admiral*, 358–9; and Joel J. Sokolsky, "Between 'Bully Pulpit' and 'Pulpit Diplomacy': The Axworthy Doctrine, Neo-Wilsonianism and Canada-US Relations," in Haglund, ed., *Over Here and Over There*, 50, 67.

58 Sokolsky, *The Americanization of Peacekeeping*, 51–2, and "Between 'Bully Pulpit' and 'Pulpit Diplomacy,'" 45, 55.

59 Little has been written about JTF2 apart from Pugliese's *Canada's Secret Commandos*, 11, 17, 18, 22–33. See also Jockel, *The Canadian Forces*, 42.

60 Horner, *SAS: Phantoms of the Jungle*; and Horner, *Making the Australian Defence Force*, 20.

61 See Breen, *Giving Peace a Chance*.

62 Sheppard, *Trends in Australian Defence*, 9.

63 Ibid., 14; Horner, *Making the Australian Defence Force*, 129; Palazzo, *The Australian Army*, 346–7; Hinge, *Australian Defence Preparedness*, xvi; and author's correspondence with Dr Ron Haycock, 8 October 2003.

64 Palazzo, *The Australian Army*, 365.

65 Hinge, *Australian Defence Preparedness*, 49; and Palazzo, *The Australian Army*, 360.

66 Horner, *Making the Australian Defence Force*, 93; and Palazzo, *The Australian Army*, 366.

67 The cutbacks were from Canadian $12 billion in 1993–94 to $9.4 billion in 1998–99.

68 David Meren, interview on the Underground Royal Commission, *A Question of Honour: Episode 4 – "The Bungle in the Jungle"* (video); Jett, *Why Peacekeeping Fails*, 11; Sloan, *The Revolution in Military Affairs*, 130–1; Delvoie, "Canada and International Security Operations," 21; Rempel, *Chatter Box*, 163–73; author's correspondence with Lieutenant-Colonel Terry Loveridge, 22 October 2003; and author's correspondence with Dr Ron Haycock, 8 October 2003.

69 Natynczyk, "Coalitions of the Willing"; Jockel, *The Canadian Forces*, 52, 61, and 123; Morton, *Understanding Canadian Defence*, 91; Gaasenbeck, *A Wake-Up Call for Canada*; Middlemiss and Sokolsky, *Canadian Defence*, 220.

70 Maloney and Llambias, *War with Iraq*, 29–30, 40.

71 Jockel, *The Canadian Forces*, 69, 86.

72 This exercise involved 15,000 troops and hundreds of Canadian, U.S., and other allied ships and aircraft.

73 Jane Boulden, "The Americanization of Peacekeeping Revisited: From Blue Helmets to Green," in Haglund, ed., *Over Here and Over There*, 106.

74 While most of the CF-18 combat sorties were focused on the air-to-ground bombing role utilizing precision-guided munitions, Hornet crews did fly 120 of their total 678 sorties in the air-to-air-combat patrol role, armed with AIM-9M Sidewinder infra-red guided missiles and AIM-7 Sparrow radar-guided missiles.

75 Rempel, *The Chatter Box*, 99, 106, 110–11.

76 Clark, *Waging Modern War*; Kagan, *Of Paradise and Power*, 50–1; Rempel, *Counterweights*, 6; Stairs, "Canada in the 1990s," 43; and author's correspondence with Lieutenant-Colonel Terry Loveridge, 22 October 2003.

77 Cosgrove cited in Hinge, *Australian Defence Preparedness*, 297; and Palazzo, *The Australian Army*, 367.

78 Breen, *Mission Accomplished*; Ryan, *Primary Responsibilities and Primary Risks*; Blaxland, *Information Era Manoeuvre*; and Horner, *Making the Australian Defence Force*, 157. "Collateral damage" is the military term referring to damage to people/sites/objects that were not part of the intended target but that were in close proximity to the target and were affected by the blast effect. It is generally taken to mean civilian casualties.

79 Hinge, *Australian Defence Preparedness*, 302.

80 See Smith and Dee, *Peacekeeping in East Timor*.

81 See Smith, *A Handmaiden's Tale*.

82 As a graduate of the last class of RMC Duntroon that did not experience tri-service integration at ADFA, I have personal knowledge of colleagues from even one year below (with experience of at least one year with the other services at ADFA) who have been able to resolve staff and procedural problems (which appeared insurmountable to me) quickly and effortlessly, owing to the well-established friendly and respectful relationships they had established at ADFA. Such benefits are rarely considered by high-level academic critiques of ADFA, but, in my opinion, they make the investment in ADFA invaluable.

83 Caligari, *The Army's Capacity to Defend Australia Offshore*, 21.

84 In thinking of amphibious operations, the reader may imagine an Iwo Jima or Guadalcanal scenario. This is not what has been envisaged by the ADF,

however, nor is it intended here. Arguably, not since the Korean War has an allied force crossed a "hot" beach where an enemy has prepared to meet it. Today, with greater situational awareness (through superior intelligence), improved technology (including helicopters), and more detailed planning, amphibious operations rarely even cross a beach, and when they do, prior intelligence and planning invariably facilitates surprise and the crossing of an undefended beach or coastal shore by air and sea.

85 Leahy, "A Land Force for the Future," 21, 25; and Bostok, "Expeditionary Objectives," 29, 32. See Australian Army, Future Land Warfare Branch, "Army Vanguard Concept"; and Ryan, *Australian Army Cooperation with the Land Forces of the United States*, 9. Ryan refers to the American-British-Canadian-Australian Armies Program, *Coalition Operations Handbook* (Arlington, Va.: Primary Standardization Office 1999).

86 Leahy, "A Land Force for the Future," 23.

87 Canada, Department of National Defence, *The Canadian Army Reading List*; and Donald E. Graves, "Introduction: The Central Military Act," in Graves, ed., *Fighting For Canada*, 16.

88 Nordick, "Fighting in Built up Areas" and "Warfighting." See also Semianiw, "Train for War and Peace," 70–1.

89 Author's correspondence with Dr Ron Haycock, 8 October 2003.

90 Hobson, "Canada – Readiness at a price."

91 Ankersen, "'Too Many Houseboats,'" 66.

92 Jockel, *The Canadian Forces*, 43–4; Canada, Department of National Defence, "Operations: Canadian Forces Joint Operations Group"; and Garnett, "The Evolution of the Canadian Approach to Joint and Combined Operations."

93 Haglund, "'Are We the Isolationists?'" 5.

94 Capling and Nossal, "The Limits of Like-Mindedness," in MacMillan and McKenzie, ed., *Parties Long Estranged*, 244–5. See also Cooper, *In Between Countries*; and Capling, *Australia and the Global Trade System*, 118–45.

95 Nye, Jr, *The Paradox of American Power*, 140, 158.

CHAPTER EIGHT

1 Evans, "From Kadesh to Kandahar," 136.

2 Blainey, "After Iraq, the Road from Baghdad," 27

3 See Peters, *Beyond Terror*.

4 Stratfor, "American Empire," downloaded from http://www.stratfor.com, 20 April 2003.

5 Leahy, "A Land Force for the Future," 24.

6 These issues were addressed by the Honourable Denis Coderre, minister of citizenship and immigration, in "National Security, Immigration and Our American Neighbours Post 9/11."

7 Stephen Clarkson, "Uncle Sam and Canada after September 11th," in Griffiths, ed., *The Canadian Forces and Interoperability*, 77.

8 Canada, Department of Foreign Affairs and Trade, *A Dialogue on Foreign Policy*, 7–8; and Handelman, "All Together Now."

9 Scobell, *Strategic Effects of the Conflict with Iraq.*

10 See, for instance, Australian Strategic Policy Institute, *Beyond Bali*, 3.

11 Pugliese, *Canada's Secret Commandos*; and Maloney, "Domestic Operations: The Canadian Approach."

12 Nye, Jr, *The Paradox of American Power*, 198; and Fortmann and Haglund, "Canada and the Issue of Homeland Security."

13 Pugliese, *Canada's Secret Commandos*, 117–18; Cohen, *While Canada Slept*, 57; and Krott, "Bolt Actions Speak Louder Than Words."

14 Australian Strategic Policy Institute, *Beyond Bali*, 5.

15 Cohen, *While Canada Slept*, 22, 26–7, 47, 161; Henault, *A Time for Transformation*, iii, 31.

16 Hill, *Australia's National Security.*

17 Sargeant, "Draft Discussion Paper: United States Defense Strategy." Copy in possession of author. Used with permission.

18 See Australia, Department of Foreign Affairs and Trade, *Advancing the National Interest.*

19 Sargeant, "Draft Discussion Paper: United States Defense Strategy."

20 Tasseron, "Facts and Invariants," 22.

21 Stratfor, "Australia's Growing Importance to U.S. Strategic Plans."

22 Author's discussions with Mr Daniel Bon, assistant deputy minister for policy in the Canadian Department of National Defence, 30 October 2002.

23 Author's discussions with Dr Joel Sokolsky, 16 October 2003; Sokolsky, *The Americanization of Peacekeeping*, 38–9; and Harvey, presentation.

24 Fisher, "How Australia's Plucky Military Does More with Less."

25 Pellerin, "Australia's Military Does More with Less"; and Krauss, "Canadian Envisions New Role for Nation."

26 Canada, Department of Foreign Affairs and Trade, *A Dialogue on Foreign Policy*, 5–6.

27 Author's discussions with Dr Joel J. Sokolsky, 5 March 2003.

28 Kupchan, *The End of the American Era*, 117–18, 131.

29 Associated Press, "Australia Put Troops into Iraq before War."

30 The Canadian Forces flew more than 5,700 hours, including some 2,700 combat-air patrols and 56 bombing sorties in the Gulf War in 1991.

In Kosovo in 1999, CF-18s flew 678 combat sorties (air-to-ground bombing and combat-air patrol), for a total of more than 2,500 flying hours.

31 Australian FA-18s flew 350 combat sorties over Iraq and dropped 122 precision-guided weapons.

32 Harris, "Historic aerial re-supply," 3.

33 Sixty air-traffic controllers were sent to Baghdad International Airport; sixteen defence specialists were committed in support of the efforts to locate and destroy weapons of mass destruction; a seventy-five-person security detachment deployed to Baghdad to protect the Australian Representative Mission; three ADF representatives were committed to work with the Office of Reconstruction and Humanitarian Assistance; and two C-130 Hercules aircraft, two PC-3 Orion aircraft, and the frigate HMAS *Sydney* also remained on station in support of the operation.

34 Molan, "Op Falconer – War against Iraq."

35 Steyn, "French Can Sneer but 'Les Anglo-Saxons' World's Best Hope"; Wattie, "Ottawa Offered to Join Iraq War"; Anderson et. al., *Coalition of the Willing or Coalition of the Coerced*; Cooper and Morton, "Chrétien Has Put Party Ahead of Country"; Thorsell, "Canada Can No Longer Ignore the World's Siren Call"; and Lunman, "Canadians 'Dead Split' on Supporting War, Poll Reports"; Douglas L. Bland, "Military Interoperability," in Griffiths, ed., *The Canadian Forces and Interoperability*, 61; and Andrew Cohen cited in Geddes, "Smart Guy, eh?"

36 A survey conducted on 1–3 April 2003 by CTV/*Globe and Mail* found only 29 per cent of those surveyed in Quebec expressing support for the U.S.-led war in Iraq, compared to 54 per cent in the rest of Canada.

37 Journalist Mark Steyn claims that TotalFinalElf's largest shareholder is a subsidiary of Power Corp. He argues that Canada refused to join the war to liberate Iraq because of Chrétien's family connections with Montreal's Power Corp chief executives Paul Desarais, Jr and André Desmarais (Chrétien's son-in-law). See Steyn, "French Can Sneer but 'Les Anglo-Saxons' World's Best Hope."

38 See Kennedy, "The Perils of Empire."

39 Brigadier (ret.) Jim Wallace argues that, since war "remains diplomacy by other means," Australia's contribution, if it was to be seen as significant, should have been in the order of 7,000 servicemen and women. See Wallace, "Iraq Lesson Can Help Correct Defence Policy."

40 The Honourable Paul Martin, "Transcript: Canada's Role in a Complex World."

41 Margaret MacMillan cited in Geddes, "Smart Guy, eh?"

42 See, for instance, Jean-Marc Léger, "More Canadians Believe Iraq War Justified: Poll." This poll suggested an increase in the number of Canadians who felt the war was justified from 33 per cent to 46 per cent in March 2003.

43 Blainey, "After Iraq, the Road from Baghdad," 27.

44 Australia, Department of Defence, *Future Warfighting Concept*, 2–3, 14.

45 Michael Evans, "General Monash's Orchestra Reaffirming Combined Arms Warfare," in Evans and Ryan, ed., *From Breitenfeld to Baghdad*, 24–5.

46 Evans, "From Kadesh to Kandahar," 140, 143, 146.

47 Geddes, "In Harm's Way."

48 General Henault cited in Rempel, ed., "Annual Report of the Chief of Defence Staff, 2002–2003," 19.

49 Canadian Alliance, *The New North Strong and Free*, 34; Morton, *Understanding Canadian Defence*, 211; and Australian Minister for Defence Media Mail List, "Operation Anode."

50 Graham, *Canada's International Policy Statement: A Role of Pride and Influence in the World – Defence*; and Australian Army, "The Hardened Networked Army."

51 Leahy, "A Land Force for the Future," 20.

OVERVIEW AND PROSPECTS

1 McKercher and Aronsen makes the point that the three components of the triangle did not always have common external interests, or even work harmoniously together to pursue their separate interests. See McKercher and Aronsen, ed., *The North American Triangle in a Changing World*, 3.

2 Australia Strategic Policy Institute, *Beyond Bali*, 4, 10.

3 See Australian Army, *The Fundamentals of Land Warfare*, 51–2.

4 Author's correspondence with Dr Ron Haycock, 8 October 2003.

5 Michael Ignatieff cited in Geddes, "Smart Guy, eh?"

6 This argument is made in some detail throughout Maloney's *Canada and UN Peacekeeping*.

7 Author's discussions, with Dr Joel Sokolsky, March 2002.

8 Cohen, *While Canada Slept*, 29.

9 In informal discussion with serving Canadian officers, numerous people have suggested that the ABCA relationship has become much more important to the Canadian Army than it was in the Cold War years, when NATO dominated Canada's defence thinking.

10 Stacey, *Canada and the Age of Conflict, Volume 2*, 299.

11 Last, "Almost a Legacy," in Horn, ed., *Forging a Nation*, 383; and Middlemiss and Sokolsky, *Canadian Defence*, 173–4.

12 Peters, "Club Dues?" 161–3. See also Gray, *Canadians in a Dangerous World*, 26, but the point he makes applies to Australia.

13 Crickard, "A Tale of Two Navies," 282.

14 Cheeseman, *Canada's Post-Cold War Military Blues*, 16; and Walker, "Poles Apart."

15 Ann Denholm Crosby, "Defining the Debate: A Response to Danford Middle-miss and Denis Stairs," in Griffiths, ed., *The Canadian Forces and Interoperability*, 96; Lieutenant-Commander Brent Hobson, "Interoperability and the Canadian Navy: A Classic Example of Hobson's Choice," in ibid., 124; Cohen, *While Canada Slept*, 173; Elliott, "The Aussie Rules of Foreign Policy"; and Gaasenbeck, *A Wake-Up Call for Canada*, 2, 20.

16 Rempel, *Counterweights*, 207.

17 Author's discussions with Brigadier Gary Bornholt, 1 May 2003, and Dr Charles Pentland, 24 April 2003.

18 Richard H. Gimblett, "Canada-US Interoperability: Towards a Home Port Division of the United States Navy," in Griffiths, ed., *The Canadian Forces and Interoperability*, 106.

19 David Mutimer, "(Inter)Operating within Niches of Security: A Response to Middlemiss and Stairs," in ibid.,169.

20 I am indebted to Lieutenant-Colonel Graeme Sligo for the suggestion of this likely angle of criticism.

21 Joel J. Sokolsky, "Glued to Its Seat: Canada, Peacekeeping and the Western Alliance in the Post-Cold War Era," in Pentland, ed., *The Transatlantic Link in Evolution*, 38.

22 Bell, "Normative Shift." Also, author's correspondence with Dr Ron Haycock, 8 October 2003.

23 Author's discussions with Dr Ron Haycock, August 2002, and Dr Joel Sokolsky, 16 October 2003.

24 Cohen, *While Canada Slept*, 200.

25 Ryan, *Australian Army Cooperation with the Land Forces of the United States*, vi, and 9.

26 Nye, Jr, *The Paradox of American Power*, xv; author's correspondence with Dr Ron Haycock, 8 October 2003, and Dr Joel Sokolsky, 16 October 2003; Kagan, *Of Paradise and Power*, 39; Biddle, "Are Allies Worth It?"; and Canada, Department of Foreign Affairs and Trade, *A Dialogue on Foreign Policy*, 8–9.

27 Author's correspondence with Dr Ron Haycock, 8 October 2003.

28 Kagan, *Of Paradise and Power*, 40–1; Crickard, "A Tale of Two Navies," 284; and Sargeant, "Draft Discussion Paper: United States Defense Strategy," para. 11.

29 Andrew F. Cooper, "Keeping in Touch: Patterns of Networking in the Canadian-Australian Diplomatic Relationship," in MacMillan and McKenzie, ed., *Parties Long Estranged*, 260, in MacMillan and McKenzie, ed., *Parties Long Estranged*, 264.

30 MacMillan and McKenzie, "Conclusion," in MacMillan and McKenzie, ed., *Parties Long Estranged*, 269.

31 Anne N. Forman, "Foreword," in Charters et al., ed., *Military History and the Military Profession*, x.

32 I am indebted to Dr Joel Sokolsky for helping to crystalize the thoughts expressed in this paragraph.

33 Author's correspondence with Brendan Sargeant, 20 October 2003.

APPENDIX SEVEN

1 Prominent among these are (in reverse chronological order): MacMillan and McKenzie, ed., *Parties Long Estranged*; Cardinal and Headon, ed., *Shaping Nations*; Cooper, *In Between Countries*; Holland, Morton, and Caligan, ed., *Federalism and the Environment*; Donaghy, *Parallel Paths*; Nossal, *Rain Dancing*; Miller, *Following the Americans to the Persian Gulf*; Cooper, Higgott, and Nossal, *Relocating Middle Powers*; Alexander and Galligan, ed., *Comparative Political Studies*; Hodgson et al., ed., *Federalism in Canada and Australia*; Hawkins, *Critical Years in Immigration*; McDougal and Whitlock, ed., *Australian/Canadian Literature in English*; Dyck, ed., *Indigenous Peoples and the Nation State*; Mathews, ed., *Public Policies in Two Federal Countries* (focusing on constitutional, economic, and cultural comparisons); Hodgins et al., ed., *Federalism in Canada and Australia*; Fox, *The Politics of Attraction*; Albinski, *Canadian and Australian Politics in Comparative Perspective*; Birch, *Federalism, Finance and Social Legislation in Canada, Australia, and the United States*; and the journal *Australian-Canadian Studies*.

2 MacMillan and McKenzie, "Introduction," in MacMillan and McKenzie, ed., *Parties Long Estranged*, 5.

3 Cooper, *In Between Countries*, ix.

4 Simpson, "Australia: Canada's secret alter ego."

5 Some contend that invasion by the Japanese in 1942 was unlikely. See, for instance, Frei, *Japan's Southward Advance*.

6 Vol. 5, no. 1 (May 1987).

7 Vol. 2, no. 1 (May 1984).

8 Vol. 13, no. 1 (1984).

9 Durham, N.C.: Duke University, Commonwealth-Studies Center, 1967.

10 Manchester, U.K.: Manchester University Press 1988.

11 Manchester, U.K.: Manchester University Press 1988.

12 London: Oxford University Press and the Royal Institute of International Affairs 1952.

13 Canberra: Australian Defence Studies Centre 2000.

14 Montreal and Kingston: McGill-Queen's University Press 2002.

15 Canberra: University College, University of New South Wales, 1997.
16 MA thesis, Dalhousie University, Halifax, 1993.

APPENDIX EIGHT

1 Adam Chapnick argues that Canada's status as a middle power is a myth. If he is correct, then his conclusions apply equally to Australia. Nevertheless, the term "middle power" captures the similar sense of identity in Australian and Canadian foreign-policy consciousness and so is a valid term for the purposes of this study. See Chapnick, "The Canadian Middle Power Myth." For a more detailed consideration of the debate, see Cooper, Higgott, and Nossal, *Relocating Middle Powers*, 16–19, who argue that there are four general approaches to the definition of middle powers: by position in the international hierarchy; by geography; in terms of the normative (like-mindedness) view of middle powers; and in terms of behaviour (including the tendency to embrace notions of "good international citizenship" to guide diplomacy). Capling, in *Australia and the Global Trade System*, 5, eschews the term "middle power," opting instead to describe Australia as a small power in the multilateral trade system, but her perspective overlooks the military dimension of middle-power status. Indeed, Australian Foreign Minister Alexander Downer, in a speech to the Australia National Press Club, adamantly asserted that Australia is "not a middling nation, but a considerable power," See Downer, "The Myth of 'Little' Australia."
2 Leahy, "A Land Force for the Future," 20. Reflecting a similar mindset, the Canadian chief of land staff in 2002, Lieutenant-General Mike Jeffery, planned for a transformation of the Canadian Army into a "rapidly deployable, medium-weight, flexible force." The plan impressed the defence minister, John McCallum, who threw his support to the army. Cited in Hobson, "Canada – Readiness at a price."
3 Martin van Creveld cogently argues that, in the Second World War at least, American divisions acted "like some huge meat-grinding machines that processed men on their way from the replacement system in the rear to becoming casualties at the front." See *Fighting Power*, 47.
4 Britain is a veto-wielding member of the UN Security Council and is the most important ally of the United States in NATO and beyond. Australians do not have pretensions to such a significant place in U.S. security relationships, but they have fought alongside American troops even when Canada and Britain have not. Australia contributed forces alongside U.S. troops in the First and Second World Wars, the occupation of Japan, the Korean War, the Vietnam War, the Gulf War (90–91), Somalia, East Timor, Afghanistan, and Iraq.

5 While Canada did not contribute forces to the war in Iraq, its troops have operated alongside U.S. troops in the First and Second World Wars, in Europe through NATO, and in the Korean War, Somalia, Haiti, Bosnia, Kosovo, East Timor, and Afghanistan. They also acted as the U.S. proxy in the Suez Crisis of 1956 and contributed in Indochina through the ICSC.

6 Berger, *The Sense of Power*, 64; and Beavis, "Canada and Imperial Defence," 42.

7 The significance of NATO to Canadian defence- and foreign-policy makers is discussed in Haglund, *The North Atlantic Triangle Revisited*; and Pentland, ed., *The Transatlantic Link in Evolution*.

8 The term "New World" originates in American political discourse, but it has wider applicability given the North American and Australasian (Australia and New Zealand) similarities.

9 Alfred van Staden, "The Security Implications of 11 September 2001: A Dutch Perspective," in Pentland, ed., *The Transatlantic Link in Evolution*, 30–1.

10 Author's discussions with Colonel Mike Cessford (CF), 28 May 2003.

11 Sokolsky, "Glued to Its Seat," in Pentland, ed., *The Transatlantic Link in Evolution*, 51.

12 Cooper, *In Between Countries*, 13.

13 New Zealand's ties with the United States through ANZUS were frozen in 1986 when the New Zealand government objected to nuclear warships entering its ports. In the late 1990s New Zealand opted to abandon its fighter-aircraft capability when it retired its A4 Skyhawks, despite "bargain basement" U.S.offers of F-16 replacement aircraft. In addition, in 2003 New Zealand was outspoken in its opposition to the U.S.-led war in Iraq.

14 For an excellent starting point in New Zealand's military history, see McGibbon, ed., *Oxford Companion to New Zealand Military History*. See also Madsen, "Comparing Australian and New Zealand Defence and Foreign Policy since 1985."

15 United Empire Loyalists moved to Canada during and after the American War of Independence, almost a century before Canada became a nation.

16 Preston and Wards, "Military and Defence Development in Canada, Australia and New Zealand," 4; and Richard Broome, "The Struggle for Australia: Aboriginal-European Warfare, 1770–1930," in McKernan and Browne, ed., *Australia: Two Centuries of War and Peace*. See also Windschuttle, *The Fabrication of Aboriginal History*, which offers a strong critique of the revisionist historians in Australia who, according to Windschuttle, have exaggerated the extent and fabricated evidence of aboriginal killings by colonists.

17 This case is argued in Liska, *Career of Empire*.

18 Martin, "Canada's Military Needs Big Boost"; and Maloney, "The Canadian Tao of Conflict," in Horn, ed., *Forging a Nation*, 275.

19 In Canada's case, this is effectively argued in Peters, "Club Dues?"

20 Populations in 2000: United States – 274 million; United Kingdom – 58.7 million; Canada – 30.6 million; Australia – 18.5 million; New Zealand – 3.8 million.

21 Delvoie, "The Commonwealth in Canadian Foreign Policy," 138, 142.

22 K.A. MacKirdy, "Canadian and Australian Self-interest, the American Fact, and the Development of the Commonwealth Idea," in Dyck and Krosby, ed., *Empire and Nations*, 116.

23 Millar, *Australia in Peace and War*, 104; and MacMillan and McKenzie, "Part 1: Decolonization and Nation Building," in MacMillan and McKenzie, ed., *Parties Long Estranged*, 11.

24 John Atchison, "Immigration in Two Federations," in Hodgins et. al., *Federalism in Canada & Australia*, 201; and Nossal, *Rain Dancing*, 259–62.

25 More than one-fifth of Canada's population is French-speaking. Nearly one-fifth of Australia's population also do not use English as their first language, but these people are not geographically concentrated and are not predominantly from one language group.

26 Gross Domestic Product per capita: Canada – $U.S.22,370; Australia – $U.S.20,340. They share second place on the human-development index. See *The Economist, Pocket World in Figures, 2003 Edition*, 26–8.

27 Andrew F. Cooper, "Keeping in Touch: Patterns of Networking in the Canadian-Australian Diplomatic Relationship," in MacMillan and McKenzie, ed., *Parties Long Estranged*, 260.

28 Middlemiss and Sokolsky, *Canadian Defence*, 9.

29 Both Canada and Australia are, strictly speaking, "dominions" of the "crown," but the term has fallen out of use with the decline in British prominence, particularly following the 1960s. While, technically, the national titles are the Dominion of Canada and the Commonwealth of Australia, the term "dominions" is used here to refer to them collectively when it is historically accurate and appropriate to do so.

30 Cooper, "Keeping in Touch."

31 Cooper, Higgott, and Nossal, *Relocating Middle Powers*, 11; and Cooper, "Keeping in Touch," 258.

32 See Peter H. Russell, "Colonization of Indigenous Peoples: The Movement toward New Relationships," in MacMillan and McKenzie, ed., *Parties Long Estranged*, 62–95. For a consideration of the way Canadian aboriginals have been perceived in Canadian society, see Haycock, *The Image of the Indian*.

33 Kim R. Nossal, correspondence with author, 5 December 2002. See also Elliott, *Irish Immigrants in the Canadas*. Elliott argues that the Irish experience in the

Americas was not as dominated by Irish Catholic nationalists as is popularly believed. Instead, in Canada in particular, the experience of the Irish was largely rural and a significant proportion of the Irish population was Loyalist and Protestant.

34 The two other obvious Westminster parliamentary comparisons, Britain and New Zealand, are unitary states. A key difference between the two federations is that, while Canadian senators are appointed by the government, Senate members in Australia are elected on a state basis, with each state having seven senators (except Tasmania and the ACT, which have two each). In addition, voting in Australia is compulsory and, in the Senate, is based on a proportional rather than a first-past-the-post system, while in the House of Representatives voting is based on the number count, including preferences. Canadian senators are appointed by the governor-in-council on the recommendation of the prime minister. The highly personalized (and thus patronage-driven) nature of the Canadian Senate is in marked distinction to Australia's more egalitarian equivalent.

35 Millar, *Australia in Peace and War*, 105–6; Albinksi, *Canadian and Australian Politics in Comparative Perspective*, 27; author's correspondence with Lieutenant-Colonel Casey Haskins, 14 October 2003; MacMillan and McKenzie, "Introduction," in McKenzie and MacMillan, ed., *Parties Long Estranged*, 7; and Adams, *Fire and Ice*, 5.

36 In particular, while the original constitution of Canada provided for greater central control than Australia's constitution did, Canada's provinces have been more assertive vis-à-vis the federal government than their Australian equivalents. Canada and Australia had a similar centralizing experience during the Second World War, but, in the case of Canada, Ontario and Quebec reasserted themselves after 1945 in a way that the Australian states never did.

37 Hodgins et. al., "Dynamic Federalism in Canada and Australia: Continuity and Change," in Hodgins, et. al., *Federalism in Canada & Australia: Historical Perspectives*, 19–51; and Cooper, *In Between Countries*, 21.

38 Capling, *Australia and the Global Trade System*, 1, 7; and MacMillan and MacKenzie, "Rivals, Allies and Models," in MacMillan and MacKenzie, ed., *Parties Long Estranged*, 97–8.

39 Privy Council Office, "Survey of Relations between Canada and the United States"; Ramsey, "More Bloodlust Than a Real War."

40 Mead, *Special Providence*, 115.

41 Reflecting the depth of the relationship, Australia and Canada have agreed to a range of bilateral treaties dating back to 1905. See http://www.ahc-ottawa.org/relations/, downloaded 21 May 2002.

42 An Australia-Japan business Co-operation Committee was inaugurated in 1963 which contributed to the establishment of PBEC, involving businessmen of Japan, Australia, the United States, Canada, and New Zealand. Millar, *Australia in Peace and War*, 274.

43 Cooper, Higgott, and Nossal, *Relocating Middle Powers*, 83–115; http://www.cscap.org and http://www.apecsec.org.sg/, downloaded 3 December 2002; and Cooper, "Keeping in Touch," 259.

44 This issue is discussed in Kupchan, *The End of the American Era*, 51–5. Kupchan cites Kennedy, *Preparing for the Twenty-First Century* (New York: Random House 1993), and Robert Kaplan, *The Coming Anarchy* (New York: Random House 2000).

45 New Zealand is ranked ninth. Countries ranked second to sixth are Scandinavian countries and the seventh is Holland. See *The Economist, Pocket World in Figures 2003 Edition*, 91.

46 Dewitt, "Directions in Canada's International Security Policy," 170, 182.

47 Cousineau, "Canadian Studies: Why Do We Promote It?" 133.

48 Cheeseman, *Canada's Post Cold-War Military Blues*, 18.

49 Maloney, "The Canadian Tao of Conflict," 282.

50 Canada, Department of National Defence, *Shaping the Future of Canadian Defence*.

51 Major-General H. Cameron Ross and Nigel R. Thalakada, "Interoperability Policy and Sovereignty: A Reaction to the 'Canadian Forces and the Doctrine of Interoperability,'" in Griffiths, ed., *The Canadian Forces and Interoperability*, 196; and Douglas L. Bland, "Military Interoperability: As Canadian as a Beaver," in ibid., 51, 57.

52 New Zealand gained observer status through Australia's membership.

53 See Johansen, *The ABCA Program*. The glossary in Johansen's monograph defines TEAL as "Quadripartite standardisation discussions at Vice/Deputy Chief of Staff or equivalent level." The term apparently originates from the period prior to Australian accession to the agreement, when the ABC organization was trilateral. It seems to derive from "Trilateral Exchange and Liaison" or "Tactics, Equipment and Logistics" but is not in common usage today except as the noun "TEAL." See also Sloan, "ABCA – the Next 20 Years," 52; and Groom, "ABCA: The American-British-Canadian-Australian Standardisation Programme."

54 Major-General Bill Leach, "ABCA and the Future Battlefield: A Canadian Perspective," in Malik, ed., *The Future Battlefield*.

55 Sloan, "ABCA – the Next 20 Years," 53.

56 This remark is based on the author's observation of ABCA exercises such as CID BOREALIS in Kingston, Canada, in 2002. See also Blaxland, *Signals Swift and Sure*, 153–6.

57 See Richelson and Ball, *The Ties That Bind*; Middlemiss & Sokolsky, *Canadian Defence*, 18; and Skaarup, "An Intelligence Advantage."

58 Ball and Horner, *Breaking the Codes*, 2.

59 Bland, ed., *Canada's National Defence: Volume I*, 155; Barclay, *Friends in High Places*, 172; and Federation of Atomic Scientists, "Strategic Air Defence, NORAD," downloaded from http://www.fas.org/nuke/guide/usa/airdef/norad-chron.htm, 9 September 2003.

60 McLin, *Canada's Changing Defense Policy*, 4–6. McLin's views are echoed in Joel J. Sokolsky, "The Politics of Defence Decisions at Century's End," in Horn and Harris, ed., *Generalship and the Art of the Admiral*, 341–59.

61 Although Canada includes ten provinces and three territories, the country has six geographic regions – the eastern Maritime Provinces, Quebec, Ontario, the prairie provinces of the west, British Columbia, and the northern territories north of 60 degrees. Australia arguably has three "regions" – desert, semi-desert, and fertile. In addition, the landscape has varied, distinctive characteristics, including tropical monsoonal in the north and Mediterranean-type climate in parts of the south, where much of the wine industry is based.

62 W. Harriet Critchley, "The Arctic," in Hunt and Haycock, ed., *Canada's Defence*, 198; and Grimshaw, "On Guard," chapter 4.

63 For instance, Australia has a population density of 2 people per square kilometre (sq. km.) and Canada's ratio is 3 per sq. km. In comparison, it is 107 per sq. km. in France, 30 per sq. km. in the United States, 243 per sq. km. in Britain, and 14 per sq. km. in New Zealand. *The Economist, Pocket World in Figures, 2003 Edition*, 106, 120, 140, 174, 220, 222.

64 Hiller, "Western Separatism in Australia and Canada," and Taylor, "Air Canada's Choice."

65 See http://www.rangers.forces.gc.ca/, downloaded 5 March 2003.

66 This point is well argued in Canada's case by Haycock in "The Labours of Athena and the Muses." While Australia operated at the strategic level during the East Timor crisis, few would describe this as a "comfortable" experience. Still, Australia has developed a significant strategic studies "industry" in recent years. This includes the Australian National University's Strategic and Defence Studies Centre, the Australian Defence Force Academy's Australian Defence Studies Centre, the service warfare studies centres such as LWSC and the Aerospace Power Studies Centre, and, more recently, the Australian Strategic Policy Institute. Canada has also benefited from the Department of National Defence-sponsored Security and Defence Forum, which includes thirteen universities across Canada, including the Queen's University Centre for International Relations. Other contributing organizations include the Ottawa-based Canadian Institute of International Affairs and the Canadian Institute for Strategic Studies in Toronto.

67 Council for Canadian Security in the 21st Century, *The People's Defence Review*, 11.

68 Australian dead buried in foreign fields number approximately 90,000.

69 U.S. figures cited in Kupchan, *The End of the American Empire*, 29. A total of 519 Australians were killed in action in Vietnam and 339 in Korea; 309 Canadians were killed in action in Korea. See Dennis et. al., ed., *Oxford Companion to Australian Military History*, 336, 620; and Wood, *Strange Battleground*, 257.

70 Canada maintains nine regular-force infantry battalions and a special-forces unit. Australia maintains only five regular infantry battalions. In addition, Australia maintains a Special Operations Command that includes the battalion-sized Special Air Service Regiment, as well as one regular commando battalion, a reserve commando battalion, and a critical-incident response unit.

71 Australia maintains a three-rifle-company airborne battalion. Canada's three-rifle company battalion was disbanded in 1995 but it has maintained the capability in dispersed company-level units.

72 Author's discussions with Lieutenant-Colonel Mick Brennan, Australian liaison officer to U.S. Communications Electronics Command, 1 May 2003.

73 Australia and Canada worked closely together during their acquisition of their FA-18 aircraft in the 1980s. Hinge, *Australian Defence Preparedness*, 286.

74 Submarines: Canada (CA) – 4, Australia (AS) – 6; destroyers: CA – 4, AS – nil; frigates: CA – 12, AS – 11; patrol/coastal combatants: CA – 12, AS – 20; major support vessels: CA – 2, AS – 2; helicopters: CA – 29 (Sea King), AS – 7 Sea Kings and 16 Sea Hawks. See IISS *Military Balance 200/2003*.

75 Crickard, "A Tale of Two Navies," 262.

76 That is, shipping (including helicopters, landing craft, and personnel) capable of deploying a force across unprepared shorelines or rudimentary coastal facilities. Canada had two infantry landing ships in the RCN during the Second World War. The Canadian Navy plans to acquire two Joint Support Ships to support naval ships, sealift, a joint force headquarters, and forces ashore. Interest is also being shown in acquiring a dedicated amphibious ship in the next few years.

77 Cohen, *While Canada Slept*, 35.

78 Ignatieff, *Blood and Belonging*, 110.

79 Albinski, *Canadian and Australian Politics in Comparative Perspective*, 19, 30; Simpson, *Faultlines*; Dickinson and Young, ed., *A Short History of Quebec*; and Lester, *The Black Book of English Canada*, 91.

80 The British conquest of New France between 1759 and 1763 was a defining event for Canada. Occasional rebellions occurred following Britain's

conquest. In 1838, for instance, one rebellion was put down after a week and fifty-eight rebels were exiled to Australia, a group that thus formed one of the earliest links between the two nascent nations.

81 For instance, the leader of the First World War anti-conscription movement in Australia was the Irish Catholic archbishop of Melbourne, Daniel Mannix. Another example was the reluctance of the Irish-Catholic-influenced Labor Party, when the Defence Act was being framed between 1901 and 1903, to contemplate the sending of forces overseas. While the 1933 census showed that Australia's population was remarkably homogenous (with 99 per cent from the British Isles), 10 per cent were of Irish origin and many others also had convict ancestry.

82 In Australia, the political spectrum is more socio-economically oriented, with the Labor Party being strongly nationalistic – a result of a significant Irish element in its ranks – and traditionally associated with socialism, the "working class," and the union movement. In Canada the left-right spectrum is less marked, with major parties tending to more centrist policies, influenced by the divergent regional cultural orientations of English and French Canada. The differences of other Canadian provinces are also more pronounced than those between Australia's more homogenous states.

83 Unlike in French Catholic Canada, the Irish Catholic experience in Australia has never been about internal national unity. Western Australia considered splitting from the Australia federation in 1933, but a referendum on this question, fuelled by a sense of western Australian economic disadvantage and exploitation by the federal government, was defeated. Western Canada experienced a slight surge in separatist sentiment in the early 1980s for similar economic reasons, and such sentiments were echoed two decades later.

84 Major David Last, "Almost a Legacy: Canada's Contribution to Peacekeeping," in Horn, ed., *Forging a Nation*, 374; McKenzie, "New Best Friend"; Mansergh, *Survey of British Commonwealth Affairs*, 137; Struthers, "War and Social Policy in Australia and Canada"; Hiller, "Western Separatism"; Canadian Press, "Klein Ready to Consider Firewall around Alberta"; and Millar, *Australia in Peace and War*, 177.

85 Bland, *Canada's National Defence: Volume I*, 176.

86 McKenzie, "New Best Friend."

87 "Remembering Our Military." Ottawa *Citizen*, 6 October 2003, downloaded from http://www.canada.com.

88 Cited in LaFeber, *The American Age*, 639.

89 85.1 per cent of Canadian exports (compared with only 9.9 per cent of Australian exports) go to the United States and 73.7 per cent of

Canadian imports (compared with 21 per cent of Australia's imports) come from the United States.

90 Albinksi, *Canadian and Australian Politics in Comparative Perspective*, 35, 39–40; and *The Economist, Pocket World in Figures, 2003 Edition*, 106, 120.

91 Rempel, *The Chatter Box*, 199.

92 Doran, *Forgotten Partnership*, 22; and Fox, *The Politics of Attraction*, 5.

93 Fox, *The Politics of Attraction*, 130, 144, 151.

94 Doran, *Forgotten Partnership*, 10.

95 Bland, *Chiefs of Defence*, 8, 133, and "Military Interoperability: As Canadian as a Beaver," in Griffiths, ed., *The Canadian Forces and Interoperability*, 58.

96 Ørvik, "Canadian Security and 'Defence Against Help.'"

97 McLin, *Canada's Changing Defense Policy*, 4.

98 Stephen Clarkson, "Uncle Sam and Canada after September 11th," in Griffiths, ed., *The Canadian Forces and Interoperability*, 78.

99 The Canadian origins of the principle are outlined in Keating, *Canada and World Order*, 28–33. See also Morton, *Understanding Canadian Defence*, 173.

100 Cited in Cohen, *While Canada Slept*, 9.

101 Griffiths, ed., *The Canadian Forces and Interoperability*, 37.

102 Douglas Bland, "Military Command in Canada," in Horn and Harris, ed., *Generalship and the Art of the Admiral*, 128.

103 The Cuban Missile Crisis, and Canada's lacklustre political response to it (in contrast to the Canadian military's enthusiasm), is particularly informative. See Haydon, *The Cuban Missile Crisis*.

104 W.J. Hudson, "Strategy for Survival," in McKernan and Browne, ed., *Australia: Two Centuries of War and Peace*, 38.

105 Between July and October 2003, the ADF contribution to the RAMSI Operation Helpem Fren comprised about 1,400 navy, army, and air force personnel providing security and logistic support to operations. Regional military contributions included around 600 personnel from New Zealand, Papua New Guinea, Tonga, and Fiji.

106 Millar, *Australia in Peace and War*, 316; Boeha and McFarlane, ed., *Australia and Papua New Guinea*, 3, 9; and Australian Minister for Defence Media Mail List, "Defence Personnel to Come Home from Solomons."

107 Cooper, Higgott, and Nossal, *Relocating Middle Powers*, 29, 149.

108 The fault-line notion is developed in Huntington, *The Clash of Civilizations and the Remaking of World Order*. On the "arc of instability,"

see H. White, "Defence and the Possibility of War." For a limited but still useful journalistic view on the Australian Secret Intelligence Service, see Toohey and Pinwill, *Oyster*.

109 Author's discussions with Dr Joel Sokolsky, 22 September 2003.

110 See Alberts, "Sovereignty, Credibility at Risk."

111 Stanley, *Canada's Soldiers*; and General J.M.G. Baril, "Preface," in Horn and Harris, ed., *Warrior Chiefs*, 9.

112 Anzac Day, an annual public holiday in Australia and New Zealand, commemorates the landing on the Gallipoli peninsula of the Australian and New Zealand Army Corps (ANZAC) on 25 April 1915.

113 Australian soldiers came to be colloquially called "diggers" because of their repeated need to dig trenches in battle. But the link stretched back to the hardy gold miners, or "diggers," in outback Australia during the nineteenth-century gold rush.

114 See Jeffrey Keshen, "The Great War Soldier as 'Nation Builder' in Canada and Australia," in and Headon, ed., *Shaping Nations*, 195–214; and Vance, *Death So Noble*.

115 Ross, *The Myth of the Digger*, 11–13, 27, 34–5.

116 David G. Haglund, "From Empire to Umpire to Empire: Canada and the Dilemmas of Military Interoperability," in Griffiths, ed., *The Canadian Forces and Interoperability*, 113.

117 For a useful synopsis of Australia's reliance on amphibious capabilities, see Parkin, *A Capability of First Resort*.

118 While the term "East Indies" no longer is in common usage, it generally refers to the Indonesian archipelago and illustrates the similarities between the West Indies and the archipelagic chain to Australia's north.

119 Despite the parallels with Australia, Canada's experiences at Juno beach in Normandy, in coastal operations in Belgium and Holland in the Second World War, in Egypt in 1956, and in Haiti in the mid-1990s – all operations that have been broadly amphibious in nature – have not led to the acquisition of amphibious capabilities. Canada's commitment to the defence of Norway during the Cold War also lacked appropriate maritime assets to transport and lodge the assigned force. General Theriault, the chief of defence staff in the mid-1980s, argued for a focus on Norway to allow for a joint Canadian defence capability to be developed. Theriault's proposal was abandoned because of allied opposition.

120 See Bland, *Chiefs of Defence*, 245–55; and Maloney and Robertson, "The Revolution in Military Affairs," 456.

121 Special Operations Command was officially launched on 5 May 2003. Modelled in part on its U.S. equivalent, which was created in 1986, it includes a

joint headquarters with offices in Canberra and Sydney, the SASR, 4th Battalion RAR (Commando), Tactical Assault Groups (West) and (East), 1 Commando Regiment, the Incident Response Regiment, and the Special Operations Combat Service Support Company.

122 Australian Defence Minister Public Relations Media Mail List, "New Special Operations Command," downloaded from mediacentre@defence.gov.au, 5 May 2003.

123 Simpson, "Australia: Canada's Secret Alter Ego."

124 Author's correspondence with Brendan Sargeant, 20 October 2003.

125 I am grateful to a fellow PHD candidate in war studies, Robert Addinall, for the ideas outlined in this paragraph.

126 Stephen M. Walt, *The Origins of Alliances* (Ithaca, N.Y.: Cornell University Press 1987), cited in Kupchan, *End of the American Era*, 71.

127 Perras makes this point concerning the Aleutians in his *Stepping Stones to Nowhere*.

128 From 1901 to 2005, Conservatives in Australia and Canada have had overlapping terms in office for fifteen years and Canadian Liberals and the Australian Labor Party have had overlapping terms for twenty-one years. The total overlap between politically similar parties from 1901 to 2005 is only thirty-six years.

129 Author's correspondence with Brendan Sargeant, 20 October 2003.

130 Canadian submarine executive officers are trained in Australia and some exchange officers work on Australian submarines. Similarly, until 2003 at least, the RAAF had exchange positions with Canadian P3 aircraft squadrons.

131 Hankey cited in Margaret MacMillan, "Sibling Rivalry: Australia and Canada from the Boer War to the Great War," in MacMillan and McKenzie, ed., *Parties Long Estranged*, 13; Morton, *Understanding Canadian Defence*, 160.

132 Bruce Grant cited in Cooper, *In Between Countries*, 14.

133 Ignatieff, *Blood and Belonging*, 14.

134 In essence, the term RMA refers to dramatic advances in technology that have had the effect of "revolutionizing" the way warfare is conducted – including the technology, organizations, and doctrines applied by armed forces. Arguably, however, it is only a new term for an often repeated phenomenon in the art of war. The most recent "revolution" concerns the use of advanced technology, including satellites, precision-guided munitions, and networked computers.

135 There is a plethora of writings on the RMA. One of the key early post-Gulf War works that influenced the debate was Alvin and Heidi Toffler's *War and Anti-War*. For an Australian perspective, see Evans, *Australia and the Revolution in Military Affairs*; for the Canadian side, see Sloan, *The Revolution in Military Affairs*.

Bibliography

CORRESPONDENCE AND INTERVIEWS
(VARIOUS DATES, AS INDICATED IN NOTES)

Mr Robert Adinall
Lieutenant-Colonel Warwick Austin
Mr Joshua Bennett
Rev. G.M.A. Blaxland
Major Michael Boire
Mr Daniel Bon
Brigadier Gary Bornholt
Lieutenant-Colonel Mick Brennan
Colonel Mike Cessford
Lieutenant-Colonel John Davidson
Mr Louis Delvoie
Dr Walter Dorn
Mr David Elder
Dr Jane Errington
Lieutenant-Colonel Chris Field
Lieutenant-Colonel Marcus Fielding
Dr Brad Gladman
Dr David Haglund
Lieutenant-Colonel Casey Haskins
Dr Ron Haycock
Dr David Horner
Lieutenant-Colonel Grant Iddon
Lieutenant Tonya Kerr
Dr David Last (Lieutenant-Colonel)

Mr Claude LeBlanc
Lieutenant-Colonel Terry Loveridge
Major Don Maclean
Brigadier-General (ret'd) Don MacNamara
Lieutenant-Colonel (ret'd) John Marteinson
Brigadier W.J.A. Mellor
Dr Frank Milne
Lieutenant-Commander Ian Moffat
Dr Kim Richard Nossal
Dr Albert Palazzo
Dr Charles Pentland
Dr Galen Perras
Dr Roy Rempel
Lieutenant-Colonel Randall Richert
Major Ian Rutherford
Dr Alan Ryan
Lieutenant Steve St Amant
Mr Brendan Sargeant
Lieutenant-Colonel Graeme Sligo
Lieutenant-Colonel Michael N. Smith
Dr Joel Sokolsky
Ms Elizabeth Speed
Ms Emily Spencer
Lieutenant-Colonel (ret) Glen Steiner
Mr Hasit Thankey
Mr Jamieson Weetman

PRIMARY AND SECONDARY LITERATURE

Adams, Michael. *Fire and Ice – The United States, Canada and the Myth of Converging Values*. Toronto: Penguin Canada 2003.
Adam-Smith, Patsy. *The ANZACS*. Melbourne: Thomas Nelson Australia 1978.
Alberts, Sheldon. "Sovereignty, Credibility at Risk: Retired Officer – Canada's Reputation Hinges on Increased Military Spending." *National Post*, 28 September 2002.
Albinski, Henry. *Canadian and Australian Politics in Comparative Perspective*. New York: Oxford University Press 1973.
Alexander, Malcolm and Brian Galligan, ed. *Comparative Political Studies: Australia and Canada*. Melbourne: Pitman 1992.
Anderson, Sarah, et. al. *Coalition of the Willing or Coalition of the Coerced*. Washington, D.C.: Institute for Policy Studies, 24 March 2003.

Anderson, Scott. "The Evolution of the Canadian Intelligence Establishment, 1945–1950." *Intelligence and National Security*, vol. 9 (July 1994).

Ankersen, Christopher. "'Too Many Houseboats': Why the Canadian Army Doesn't 'Do' Change Well." *Army Doctrine and Training Bulletin*, vol. 4 (fall 2001).

Associated Press. "Australia Put Troops into Iraq before War." *Globe and Mail*, 10 May 2003.

Austin, Ron. *The White Gurkhas: The Australians at the Second Battle of Krithia*. McCrae, Queensland: Globe Press 1989.

Australia. Defence Public Relations Media Release. "Hornets Come Home." Downloaded from mediacentre@defence.gov.au, 15 May 2003.

– "New Special Operations Command." Downloaded from mediacentre@defence.gov.au., 5 May 2003.

– "Operation Catalyst: Australia's Defence Contribution to Iraq's Rehabilitation." Downloaded from mediacentre@defence.gov.au., 30 April 2003.

Australia. Department of Defence. *Defence Report 1989–99*. Canberra: Australian Government Publishing Service 1984.

– *Future Warfighting Concept* (Canberra, 2003).

Australia. Department of Defence Media Release. PACC 95/03, "Investigation into Allegations against Australian Soldiers in East Timor Concludes." 16 April 2003.

Australia. Department of Foreign Affairs and Trade. *Advancing the National Interest*. Canberra: Commonwealth of Australia, February 2003. Available at http://www.dfat.au/ani/.

– http://www.ahc-ottawa.org/relations. Downloaded 21 May 2002.

Australian Army. *The Fundamentals of Land Warfare – LWD1*. Puckapunyal: Land Warfare Development Centre 2002.

– Future Land Warfare Branch. "Army Vanguard Concept No. 1 MOLE." Downloaded from http://www.army.gov.au/Vanguard/main.htm, 15 June 2003.

– Army Headquarters. "The Hardened and Networked Army." Downloaded from http://www.defence.gov.au/army/HNA/default2.htm, 17 February 2006.

Australian-Canadian Studies (Griffith University, Nathan, Queensland).

Australian Minister for Defence Media Mail List. "Defence Personnel to Come Home from Solomons." 27 October 2003 (e-mail from mediacentre@defence.gov.au; item 136/2003).

– "Operation Anode: ADF Contribution to Regional Assistance Mission to the Solomon Islands." 22 July 2003.

– "Operation Catalyst Comes into Effect Tomorrow." 15 July 2003 (Item 89/2003).

Australian Strategic Policy Institute. *Beyond Bali: ASPI's Strategic Assessment 2002*. Canberra: November 2002.

Axworthy, Lloyd. "Canada and Human Security: the Need for Leadership." *International Journal*, vol. 52 (spring 1997).

Axworthy, Tom. Presentation to Conference of Defence Associations seminar. Ottawa, 27 February 2003.

Bacevich, A.J. *American Empire: The Realities & Consequences of U.S. Diplomacy.* Cambridge, Mass.: Harvard University Press 2002.

– *The Pentomic Era: The U.S. Army between Korea and Vietnam.* Washington, D.C.: National Defense University Press 1986.

Ballard, Geoffrey. *On ULTRA Secret Service: The Story of Australia's Signals Intelligence Operations during World War II.* Melbourne: Spectrum Publications 1991.

Ball, Desmond. "The Strategic Essence." *Australian Journal of International Affairs*, vol. 55, n. 2 (2001).

– and David Horner. *Breaking the Codes: Australia's KGB network.* Sydney: Allen and Unwin 1998.

Barclay, Glen St J. *A Very Small Insurance Policy: The Politics of Australian Involvement in Vietnam, 1954–1967.* St Lucia: University of Queensland Press 1988.

– *Friends in High Places: Australian-American Diplomatic Relations since 1945.* Melbourne: Oxford University Press 1985.

Barratt, Glyn. *Russian Shadows on the British Northwest Coast of North America, 1810–1890: A Study of Rejection of Defence Responsibilities.* Vancouver: University of British Columbia Press 1983.

Barrett, John. "No Straw Man: C.E.W. Bean and Some Critics." *Australian Historical Studies*, vol. 23 (April 1988).

Bartu, Peter. "'The Fifth Faction': The United Nations Intervention in Cambodia 1991–1993." Monash University, PHD thesis, 1998.

Bashow, Lieutenant-Colonel David. "Who Killed von Richtofen?" *Canadian Military Journal*, vol. 4 (spring 2003).

Bassett, Jan. *Guns and Brooches: Australian Army Nursing from the Boer War to the Gulf War.* Melbourne: Oxford University Press 1992.

Beavis, Major-General L.E. "Canada and Imperial Defence." *Australian Army Journal*, no. 221 (October 1967).

Beck, J.M. *Pendulum of Power: Canada's Federal Elections.* Scarborough, Ont.: Prentice-Hall 1968.

Beeson, Mark. "Debating Defence: Time for a Paradigm Shift?" *Australian Journal of International Affairs*, vol. 54, no. 3 (2000).

Bell, Coral. "Normative Shift." *National Interest*, no. 70 (winter 2002). Downloaded from www.nationalinterest.org/issues/70/Bell.html, 1 July 2003.

Bell, Roger. *Unequal Allies: Australian-American Relations and the Pacific War.* Melbourne: Melbourne University Press 1977.

Bercuson, David. *Blood on the Hills: The Canadian Army in the Korean War.* Toronto: University of Toronto Press 1999.

– *Significant Incident: Canada's Army, the Airborne and the Murder in Somalia.* Toronto: McLelland and Stewart 1996.

– and J.L. Granatstein. *Dictionary of Canadian Military History.* Toronto: Oxford University Press 1992.

Berger, Carl. *The Sense of Power: Studies in the Ideas of Canadian Imperialism, 1867–1914.* Toronto: University of Toronto Press 1970.

Bermant, Chaim. *The Cousinhood.* New York: Macmillan 1972.

Berton, Pierre. *Marching as to War: Canada's Turbulent Years, 1899–1953.* [Toronto]: Anchor Books 2002.

Bezeau, Mervin Vincent. "The Role and Organization of Canadian Militia Staff, 1904–1945." Royal Military College (Kingston, Ont.), MA thesis, 1978.

Biddle, Stephen. "Are Allies Worth It?" Downloaded from http://www.carlisle.army.mil/ssi/about/2003/mar/allies.pdf., 31 March 2003.

Birch, A.H. *Federalism, Finance and Social Legislation in Canada, Australia, and the United States.* London: Oxford University Press 1955.

Blackburn, Air Commodore John N., Commodore Lee Cordner, and Brigadier Michael A. Swan. "'Not the Size of the Dog in the Fight ...': RMA – The ADF Application." *Australian Defence Force Journal,* no. 144 (September/October 2000).

Blainey, Geoffrey. "After Iraq, the Road from Baghdad: Interview with Victor Davis Hanson." *Policy* (Centre for Independent Studies), vol. 19 (spring 2003).

– *The Tyranny of Distance: How Distance Shaped Australia's History.* Melbourne: MacMillan 1968.

Bland, Douglas L., ed. *Canada's National Defence, Volumes I and II.* Kingston, Ont.: School of Policy Studies, Queens University 1997–98.

– *Chiefs of Defence: Government and the Unified Command of the Canadian Armed Forces.* Toronto: CISS 1995.

– Presentation to Conference of Defence Associations seminar. Ottawa, 21 February 2002.

– "A Sow's Ear from a Silk Purse: Abandoning Canada's Military Capabilities." *International Journal,* vol. 54 (winter 1998–99).

Blaxland, Gregory. *Amiens: 1918.* London: Frederick Muller 1968.

– *Egypt and Sinai: Eternal Battleground.* New York: Funk and Wagnalls 1966.

– *The Regiments Depart: A History of the British Army, 1945–1970.* London: William Kimber 1971.

Blaxland, John C. *Information Era Manoeuvre: The Australian-Led Mission to East Timor.* Working Paper no. 118. Canberra: Land Warfare Studies Centre, June 2002.

– *Organising an Army: The Australian Experience, 1957–1965.* Canberra: Strategic and Defence Studies Centre, Australian National University 1989.

– *Signals Swift and Sure: A History of the Royal Australian Corps of Signals, 1947–1972.* Melbourne: Royal Australian Corps of Signals 1999.

Boeha, Beno, and John McFarlane, ed. *Australia and Papua New Guinea: Crime and the Bilateral Relationship*. Canberra: Australian Defence Studies Centre, Australian Defence Force Academy 2000.

Bostok, Ian. "Expeditionary Objectives: The Australian Defence Force Confronts Its Biggest Shift in Operational Focus in a Generation." *Jane's International Defence Review*, February 2003.

Boutros-Ghali, Boutros. *An Agenda for Peace: Preventive Diplomacy, Peacemaking and Peace-keeping*. New York: United Nations 1992.

Bowes, Lieutenant-Colonel R.L. Directorate of Army Doctrine. *Canadian Army of Tomorrow Capstone Operating Concept*, 26 May 2003. Downloaded from http://armyapp.forces.gc.ca/lfdts/files/abca/june2003/AoT-Operating-Concept-26-May-03.doc., 3 July 3003.

Boyce, P.J., and J.R. Angel, ed. *Independence and Alliance: Australia in World Affairs 1976–80*. Sydney: George Allen and Unwin and the Australian Institute of International Affairs 1983.

Bradford, R.D. "The Modern Field General Staff: A Consideration of the Respective Conditions of Its Emergence and Maturation." Royal Military College (Kingston, Ont.), MA thesis, 1994.

Breen, Bob. *The Battle of Kapyong: 3rd Battalion, The Royal Australian Regiment Korea, 23–34 April 1951*. Sydney: Army Doctrine Centre 1992.

– *First to Fight: Australian Diggers, N.Z. Kiwis and U.S. Paratroopers in Vietnam, 1965–1966*. Sydney: Allen and Unwin 1988.

– *Giving Peace a Chance – Operation Lagoon, Bougainville 1994: A Case Study of Military Action and Diplomacy*. Canberra Papers on Strategy and Defence no. 142. Canberra: Strategic and Defence Studies Centre, Australian National University 2001.

– *A Little Bit of Hope: Australian Force Somalia*. Sydney: Allen and Unwin 1998.

– *Mission Accomplished: East Timor, The Australian Defence Force Participation in the International Forces East Timor (INTERFET)*. Sydney: Allen and Unwin 2001.

Bridges Papers. Royal Military College (Kingston, Ont.) Massey Library.

Broad, Graham. "'Not Competent to Produce Tanks': The Ram and Tank Production in Canada, 1939–1945." *Canadian Military History*, vol. 11 (winter 2002).

Broinowski, Alison. *Howard's War*. Carlton: Scribe Publications 2003.

Bryant, Arthur. *The Turn of the Tide 1939–1943: A Study Based on the Diaries and Autobiographical Notes of Field Marshal the Viscount Alanbrooke*. London: Collins 1957.

Bullock, David L. *Allenby's War: The Palestine-Arabian Campaigns 1916–1918*. London: Blandford Press 1988.

Burns, Lieutenant-General E.L.M. *Between Arab and Israeli*. Beirut: Institute for Palestine Studies 1969.

Byers, Daniel T. "Mobilizing Canada: The National Resources Mobilization Act, the Department of National Defence, and Compulsory Military Service in Canada." McGill University, PHD thesis 2000.

Cain, Frank, ed. *Arming the Nation: A History of Defence Science and Technology in Australia*. Canberra: Australian Defence Studies Centre, Australian Defence Force Academy 1999.

Caligari, John. *The Army's Capacity to Defend Australia Offshore: The Need for a Joint Approach*. Working Paper no. 348. Canberra: Strategic and Defence Studies Centre, Australian National University, July 2000.

Callinan, Bernard. *Independent Company: The Australian Army in Portuguese Timor 1941–43*. Reprint. Melbourne: William Heinemann Australia 1984.

Canada. Department of External Affairs. *Documents on Canadian External Relations (DEA, DCER)*, vol. 1 (1909–18); vol. 2 (1919); vol. 3 (1919–25); vol. 4 (1926–30); vol. 6 (1936–39); vol. 7 (1939–41); vol. 9 (1942–43). Ottawa, 1967–80.

– *Foreign Policy for Canadians: Foreign Policy for Canadians, Europe, International Development, Latin America, Pacific, United Nations*. Ottawa: Queen's Printer 1970.

Canada. Department of Foreign Affairs and Trade. *A Dialogue on Foreign Policy*. Ottawa, 2003.

Canada. Department of National Defence. *The Canadian Army Reading List: A Guide to Professional Reading* (Version 1, Land Forces Doctrine and Training System). Kingston, September 2001.

– *Challenge and Commitment: A Defence Policy for Canada*. Ottawa: Supply and Services Canada, June 1987.

– http://www.forces.gc.ca/site/operations/currentopse.asp. Downloaded 11 September 2003.

– "Operations: Canadian Forces Joint Operations Group." Downloaded from http://www.forces.gc.ca/site/operations/CFJOG/index_e.asp., 11 September 2003.

– *Shaping the Future of Canadian Defence: A Strategy for 2020*. Ottawa: Department of National Defence, June 1999.

Canada. Privy Council Office. "Survey of Relations between Canada and the United States," 20 June 1951. Copy in author's possession.

Canada 21 Council. *Canada 21: Canada and Common Security in the Twenty-First Century*. Toronto: Centre for International Studies 1994.

Canadian Alliance. *The New North Strong and Free: Protecting Canadian Sovereignty and Contributing to Global Stability* (Defence Policy White Paper of the Official Opposition). Ottawa: House of Commons, spring 2003.

Canadian Press. "Klein Ready to Consider Firewall around Alberta: Province Could Set up Its Own Programs without Leaving Canadian Confederation." *Globe and Mail*, 16 April 2003.

Capling, Anne. *Australia and the Global Trade System*. Melbourne: Cambridge University Press 2001.

Cardinal, Linda, and Headon, David, ed. *Shaping Nations: Constitutionalism and Society in Australia and Canada*. Ottawa: University of Ottawa Press 2002.

Carlyon, Norman D. *I Remember Blamey*. Melbourne: Macmillan 1980.

Chapnick, Adam. "The Canadian Middle Power Myth." *International Journal*, vol. 55 (spring 2000).

Charters, David A., Marc Milner, and J. Brent Wilson. *Military History and the Military Profession*. Westport, Conn.: Praeger 1992.

Cheeseman, Graeme. *Canada's Post-Cold War Military Blues and Its Lessons for Australia*. Working Paper no. 60. Canberra: Australian Defence Studies Centre, August 2000.

Clark, Major Robert H. "Canadian Weapons Acquisition: The Case of the Bomarc Missile." Royal Military College (Kingston, Ont.), MA thesis, 1983.

Clark, General Wesley K. *Waging Modern War*. New York: Public Affairs 2002.

Coates, John. *Bravery above Blunder*. Sydney: Oxford University Press 2000.

Coderre, The Honourable Denis, Minister of Citizenship and Immigration. "National Security, Immigration and Our American neighbours Post 9/11." Delivered at "On Guard For Three?" Symposium, Royal Military College (Kingston, Ont.), 4 April 2003 (partial transcript downloaded from http://www.cic.gc.ca, 3 May 2003).

Cohen, Andrew. "We Lost Our Place." *Globe and Mail*, 15 May 2003.

– *While Canada Slept*. Toronto: McClelland and Stewart 2003.

Cohen, Eliot A., and John Gooch. *Military Misfortunes: The Anatomy of Failure in War*. New York: Free Press 1990.

Cook, Tim. "Documenting War and Forging Reputations: Sir Max Aitken and the Canadian War Records Office in the First World War." Paper presented at the Wilfrid Laurier University Military History Conference, Waterloo, Ont., 3 May 2002.

Cooper, Andrew F. *In Between Countries: Australia, Canada, and the Search for Order in Agricultural Trade*. Montreal and Kingston: McGill-Queen's University Press 1997.

– and Richard A. Higgott and Kim R. Nossal. *Relocating Middle Powers: Australia and Canada in a Changing World Order*. Vancouver: University of British Columbia Press 1993.

Cooper, Barry, and David Bercuson. "A Messy War Awaits Us in Afghanistan." *National Post*, 13 August 2003. Downloaded from http://www.national post.com, 16 August 2003.

– and Ted Morton. "Chrétien Has Put Party Ahead of Country." *National Post*, 28 March 2003.

Coulthard-Clark, C.D. *Duntroon: The Royal Military College of Australia 1911–1986*. Sydney: Allen and Unwin 1986.

– *A Heritage of Spirit: A Biography of Major-General Sir William Throsby Bridges K.C.B., C.M.G.* Melbourne: Melbourne University Press 1979.

– *The* RAAF *in Vietnam: Australian Air Involvement in the Vietnam War, 1962–1975.* St Leonards.: Allen and Unwin and Australian War Memorial 1995.

Council for Canadian Security in the 21st Century. *The People's Defence Review.* Toronto, September 2002.

Cousineau, Marc. "Canadian Studies: Why Do We Promote It?" *Australian-Canadian Studies,* vol. 9, no. 1 (1991).

Cowan, Dr John S. "RMC and Ideas." Convocation Address at Royal Military College (Kingston, Ont.), 15 November 2002.

Creveld, Martin van. *Fighting Power: German and U.S. Army Performance, 1939–1945.* Westport, Conn.: Greenwood Press 1982.

Crickard, Rear-Admiral (ret'd) Fred W. "A Tale of Two Navies: United States Security and Canadian and Australian Naval Policy during the Cold War." Dalhousie University, MA thesis, 1993.

Delaney, Major Douglas. "The Soldiers' General: Bert Hoffmeister as Military Commander." Royal Military College (Kingston, Ont.), PHD thesis, 2003.

Delvoie, Louis A. "Canada and International Security Operations: The Search for Policy Rationales." *Canadian Military Journal,* vol. 1 (summer 2000).

– "The Commonwealth in Canadian Foreign Policy." In *The Round Table,* vol. 310 (Butterworth, U.K., 1989).

– "Curious Ambiguities: Canada's International Security Policy." *Policy Options* (Institute for Research on Public Policy), January/February 2001.

Dennis, Peter, et al., ed. *The Oxford Companion to Australian Military History.* Melbourne: Oxford University Press 1995.

– and Jeffrey Grey. *Emergency and Confrontation: Australian Military Operations in Malaya and Borneo, 1950–1966.* St Leonards: Allen and Unwin and the Australian War Memorial 1996.

– *The Second Fifty Years – The Australian Army 1947–1997: Proceedings of the 1997 Chief of Army's History Conference.* Canberra: School of History, University College, Australian Defence Force Academy 1997.

Devine, Miranda. "The Joke Is on the Pacifists." Sydney *Morning Herald,* 10 April 2003.

Dewitt, David B. "Directions in Canada's International Security Policy: From Marginal Actor at the Centre to Central Actor at the Margins." *International Journal,* vol. 55 (spring 2000).

Directorate of History and Heritage, Department of National Defence. Army Headquarters (AHQ). Reports, 1948–1959 (downloaded from http://www.dnd.ca/hr/dhh/, 5 March 2002).

– Report no. 16: C.P. Stacey – The Canadian Army Pacific Force, 1944–1945, 7 Jan. 53 (15 July 1947).

– Report no. 22: C.P. Stacey – The Reorganization of the Canadian Militia 1919–20 (31 Jan. 1949).

– Report no. 53: C.P. Stacey – Canadian Org in Theatres of Operations, 1939–1945 (11 June 1952).
– Report no. 57: C.P. Stacey – A Summary of Major Changes in Army Org, 1939–1945 (22 Dec. 1952).
– Report no. 64: The Reorganization of the Canadian Militia, 1936 (20 Aug. 1963).
– Report no. 73: C.P. Stacey – A Survey of Army Research and Development, 1939–45 (14 Feb. 1955).
– Report no. 75: C.P. Stacey – Military Coop within the Commonwealth, 1939–1945 (13 Nov. 1956).
Directorate of History and Heritage, Department of National Defence. DHH 112.1009 (D4). Recruiting and Use of Cdn Tps for Australia, 1945.
– DHH 171.009 (D79). Jungle Warfare Liaison Letters.
– DHH 314.009 (D88). Australian Personnel on Loan to Canada – 16 June 44 – 28 Sept. 45
– DHH 314.009 (D51). Canadian Army Observers – S & SW Pacific Theatres – May 43 – Nov. 44.
– DHH 322.009 (D713). Reports by Cdn Officers on Attachments to Australian Forces – 1944/45.
– DHH 322.009 (D11). Japanese Personnel Enlistment and Discharge.
Dickinson, John, and Brian Young, ed. *A Short History of Quebec*, 3rd ed. Montreal and Kingston: McGill-Queen's University Press 2003.
Donaghy, Greg. *Parallel Paths: Canadian Australian Relations since the 1890s*. Ottawa: Department of Foreign Affairs and International Trade 1995.
– *Uncertain Horizons: Canadians and Their World in 1945*. Ottawa: Canadian Committee for the History of the Second World War 1997.
Doran, Charles F., et. al. *Forgotten Partnership: U.S.-Canada Relations Today*. Baltimore: Johns Hopkins University Press 1984.
– *Pacific Partners: Canada and the United States*. Washington, D.C.: Institute for Foreign Policy Analysis/Fletcher School of Law and Diplomacy, Tufts University, and Brassey's 1994.
Doughty, Robert A. *The Evolution of US Army Tactical Doctrine, 1946–76*. Papers, Combat Studies Institute. Leavenworth, Kan., and Washington, D.C.: Fort Leavenworth and Center for Military History, United States Army 1979.
Douglas, W.A.B. and Greenhous, Brereton, *Out of the Shadows: Canada in the Second World War*, rev. ed. Toronto: University of Toronto Press 1995.
Downer, The Hon. Alexander, MP. "The Myth of 'Little' Australia." Downloaded from http://www.foreignminister.gov.au/speeches/2003/031126_press_club.html, 18 January 2004.
Dupont, Alan. "Three Blocks and You're Out." Sydney *Morning Herald*, 19 April 2003.

Dyck, Harvey L., and H. Peter Krosby, ed. *Empire and Nations: Essays in Honour of Frederick H. Soward*. Toronto: University of Toronto Press and University of British Columbia 1969.

Dyck, Noel, ed. *Indigenous Peoples and the Nation State: Fourth World Politics in Canada, Australia and Norway*. Social and Economic Papers no. 14. Saint John's, Nlfd.: Institute of Social and Economic Research, Memorial University of Newfoundland 1985.

Dziuban, Colonel Stanley W. *Military Relations between the United States and Canada 1939–1945*. United States Army in World War II, Special Studies. Washington, D.C.: Center of Military History, United States Army 1990.

Eayrs, James. *In Defence of Canada. Volume 1: From the Great War to the Great Depression*. Toronto: University of Toronto Press 1964.

– *In Defence of Canada, Volume 2: Appeasement and Rearmament*. Toronto: University of Toronto Press 1965.

– *In Defence of Canada, Volume 3: Growing up Allied*. Toronto: University of Toronto Press 1980.

– *In Defence of Canada, Volume 4: Indochina: Roots of Complicity*. Toronto: University of Toronto Press 1983.

The Economist. Pocket World in Figures 2003 Edition. London: Profile Books 2002.

Edwards, Peter, and Gregory Pemberton. *Crises and Commitments: The Politics and Diplomacy of Australia's Involvement in Southeast Asian Conflicts, 1948–1965*. North Sydney: Allen and Unwin and Australian War Memorial 1992.

Edwards, Robert H., and Ann L. Griffiths., ed. *Intervention and Engagement: A Maritime Perspective – Proceedings of a Conference Hosted by the Centre for Foreign Policy Studies, Dalhousie University, and the Canadian Forces Maritime Warfare Centre, Halifax, 7–9 June 2002*. Halifax: Centre for Foreign Policy Studies, Dalhousie University 2002.

Elliott, Bruce S. *Irish Immigrants in the Canadas: A New Approach*. Montreal and Kingston: McGill-Queen's University Press 1988.

Elliott, Michael. "The Aussie Rules of Foreign Policy: A Nation That's Similar to Canada Has Found a Different and Better Route." *Time* (Canadian ed.), 26 May 2003.

English, John A. "European Defence, Divide and Fall: Recklessness on Both Sides of the Atlantic Is Threatening to Undermine NATO. *The Economist*, 25 October 2003.

– *Failure in High Command: The Canadian Army and the Normandy Campaign*, Ottawa: Golden Dog Press 1995.

– *Lament for an Army: The Decline of Canadian Military Professionalism*. Toronto: Canadian Institute of International Affairs and Irwin Publishing 1998.

Evans, Gareth. *Cooperating for Peace: The Global Agenda for the 1990's and Beyond*. St Leonards: Allen and Unwin 1993.

Evans, Michael. *Australia and the Revolution in Military Affairs*. Working Paper no. 115. Canberra: Land Warfare Studies Centre, August 2001.

– *Forward form the Past: The Development of Australian Army Doctrine 1972 – Present*. Study Paper no. 301. Canberra: Land Warfare Studies Centre, August 1999.

– "From Kadesh to Kandahar: Military Theory and the Future of War." *Naval War College Review*, vol. 56 (summer 2003).

– *The Role of the Australian Army in a Maritime Concept of Strategy*. Working Paper no. 101. Canberra: Land Warfare Studies Centre, September 1998.

– *From Deakin to Dibb: The Army and the Making of Australian Strategy in the 20th Century*. Working Paper no. 113. Canberra: Land Warfare Studies Centre, Canberra, June 2001.

– and Alan Ryan, ed. *From Breitenfeld to Baghdad: Perspectives on Combined Arms Warfare*. Working Paper no. 122. Canberra: Land Warfare Studies Centre, July 2003.

Faraday, Bruce. "Half the Battle: The Administration and Higher Organisation of the AIF 1914–1918." Canberra: University College, University of New South Wales, PHD thesis, 1997.

Farrar-Hockley, Anthony. *The Edge of the Sword*. London: Muller 1954.

Federation of Atomic Scientists. "Strategic Air Defence, NORAD Selected Chronology." Downloaded from http://www.fas.org/nuke/guide/usa/airdef/norad-chron.htm, 9 September 2003.

Field, Laurie. *The Forgotten War: Australia and the Boer War*. Melbourne: Melbourne University Press 1979 and 1995.

Fife, Robert. "Mulroney Slams PM's View on War." *National Post*, 24 March 2003.

Findlay, Trevor. *The Use of Force in UN Peace Operations*. Stockholm and Oxford, U.K.: Stockholm International Peace Research Institute and Oxford University Press 2002.

Fisher, Matthew. "How Australia's Plucky Military Does More with Less." Ottawa *Citizen*, 7 August 2003. Downloaded from http://www.canada.com.

Fitzgerald, Todd, and Michael Hennessy. "An Expedient Reorganization: The NDHQ staff System in the Gulf War." *Canadian Military Journal*, vol. 4 (spring 2003).

Fortman, Michael and David Haglund. "Canada and the Issue of Homeland Security: Does the 'Kingston Dispensation' Still Hold?" *Canadian Military Journal*, vol. 3 (spring 2002).

Fox, Annette Baker. *The Politics of Attraction: Four Middle Powers and the United States*. New York: Columbia University Press 1977.

Frei, Henry P. *Japan's Southward Advance and Australia: From the Sixteenth Century to World War II*. Carlton: Melbourne University Press 1991.

Friedman, Thomas. *The Lexus and the Olive Tree: Understanding Globalization*. New York: Anchor Books 2000.

Frost, Frank. *Australia's War in Vietnam*. Sydney: Allen and Unwin 1987.

Gaasenbeck, Matthew (chairman). *A Wake-up Call for Canada – The Need for a New Military* (a proposal by the Defence Studies Committee of the Royal Canadian Military Institute). Toronto, 2001.

Gammage, Bill. *The Broken Years: Australian Soldiers in the Great War*. Ringwood, Australia: Penguin 1990.

Gardam, John. *Canadians in War and Peacekeeping*. Burnstown, Ont.: General Store Publishing 2000.

Garnett, Vice-Admiral (ret'd) G.L. "The Evolution of the Canadian Approach to Joint and Combined Operations at the Strategic and Operational Level." *Canadian Military Journal*, vol. 3 (winter 2002–03).

Geddes, John. "In Harm's Way." *Maclean's*, 13 October 2003.

– "Smart Guy, eh?" *Macleans*, 23 June 2003.

Gibson, F.W. "The Alaskan Boundary Dispute." Queen's University, MA thesis, 1944.

Godefroy, A.B. *For Freedom and Honour? The Story of the 25 Canadian Volunteers Executed in the Great War*. Nepean, Ont.: CEF Books 1998.

Goodspeed, D.J. *The Road Past Vimy: The Canadian Corps 1914–1918*. Toronto: Macmillan 1969.

Goot, Murray, and Rodney Tiffen, ed. *Australia's Gulf War* (Melbourne: Melbourne University Press 1992.

Gordon, Harry. *The Embarrassing Australian: The Story of an Aboriginal Warrior*. Melbourne: Lansdowne Press 1962.

Gotlieb, Alan. "The Chretien Doctrine: By Blindly Following the UN, the Prime Minister Is Hurting Canada." *Macleans*, 31 March 2003.

Gowans, Captain P.T.F. "Canadian Defence Integration." *Australian Army Journal*, no. 184 (September 1964).

Graham, The Honourable Bill. *International Policy Statement: A Role of Pride and Influence in the World – Defence*. Ottawa, 2005. Downloaded from http://www.forces.gc.ca/site/Reports/dps/pdf/dps_e.pdf, 17 February 2005.

Granatstein, J.L. *Canada's Army: Waging War and Keeping Peace*. Toronto: University of Toronto Press 2002.

– *The Generals: The Canadian Army's Senior Commanders in the Second World War*. Toronto: Stoddard 1995.

– "The Importance of Being Less Earnest: Promoting Canada's National Interests through Tighter Ties with the U.S." C.D. Howe Institute, Benefactors Lecture,

Toronto, 21 October 2003). Downloaded from http://www.cdhowe.org/pdf/ benefactors_lecture_2003.pdf., 27 October 2003.

– "Why Go to War? Because We Have to." *National Post*, 20 February 2003.

– and Robert Bothwell. *Pirouette: Pierre Trudeau and Canadian Foreign Policy*. Toronto: University of Toronto Press 1990.

– and David Stafford. *Spy Wars: Espionage and Canada from Gouzenko to Glasnost*. Toronto: McClelland and Stewart 1992.

– and Peter Neary. *The Good Fight: Canadians and World War II*. Toronto: Copp Clark 1995.

Graves, Donald E., ed. *Fighting for Canada: Seven Battles, 1758–1945*. Toronto: Robin Brass Studio 2000.

Gray, Colin S. *Canadians in a Dangerous World*. Toronto: Atlantic Council of Canada 1994.

Gray, Hub. *Beyond the Danger Close: The Korean Experience Revealed – 2nd Battalion Princess Patricia's Canadian Light Infantry*. Calgary, Alta.: Bunker to Bunker Publishing 2003.

Greenhous, Brereton. *Dieppe, Dieppe*. Montreal: Art Global Press 1996.

Grey, Jeffrey. *The Australian Army*. Melbourne: Oxford University Press 2001.

– *The Commonwealth Armies and the Korean War: An Alliance Study*. Manchester, UK: Manchester University Press 1988.

– *Up Top: the Royal Australian Navy and Southeast Asian Conflicts, 1955–1972*. St Leonards: Allen and Unwin and Australian War Memorial 1998.

– and Peter Dennis, ed. *The Korean War: The Chief of Army's Military History Conference 2000*. Canberra: Army History Unit 2000.

Griffith, Paddy. *Battle Tactics of the Western Front: The British Army's Art of Attack 1916–18*. New Haven, Conn., and London: Yale University Press 1994.

Griffiths, A.L., ed. *The Canadian Forces and Interoperability: Panacea or Perdition?* Halifax: Centre for Foreign Policy Studies, Dalhousie University 2003.

Grimshaw, Major Louis E. "On Guard: A Perspective on the Roles and Functions of the Army in Canada." Royal Military College (Kingston, Ont.), MA thesis, 1989.

Groom, Lieutenant-Colonel Kenneth G. "ABCA: The American-British-Canadian-Australian Standardisation Programme," *Australian Army Journal*, no. 177 (February 1964).

Gubb, M. *The Australian Military Response to the Fiji Coup: An Assessment*. Working Paper no. 171. Canberra: Strategic and Defence Studies Centre 1988.

Hadly, Michael L., and Roger Sarty. *Tin-Pots & Pirate Ships: Canadian Naval Forces & German Sea Raiders 1880–1918*. Montreal and Kingston: McGill-Queen's University Press 1991.

Haglund, David. "'Are We the Isolationists?': North American Isolationism in a Comparative Context." *International Journal*, vol. 58 (winter 2002–03).

- "North American Cooperation in an Era of Homeland Security." *Orbis* (Foreign Policy Research Institute), vol. 47 (fall 2003).
- *The North Atlantic Triangle Revisited: Canadian Grand Strategy at Century's End.* Toronto: Canadian Institute of International Affairs and Irwin Publishing 2000.
- ed. *Over Here and over There: Canada-US Defence Cooperation in an Era of Interoperability.* Queen's Quarterly, Special Edition, 2001.

Hancock, W.K. *Survey of British Commonwealth Affairs*, 2 vols. London: Oxford University Press and Royal Institute of International Affairs 1940 and 1942.

Handelman, Stephen. "All Together Now." *Time* (Canadian ed.), 26 May 2003.

Harries, Owen, "Understanding America." Centre for Independent Studies Lecture. Downloaded from http://www.cis.org.au/Events/CISlectures/2002/Harries030402.htm., 18 November 2002.

Harris, Major Mike. "Historic aerial re-supply." *Army: The Soldiers Newspaper*, 24 April 2003.

Harris, Stephen J. *Canadian Brass: The Making of a Professional Army, 1860–1939.* Toronto: University Press 1988.

Harvey, Frank. Presentation to Conference of Defence Associations seminar. Ottawa, 27 February 2003.

Hawkins, Freda. *Critical Years in Immigration: Canada and Australia Compared.* Montreal and Kingston: McGill-Queen's University Press 1989.

Haycock, Ronald G. "Early Canadian Weapons Acquisition: 'That Damned Ross Rifle.'" *Canadian Defence Quarterly*, vol. 14 (winter 1984–85).
- *The Image of the Indian: the Canadian Indian as a Subject and a Concept in a Sampling of the Popular National Magazines Read in Canada, 1900–1970.* Waterloo, Ont.: Waterloo Lutheran University 1971.
- "The Labours of Athena and the Muses: Historical and Contemporary Aspects of Canadian Military Education." *Canadian Military Journal*, vol. 2 (summer 2001).
- "The 'Myth' of Imperial Defence: Australian-Canadian Bilateral Military Co-operation, 1942." *War and Society*, vol. 2 (May 1984).
- *Sam Hughes: The Public Career of a Controversial Canadian 1885–1916.* Waterloo, Ont., and Ottawa: Wilfrid Laurier University and Canadian War Museum 1986.

Haydon, Commander (ret'd) Peter T. *The Cuban Missile Crisis: Canadian Involvement Reconsidered.* Toronto: Canadian Institute of Strategic Studies 1993.

Hellyer, Paul. *Damn the Torpedoes: My Fight to Unify Canada's Armed Forces.* Toronto: McClelland and Stewart 1990.

Henault, General Ray. *A Time for Transformation: Annual Report of the Chief of the Defence Staff, 2002–2003.* Ottawa: Directorate General of Public Affairs, National Defence Headquarters 2003.

Hensley, Gerald. "Will New Zealand Ever Rejoin ANZUS?" *Policy* (Centre for Independent Studies), vol. 19 (spring 2003).

Hetherington, John. *Blamey: Controversial Soldier.* Canberra: Australian War Memorial 1973.

Heydon, Peter. *Quiet Decision: A Study of George Foster Pearce.* Melbourne: Melbourne University Press 1965.

Hill, A.J. *Chauvel of the Light Horse: A Biography of General Sir Harry Chauvel, G.C.M.G., K.C.B.* Melbourne: Melbourne University Press 1978.

Hill, Senator Robert. *Australia's National Security: A Defence Update 2003.* Donwloaded from http://www.defence.gov.au., 26 February 2003.

– "Australia's National Security: A Defence Update 2003." Downloaded from http://www.defence.gov.au, 15 February 2006.

Hillen, John. *Blue Helmets: The Strategy of UN Military Operations*, 2nd ed. Washington, D.C.: Brassey's 2000.

Hiller, Harry. "Western Separatism in Australia and Canada: The Regional Ideology Thesis." *Australian-Canadian Studies*, vol. 5, no. 2 (1987).

Hilliker, J.F. "Distant Ally – Canadian Relations with Australia during the Second World War." *Journal of Imperial and Commonwealth History*, vol. 13, no. 1 (1984).

Hillmer Norman, and J.L. Granatstein. *Empire to Umpire: Canada and the World to the 1990s.* Mississauga, Ont.: Copp Clark Longman 1994.

Hinge, Alan. *Australian Defence Preparedness: Principles, Problems and Prospects.* Canberra: Australian Defence Studies Centre, Australian Defence Force Academy 2000.

Hitsman, J. McKay. *Inspection Services in Canada.* Ottawa: Queen's Printer 1959.

Hobson, Sharon. "Canada – Readiness at a Price." *Jane's Defence Weekly*, 17 September 2003.

Hodgins, Bruce W., Don Wright, and W.H. Heick, ed. *Federalism in Canada and Australia: The Early Years.* Waterloo, Ont.: Wilfrid Laurier University Press 1978.

Hodgson, B.W., et al., ed. *Federalism in Canada and Australia: Historical Perspectives 1920–1988.* Peterborough, Ont.: Trent University, Frost Centre for Canadian Heritage and Development Studies 1989.

Holland, Kenneth M., F.L. Morton, and Brian Galligan, ed. *Federalism and the Environment: Environmental Policy Making in Australia, Canada and the United States.* Westport, Conn.: Greenwood Press 1996.

Holmes, John W. *The Shaping of Peace: Canada and the Search for World Order 1943–1957.* Vol. 1. Toronto: University of Toronto Press 1979.

Hooker, M.A., "Serving Two Masters: Ian Mackenzie and Civil-Military Relations, 1935–1939." *Journal of Canadian Studies*, vol. 21 (spring 1986).

Hopkins, Major-General R.N.L. *Australian Armour: A History of the Royal Australian Armoured Corps, 1927–1972.* Canberra: Australian War Memorial and Australian Government Publishing Service 1978.

Horn, Lieutenant-Colonel Bernd. *Bastard Sons: An Examination of Canada's Airborne Experience 1942–1995*. St Catharines: Vanwell Publishing 2001.

– ed. *Forging a Nation: Perspectives on the Canadian Military Experience*. St Catharines: Vanwell Publishing 2002.

– and Stephen Harris, ed. *Generalship and the Art of the Admiral: Perspectives on Canadian Senior Military Leadership*. St Catharines, Ont.: Vanwell Publishing 2001.

– *Warrior Chiefs: Perspectives on Senior Canadian Military Leaders*. Toronto: Dundurn Press 2001.

Horner, D.M. *Blamey: The Commander-in-Chief*. Sydney: Allen and Unwin 1998.

– "Chronicling the Peacekeepers: Report on the Feasibility of an Official History of Australian Peacekeeping Operations." Prepared for Australian War Memorial, 27 May 2003.

– *Defence Supremo: Sir Frederick Shedden and the Making of Australian Defence Policy*. Sydney: Allen and Unwin 2000.

– *The Gulf Commitment: The Australian Defence Force's First War*. Melbourne: Melbourne University Press 1992.

– *The Gunners: A History of Australian Artillery*. Sydney: Allen and Unwin 1995.

– *High Command: Australia & Allied Strategy, 1939–1945*. Sydney and Canberra: Australian War Memorial and Allen and Unwin 1982.

– *Making the Australian Defence Force: The Australian Centenary History of Defence, Volume IV*. Melbourne: Oxford University Press 2001.

– *SAS: Phantoms of the Jungle: A History of the Australian Special Air Service*. Sydney: Allen and Unwin 1989.

– and Desmond Ball. *Australia's Secret Space Programs*. Canberra Papers on Strategy and Defence, no. 43. Canberra: Strategic and Defence Studies Centre, Australian National University 1988.

"Howard Backs Away from 'Anglosphere' Alliance." Sydney *Morning Herald*, 6 May 2003. Downloaded from www.smh.com.au.

Hudson, W.J. *Blind Loyalty: Australia and the Suez Crisis, 1956*. Carlton: Melbourne University Press 1989.

Hunt, B.D., and R.G. Haycock, ed. *Canada's Defence: Perspectives on Policy in the Twentieth Century*. Toronto: Copp Clark Pitman 1993.

Huntington, Samuel. *The Clash of Civilizations and the Remaking of the World Order*. New York: Simon and Schuster 1996.

Hyatt, A.M.J. *General Sir Arthur Currie: A Military Biography*. Toronto: University of Toronto Press 1987.

Ignatieff, Michael. *Blood and Belonging: Journeys into the New Nationalism*. Toronto: Viking 1993.

Inglehart, Ronald. World Values Survey, University of Michigan, http://wvs.isr.umich.edu/, downloaded 26 May 2003.

– and Christian Welzel. *Modernization, Cultural Change and Democracy*. New York and Cambridge: Cambridge University Press 2005.

Inglis, K.S. *The Rehearsal: Australians at War in the Sudan, 1885*. Sydney: Rigby 1985.

International Institute for Strategic Studies. *The Military Balance 2002–2003*. London: Oxford University Press 2002.

James, Lieutenant-Colonel N.F. "A Brief History of Peacekeeping." *Australian Defence Force Journal*, no. 104 (January/February 1994).

Jett, Dennis C. *Why Peacekeeping Fails*. New York: Palgrave 2001.

Jockel, Joseph. *The Canadian Forces: Hard Choices, Soft Power*. Toronto: Canadian Institute of Strategic Studies 1999.

Johansen, Grant A. *The ABCA Program: Rhetoric to Reality*. Occasional issue no. 44. Strategic and Combat Studies Institute, Wiltshire, UK, January 2002.

Johnston, Mark, and Peter Stanley. *Alamein: The Australian Story*. Australian Army History Series. Melbourne: Oxford University Press 2002.

Jones, David Martin. "Regional Illusion and Its Aftermath." *Policy* (Centre for Independent Studies), vol. 19 (spring 2003).

Jordan, Amos A., William J. Taylor, Jr, and Michael J. Mazarr. *American National Security*, 5th ed. Baltimore and London: Johns Hopkins University Press 1999.

Kagan, Robert. *Of Paradise and Power: America and Europe in the New World Order*. New York: Knopf 2003.

Keating, Tom. *Canada and World Order: The Multilateralist Tradition in Canadian Foreign Policy*. Toronto: McClelland and Stewart 1993.

Keegan, John. *A History of Warfare*. New York: Vintage Books 1993.

Kendle, J.E. *The Colonial and Imperial Conferences 1887–1911*. Royal Commonwealth Society Imperial Studies no. 28. London: Longmans 1967.

Kennedy, Paul. "The Perils of Empire." Washington *Post*, 19 April 2003.

Kissinger, Henry. *White House Years*. Boston: Little, Brown 1979.

Krause, Lieutenant-Colonel Michael. "Lest We Forget: Combined Arms Assault in Complex Terrain." *Australian Army Journal*, vol. 1, no. 1 (2003).

Krauss, Clifford. "Canadian Envisions New Role for Nation." New York *Times*, 19 October 2003. Downloaded from http://www.nytimes.com/2003/20/19/international/americas/19CANA.html.

Kronenberg, Vernon J. "All Together Now: Canadian Defence Organization 1964–1971." Carleton University, MA thesis, 1971.

Krott, Rob. "Bolt Actions Speak Louder Than Words: Canadian Snipers in Afghanistan." *Soldier of Fortune*, September 2002.

Krulak, General C.C. "The Strategic Corporal: Leadership in the Three Block War." *Marines Magazine*, vol. 28 (January 1999).

Kupchan, Charles A. *The End of the American Era: U.S. Foreign Policy and the Geopolitics of the Twenty-First Century*. New York: Knopf 2003.

LaFeber, Walter. *The American Age: US Foreign Policy at Home and Abroad*, 2nd ed. New York and London: W.W. Norton 1994.

Last, Major David. "Almost a Legacy: Canada's Contribution to Peacekeeping." In Lieutenant-Colonel Bernd Horn, ed., *Forging a Nation: Perspectives on the Canadian Military Experience*. St Catharines, Ont.: Vanwell Publishing 2002.

Leahy, Lieutenant-General Peter. "A Land Force for the Future: The Australian Army in the Early 21st Century." *Australian Army Journal*, vol. 1, no. 1 (2003).

Léger, Jean-Marc. "More Canadians Believe Iraq War Justified: Poll." *Globe and Mail*, 10 May 2003, downloaded from www.globeandmail.com., 11 May 2003.

Lester, Normand. *The Black Book of English Canada*. Toronto: McClelland and Stewart 2002.

Letts, Major R.D. "Exercise Winter Sun." *Australian Army Journal*, no. 326 (July 1976).

Library and Archives of Canada. "Lester Bowles Pearson Biography." Downloaded from http://www.nlc-bnc.ca/primeministers/h4-3356-e.htmlon, 9 October 2003.

– RG 24, vol. 3900 NSS 1037–1–20 – Canadian Assistance to Australia.

– RG 25, vol. 3116 – Canadian Australian Relations – 4533–40.

Liska, George. *Career of Empire: America and Imperial Expansion over Land and Sea*. Baltimore: Johns Hopkins University Press 1978.

Londey, Peter. *Other People's Wars: A History of Australian Peacekeeping*. Sydney: Allen and Unwin 2004.

Long, Gavin. *To Benghazi*. Canberra: Australian War Memorial 1952.

– *Greece, Crete and Syria*. Canberra: Australian War Memorial 1953.

– *The Six Years War: Australia in the 1939–45 War*. Canberra: Australian War Memorial and Australian Government Publishing Service 1973.

Loomis, D.G. *The Somalia Affair: Reflections on Peacemaking and Peacekeeping*. Ottawa: DGL Publications 1996.

Lunman, Kim. "Canadians 'Dead Split' on Supporting War, Poll Reports." *Globe and Mail*, 7 April 2003.

Lupfer, Timothy T. *The Dynamics of Doctrine: The Changes in German Tactical Doctrine during the First World War*. Leavenworth Papers. Fort Leavenworth, Kan.: Combat Studies Institute, July 1981.

MacKenzie, Major-General Lewis. *Peacekeeper: The Road to Sarajevo*. Vancouver: Douglas and McIntyre 1993.

Maclaren, Roy. *Canadians on the Nile, 1882–1898: Being the Adventures of the Voyageurs on the Khartoum Relief Expedition and Other Exploits*. Vancouver: University of British Columbia Press 1978.

MacMillan, Margaret. *Paris 1919: Six Months That Changed the World*. New York: Random House 2002.

– and Francine McKenzie, ed. *Parties Long Estranged: Canada and Australia in the Twentieth Century*. Vancouver: University of British Columbia Press 2003.

Madsen, Flight Lieutenant S.A. "Comparing Australian and New Zealand Defence and Foreign Policy since 1985." *Australian Defence Force Journal*, no. 136 (May/June 1999).

"Mahatir: Jews Rule the World." CNN.com, 16 October 2003, downloaded from http://cnn.worldnews.printthis.clickability.com.

Malik, J. Mohan, ed. *The Future Battlefield*. Geelong: Deakin University Press and Directorate of Army Research and Analysis 1997.

Mallett, Ross. "The Interplay between Technology, Tactics and Organisation in the First AIF." University College, University of New South Wales, MA thesis, 1999.

Maloney, Sean M. "Canada's Ill-Conceived Mission to Kabul." *National Post*, 14 August 2003, downloaded from http://www.national post.com, 16 August 2003.

– *Canada and UN Peacekeeping: Cold War by Other Means, 1945–1970*. St Catharines, Ont.: Vanwell Publishing 2002.

– "Domestic Operations: The Canadian Approach." In *Parameters: US Army War College Quarterly*, vol. 27 (autumn 1997).

– "Missed Opportunity: Operation Broadsword, 4 Canadian Mechanised Brigade and the Gulf War, 1990–1991." *Army Doctrine and Training Bulletin*, vol. 5 (spring 2002).

– *War without Battles: Canada's NATO Brigade in Germany, 1951–1993*. Toronto: McGraw-Hill Ryerson 1997.

– and John Llambias. *Chances for Peace: Canadian Soldiers in the Balkans, 1992–1995*. St Catharines, Ont.: Vanwell Publishing 2002.

– *War with Iraq: Canada's Strategy in the Persian Gulf 1990–2002*. Martello Paper 24. Kingston, Ont.: Queen's University, Centre for International Relations 2002.

– and Scott Robertson. "The Revolution in Military Affairs: Possible Implications for Canada." *International Journal*, vol. 54 (summer 1999).

Mandelbaum, Michael. *The Ideas That Conquered the World: Peace, Democracy and Free Markets in the Twenty-first Century*. New York: Public Affairs 2002.

Mansergh, Nicholas. *The Commonwealth Experience, Volume Two: From British Commonwealth to Multi-Racial State*. London: Macmillan 1982.

– *Survey of British Commonwealth Affairs: Problems of External Policy 1931–1939*. London: Oxford University Press and Royal Institute of International Affairs 1952.

Marteinson, John. *We Stand on Guard: An Illustrated History of the Canadian Army*. Montreal: Ovale 1992.

Martin, The Honourable Paul. "Transcript: Canada's Role in a Complex World." Downloaded from http://www.paulmartintimes.ca/home/stories_e.asp?id=526, 2 May 2003.

Martin, Keith, MP. "Canada's Military Needs Big Boost." Toronto *Star*, 14 August 2003, downloaded from www.thestar.com, 16 August 2003.

Mathews, R.L., ed. *Public Policies in Two Federal Countries: Canada and Australia*. Canberra: Centre for Research on Federal Financial Relations, Australian National University 1982.

Matloff, Maurice. *United States Army in World War II: Strategic Planning for Coalition Warfare, 1943–1944*. Washington, D.C.: Center for Military History, United States Army 1994.

– and Edwin M. Snell. *United States Army in World War II: Strategic Planning for Coalition Warfare, 1941–1942*. Washington, D.C.: Center for Military History, United States Army 1999.

McCarthy, D.S. "The Once and Future Army: An Organizational, Political and Social History of the Citizen Military Forces, 1947–1974." University College, Australian Defence Force Academy, University of New South Wales, PHD thesis, 1997.

McCarthy, John. *Last Call of Empire: Australia and the Empire Air Training Scheme*. Canberra: Australian War Memorial 1988.

McCulloch, Ian M. "The 'Fighting Seventh': The Evolution of Tactical Command." Royal Military College (Kingston, Ont.), MA thesis, 1997.

McDougal, Russell, and Gillian Whitlock. *Australian/Canadian Literature in English: Comparative Perspectives*. Melbourne: Methuen 1987.

McDougall, Walter A. *Promised Land, Crusader State: The American Encounter with the World since 1776*. Boston: Mariner Books 1997.

McFarlane, John. *Ernest Lapointe and Quebec's Influence on Canadian Foreign Policy*. Toronto: University of Toronto Press 1999.

McGibbon, Ian, ed. *The Oxford Companion to New Zealand Military History*. Auckland: Oxford University Press 2000.

McKenzie, Francine. "New Best Friend." *The Globe and Mail*, 2 May 2003.

– *Redefining the Bonds of Commonwealth, 1939–1948: The Politics of Preference*. Cambridge Imperial and Post-Colonial Studies. Houndmills, U.K.: Palgrave Macmillam 2002.

McKercher, B.J.C., and Lawrence Aronsen, ed. *The North Atlantic Triangle in a Changing World: Anglo-American-Canadian Relations, 1902–1956*. Toronto: University of Toronto Press 1996.

McKernan, M., and M. Browne, ed. *Australia: Two Centuries of War and Peace*. Canberra: Australian War Memorial and Allen and Unwin 1988.

McLennan, A.D. "Engagement with Asia Revisited." *Policy: A Review of Public Policy and Ideas*, vol. 19 (autumn 2003).

McLin, Jon B. *Canada's Changing Defense Policy: The Problems of a Middle Power in Alliance.* Baltimore: Johns Hopkins University Press and Washington Center of Foreign Policy Research, School of Advanced International Studies 1967.

McNeill, I.G. *To Long Tan: The Australian Army and the Vietnam War 1950–1966.* Sydney: Allen and Unwin 1993.

– *The Team: Australian Army Advisers in Vietnam, 1962–1972.* Canberra: Australian War Memorial and University of Queensland Press 1984.

– and Ashley Ekins. *On the Offensive: The Australian Army in the Vietnam War, 1967–1968.* St Leonards: Allen and Unwin and Australian War Memorial 2003.

McNeill, William H. *The Pursuit of Power: Technology, Armed Force and Society since A.D. 1000.* Oxford, UK: Basil Blackwell 1983.

Mead, Walter Russell. *Special Providence: American Foreign Policy and How It Changed the World.* New York: Alfred A. Knopf 2001.

Michaud, Nelson, and Kim R. Nossal, ed. *Diplomatic Departures: The Conservative Era in Canadian Foreign Policy, 1984–93.* Vancouver: University of British Columbia Press 2001.

Middlemiss, D.W., and J.J. Sokolsky. *Canadian Defence: Decisions and Determinants.* Toronto: Harcourt Brace Jovanovich 1989.

Millar, T.B., ed. *Australian Foreign Minister: The Diaries of R.G. Casey 1951–1960.* London: Collins 1972.

– *Australia in Peace and War: External Relations, 1788–1977.* Canberra and New York: Australian National University Press and St Martin's Press 1978.

Miller, Carman. *The Canadian Career of the Fourth Earl of Minto: The Education of a Viceroy.* Waterloo, Ont.: Wilfrid Laurier University Press 1980.

– *Painting the Map Red: Canada and the South African War 1899–1902.* Montreal and Kingston: McGill-Queen's University Press and Canadian War Museum 1993.

Miller, Ronnie. *Following the Americans to the Persian Gulf: Canada, Australia and the Development of the New World Order.* London and Toronto: Associated University Presses 1994.

Minifie, James M. *Peacemaker or Powder-Monkey.* Toronto: McClelland and Stewart 1960.

Molan, Major-General Jim. "Op Falconer – War against Iraq – Winning Concepts." *Army: The Soldiers Newspaper,* 24 April 2003.

Monash, Lieutenant-General Sir John. *The Australian Victories in France in 1918.* London: Hutchinson 1920.

Morton, Desmond. *A Military History of Canada,* 4th ed. Toronto: McClelland and Stewart 1999.

– *Ministers and Generals: Politics and the Canadian Militia, 1868–1914.* Toronto: University of Toronto Press 1970.

– *Understanding Canadian Defence*. Toronto: Penguin McGill 2003.

– and J.L. Granatstein. *Marching to Armageddon: Canadians and the Great War, 1914–1919*. Toronto: Lester and Orpen Dennys 1989.

Morton, Peter. *Fire across the Desert: Woomera and the Anglo-Australian Joint Project 1946–1980*. Canberra: Australian Government Publishing Service 1989.

Munro, John A., and Alex I. Inglis, ed. *Mike: The Memoirs of the Right Honourable Lester B. Pearson, Volume 2, 1948–1957*. Toronto: University of Toronto Press 1973.

Natynczyk, Colonel W.J. "Coalitions of the Willing: Where's the Will." US Army War College Research Project, April 2002.

Nicholson, G.W.L. *The Official History of the Canadian Army in the Second World War, Vol. II, The Canadians in Italy*. Ottawa: Queen's Printer 1956.

Nordick, Brigadier-General Glenn. "Fighting in Built up Areas: We Can Do This, So Let's Get on with It." *Army Doctrine and Training Bulletin*, vol. 4 (fall 2001).

– "Warfighting: The Way Ahead for the Canadian Land Force Command and Staff College." *The Army Doctrine and Training Bulletin*, vol. 5 (spring 2002).

Nossal, Kim Richard. "Chunking Prism: Cognitive Process and Intelligence Failure." *International Journal*, no. 32 (summer 1977).

– *The Politics of Canadian Foreign Policy*, 3rd ed. Scarborough, Ont.: Prentice Hall 1997.

– *Rain Dancing: Sanctions in Canadian and Australian Foreign Policy*. Toronto: University of Toronto Press 1994.

– "Seeing Things? The Adornment of 'Security' in Australia and Canada." *Australian Journal of International Affairs*, vol. 49 (May 1995).

Nye, Jr, Joseph S. *The Paradox of American Power: Why the World's Only Superpower Can't Go It Alone*. New York: Oxford University Press 2002.

O'Brien. John B. "Empire v. National Interests in Australian-British Relations during the 1930s." *Historical Studies*, vol. 22, no. 89 (1987).

Odgers, George. *Across the Parallel: The Australian 77th Squadron with the United States Air Force in the Korean War*. Melbourne: William Heinemann 1953.

Off, Carol. *The Lion, The Fox and the Eagle: A Story of Generals and Justice in Rwanda and Yugoslavia*. Toronto: Vintage 2000.

O'Neill, Robert. *Australia in the Korean War: 1950–1953*, 2 vols. Canberra: Australian War Memorial 1981 and 1985.

Ørvik, Nils. "Canadian Security and 'Defence against Help.'" *International Perspectives*, May/June 1983.

Palazzo, Albert. *The Australian Army: A History of Its Organisation, 1901–2001*. Melbourne: Oxford University Press 2001.

– "Failure to Obey: The Australian Army and the First Line Component Deception." *Australian Army Journal*, no. 1 (2003).

Parkin, Russell. *A Capability of First Resort: Amphibious Operations and Australian Defence Policy, 1901–2001*. Working Paper no. 117. Canberra: Land Warfare Studies Centre May 2002.

Parrish, Thomas, ed. *The Simon and Schuster Encyclopaedia of World War II*. New York: Simon and Schuster 1978.

Patman, Robert G. "Beyond the 'Mogadishu Line': Some Australian Lessons for Managing Intra-State Conflicts." *Small Wars and Insurgencies*, vol. 12 (spring 2001).

Pellerin, Alain. "Australia's Military Does More with Less – Why Not Canada's?" Ottawa: Report of Executive Director, Conference of Defence Associations, 8 August 2003.

Pemberton, Gregory. *All the Way: Australia's Road to Vietnam*. Sydney: Allen and Unwin 1987.

Pentland, Charles C., ed. *The Transatlantic Link in Evolution: What Has Changed since 11 September 2001?* Martello Paper 25. Kingston, Ont.: Queen's University, Centre for International Relations 2003.

Perras, Galen Roger. *Franklin Roosevelt and the Origins of the Canadian-American Security Alliance, 1933–1945*. Westport, Conn.: Praeger 1998.

– "'They Need a Few Beatings and a Bit of Kicking around and Then You Couldn't Beat Them': Canadian Diplomats and Australians, 1939–1945." Paper presented at the Conference of Australian Studies Association of North America, Toronto, March 1998.

– *Stepping Stones to Nowhere: The Aleutian Islands, Alaska and American Military Strategy, 1867–1945*. Vancouver: University of British Columbia Press 2003.

Perry, F.W. *The Commonwealth Armies: Manpower and Organisation in Two World Wars*. Manchester, UK: Manchester University Press 1988.

Peters, Ralph. *Beyond Terror: Strategy in a Changing World*. Mechanicsburg, Penn.: Stackpole Books 2002.

Peters, William N. "Club Dues? The Relevance of Canadian Expeditionary Forces." Royal Military College (Kingston, Ont.), MA thesis, 1999.

Pope, Maurice A.. *Soldiers and Politicians: Memoirs*. Toronto: University of Toronto Press 1962.

Preston, Richard A. *Canada and "Imperial Defense": A Study of the Origins of the British Commonwealth's Defense Organization, 1867–1919*. Durham, N.C.: Duke University, Commonwealth-Studies Center 1967.

– *Canada's RMC: A History of the Royal Military College*. Toronto: University of Toronto Press 1969.

– and Ian Wards. "Military and Defence Development in Canada, Australia and New Zealand: A Three-Way Comparison." *War & Society*, vol. 5, no. 1 (1987).

Prior, Robin, and Trevor Wilson. *Command on the Western Front: The Military Career of Sir Henry Rawlinson, 1914–1918*. Oxford, UK: Blackwell 1992.

– *Passchendaele, the Untold Story*. Melbourne: Scribe Publications 2003.

Pugliese, David. *Canada's Secret Commandos: The Unauthorized Story of Joint Task Force Two*. Ottawa: Esprit de Corps Books 2002.

Pulsifer, Cameron. "Canada's First Armoured Unit, Raymond Brutinel and the Canadian Motor Machine Gun Brigades of the First World War." *Canadian Military History*, vol. 10 (winter 2001).

Ramsey, Alan. "More Bloodlust Than a Real War." Sydney *Morning Herald*, 12 April 2003.

Rawling, Bill. *Surviving Trench Warfare: Technology and the Canadian Corps, 1914–1918*. Toronto: University of Toronto Press 1992.

Reid, Escott. *On Duty: A Canadian at the Making of the United Nations, 1945–1946*. Toronto: McClelland and Stewart 1983.

"Remembering Our Military." Ottawa *Citizen*, 6 October 2003. Downloaded from http://www.canada.com.

Rempel, Roy. "Annual Report of the Chief of Defence Staff, 2002–2003." Defence Associations National Network (Ottawa), *National Network News*, vol. 10 (summer 2003).

– *The Chatter Box: An Insider's Account of the Irrelevance of Parliament in the Making of Canadian Foreign and Defence Policy*. Toronto: Breakout Educational Network and Dundurn Press 2002.

– *Counterweights: The Failure of Canada's German and European Policy, 1955–1995*. Montreal and Kingston: McGill-Queen's University Press 1997.

Reynolds, Wayne. *Australia's Bid for the Atomic Bomb*. Carlton: Melbourne University Press 2000.

– "The Wars That Were Planned: Australia's Forward Defence Posture in Asia and the Role of Tactical Nuclear Weapons, 1945–1967." *Australian Journal of International Affairs*, vol. 53, no. 3 (1999).

Richelson, Jeffrey T., and Desmond Ball. *The Ties That Bind: Intelligence Cooperation between the – UKUSA Countries – the United Kingdom, the United States of America, Canada, Australia and New Zealand*. Sydney and Boston: George Allen and Unwin 1985.

Richert, Major R.J. "An Essay on the Vulnerability of Australia's Centers of Gravity to Asymmetric Attack." Eessay submitted to Air Command and Staff College, RAAF, Fairbarn, 1999.

Richter, Andrew. *Avoiding Armageddon: Canadian Military Strategy and Nuclear Weapons 1950–1963*. Vancouver and Toronto: University of British Columbia Press 2002.

– "Strategic Ambitions and Fiscal Realities: Give the Navy Priority." *Policy Options* (April 2002), downloaded from http://www.irpp.org/po/archive/apro2/richter.pdf., 18 October 2003.

Ritchie, Charles. *Diplomatic Passport: More Undiplomatic Diaries, 1946–1962*. Toronto: Macmillan 1981.

Robertson, John. *Anzac and Empire*. Sydney: Hamlyn 1990.

– and John McCarthy. *Australian War Strategy, 1939–1945: A Documentary History*. St Lucia: University of Queensland Press 1985.

Robson, L.L. "Beyond a Pale Horse: Australian War Studies." *Australian Historical Studies*, vol. 23 (April 1988).

– *The First A.I.F.: A Study of Its Recruitment, 1914–1918*. Melbourne: Melbourne University Press 1970.

Roggeveen, Sam. "Amphibious Warfare in the ADF: The Poverty of Non-Offensive Defence Strategy in the Australian Context." *Australian Defence Force Journal*, no. 120 (September/October 1996).

Rosner, Gabriella. *The United Nations Emergency Force*. New York: Columbia University Press 1963.

Ross, A.T. *Armed and Ready: The Industrial Development and Defence of Australia, 1900–1945*. Sydney: Turton and Armstrong 1995.

Ross, Jane. *The Myth of the Digger: The Australian Soldier in Two World Wars*. Sydney: Hale and Iremonger 1985.

Rudner, Martin. "Canada's Communications Security Establishment from Cold War to Globalization." *Intelligence and National Security*, vol. 16, no. 1 (2001).

Ryan, Alan. *Australian Army Cooperation with the Land Forces of the United States: Problems of the Junior Partner*. Working Paper no. 121. Canberra: Land Warfare Studies Centre, January 2003.

– *Primary Responsibilities and Primary Risks: Australian Defence Force Participation in the International Force East Timor*. Study Paper no. 304. Canberra: Land Warfare Studies Centre, November 2000.

Sargeant, Brendan. "Draft Discussion Paper: United States Defense Strategy – Contemporary Developments and Possible Implications for Australian Defence Policy." Australian Embassy, Washington, D.C., March 2003.

Saul, John Ralston. *Voltaire's Bastards: The Dictatorship of Reason in the West*. Toronto: Penguin Books 1993.

Schindlmayr, Thomas, and Commander Peter Ong. "Attaining 54,000?" *Australian Defence Force Journal*, no. 153 (March/April 2002).

Schlesinger, Arthur Jr. *The Disuniting of America*. New York: Norton 1992.

Schreiber, Shane. *Shock Army of the British Empire: The Canadian Corps in the Last 100 Days of the Great War*. Westport, Conn.: Praeger 1997.

Scobell, Andrew. *Strategic Effects of the Conflict with Iraq: Australia and New Zealand*. Carlisle: Strategic Studies Institute 2003. Downloaded from http://www.carlisle.army.mil/ssi/index.html, 22 April 2003.

Scowen, Peter. *Rogue Nation: The America the Rest of the World Knows*. Translated from French. Toronto: McClelland and Stewart 2003.

Semianiw, Colonel Walter. "Train for War and Peace." *Canadian Military Journal,* vol. 3 (spring 2002).

Sexton, Michael. *War for the Asking: How Australia Invited Itself to Vietnam.* Reprint. Sydney: New Holland 2002.

Sheppard, Allan. *Trends in Australian Defence: A Resources Survey.* Canberra: Australian Defence Studies Centre, Australian Defence Force Academy 1999.

Simpson, Jeffrey. "Australia: Canada's Secret Alter Ego." *Globe and Mail,* 17 September 2002.

– *Faultlines: Struggling for a Canadian Vision.* Toronto: Harper Collins 1993.

Singleton, John, and Paul L. Robertson. *Economic Relations between Britain and Australasia, 1945–1970.* Cambridge Imperial and Post-Colonial Studies. Houndmills, U.K.: Palgrave Macmillan 2002.

Skaarup, Major H.A. "An Intelligence Advantage: Collective Security Benefits Gained by Canada through the Sharing of Military Intelligence with the United States." Royal Military College (Kingston, Ont.), MA thesis, 1997.

Sligo, Lieutenant-Colonel Graeme. "The Staff College at Armour Heights, 1943–2003." Draft paper in possession of author.

Sloan, Lieutenant-Colonel C.E.E.. "ABCA – The Next 20 Years." *Defence Force Journal,* no. 67 (November/December 87).

Sloan, Elinor C. *The Revolution in Military Affairs.* Montreal and Kingston: McGill-Queen's University Press 2002.

Smith, Hugh, ed., *International Peacekeeping: Building on the Cambodian Experience.* Canberra: Australian Defence Studies Centre, Australian Defence Force Academy 1994.

Smith, Michael G., and Moreen Dee. *Peacekeeping in East Timor: The Path to Independence.* International Peace Academy Occasional Papers Series. Boulder, Colo., and London: Lynne Rienner Publishers 2003.

Smith, Susan. *A Handmaiden's Tale: An Alternative View of Logistics Lessons Learned from INTERFET.* Working Paper no. 65. Canberra: Australian Defence Studies Centre, April 2001.

Snider, Michael, and Sean Maloney. "Firefight at the Medak Pocket." *Macleans,* 2 September 2002.

Sokolsky, Joel J. *The Americanization of Peacekeeping.* Martello Paper 17. Kingston, Ont.: Queen's University, Centre for International Relations 1997.

"Special Report: American Values." *The Economist,* 4 January 2003.

"Special Report: World Trade – The Doha Squabble." *The Economist,* 29 March 2003.

Stacey, Colonel C.P. *Canada and the Age of Conflict – Volumes 1 and 2.* Toronto: Macmillan and University of Toronto Press, 1977 and 1981.

- *Six Years of War: The Army in Canada, Britain and the Pacific*. Volume 1. Official History of the Canadian Army in the Second World War. Ottawa: Queen's Printer 1966.
- and Barbara Wilson. *The Half-Million: The Canadians in Britain, 1939–1946*. Toronto: University of Toronto Press 1987.

Stairs, Denis. "Canada and the Korean War Fifty Years on." *Canadian Military History*, vol. 9 (summer 2000).
- "Canada in the 1990s: Speak Loudly and Carry a Bent Twig." *Policy Options* (Institute for Research on Public Policy), January/February 2001.
- *The Diplomacy of Constraint: Canada, the Korean War and the United States*. Toronto: University of Toronto Press 1974.

Stanley, George F.G. *Canada's Soldiers: The Military History of an Unmilitary People*. Toronto: Macmillan 1960.

Steyn, Mark. "French Can Sneer but 'Les Anglo-Saxons' World's Best Hope: France, Germany, Russia, Belgium and Canada Are Not on the Side of Morality or the Iraqi People." Chicago *Sun-Times*, 13 April 2003.

Stratfor [e-mail news service]. "American Empire." Downloaded from http:// www.stratfor.com, 20 April 2003.
- "Australia's Growing Importance to U.S. Strategic Plans" (4 June 2003). See www.stratfor.com.

Stretton, Alan. *Soldier in a Storm: An Autobiography of Alan Stretton*. Sydney and London: Collins 1978.

Struthers, James. "War and Social Policy in Australia and Canada." *Australian-Canadian Studies*, vol. 6, no. 1 (1988).

Tasseron, Major Jeff. "Facts and Invariants: The Changing Context of Canadian Defence Policy." *Canadian Military Journal*, vol. 4 (summer 2003).

Taylor, Peter Shawn. "Air Canada's Choice: The Parallel Histories of Qantas and Air Canada." *Financial Post*, 28 March 2003.

Taylor, S., and B Nolan. *Tarnished Brass*. Toronto: Lester Publishing 1996.

Thompson, John Herd, and Stephen J. Randall. *Canada and the United States: Ambivalent Allies*. 3rd ed. Montreal and Kingston: McGill-Queen's University Press 2002.

Thomson, Alistair. "'The Vilest Libel of the War?' Imperial Politics and the Official Histories of Gallipoli." *Australian Historical Studies*, vol. 25, no. 101 (1993).

Thorsell, William. "Canada Can No Longer Ignore the World's Siren Call." *Globe and Mail*, 7 April 2003.

Toffler, Alvin and Heidi. *War and Anti-War: Making Sense of Today's Global Chaos*. New York: Warner Books 1993.

Toohey, Brian, and William Pinwill. *Oyster: The Story of the Australian Secret Intelligence Service*. Melbourne: William Heinemann 1989.

Travers, Tim. *The Killing Ground: The British Army, the Western Front and the Emergence of Modern Warfare, 1900–1918*. London: Allen and Unwin 1987.

Troen, S.I., and S. Shemesh, ed. *The Suez-Sinai Crisis 1956: Retrospective and Reappraisal*. New York: Columbia University Press 1990.

Twolan, David Shawn. "Defence Policy Making in Canada: The Failure of the White Paper." Queen's University, MA thesis, May 1992.

Underground Royal Commission. *A Question of Honour: Episode 4 – "The Bungle in the Jungle."* Video. Toronto: Stornoway Productions 2002.

United Nations. "SHIRBRIG Multi-National Standby High Readiness Brigade for United Nations Operations." Downloaded from http://www.shirbrig.dk, 4 June 2003.

United States Army. *Papuan Campaign: The Buna-Sanananda Operation 16 November 1942–23 January 1943*. Washington, D.C.: Center of Military History 1990.

– *United States Army in the World War, 1917–1919: Military Operations of the American Expeditionary Forces, Volume 7*. Washington, D.C.: United States Army, Center of Military History 1990.

– *United States Army in the World War, 1917–1919: Training and Use of American Units with the British and French, Volume 3*. Washington, D.C.: Center of Military History 1989.

Urquhart, Hugh M. *Arthur Currie: A Biography of a Great Canadian*. Toronto: J.M. Dent and Sons 1950.

Vance, Jonathan F., *Death So Noble: Memory, Meaning, and the First World War*. Vancouver: University of British Columbia Press 1997.

Varey, David K. "Clash of Strategies: The Foreign Office, the Global Balance of Power, and the Treasury's Bid for an Anglo-Japanese Rapprochement, 1931–1934."

Wahlert, Glenn, ed. *Australian Army Amphibious Operations in the South-West Pacific: 1942–45*. Edited Papers of the Australian Army History Conference held at the Australian War Memorial, 15 November 1994. Sydney: Army Doctrine Centre 1995.

Walker, Major R.J. "Poles Apart: Civil Military Relations in the Pursuit of a Canadian National Army." Royal Military College, MA thesis, 1991.

Wallace, Jim. "Iraq Lesson Can Help Correct Defence Policy." *The Age*, 20 April 2003.

Watt, Alan. *The Evolution of Australian Foreign Policy, 1938-1965*. Cambridge, UK: Cambridge University Press 1967.

Wattie, Chris. "Ottawa Offered to Join Iraq War." *National Post*, 27 November 2003.

Welburn, M.C.J. *The Development of Australian Army Doctrine 1945–1964*. Papers on Strategy and Defence no. 108. Canberra: Strategic and Defence Studies Centre, Research School of Pacific and Asian Studies, Australian National University, 1994.

White, Hugh. "Defence and the Possibility of War." *Australian Journal of International Affairs*, vol. 56, no. 2 (2002).

Wigley, Philip G. *Canada and the Transition to Commonwealth: British-Canadian Relations, 1917–1926*. Cambridge, UK: Cambridge University Press 1977.

Wigmore, Lionel, and Bruce Harding. Second ed., revised and condensed by Jeff Williams and Anthony Staunton. *They Dared Mightily*. Canberra: Australian War Memorial 1986.

Wilcox, Craig. *Australia's Boer War: The War in South Africa, 1899–1902*. Melbourne: Oxford University Press and Australian War Memorial 2002.

Windschuttle, Keith. *The Fabrication of Aboriginal History*. Sydney: Macleay Press 2002.

Windsor, Lee. "Professionalism under Fire: Canadian Implementation of the Medak Pocket Agreement, Croatia 1993." *Army Doctrine and Training Bulletin*, vol. 4 (fall 2001).

Winks, Robin W. *Canada and the United States: The Civil War Years*. Baltimore: Johns Hopkins Press 1960.

Wood, Captain G.A. "Employment of ... Commonwealth and U.S. Field Artillery." *Australian Army Journal*, no. 42 (November 1952).

Wood, Lieutenant-Colonel Herbert Fairlie. *Strange Battleground: Official History of the Canadian Army in Korea*. Ottawa: Queen's Printer 1966.

Wood, John, ed. *The Chance of War: Canadian Soldiers in the Balkans, 1992–1995*. Toronto: Breakout Educational Network and Dundurn Press 2003.

– *Talking Heads Talking Arms, Volume 2: Whistling Past the Graveyard, Conversations about Canada's Armed Forces at the Beginning of the 21st Century*. Toronto: Breakout Educational Network and Dundurn Press 2003.

Index

Index